Symptoms of Modernity

Symptoms
of Modernity

Jews and Queers
in Late-Twentieth-Century Vienna

Matti Bunzl

UNIVERSITY OF CALIFORNIA PRESS
Berkeley / Los Angeles / London

Erich Lifka's "Landesgericht zwei, Wien" appears by permission of
Foerster Media.
Erich Fried's "An Österreich" appears by permission of Claassen Verlag,
Munich.
English-language translation of Erich Fried's "To Austria" reprinted
from *Contemporary Jewish Writing in Austria: An Anthology,* edited by
Dagmar C. G. Lorenz, by permission of the University of Nebraska Press.
© 1999 by the University of Nebraska Press.

University of California Press
Berkeley and Los Angeles, California

University of California Press, Ltd.
London, England

Library of Congress Cataloging-in-Publication Data
Bunzl, Matti, 1971–.
   Symptoms of modernity : Jews and queers in late-twentieth-century
Vienna / Matti Bunzl.
      p.   cm.
   Includes bibliographical references.
   ISBN 0–520–23842–7 (cloth : alk. paper) — ISBN 0–520–23843–5
(pbk. : alk. paper)
   1. Jews—Austria—Vienna—Social conditions—20th century.   2. Gays—
Austria—Vienna—Social conditions—20th century.   3. Vienna (Austria)—
Ethnic relations.   4. Vienna (Austria)—Social life and customs—20th
century.   5. Austria—History—1955-   6. Austria—Social policy.
7. Nationalism—Social aspects—Austria.   I. Title.
DS135.A92 V52216   2004
305.892'4043613'09049—dc21   2003002458

Manufactured in the United States of America
13   12   11   10   09   08   07   06   05   04
10   9   8   7   6   5   4   3   2   1

The paper used in this publication is both acid-free and totally chlorine-
free (TCF). It meets the minimum requirements of ANSI/NISO Z39.48–1992
(R 1997) *(Permanence of Paper).*☉

For Billy Vaughn

Illustrations for *Symptoms of Modernity* are posted at
www.staff.uiuc.edu/~bunzl/index.html

Contents

Preface and Acknowledgments

This book is an account of Central European modernity that takes the form of a comparative ethnography of Jews and queers in late-twentieth-century Vienna. I focus on these two groups as the foundational bearers of negative identification in the constitution of the modern nation-state. In its Central European (that is, German) variant, the nation-state was invented in the late nineteenth century as an ethnically homogenous and intrinsically masculinist entity, a narrative whose cultural coherence depended on the systematic abjection of Jews and homosexuals. Through the modern twin discourses of antisemitism and homophobia, these groups were mobilized and fortified as the constitutive outsides of respectable Germanness, thereby allowing the retrospective fixing of the nation-state as a fantasized public space of ethnic and sexual purity. Jews and queers thus figured as symptoms of modernity, abject by-products whose irreducible Otherness underwrote the fictions of the modern nation-state. Following Zygmunt Bauman, I read the Holocaust in this analytic context as a quintessentially modern event, taking the exclusionary principles of German nation-building to its catastrophic conclusion. The nation had been imagined in constitutive opposition to Jews and queers; the Holocaust was designed to effect their complete eradication from the German (and Austrian) public sphere.

As an empirical project, *Symptoms of Modernity* begins in the wake of the Holocaust. I read the postwar period of Austrian history as a moment of late Central European modernity. Although the systematic murder of the nation's Others had ended, Austrianness continued to be fantasized in constitutive opposition to Jews and homosexuals. Their violent and systematic exclusion from the public sphere reproduced the logic of modern abjection, underwriting a national imagery purged of those located outside it. This situation started to change in the late 1970s, when Jews and queers began to contest their enforced exclusion from Austria's public sphere. In the following decades, these efforts steadily intensified, and by the 1990s, in the cultural context of an increasingly transnational world that undermined the ideological stronghold of the nation-state, both groups emerged as prominent components of Vienna's urban topography. Even more remarkably, the state, formerly the principal agent in the violent abjection of Jews and homosexuals, became the strongest champion of Jewish and queer participation in Vienna's cultural landscape. By the turn of the twenty-first century, Jewish and queer visibility was greater than at any other point in Austrian history, a situation that had dramatic effects on processes of publicized subjectification. Jews and queers, in other words, "came out" in unprecedented numbers.

As I explicate in the conclusion of the book, this phenomenon presents an occasion for further theoretical reflection. I suggest that the emergence of Jews and queers into Vienna's public sphere should be read as a signpost of postmodernity. This is meant literally, in that the unprecedented prominence of these groups within the city's urban landscape signals a genuine departure from the modern logic of Jews' and homosexuals' foundational abjection. In a globalizing world, the principal Others of the modern nation-state no longer figure as constitutive outsides. On the contrary, they have been incorporated as fundamental elements of a diversified public sphere. For the symptoms of modernity, this process has a liberating quality, anchored as it is in a dialectical convergence of resistive and reproductive authentification. This cultural dynamic is essentially uncontested; in the Austrian context, not even Jörg Haider's Freedom Party seeks to guard the nation's traditional boundaries any longer. Instead, the political struggle over cultural self-definition has moved to a supranational realm, where Europe's right-wing parties model the integrating continent in virulently exclusionary terms. It will be up to Europe's moderate and progressive forces to ensure the codification of a polity that is not imagined through the reproduction of national exclusion on a supranational level; otherwise, a new set of Others will emerge as the abject symptoms of Europe's postmodernity.

Fieldwork and archival work for this project were carried out in winter 1994, summer 1995, April to November 1996, summer 1997, spring 1998, summer 1999, January to June 2000, and summer 2001. It is a great pleasure to thank the institutions that facilitated my research: the Social Science Division of the University of Chicago, Vienna's Internationales Forschungszentrum Kulturwissenschaften (IFK), the Österreichische Akademie der Wissenschaften, and the Department of Anthropology and Research Board at the University of Illinois at Urbana-Champaign.

My work in Vienna was greatly facilitated by the kindness of several friends and interlocutors. Specifically, I would like to thank Ruth Beckermann, Andreas Brunner, Stefan Dobias, Helmut Graupner, Naomi Lassar, Srulik Pollak, Doron Rabinovici, and Diana Voigt. Karl Albrecht-Weinberger made the archive of Vienna's Jewish Museum available to me, while Michael Toth and Kurt Krickler gave me generous access to the archives of Safeway and HOSI, respectively. Hannes Sulzenbacher shared with me his treasured collection of sources on Austria's lesbian/gay past. In addition, I benefited from the expertise of the staff at the following public libraries and archives: Archiv der Arbeiterkammer, Bibliothek des Jüdischen Museum Wien, Bibliothek der Rosa Lila Villa, Wiener Universitätsbibliothek, and Österreichische Nationalbibliothek.

Over the years, I have incurred many intellectual debts. At the University of Chicago, I was fortunate to have George Stocking as an extraordinary mentor. My fellow students also inspired me. The members of the Anthropology of Europe Workshop and the Lesbian/Gay Studies Workshop were important intellectual companions. I owe particular gratitude to Ira Bashkow, Daphne Berdahl, and David Churchill, my close friends, who made graduate school a pleasure and who continue to be my models of scholarly excellence.

The University of Illinois at Urbana-Champaign has been a most conducive environment for the completion of this project. It is hard to do justice to the intellectual excitement and camaraderie that characterize this wonderful institution. My colleagues in the Department of Anthropology, the Program in Jewish Culture and Society, the Department of History, and the Unit for Criticism and Interpretive Theory have all contributed to this book in innumerable ways. Lisa Lampert, Harry Liebersohn, Andy Orta, and Adam Sutcliffe were particularly generous, listening to my ideas with endless patience. The University of Illinois also provided the funds for a research assistant, and it is a pleasure to acknowledge the formidable work of Nora Glatzel, who transcribed countless tapes of ethnographic interviews.

Over the years, many friends and colleagues in the United States and Europe have discussed portions of this book with me. Among those who changed the way I think about the material presented in this study are

Steven Beller, Michael Berkowitz, Philip Bohlman, Dan Diner, Pieter Judson, Albert Lichtblau, Richard Handler, Marsha Rozenblit, Dan Segal, and Ruth Wodak. As this project neared completion, I was fortunate to find a most generous editor in Stan Holwitz. He has made the publication process with the University of California Press a truly pleasant experience.

Over the years, the various branches of my family have provided much emotional support. My grandparents, Felix Bar-Geva and the late Frida Bar-Geva and Viktor Bunzl, were a constant source of inspiration. My mother, Liora Bunzl, has always been there. Sarah Vaughn and Jackie Vaughn have welcomed me into their lives and made me part of their family. My career would not have been possible without the love and support of my father, John Bunzl. As a scholar, he not only introduced me to the life of the mind but has remained a constant interlocutor. I am deeply grateful to him.

Finally, my partner, Billy Vaughn, has made all of my endeavors possible. I cannot count the ways in which he has inspired and sustained me over the years. He not only read and commented on every word of this book, but gave me the strength and security to pursue it in the first place. It is as a small token of my love and gratitude that I dedicate this book to him.

Urbana, July 2002

Symptoms of Modernity

On June 29, 1996, a small group of lesbian and gay Jews took to the streets of Vienna to join the city's first-ever Gay Pride Parade. Re'uth, as the group called itself after the Hebrew word for friendship, had come into existence in 1991. Comprising about two dozen members, the organization hoped to provide an affirmative space for Vienna's queer Jews. But Re'uth not only functioned as a social group for lesbian/gay Jews and their friends; the organization also saw itself as a crucial bridge between two minority communities. Indeed, ever since its founding, Re'uth's members endeavored to raise awareness for Jewish concerns among queers and for lesbian/gay issues among Jews. So when a group of queer activists organized Vienna's inaugural Gay Pride Parade under the name Regenbogen Parade (Rainbow Parade), Re'uth's members were eager to participate. The event would present a unique opportunity to showcase the existence of lesbian/gay Jewish life and publicize the group's activities.

To maximize visibility during the parade, Re'uth designed a banner that symbolized the interarticulation of the group's ethnic and sexual identification. Recalling the design of Israel's national flag, the banner featured a prominent Star of David, a powerful and ambivalent sign in the context of Central Europe's recent past. While historically a sign of affirmative Jewish nationness, Austria's Jews were required to wear the star of David as a means of abject identification during the Nazi period.[1]

As such, it not only functioned as the most visceral icon of Jewish stigmatization, but as the very emblem of antisemitic persecution. Re'uth paired the Star of David with yet another historically ambivalent sign. Superimposed on the Jewish icon was the Pink Triangle, the badge of identification gay men were forced to wear in Nazi concentration camps.[2] While the emblem had been appropriated and rearticulated by the lesbian/gay movement, it was nevertheless a daring choice. In conjunction with the Star of David, the Pink Triangle referenced and critiqued a local history of multiple persecutions. In contrast to, for example, a menorah and a Rainbow Flag, Re'uth's design thus made an overtly political statement. Jews and queers, Re'uth suggested, on the level of both symbolism and collective physical embodiment, had been victims of Central Europe's genocidal history; but in late-twentieth-century Vienna, even the doubly marginalized group of queer Jews demanded and claimed an affirmative presence in the city's public sphere. Indeed, since 1996, Re'uth participated in every Regenbogen Parade; since the event was successfully institutionalized as the highlight of Austria's queer calendar, the group and its banner became annual fixtures of Vienna's symbolic landscape.

Jews and Queers in Late-Twentieth-Century Vienna

On a basic level, this book presents an anthropological analysis of the historical conditions that enabled the public emergence of queer Jews. To account for this phenomenon, however, it does not suffice to chart the history of Re'uth or to present the ethnography of a tiny group of lesbian/gay Jews. Rather attention needs to be focused on the respective histories of Jews and queers in Vienna. In their interarticulation, these histories can account for the emergence of Re'uth into the city's public sphere. Even more importantly, however, they can tell us much about the historical transformations in the cultural fields, not only of Vienna itself, but of Austria and Central Europe more generally.

In the final years of the twentieth century, Vienna's social fields were characterized by a rapid process of cultural pluralization. This situation marked a significant shift from the postwar era. In the wake of the devastations of World War II and the Holocaust, Vienna had ossified into a museum commemorating the imperial capital's former splendor and thwarting the emergence of vibrant social spheres. Governed by a social democratic logic of embourgeoisement that articulated with Austria's social conservatism, the aging city evidenced a remarkable degree of ethnic and cultural homogeneity.³ While other European metropolises boasted political diversity and radical cultural scenes, Vienna was characterized by the sheer conventionality of its provincialism.⁴ In the face of a political field governed by the postwar consensus of *Sozialpartnerschaft,*⁵ even the furors of 1968 produced little more than a whimper, confirming rather than challenging the status quo of the country's postwar arrangements.

It was not until the 1980s that Vienna's apparent ethnic and cultural seamlessness began to break down. In 1979, the opening of the United Nations headquarters brought a massive influx of foreigners to the city, leading to the gradual emergence of a transnational infrastructure beyond the city's tourist economy. The appearance in the 1980s of foreign-language bookstores and movie theaters heralded the decentering of Vienna's cultural homogeneities at the very moment that saw the advent of a highly visible youth culture, identified first and foremost with the successful creation of Vienna's *Bermudadreieck.*⁶

Nowhere was the radical nature of Vienna's transformation more evident, however, than in the emergence of Jews and queers into the city's public sphere. A gradual process that commenced in the late 1970s, gathered steam in the 1980s, and exploded in the 1990s, it marked the most explicit break with postwar Austria's social realities. Their articulation through a symbolic logic of cultural homogeneity had undermined and thwarted any ready articulation of difference, affecting Jews and queers in analogous ways throughout Austria's Second Republic.⁷

Jews experienced Austria's publicly enforced ethnic and cultural homogeneity as an ongoing form of symbolic violence. Enacted through governmental inaction, hostile bureaucracies, and other unofficial channels refracting the country's widespread antisemitic sentiments, this violence enforced an accomodationist stance marked by Jews' retreat into a private sphere of nonthreatening difference.⁸ Throughout the first four decades of the Second Republic, Vienna's Jewish population of slightly less than ten thousand remained essentially invisible, self-censoring their individual profiles to conform to Austrian hegemonies that demanded their constitutive absence from the country's public and semipublic spheres.

If the postwar period was characterized by the absence of Jews from Vienna's public sphere, the late 1980s and 1990s witnessed a momentous change. In the contradictory wake of the Waldheim affair, Vienna's Jews began to assert a public identity, a process indicated most prominently by the creation of several institutions designed to effect the affirmative anchoring of the city's Jewish population in Vienna's cultural geography. In particular, the creation in the early 1990s of regular Jewish culture festivals and the concurrent inception of an annual Jewish street fair signaled a new public self-understanding of Vienna's Jewish community. At about the same time, the state, in the form of Vienna's municipal administration as well as Austria's federal government, began to champion a Jewish presence in the public sphere. Such institutions as Vienna's Jewish Museum and a Jewish Institute for Adult Education were founded as a result.

While predicated on radically different histories of social and cultural Otherness, the trajectory is surprisingly similar in the case of lesbians and gay men. There, too, the first decades of Austria's Second Republic were characterized by the violently enforced privatization of an abjectly marked difference. While an infrastructure of informal gathering places existed alongside a small commercial scene of predominantly gay male locales, the social situation was stamped by the legal interdiction of all homosexual acts. Codified in the regularly executed §129 Ib, which carried the threat of multiyear prison sentences, the so-called *Totalverbot* (total ban) effectively removed lesbians and gay men from the public sphere and public consciousness.[9] While the abolition of the *Totalverbot* eased the threat of legal sanctions in the early 1970s, a number of anti-lesbian/gay statutes continued to undermine the creation of affirmative queer lifeworlds.

Whether or not the absence of queer visibility in Austria's Second Republic should be regarded as a direct correlate of the country's anti-lesbian/gay legislation remains debatable. It is a fact, however, that in the context of Catholic oppression and widespread social conservatism, the post-Stonewall years failed to usher in an age of widespread lesbian/gay liberation. Until well into the 1980s, lesbian public spaces were absent altogether, while Vienna's gay male scene was synonymous with clandestine locales — a number of parks, several public bathrooms, and a few carefully hidden bars that monitored their nightly clientele through the use of doorbells.

Despite the persistent pressures of a homophobic cultural field, the situation changed rapidly in the early 1990s. Within a few years, Vienna saw the creation of a number of seminal institutions that signified and underwrote the formation of publicly queer identities. Ranging from queer culture festivals to light and airy cafés that invited the larger public into the lesbian/gay world, these institutions emerged as visible signposts of a world beyond the social and cultural closet. Among these efforts, Vienna's Rainbow Parade quickly came to occupy center stage; and in the wake of the queer spectacle's widespread resonance in the city's cultural fields, Vienna's municipal government began to address lesbian/gay concerns, most importantly through the creation of a lesbian/gay antidiscrimination office in city hall.

For over four decades, Austria's Second Republic had been marked by the abject silencing of lesbians and gay men, but in the pluralizing moment of the 1990s, queers emerged as a constitutive part of Vienna's cultural topography. Much like the case of Jews, their cultural identity was no longer fixed within a social imaginary of concealed Otherness, but instead became an integral aspect of the city's lived reality. For most of Austria's Second Republic, Vienna's metropolitan institutions had sustained little beyond the private existence of Jews and homosexuals; by the end of the twentieth century, the city's urban landscape not only afforded but invited the affirmative articulation of Jewish and queer difference.

The Anthropologies of Jews and Queers

In tracing the respective trajectories of Jews and queers in the last decades of the twentieth century, this book contributes to the anthropological literature on both groups. In regard to the anthropology of Jews, this study seeks to intervene in a relative silence. As Virginia Dominguez has noted, anthropology seems to have a "professional problem with Jewishness." Having kept the subject at "arm's length," Jews were "often selectively forgotten or dismissed as 'the Other within.'"[10] Indeed, the ethnographic study of Jews and Judaism has remained quite marginal to the discipline at large. In part, this is related to its prolonged identification with the study of Israel and its immigrant populations. Over the last decades, the vast bulk of ethnographic research has in fact been carried out in Israel.[11] Unwittingly perhaps, this situation reproduces the traditional Zionist opposition between a culturally doomed diaspora and a socially thriving Israel, often figured as the only viable place of post-Holocaust Jewish existence. The ethnographic impression of a vanished diaspora has only been heightened by the many studies focusing on Israel's various immigrant groups and their complex social relations.[12] Philip Bohlman's important study of the musical culture of German immigrants, to cite just one example, is thus paradigmatic of an ethnographic genre that figures Israel as the cultural telos of a destroyed or vacated diaspora — the logical site for the post-Holocaust articulation of, in this case, German-Jewish culture.[13]

If anything, this conceptual dichotomization between a vibrant Israeli society and a vanishing diaspora has been heightened by the small body of ethnographic work conducted among Jews outside of Israel. Dominguez has pointed to the deeply nostalgic nature of many of these studies, which often seek to recuperate "lost worlds" and "dying customs."[14] Even work undertaken in the United States has been pervaded by a sense of mournful loss. The two seminal ethnographies of American-Jewish existence — Barbara Myerhoff's *Number Our Days* and Jack Kugelmass's *The Miracle of Intervale Avenue* — both explore elderly communities, whose inevitable disappearance motivated a form of "salvage anthropology."[15]

While ethnographers of American Jewry have recently begun to address contemporary rearticulations of Jewish identities,[16] anthropological research on European Jewry has been thoroughly dominated by the paradigm of mournful nostalgia. The work of Jonathan Boyarin, the leading anthropologist of European Jewry, is axiomatic. Following such earlier ethnographic works as *Life Is with People* and *Image Before My Eyes,* Boyarin figured his work on Polish emigrants in Paris as an "ethnography of memory," a deliberate attempt to bridge the "total break" separating his Yiddish-speaking interlocutors from their shtetl upbringing.[17] Motivated by a "deep nostalgia for a world that has disappeared," Boyarin thus sought to harness the "power of the past" for an "ethnographic presence."[18]

But Boyarin is not the only anthropologist of European Jewry who deploys ethnography to account for the cultural absence of a lost world. In their ethnographic interviews with Jews who returned to Germany after the Holocaust, John Borneman and Jeffrey Peck sought to isolate that which is "genuinely" German-Jewish. The large presence of immigrants from Eastern Europe in contemporary Germany thus effectively constituted an obstacle in their ethnographic quest.[19] What emerges from this conceptualization is a common approach that tends to privilege an "authentic" identity configuration anchored in a pristine past of cultural purity over a messy cultural present marked by traumatic loss and ongoing population flux. It is in this context that we have next to no ethnographic data on the *contemporary* lifeworlds of European Jewry.[20] To be sure, these lifeworlds have little in common with the glorious pasts imagined under the conceptual rubrics of Eastern Europe's shtetls or Western Europe's cosmopolitan salons. But it is the very social hybridity and cultural inventiveness of the European Jewish present that should attract the attention of anthropologists.

In part, then, this book serves as a conceptual corrective to the available ethnographic literature on European Jewry. It neither aims for the nostalgic reconstruction of a "genuine" Austrian-Jewish culture, nor advocates the investigation of "authentic" historical and cultural continuities. Much like the case of Germany, Austria's postwar Jewish community was in large part the product of waves of Eastern European immigration. But rather than viewing this situation as an analytic liability, I am fascinated by the complex strategies of cultural integration Jews developed to feel "native" in their adopted home of Vienna. The heterogeneity of post-Holocaust Austrian Jewry thus emerged as a constitutive aspect of the ethnographic question at hand. For only the engagement with postwar arrivals from the East could ultimately render the following analysis an ethnography of a Jewish present, rather than a eulogy for a Jewish past.

Much like the anthropology of Jews and Judaism, ethnographic work on same-sex sexualities has been relatively marginal to the anthropological project at large. While incidental observations on non-Western same-sex sexual behavior sprinkle the ethnographic record, there were few attempts at systematization prior to the late 1960s.[21] Before then, a number of Boasian anthropologists had invoked the question of homosexuality to advocate a relativist position;[22] but it was only with the rise of the lesbian/gay liberation movement in the 1970s and 1980s that the study of homosexuality began to be integrated into the anthropological project at large.[23]

Paralleling trends in feminist anthropology, early efforts in the anthropology of homosexuality focused on the recovery of previously hidden cultural realities. In a politically motivated project of "ethnocartography," scholars sought to document the prevalence of "homosexuals" in other societies and aimed to show their culturally normative status.[24] Efforts undertaken in this vein focused on Melanesia and Native North America, ethnographic locales where the preponderance of same-sex sexual practices and gendered ambiguity invited the transcultural study of homosexuality.[25]

In the course of the 1980s, the transcultural figuration of homosexuality came under severe theoretical attack. In the wake of the constructionist critique of essentialist conceptions of sexuality, critics began to interrogate the validity of extending such Western notions as "homosexuality" to other socio-sexual fields. As a distinct identity configuration, homosexuality was after all a culturally specific invention of the late nineteenth century, suffused with European conceptions of a distinctly individualized sexuality.[26] In this light, Melanesian rituals involving same-sex sexual activity, for example, looked less like Western homosexual practices than the local articulation of such social relations as age and hierarchy.[27] In general, the critique of Western essentialisms has been extraordinarily productive for the ethnographic investigation of same-sex sexual practices, engendering research in a wide range of culture areas.[28]

While constructionist critiques have engendered important work on the cultural specifics of non-Western same-sex sexual practices, they have also brought renewed attention to the social organization of Western sexualities themselves. Denaturalized as products of historically and culturally specific social relations, they have become the object of social historians and ethnographers. In this vein, the cultural creation and social implementation of the hegemonic homo/hetero binary has been reconstructed,[29] at the same time as a steadily growing number of ethnographies have chronicled the realities of lesbian/gay existence in the extended present.[30]

Unwittingly, however, this important work on modern Western sexualities has introduced a new form of essentialism. In light of the constitutive privileging of North American sexualities in the available literature, a deep ethnocentric bias has come to pervade our understanding of lesbian/gay identities in the West. This bias implicitly posits the homogeneity of "Western" sexualities by figuring North American realities as their essential markers. The problem lies less with the historical framing of the homo/hetero divide, which was in fact operative across the transatlantic divide, than with the historical specificities of late-twentieth-century American lesbian/gay existence. This existence owes its cultural configuration to the Stonewall rebellion of 1969 and the subsequent rise of the American lesbian/gay liberation movement. Operating in a cultural field that allowed the celebration of ethnic pluralism, the movement could adopt and disseminate a teleological script that led from the oppression of pre-Stonewall days to the social emancipation and personal authentification achieved in the wake of the 1969 uprising. If ethnographers like Kath Weston have documented the forging of kinship relations as a new form of lesbian/gay association in 1980s San Francisco, they ultimately observed the fallout of a political project that sought to replace individual stigmatization with communal affirmation.[31] After all, the conception of socially veiled lesbian/gay identities, captured so perfectly by the slogan "gay pride," has been most fully realized in the ethnicized lifeworlds of North America's "gay ghettos" — the privileged sites for the collective articulation of lesbian/gay cultural difference.

The model of lesbian/gay history articulated in the empirical context of North America is powerful, but we have to guard against its extension to such "Western" locales as Austria. There, as in much of continental Europe, the 1970s failed to usher in a clear-cut transition from a conception of homosexuality as personal deviance to a socially based, affirmative lesbian/gay identity. The absence of a politically grounded, mass-based lesbian/gay liberation movement resulted from both the country's social conservatism and its anti-lesbian/gay legislation. In consequence, the cultural field continued to construct persons attracted to the same sex as morally deviant, psychologically aberrant, and criminal until well into the 1990s.

While the last years of the twentieth century brought momentous shifts underwriting the new visibility of queers, this phenomenon was not predominantly the result of liberationist activities. Indeed, when a small lesbian/gay liberation movement emerged in late 1970s Austria, few homosexuals followed its demand to "come out." Even beyond the turn of the century, the recent changes notwithstanding, the majority of Austrian lesbians and gay men chose to remain "in the closet." In contrast to North America, there were no identifiably gay neighborhoods in Vienna, and while the lesbian/gay infrastructure grew rapidly in the 1990s, it was indicative that queers were as likely to refer to it as "die Szene" (the scene) as they were to think of it in terms of the ethnicized notion of "community."

Given this situation, this book seeks to broaden the currently available ethnographic literature on "Western" sexualities.[32] By documenting the specific social relations circumscribing Austrian lesbian/gay subjectivities, I hope to destabilize an analytic logic that equates "Western" sexualities with their specifically North American articulations. Concretely, I aim to explore the queer trajectories engendered in the absence of both a mass-based lesbian/gay liberation movement and the cultural pluralism enshrined in America's constitutional context. The specific forms of cultural existence created in such an environment can help us to rethink and complicate the very notion of "Western" sexuality.

Having located this book in the anthropological literatures on Jews and queers, I want to caution against its bifurcated reception. While my arguments on Jewish and lesbian/gay culture are in conversation with existing work on the respective groups, the book's raison d'etre clearly lies in their comparison. In this manner, it contributes to the small literature written at the intersection of Jewish and queer studies.[33] Much more importantly, however, it is my contention that the comparative study of Jews and queers — of which this book is a first-ever attempt — allows us to pose questions that far exceed the groups' particular histories. Ultimately, this book thus redeploys the ethnographic analyses of Jews and queers to advance an argument about the trajectory of modernity in the German-speaking world. Jews and queers are symptoms of that modernity, and as such, their histories can elucidate its course over the twentieth century.

The Logic of Comparison

Over the last decades, few cultural anthropologists have been engaged in overtly comparative projects. In general terms, this situation seems a direct result of the "crisis of anthropology" — the protracted moment in the late 1960s and 1970s when many of the discipline's practitioners began to question the politics of anthropology's epistemologies. In this light, the grand comparative schemes underlying such projects as the Human Relations Area Files (HRAF) came under intense scrutiny. To anthropology's critics, the positivist belief in HRAF's value-neutral objectivism seemed at best naive, and at worst complicit with post- and neocolonial forms of domination. Instead of an epistemology that subjugated Others by rendering them in the depersonalized form of easily manipulated data, critical anthropologists advocated an intersubjective and hence inherently reflexive approach to fieldwork and the writing of ethnography.[34] Anthropology's initial critics were vilified for their antipositivist stance, but in the context of a larger scholarly field moving toward interpretive approaches in the social sciences, their demands were largely realized in the anthropology of the 1980s.[35] By the time practitioners began to think of their work in terms of "poetics and politics" and "cultural critique," anthropology had thoroughly abandoned projects of comparison and generalization.[36] Instead, the discipline embraced a hermeneutic of dialogism, anchored in the pursuit of cultural specificity and personal reflexivity.[37]

It is ironic that the most influential theorist in cultural anthropology's reflexive turn was also the last major advocate of comparison. Clifford Geertz paved the way for the hermeneutic revolution, famously introducing such seminal notions as "thick description" and the metaphor of culture as text.[38] Geertz's students and followers took his interventions in the direction of ever-increasing particularity. Geertz himself, however, never put interpretive anthropology in opposition to comparison. Quite on the contrary, he advocated the practice of comparison from the time of his dissertation research on the religions of Java, through his crosscultural comparisons of Islam, and on to his retrospective reflections.[39] In his enduring commitment to a hermeneutically based comparative project, Geertz continued a long American tradition of "controlled comparison." That tradition led back through such figures as Fred Eggan, Clyde Kluckhohn, Margaret Mead, and Ruth Benedict to the founding father of American anthropology, Franz Boas.[40]

Boas had articulated a comparative program in opposition to nineteenth-century evolutionary anthropology. Trained in the German historicist tradition of Humboldtian social thought, the immigrant scholar found the positivist assumptions of late-nineteenth-century America's leading anthropologists conceptually untenable.[41] In a famous critique that anticipated arguments advanced during the crisis of anthropology, he attacked the arrangement of the ethnological exhibits at the U.S. National Museum.[42] There curator Otis Mason had deployed a standard evolutionary paradigm in presenting artifacts in hypothetical sequences of development. Boas strenuously opposed such decontextualized comparativism. First and foremost, he argued, "each ethnological specimen" needed to be studied "individually in its history and in its medium." Otherwise, "we cannot understand its meaning."[43]

But while Boas thus advocated a culturally specific historicism as the principal mode of ethnographic knowledge production, he continued to champion a modified form of comparativism. In his seminal 1896 paper "The Limitations of the Comparative Method in Anthropology," he concretized his position, rendering the validity of comparative investigations contingent on the nature of the phenomena under question. Only if phenomena were shown to originate in analogous processes, Boas argued, could they be compared in meaningful ways. As he put it, "Before extended comparisons are made, the comparability of the material must be proved."[44]

In the Boasian framework, two basic modes of comparison were possible: one that focused on difference and one that focused on similarity. The first mode allowed for the articulation of cultural relativism through the recognition of particular social formations. Ruth Benedict and Margaret Mead advanced their seminal arguments on cultural patterns and the specificity of sex/gender systems in this very vein.[45] Having identified the phenomena under question as reflections of specific cultural configurations, their comparison undermined universalized conceptions of human behavior, gender, and sexuality. More recently, Geertz employed this mode of comparison in his crosscultural study of Islam.[46] Holding the religious system constant across the divide between Morocco and Indonesia, the object of study was the observed differences. Those emerged as a function of historical and cultural specificity, a relativistic finding that countered conceptions of Islamic homogeneity. In this Weberian analysis of the dialectic between religion and culture, the systematic presentation of distinctions thus stood at the heart of the comparative project.[47]

By contrast, the present book is indebted to the second mode of Boasian comparativism. That mode, which focuses on the identification of cultural similarities, actually took precedence in Boas's own work. Faced with vast amounts of ethnological evidence, he hoped to systematize inquiries into the history of American Indians by identifying commonalities among different groups. These commonalities, he argued, allowed for the careful reconstruction of the "processes by which certain stages of culture have developed."[48] Comparison was thus a precondition for generalization, enabling the anthropologist to identify larger historical patterns. In contrast to the comparative method of evolutionary anthropologists, however, these patterns were not global expressions of a universal human mind. Rather they were local phenomena, indicative of the cultural processes of "well-defined, small geographical territories."[49]

The present book derives its comparative logic from this Boasian approach. Much like Boas, I am interested in exploring larger historical processes; like him, I turn to the comparative investigation of specific cultural patterns to arrive at careful generalizations about them. Exploring commonalities between Jews and queers is particularly promising in this regard. On a surface level, after all, the two groups could hardly be more dissimilar. Jews are an ethnic and religious group that, in particular historical conjunctures, has also been figured in racial and national terms. Queers, by contrast, are a social group constructed on the basis of sexual orientation. Jewishness is reproduced through familial relations; queerness is not inherited, ongoing genetic research attempting to prove the contrary notwithstanding. It would be easy to continue expounding on the groups' differences, but that would merely highlight the fact that most of them are patently obvious.

What is not at all obvious, however, is the groups' structural similarities. Those, of course, are at the heart of this book, and their systematic elucidation promises new insights into the historical trajectory of twentieth-century Central Europe. In this comparative framework, Jews and queers not only occupy analogous positions as victims of Nazi persecution and oppressed minorities in Austria's Second Republic. Even more importantly from a Boasian perspective of historical reconstruction, they share a common genealogy of cultural abjection, anchored in late-nineteenth-century Central European modernity.

Symptoms of Modernity

It is a central argument of this book that the historical trajectories of Jews and queers have been linked by a joint logic of social articulation. As the following discussion will show, Central Europe's Jews and homosexuals both emerged in their modern configuration in the late nineteenth century. This common origin was not a historical coincidence. Rather, it was a function of nationalism, the normalizing process that imagined modern collectivities as ethnically homogeneous and inherently masculinist entities. As this coarticulated narrative of cultural and sexual purity was fashioned in the moment of late-nineteenth-century German nation-building, it depended on the foundational construction of constitutive outsides. Surveilled by the twin technologies of antisemitism and homophobia, Jews and homosexuals thus became central players in the social drama of modernity. Constituted as always already outside the margins of respectability, their abjection gave coherence to the fiction of German nationness.

It might seem far-fetched to date the modern configuration of Jewishness to the late nineteenth century. Jews, after all, have existed for millennia, and their entry into modernity is usually linked to the *Haskala* of the late eighteenth century. It was at that point that Jews began to enter Central European society as part of a larger emancipatory effort at social transformation.[50] Characterized by a quest for cultural normalization, that effort was supported and aided by enlightened German authorities hoping to harness Jewish resources for the greater good. The resulting ideology of German-Jewish emancipation centered on a logic of acculturation. While Jews were seen as debilitated by centuries of rabbinic solipsism and the harsh life of the ghetto, they could be reformed through *Bildung,* which would render them productive citizens of the German cultural nation. Jews themselves embarked on this process of transformation with great zeal; by the middle of the nineteenth century, they had become fully German.[51]

German Jews continued to adhere to the emancipatory ideals of the late eighteenth century. German support for Jewish normalization, however, was eroding, and by the end of the nineteenth century, the ideology of German-Jewish emancipation was under siege by an antisemitic movement.[52] In place of the progressive program that envisioned Jews as potential equals, the new ideology regarded them across a chasm of invariant and pathologized difference. This is not to say that Jew-hatred was an entirely modern phenomenon. On the contrary, in the European realm it had persisted for nearly two millennia, fueled by Christian doctrine and various local arrangements that placed Jews outside the social sphere.[53] But premodern society had been inherently more segmentary, rendering Jews one group among several whose connections to the body politic were intrinsically tenuous. Moreover, even if Jews existed on the margins of the social order, Christian dogma allowed for a more or less ready recuperation in the event of their conversion.

What ultimately distinguished the late nineteenth century's modern variant of antisemitism from its antecedents was its constitutive anchoring in the concept of race.[54] A function of modernity's striving toward rational classification, the idea of race transformed the notion of Jewish Otherness from a religious and cultural model of explanation to one grounded in the immutable destiny of biology. As Hannah Arendt put it, "Jews had been able to escape from Judaism into conversion; from Jewishness there was no escape."[55] Indeed, within the span of a few decades, elaborate technologies of racial differentiation developed, fixing the new conception through recourse to such emerging scholarly fields as anthropology and eugenics. This materialist "science of race," which fit Jews with a distinct body, sexuality, and behavioral traits, was at once engendered and augmented by an ideological superstructure.[56] This superstructure was the "mystery of race," to use George Mosse's designation for such figures as Richard Wagner and Houston Stewart Chamberlain, who championed the modern notion of invariant Jewish Otherness in the course of the late nineteenth century.[57] It was in the context of their interpretive elaborations of Jewish difference that the Jew came to be figured as a new type of being, forever standing outside the constitutive boundaries of respectability and therefore wholly antithetical to the German nation.

The genealogy of the "homosexual" can also be traced to the cultural logic of late-nineteenth-century modernity. As Michel Foucault has proposed in somewhat speculative fashion and as a number of other scholars have documented empirically, the homosexual's invention was predicated on the emergence of sexuality as an irreducible and constitutive aspect of the self.[58] Created by the ascending bourgeoisie as a technology of individuation, the domain of sexuality quickly became an object of intense scrutiny, not only by individuals who learned to police their bodies, but by an entire industry that came to monitor the new domain. Anchored in the new discipline of sexology but encompassing such older forms of surveillance as the law and the Church, this industry developed, and thereby created, a modern typology of psycho-sexual deviance. It is Foucault's famous argument that the modern homosexual originated at this very intersection of power and knowledge. As the actualized subjectivity created by an enlightened desire for scientific classification, the figure represented a break with former times. The early modern sodomite had been "a temporary aberration," but with the emergence of a sexual science around 1870, "the homosexual was now a species."[59] Indeed, it was through the popular dissemination of sexological publications that a notion of homosexual difference gained currency, both among those who were "afflicted" and those who learned to regard the afflicted as wholly Other.[60]

More than anyone else, we owe the exploration of this process to Mosse. In his groundbreaking book *Nationalism and Sexuality,* he traced the bourgeois deployment of respectability as the principal vehicle of an exclusively nationalizing project.[61] This project was anchored in a romantic ideology of manliness, deployed to safeguard the existing social order in a rapidly changing world. In this light, the presence of the male homosexual as a distinctly effeminate species allowed the clear separation of that which was properly national and that which was not.[62] In conjunction with an operative imaginary that figured lesbians as transgressively manly, this cultural logic effectively located the "homosexual" in constitutive opposition to an emerging national imaginary. As a species whose collective gender insubordination impaired the orderly reproduction of the nation, homosexuals threatened to undermine the state from within. As Mosse put it, "the secrecy that accompanied deviant sexuality resembled a conspiracy sowing hatred against the state; men and women who practiced such vices lacked either moral sense or civic responsibility."[63] It is in that sense that the medical, juridical, and moral demarcation and persecution of homosexuals became intelligible as an integral part of late nineteenth-century German nation-building.

Mosse's analytic approach also highlighted the interarticulation of the discourses that constituted Jews and homosexuals as national Others. While *Nationalism and Sexuality* was primarily concerned with the figure of the "homosexual," he also traced the processes that placed the "Jew" outside the bounds of masculinist respectability. In doing so, Mosse identified a shared set of stereotypes — effeminacy, sexual perversion, reproductive dysfunction, physical deformation — that located Jews and homosexuals in common opposition to the fiction of nationness.[64]

Much like Mosse, I see the overlapping attributions of Jews and homosexuals through the prism of nationalism and the nation-state. As such, the groups' supposed similarities become intelligible through their common location vis-à-vis the nation. As agents of racial and sexual insubordination, they not only threatened the nation's integrity, but also undermined its very constitution. For Mosse, this constellation was somewhat accidental, however. While he figured nationalism as an essentially modern phenomenon, he regarded neither Jews nor homosexuals as products of modernity. Predating the rise of nationalism, they had always been positioned outside the normative boundaries of the social order. And when the bourgeoisie harnessed the concept of respectability as the central element of its nationalizing project, they became its inevitable Others.

In light of the previous discussion, I offer a more overtly constructivist interpretation. In contrast to Mosse, I see the emergence of Jews and homosexuals as a quintessentially modern phenomenon. As such, their very creation underpinned the rise of nationalism and the nation-state. Codified as an ethnically homogenous and intrinsically masculinist entity, the German nation presupposed the presence of constitutive outsides for its operative narration. This was an inherently dialectical process. On the one hand, the two groups were imagined as the primary bearers of racial and sexual impurity. On the other hand, these stereotypes were then marshaled to demarcate the symbolic space of the nation. In early modern times, Jews did not have a privileged position vis-à-vis the body politic, while homosexuals had not existed as a distinct species. It was only with the rise of nationalism that they came to function as social signifiers. Giving coherence to the fiction of German nationness, Jews and homosexuals were thus the abject by-products of the normalizing process that defined the late nineteenth century.[65]

In this analytic framework, Jews and homosexuals emerge as symptoms of modernity. This proposition encompasses both meanings of *symptom:* that of dysfunction and that of sign. The first meaning signals the groups' abject status vis-à-vis the nationalized body politic. Against the idealized vision of racial and sexual homogeneity, Jews and homosexuals appeared as principal bearers of pathological disorder. Their presence undermined the healthy reproduction of a nationally pure society, suggesting forms of social engineering in an effort to safeguard the well-being of the collectivity.[66]

In his brilliantly provocative book *Modernity and the Holocaust,* Zygmunt Bauman proposed to read Nazi ideology in these very terms.[67] Building on Max Horkheimer's and Theodor Adorno's argument in the *Dialectic of Enlightenment,* Bauman presented the Holocaust as the telos of a modernizing project constituted at the intersection of rationalized classification and social improvement.[68] Opposing the commonly held conception of the Holocaust as a "cancerous growth on the body of civilized society, a momentary madness among sanity," he thus refigured the event in terms of the nation-state's exclusionary logic:[69]

In a world that boasts the unprecedented ability to improve human conditions by reorganizing human affairs on a rational basis, racism manifests the conviction that a certain category of human beings cannot be incorporated into the rational order, whatever the effort.[70]

As a moment of total social engineering, the Holocaust thus emerged as the pinnacle of modern German nation-building. "Separating and setting apart useful elements destined to live and thrive, from harmful and morbid ones, which ought to be exterminated," it became intelligible as the systematic effort to cleanse the body politic of those groups deemed wholly irredeemable.[71]

The interpretation I offer in this book builds on Bauman's argument. Like him, I read the Holocaust as the catastrophic realization of the structures built into modernity's nationalizing project. Unlike Bauman, however, I do not restrict myself to the question of racial Otherness. To fully understand the cultural logic of nationalism's exclusionary project, it is essential to account for the systematic persecution of homosexuals during the Third Reich. This persecution was ultimately a function of the group's initial construction as a foundational threat to the nation's integrity. Along with Jews, homosexuals had emerged as the pathological by-products of late-nineteenth-century nation-building; when the Nazis endeavored to complete the project in a merciless act of social engineering, the principal symptoms of modernity became its ultimate sacrifice.[72]

The Nazis, of course, very nearly succeeded in realizing their modernist vision of a racially and sexually homogeneous society. But as Germans and Austrians wrestled with the devastation brought on by World War II, the symptoms of modernity had already begun to make their reappearance in the countries' urban centers. This book endeavors to trace their postwar history. By charting the trajectory of Jewish and lesbian/gay life in post-Holocaust Vienna, I seek to document acts of resistance and accommodation and hope to reconstruct cultural patterns.

But I am also pursuing a larger theoretical project, one that is rooted in the analytic framework sketched out in this introduction. Referencing the second meaning of *symptom* — the notion of symptom as sign — that project treats Jews and queers as social indices of Central European modernity's ongoing trajectory. As symptoms of that modernity, Jews and homosexuals were the abject products underwriting its originary constitution and the principal targets of its genocidal actualization. More generally, the two groups have borne the foundational imprint of the nation-state's cultural logic; as its constitutive Others, their trajectories have been intimately linked to its development in the course of the twentieth century. This was particularly true of the post-Holocaust world whose configuration continued to be articulated through the cultural logic of modernity. Jews and queers continued to function as symptoms of this process; it is in that sense that an account of their postwar histories allows for a theorization of late modernity's cultural patternings. Before I can begin to trace the symptoms' trajectory from modern exclusion to postmodern celebration, however, I need to address some of the peculiarities of Austrian history.

Austrian Specificities

On the surface, Austria might seem an unlikely site for a study that takes the cultural logic of nationalism and the nation-state as its central object. For most of its recent history, after all, the country has existed apart from the principal German nation-state. Moreover, Austria's political roots lie in the supranational Habsburg Monarchy rather than a nineteenth-century history of invented national tradition. As such, the country hardly fits the conventional model of European nation-building, anchored as it is in an ethnic collective's gradual attainment of political sovereignty.[73] This process took place in the German-speaking world, of course, but it excluded rather than embraced Habsburg's Germans.[74]

The consequence of this repudiation, however, was not renewed loyalty to Habsburg's dynastic principles. Quite on the contrary, in the context of Austria-Hungary's escalating national problem, the region's ethnic Germans embraced the exclusionary tenets of nationalism with particular vigor. Pieter Judson has explored this process in a number of settings, documenting how metropolitan nation-builders fostered the creation of German national sentiments at the margins of the Habsburg monarchy.[75] Even more to the point, Judson has traced the trajectory of imperial Austria's liberal parties.[76] The principal agents of constitutional reform in the mid-nineteenth century, by the 1880s they had abandoned their universalist quest for a harmonious community of free peoples. Instead, they forged a German-nationalist politics increasingly based on ethnic distinction.

The liberal parties' embrace of German nationalism was indicative of larger political trends that came to define the body politic according to modernity's exclusionary principles. Georg von Schönerer was the "pioneer" of the modern "politics in a new key."[77] In his radical brand of German nationalism, Jews were produced as the constitutive Other of the national collectivity. As early as the mid-1870s, he had interlaced the new racial antisemitism with a populist critique of Habsburg's liberal economic system to agitate against the deleterious effects of Jewish capitalism. And by the 1880s, this stance had hardened into a full-blown political program that demanded the "removal of Jewish influence from all sections of public life."[78]

Although Schönerer's quest for political influence faltered in 1888, the void was filled shortly thereafter by Karl Lueger, who developed his opportunistic brand of antisemitism into a palpable political vision.[79] Campaigning in Vienna in the early 1890s, Lueger united a coalition of lower-middle-class artisans and middle-class civil servants against a liberal establishment coded as inherently Jewish. In this political program, the Jews of Austria emerged as a monolithic group whose international connections threatened to overpower the "laboring Christian *Volk*."[80] By 1897, the success of Lueger's antisemitic platform secured him the position of mayor of Vienna, and even though he never fully implemented the measures proposed in his antisemitic campaign promises, he fundamentally contributed to the regularization of a public discourse that constructed Jews as a group existing in self-evident opposition to the national collectivity.

Austria's late nineteenth century witnessed the constitution of Jews as the modern national field's abject Other, but it was also the period when homosexuals emerged as a clearly marked threat to the social order. This process was predicated on the intersection of juridical and medical technologies. In 1852, Austria's new penal code had systematized older regulations regarding sexual conduct. The reform brought the codification of §129 Ib, which interdicted "lechery with the same sex" and threatened violators with prison sentences of one to five years.[81] Ushering in an era of increased persecution that steadily intensified in the last decades of the monarchy, the new legislation not only broke with the early nineteenth century's more liberal approach to sodomy, but it was part and parcel of a modern regime that sought to curb sexual deviance in the interests of the collectivity. Austrian doctors and psychiatrists aided in this project of abject classification. More than anyone else, it was Richard von Krafft-Ebing who embodied the modern quest for sexual identification.[82] The author of the best-selling *Psychopatia Sexualis,* which was published initially in 1886 and went through twelve ever-expanding editions over the next seventeen years, he named and analyzed an entire range of nonprocreative sexualities, homosexuality foremost among them. In conjunction with a number of well-publicized sex scandals, both in Austria and abroad, this discursive apparatus served to establish the "homosexual" as a common threat to the modern order of late imperial Vienna.[83]

The nationalization of the Habsburg Monarchy's German-speaking areas had brought forth the symptoms of modernity, and their salience increased further in the wake of World War I. The Great War, of course, culminated in the dissolution of the empire, which was succeeded in turn by a number of nation-states — products, so it seemed, of decade-long struggles for ethnic autonomy.[84] In one sense, Austria was simply the territory left over after the new countries' creation. In another sense, however, it too was now an ethnically defined nation-state, a status signaled most clearly by its official name: Deutsch-Österreich (German-Austria).[85] Most of the new country's citizens had considered themselves German long before the constitution of the so-called First Republic, and in light of the lost access to the vital economic resources in the East, there was widespread support for a formal annexation by Germany. That course of action, however, was disallowed by the allies, leading to an ambiguous attempt at nation-building that oscillated between Catholic imperial nostalgia and German national commitments.

The trajectory of modernity's symptoms gives an indication of the First Republic's cultural configuration. For Jews, the end of the imperial order had particularly grave consequences.[86] While they had been the target of steadily growing political antisemitism, their strict dynastic loyalty had served as a means of protection. In their status as a nonnational minority, Jews were unique among Habsburg's constituencies in that they were not engaged in a struggle for political autonomy.[87] Quite on the contrary, the supranational design allowed for a situation in which they could be "culturally German, Czech, Magyar, or Polish, politically Austrian, and ethnically Jewish all at the same time."[88] Jews, in this light, appeared and saw themselves as the ideal citizens of the Habsburg Monarchy.[89]

This was hardly the case in regard to the monarchy's German successor state. In Austria's First Republic, Jews no longer embodied a core principle like dynastic loyalty. Quite on the contrary, they found themselves on the margins of a social order that defined itself in ethnic terms. Jews, of course, had functioned as a constitutive Other in the late imperial fortification of German nationalism; now that an Austrian state had been created on its basis, they quickly emerged as a negative target of nation-building. It was in this sense that antisemitism came to play a foundational role in interwar Austrian politics.[90] In a cultural field whose connection to the German nation-state could not be actualized, it served as a principal means of national identification. Indeed, all the major parties of Austria's First Republic deployed antisemitism in constitutive ways, leading the phenomenon's foremost historian to comment that interwar "antisemitism was probably more intense in Austria than anywhere else in western or central Europe."[91]

But Austria's new status as a German nation-state not only put Jews in more pronounced opposition to the state's apparatuses. Homosexuals, too, were an increasing target of abject surveillance. While a small lesbian/gay scene developed in the course of the 1920s in a cultural pattern that mirrored that of the Weimar Republic, its patrons faced the constant threat of legal persecution.[92] In contrast to interwar Germany, where only male-to-male same-sex sexuality was outlawed, this threat extended to both men and women, and it became ever more severe as Austrian police began to monitor and systematically raid lesbian/gay establishments. Since the late 1870s, §129 Ib had been applied even in cases of attempted same-sex actions; in conjunction with the state's increased surveillance of lesbian/gay sites, the number of convictions during the First Republic grew into the hundreds.[93]

If the nationalizing process of modernity intensified and accelerated during Austria's First Republic, it was fully realized in the 1938 *Anschluss* to Nazi Germany. The Third Reich had embarked on a quest for national purification, and Austria's population joined its fellow Germans with nearly unqualified enthusiasm. Indeed, the number of native Austrians serving in key positions of the Nazi machinery was disproportionately high; with popular support growing steadily, the NSDAP counted almost 700,000 members in the former Austria by the year 1942.[94] Identification with the German cause remained at a consistently high level during World War II. And since the overwhelming majority of Austria's population never perceived the National Socialist state as an alien regime, the end of the war was widely seen as a national defeat rather than liberation from a foreign yoke.[95]

The massive support for Nazi Germany's project had dire consequences for those groups constituted as its inherent Others. The abject reproduction of modernity's symptoms had already intensified during the First Republic; when the *Anschluss* rendered Austria a part of the Third Reich, its population became ready collaborators in the deadly project of social engineering. If anything, the support for Nazi Germany's exclusionary quest was even greater in the former Austria than in the rest of the Third Reich.

Jews, of course, were the most immediate victims of this genocidal project. In Vienna and other Austrian cities, the *Anschluss* was already accompanied by events resembling pogroms: public humiliation, abuse, physical attacks, beatings, murders, and robberies on a mass scale. Perpetrated predominantly by the civilian population, the events even surprised Nazi functionaries, who envisioned a more orderly process of Jewish disenfranchisement.[96] A few months later, the so-called *Reichskristallnacht* of November 1938 was more violent and caused more bloodshed among Vienna's Jewish population than in any other city in the Reich. Against this backdrop of popular Viennese antisemitism, Adolf Eichmann devised the administrative structures that would render all of Germany *judenrein*. As Doron Rabinovici has documented, Vienna's euphemistically named "Central Agency for Jewish Emigration" became the model for all of Nazi Germany's Jewish administration.[97] Eichmann's Viennese operation worked efficiently, forcing thousands of Jews to leave the city while ensuring that their property was "aryanized." By October 1939, the number of Jews living in Vienna had been cut in half, and when the outbreak of World War II altered the situation, Eichmann's agency became the medium of destruction. In 1941, large-scale deportations of the remaining Jews commenced; by 1945, 65,000 Austrian Jews had lost their lives in the Holocaust.[98]

We know much less about the Nazi persecution of Austria's homosexuals.[99] But there, too, it seems that the *Anschluss* unleashed modes of subjugation whose intensity exceeded other locales in the Third Reich.[100] Following the *Anschluss,* there was an immediate increase in court cases prosecuted in ostensible violation of §129 Ib. At the same time, the Nazi secret police (Gestapo) stepped up its campaign for sexual normalization by establishing a standard office of homosexuality and abortion in Vienna. Aided by a population whose commitment to the Nazi project rendered them willing informers, many thousands of suspected homosexuals passed through that office over the next years. While the Nazis never developed a uniform policy in regard to their persecution, it is clear that many of them were sent to concentration camps. Forced to wear the pink triangle, homosexuals faced particular scorn, and thousands of them died in the interest of the nation's sexual purification.

Austria's role in the Third Reich remains an issue of scholarly debate. Much of that debate has focused on the degree to which Hitler's genocidal ideology was the product of his Austrian upbringing. The question is far from settled, but Brigitte Hamann has made a convincing case for the centrality of Hitler's years in turn-of-the-century Vienna.[101] Hamann focused on his "apprenticeship" with leading figures of the antisemitic movement. In light of the previous analysis, I would submit that this is only a partial explanation for a more systematic encounter with the exclusionary project of German nation-building. Whether or not Hitler's hatred for the symptoms of modernity had its origin in early-twentieth-century Vienna, it is clear that its cultural logic replicated the negative contours of the nation imagined then and there. That nation cohered through the abject production of Jews and homosexuals — a principle that in turn necessitated their systematic eradication in a project of total eugenic purification.

Outline of the Book

This book traces the trajectory of Central European modernity. Having proposed late-nineteenth-century nationalism as the origin and the Holocaust as the catastrophic climax of that modernity, it turns to the postwar period to elucidate its further development. In this analytic framework, the first decades of Austria's Second Republic could be regarded as a moment of late modernity. For, contrary to official discourses, the year 1945 hardly constituted a total break with the Third Reich. While Nazi Germany's defeat ended the systematic extermination of Jews and homosexuals, the Second Republic reproduced a cultural logic that constructed the body politic through the abjection of modernity's Others.

Part 1 addresses this cultural logic and traces its various manifestations in postwar Austria's social fields. Under the heading of "Subordination," its two chapters cover the respective legal and political dimensions of Jews' and homosexuals' ongoing discrimination and documents the ways in which the state's hegemonic discourse was rendered and magnified by the country's mass media. These analyses are followed by ethnographic reconstructions of Jews' and homosexuals' inherently privatized life-worlds as the social expression of the groups' constitutive silencing.

Part 2, entitled "Resistance," traces the various forms of opposition devised by Jews and queers to offset their exclusion from the public sphere. Reflecting a context of generational shifts and altered political landscapes, the two chapters are anchored in the 1970s, the decade that witnessed the respective beginnings of Jews' and queers' self-consciously public mobilization. Early on, these efforts were articulated in political terms; when those were extended into a broadly cultural agenda in the course of the 1980s and 1990s, they resulted in the mass-based emergence of Jews and queers into Vienna's social landscape.

Part 3 also addresses the installation of Jews and queers in Vienna's public sphere. Under the title "Reproduction," its two chapters focus not on the groups' autonomous efforts, however, but on the affirmative role of the state. Central to my argument is an analysis of the geopolitical transformations of the late 1980s and early 1990s. These transformations profoundly altered the trajectory of Austrian nationness, which in turn brought fundamental changes in the treatment of its principal Others. I examine these changes in regard to their political and cultural dimensions and close with ethnographic sketches of Jewish and queer existence at the turn of the twenty-first century.

In the conclusion of the book, I situate the Austrian case in the context of Central Europe and the continent at large. I do so in order to propose a larger theoretical argument centered around my contention that the trajectory of Vienna's Jews and queers signaled the passing of a European modernity anchored in the exclusionary principles of the nation-state. But while this development brought the affirmative integration of modernity's abject symptoms, it pointed to the possibility of new subordinations — a threat that informs the book's concluding discussion of the New Europe and its postmodern trajectory.[102]

A Note on Terminology

Before proceeding further, a word seems in order about the operative designations framing this book. In regard to Jews, the situation is straightforward. Much like in the Anglo-American context, the terms *Juden* (Jews) and *Jude/Jüdin* (Jew [masculine and feminine]) function both on an emic and etic level. While derogatory diminutives such as *Jud* do exist in specific antisemitic contexts, there ultimately is a valuational convergence between the group's hegemonic designation and its self-appellation. And while the terms' referential field continues to be anchored in a notion of race, thereby reflecting the genocidal contingencies of Central European modernity, they are not in and of themselves the object of ongoing contestation. In other words, both Jews and non-Jews deploy *Juden* and *Jude/Jüdin* in an unconscious and readily naturalized manner, rendering the use of the term *Jews* as the logical choice for the present analytic context.

The situation is more complicated in regard to the other group under investigation — a condition reflected in my use of *queers* as the principal term of my analysis. The choice has a political valence. Like many other scholars, I am very careful with the terms *homosexual* and *homosexuals,* generally using them to signal an operative history of abject medical, legal, and national subjectification. In contrast to *homosexual* and its variants, I readily use such designations as *lesbian/gay (lesbisch/schwul)* or *lesbians and gay men (Lesben und Schwule)*. Not only do these terms signal to the emancipatory project of the lesbian/gay movement, but Austria's lesbians and gay men themselves frequently use them for the purpose of self-identification.

More recently, however, the terms have become somewhat problematic. Over the last ten years, the designation *lesbian/gay* has been increasingly criticized for its exclusion of such groups as bisexuals and transgendered people. In the United States, this has contributed to the popularization of *queers* and *queer* — inclusive terms of sexual subversion that emerged in the context of radical AIDS work and marked the powerful potential of discursive reappropriation. A similar process of resistive pluralization and transidentification characterized Austria's late 1990s, when *lesbisch/schwul* was increasingly replaced by the deliberately inclusive *les/bi/gay/trans* (an American-inflected phrase short for "lesbian/bisexual/gay/transgender"). *Queer,* which had itself appeared in Austria by the turn of the century, seems the most effective rendition of this rather cumbersome term.

But while I use *queer* for reasons of politics and aesthetic economy, I am anxious to retain the semantic history and conceptual specificity of its antecedents. Former "homosexuals" could become "queers," but they were still the bearers of an abject history of national identification. Even in their postmodern rearticulation, in other words, they were still symptoms of modernity.

PART ONE

Subordination

CHAPTER I

Myths and Silences

It would be unkind not to speak about your guilt
that bends you to the ground and threatens to crush you.
And this very guilt of yours becomes entirely my own
like your mountains and your misery.
One day you shall not just point your finger at me:
Punish the evil neighbor who compelled me!
It is you who must confess to your guilt
and name your own name in court.
It fills me with fear to return to you,
to atone with you, I who never struck a blow.
I will defend myself against false penitents,
and you will be smooth with deceit again and again!
Probably I might teach you this or that,
and learn as well. . . . But am I strong enough?
Yet, the train takes me on a homebound course.
You are my risk — and I must take my chance with you.

Erich Fried, To Austria

Written in the aftermath of the Holocaust, Erich Fried's poem *To Austria* was an eloquent and painful indictment of post–World War II Austrian hegemonies. In a poetic corpus that often addressed the memory of pre-Nazi culture, Nazi atrocities, and the victims of the Shoah, the text stood out for its incisive analysis of the postwar relations between Austrians and Jews. In a few lines, it not only captured the structures of subordination, unacknowledged guilt, and persistent deceit that characterized those relations, but also charted the inherently ambivalent feelings of Jews vis-à-vis Austria's Second Republic.

Fried's analysis of postwar Jewish marginalization had a strongly autobiographical quality. The poet, who was born in Vienna in 1921, had survived the war in London, and like a number of other émigré intellectuals, he had contemplated a permanent return to his country of origin. Visits to postwar Vienna, however, proved disappointing, as Fried quickly realized that he would always remain an "outsider or at best a newcomer."[1]

As the following analysis will show, Fried's experience in post-Holocaust Austria was paradigmatic. In a cultural field constituted in continued abjection of a Jewish Other, there was no conceptual space for real-life Jews. Whether they were "rémigrés" like Fried or post-Holocaust arrivals from Eastern Europe, Austria's Jews faced a state apparatus that systematically excluded them from the national imaginary. That imaginary was no longer predicated on the Jews' genocidal removal, but it still presupposed their foundational absence from the public sphere. Indeed, as symptoms of modernity, postwar Austria's Jews remained unseen during the first decades of the Second Republic. But in their privatized world of cultural difference, they began to develop the counteridentifications that would underwrite their latter-day resistance against the homogenizing forces of the nation-state.

Victim Myths and Postwar Austrian Nationness

Austria's status as a nation-state had been somewhat tenuous during the interwar years. As the Habsburg Monarchy's German successor state, the country claimed a German national identity. But while the majority of the population regarded the country in those terms, efforts were also underway to constitute a distinct Austrian nationality. Championed in radically different political contexts by factions of the Christian Social Party and Austria's Communists, the project of Austrian nation-building faltered, however. In 1934, the civil war between the Social Democratic *Schutzbund* and the Christian social *Heimwehr* destroyed the fiction of a unified Austrian polity, and the subsequent establishment of the totalitarian *Ständestaat* further undermined the viability of Austrian nationness. As a result, even Social Democratic politicians welcomed the 1938 *Anschluss* to Germany as a development of historical inevitability.[2]

When Austria was reestablished after World War II, the project of Austrian nation-building assumed renewed urgency. Culturally the country would still define itself as German, but in the wake of the Holocaust, it was much more opportune to emphasize the qualities that distinguished Austria from Germany proper. It was in this context that the narrative of Austria as Nazi Germany's first victim was offered by the reconstituted state as the core of a newly invented Austrian national identity. While hardly the collective basis of a classic nation-state, Austria's "victim myth" nonetheless imagined the national community in terms more stridently exclusionary of Jews than any other European country.[3] Subordinating Jews on constitutive grounds in an articulation of unabated antisemitism, it located Jews outside the boundaries of the nation-state.

Ironically, the victim myth had its origin in the international struggle against Nazism. In the Moscow declaration of 1943, the allies had deemed Austria the "first victim" of Hitler's aggression, in a strategic move intended to stimulate Austrian resistance against the Third Reich.[4] Eager to capitalize on the status of victim, the political elite of postwar Austria seized on the allies' original formulation, enshrining it in the country's declaration of independence. Signed on April 27, 1945 by representatives of the three "anti-fascist" parties — the Socialist Party (SPÖ), the Christian Conservative People's Party (ÖVP), and the Communist Party (KPÖ) — the declaration interpreted the years between 1938 and 1945 as the violent imposition of a foreign regime.[5] That narrative was further codified in an official state document published a year later. Subtitled "Justice for Austria," the *Rot-Weiss-Rot-Buch* gave an account of the country's "occupation" in order to justify the thesis of Austria's victimization at the hands of National Socialist aggression. Abandoned by the world, Austria — it was claimed — was left in a "state of confusion," defenseless against the ensuing "political destruction and economic exploitation." A possible short-lived euphoria following the *Anschluss* in March 1938 was said to have been superseded by general disillusionment, sparking an ever-growing "spirit of resistance." Moreover, according to the authors, the "overwhelming majority of the population had never been national socialist," thus allowing the conclusion that the country's restoration as an independent and democratic state should proceed without making the "*Anschluss* and its concomitant circumstances . . . the basis for the political treatment of Austria."[6]

As a principal vehicle of postwar Austrian nation-building, the country's official historiography was designed to externalize the Third Reich and such concomitant circumstances as the Holocaust. As such, the years between 1938 and 1945 were seen as an interruption of Austrian history, which had properly ceased on the day of the *Anschluss*. In order to sustain this narrative, it was not only necessary to ignore the widespread involvement of native Austrians in the Nazi machinery, but also to discount

National Socialism's high level of popular support. Since that support persisted long after the terrorist nature of the Nazi regime had become apparent, it needed to be downplayed to sustain the narrative of widespread anti-Nazi sentiments.[7]

Austrian *Entnazifizierung* (denazification) proceeded along these very lines. Figured as implicit victims rather than perpetrators, the state dealt with former Nazis in decidedly cavalier terms. As early as 1945, the main strategy regarding the several hundred thousand Nazi Party members was thus one of integration rather than exclusion.[8] Nazis were quickly restored to positions of power,[9] and beginning in 1949 — when the former members of the NSDAP were allowed to vote again in general elections, after having being barred in 1945 — both SPÖ and ÖVP fought over their votes with the tacit promise that their role in the Third Reich could be reconciled within the framework of the new Austria.[10]

Austria's founding myth was reinforced by the country's treatment at the hands of the international community. Spared the German fate of partition, ostracism, and the burden of paying adequate reparations, Austria and its citizens were not confronted with their role in the Third Reich.[11] As a consequence, the majority of Austria's population never developed a sense of responsibility for the Third Reich and the Holocaust. Instead, they organized their historical memory around the trope of victimization.[12] Promoted in principle by all major political forces, the country's official historiography thus served to coalesce and sanctify a narrative of collective innocence.

For over forty years, Austria's victim myth remained essentially unchallenged in national and international discourse. Along with the country's neutrality and the political system of social partnership, it came to serve as the central tenet of postwar Austrian nationness.[13] In combination, these three principles constituted Austria as an "island of the blessed" rather than a conquered aggressor whose might needed to be quelled through allied occupation. The very logic of the Cold War order that had divided Germany between East and West thus not only allowed Austria to remain intact but created it as a viable national entity.[14]

Jews and the Nation of Victims

Jews disturbed the ongoing articulation of Austria's victim myth. As the actual victims of Nazi oppression, they not only functioned as embodied signs of the country's co-responsibility for the Holocaust, but undermined the conceptual stability of Austria's postwar arrangements. Those arrangements constituted the nation-state as a collective victim of Nazism — a narrative that could never integrate the Jewish experience of the Shoah. To forge postwar Austria's national imaginary, Jewish voices thus needed to be silenced in the interest of preserving the fiction of a homogeneous victim society. As the presence of Jews in and of itself seemed antithetical to the logic of the imagined community, the state once again became an agent of abject identification. Through a series of political and administrative technologies, postwar Austria sought to purge its national sphere of any Jewish traces. It was a process that at once reproduced Jews' original exclusion on German national grounds and rearticulated it according to the postwar logic of Austrian victimization. The result was a mutual reinforcement that posited Jews as the constitutive Other of a newly purified national collectivity. Jews once more gave coherence to the narration of the nation-state.

In this sense, 1945 was hardly a *Stunde Null* (zero hour). Even though the social exclusion of Austria's Jews had just been taken to its catastrophic extreme, antisemitic structures remained effectively unchallenged in the wake of Austria's liberation. The cultural expressions of these structures extended from the realities of everyday life to utterances by the country's elected officials. In regard to the former, traditional resentments combined with the economic depravations of the day to incite a pogrom-like atmosphere. As former Nazis were quickly normalized in postwar Austria's national community, virulent antisemitism was manifest in numerous settings, ranging from film screenings and university lectures to Vienna's soccer fields and the city's transportation system.[15]

The severity of postwar antisemitism was exacerbated by the denial of its very existence. Austria's politicians, for their part, had a vested interest in negating a phenomenon that clearly contradicted the tenets of the country's victim myth. In 1947, Vienna's Socialist mayor Theodor Körner, for example, defended the city and its population against the accusation of persistent antisemitism. Denouncing the numerous reports of anti-Jewish incidents as "deliberate lies and thoughtless chatter," he noted that the "Viennese" was "intrinsically no antisemite." After all, he was a "citizen of the world," and as such, "antisemitic tendencies were completely alien to him."[16] Körner's defense of postwar Vienna was part and parcel of a larger political strategy in regard to the Jewish question. Having constituted the imagined community in terms of collective victimization, Austria's politicians needed to disallow any categorical distinctions between Austrian and Jewish victims. The result of this situation was an act of cynical universalization. Jews, it was suggested, could be reinte-grated into the national imaginary if they accepted their position as fel-low victims. "We have all suffered," was the way Chancellor Leopold Figl put it in 1946. "The Jews, too, of course," but now, "we wish only to be Austrians, irrespective of what religion we belong to."[17]

Figl's paradigmatic sentiment may have implied a theory of postwar Jewish integration; the practical situation, however, rendered it an impos-sibility. The crux of the matter was the question of return and restitution. The state might have imagined Austrians and Jews as fellow victims of Nazi Germany, but the reality of forced emigration and widespread dis-possession placed the two groups in stark opposition. Even if the state of Austria had not instigated the process of violent exclusion, the country's population had been its clear benefactors, the Jews its obvious victims. In this context, the Jews' possible return raised the specter of restitution, which in turn sparked a reactionary movement. In 1946, a survey found that 46 percent of Austrians opposed the return of the country's Jews, and in 1948, the *Verband der Rückstellungsbetroffenen* (Organization of Those Affected by Restitution) constituted itself to capitalize on this popular sentiment and to lobby on behalf of the rights of "Aryanizers."[18] Given the virulently antisemitic climate, their defense of Austrians' claims on for-merly Jewish property resonated widely, effectively constructing Jewish demands for restitution as an alien threat to the nation's economic via-bility. The sentiment was echoed by the political elite. Interior Secretary Oskar Helmer warned against the imminent danger of "Jewish expan-sion," while President Karl Renner noted that in its "present mood," Austria would not tolerate the restoration of "Jewish monopolies."[19] The mass media, too, was complicit in this project of exclusionary nation-building; for years, Jews appeared in the Austrian press only as the aggressive agents of foreign claims on an embattled Second Republic.[20]

This effective reversal of the roles of victim and perpetrator articulated with the cultural logic of the Second Republic. As such, it served as an extension of the victim myth and its construction of Austria as a hapless casualty of foreign intrusion. Having been victimized by Nazi Germany, Austria was now the target of unjust Jewish claims that needed to be diffused in order to preserve the country's reputation. In this light, the Austrian government decided to approach the question of restitution through a strategy of protraction, famously captured in the phrase "I am in favor of stretching out the issue."[21] Refusing to enter formal negotia-tions until 1953, the Austrian government never altered its position fun-damentally, continuing to insist that the country and its citizens should not be held responsible for Nazi crimes. According to the Jewish negotiator Gustav Jellinek, the state's position was that "Austria cannot be blamed for all those bad things, and where there is no guilt, there is no obligation to give compensation."[22] For a nation whose ongoing narration depended on the rearticulation of the victim myth, genuine amends remained an impossibility. On the contrary, the abjection of Jews needed to continue to sustain the fiction of collective victimization.

Structural Exclusions

The symbolic economy of the Second Republic fortified a national Self in constitutive opposition to an externalized Jewish threat. But if Jews thus appeared as an inherently alien entity, their physical presence in postwar Austria undermined the constitution of a purified victim society. As racialized targets of Nazi genocide, their collective experience of the Holocaust could never articulate with the country's fiction of political victimization; as such, they potentially impeded the postwar nation's successful narration. The Jewish community of post-Holocaust Vienna never counted more than ten thousand people, but given their disruptive position vis-à-vis Austria's victim myth, they had to be kept outside the bounds of normal nationness. In this situation, postwar Austria's Jews were the subject of an ongoing process of structural exclusion. Enacted and policed by the state apparatus and the country's mass media, it constituted them beyond the imagined community and barred them from the public sphere of national reproduction.

The constitutive exclusion of Jews was codified during the originary moments of Austria's Second Republic. As the resurrected nation imagined itself in a new legal code, the surviving victims of Nazism received special attention. In light of the new state's symbolic economy, however, all suffering was not equal. When the legislature passed the first *Opferfürsorgegesetz* (the law regulating support for war victims) in 1945, only political victims of Nazism were eligible to receive financial support.[23] In the postfascist society imagined by the Second Republic's founders, their suffering symbolized the fate of the country at large and therefore stood at the heart of postwar nation-building. This was in contrast to those who had "merely" been racially persecuted. For them, there was no obvious space in a society of political victims. To be eligible for benefits under the *Opferfürsorgegesetz,* returning concentration camp survivors had to prove that they were not just Jews, but political opponents of National Socialism as well. In and of itself, being a Jew did not confer membership in the imagined victim society. Quite on the contrary, Jewish émigrés were not entitled to support at all, since they had ostensibly escaped Nazi victimization.[24]

The foundational inequality of this legislation was challenged almost immediately. In 1946, Jewish survivors established an organization defending the rights of racially persecuted Nazi victims; in the context of the country's Allied occupation, their demands led to the passing of a second *Opferfürsorgegesetz* in 1947.[25] The new law did provide a degree of support for Jews; but since political victims remained starkly privileged, it became an ongoing site of contestation. Consequently, the *Opferfürsorgegesetz* was amended frequently over the next few years. In 1949, for example, Jews attained equal benefits, but only if they had spent either six months in a concentration camp or a year in "regular" prison. Later that year, the inequality was leveled somewhat further when Jews with diminished earning capacities finally became eligible for support. The different valuation remained in place, however, as Jews were required to demonstrate a higher degree of disability than political victims. It was not until the sixteenth revision of the *Opferfürsorgegesetz,* in 1964, that full legal equality was achieved.[26]

If postwar Austria's legal code subordinated Jews vis-à-vis the imagined victim community, the public celebration of nationness systematically enacted their performative exclusion. Simply put, Jews had no space in the Austrian state's ritualized narrations of Self. Invariably grounded in a constitutive affirmation of the country's victim status, these public narrations did not merely overlook Jews. Rather, a Jewish presence had to be actively suppressed to sustain the fiction of postwar Austria's imagined community.

The twenty-fifth anniversary of the *Anschluss* was a paradigmatic example of the manner in which the Austrian state's memorial apparatus effectively produced Jewish silence.[27] Much like other historically meaningful dates, the state used March 1963 to publicly affirm the project of postwar Austrian nationness. Embedded in a series of commemorative events that included sessions by the Austrian parliament and Vienna's state legislature, a grand ceremony on the capital's *Heldenplatz* constituted the climax of the activities.[28] There, at the very site of Hitler's triumphant 1938 speech, the pillars of Austria's Second Republic — the antifascist parties, the church, and the military — performed their access to and claim on the state. Broadcast live on television and radio, the event featured only one speech. Delivered by Chancellor Alfons Gorbach (ÖVP), it presented a classic statement of Austria's victim narrative. Blaming the world community for its ostensible abandonment of Austria in 1938, it reaffirmed the country's innocence in regard to the atrocities committed by the Third Reich. Even more importantly, however, the speech presented a paradigmatic argument about the Second Republic as a state brought forth by the common victimization of former enemies. In this narrative, the bitter opponents from the country's 1934 civil war, Christian Socials and Social Democrats, forged a bond of Austrian patriotism in opposition to Nazi oppression. A Socialist speaker might have glossed the civil war with slightly more animus, but Gorbach's main thrust was readily acceptable to all constituencies of postwar Austrian nationness. In calling for an emphasis on "that which unites us over that which divides us," he constructed Austria as a homogeneous society of political victims; insofar as he pleaded with the nation to "forgive and forget," he also managed to incorporate former Nazis into the state's imagined community.[29]

The Jewish community was constitutively excluded from such ritualized narrations. Given the experience of the Holocaust, its members found it impossible to simply "forgive and forget," not least because it marked a divide that could not be overcome through the invocation of a common victimization. Even more relevant for the Jews' structural exclusion from the nation's public sphere, however, were the actions of the state itself. Since Jews would disrupt the ritualized narration of postwar Austrian nationness, they were effectively silenced. In the decades following World War II, Jews never spoke at official state events and rarely even attended them. Instead, they stood apart, symbolically and spatially, from the public articulation of Austrianness.

Again, the events of March 1963 were paradigmatic. While the state performed its official ritual of national affirmation, the Jewish community enacted its silencing with a simple and private ceremony. Excluded from the *Heldenplatz* as a site of state power, the *Israelitische Kultusgemeinde* (IKG), the administrative and governing body of Vienna's Jews, assembled its employees for a quiet session in remembrance of the Jewish dead.[30]

Everyone took their seats in silence and with a somber mood. Not a word was said, no speech was given. An employee who had suffered unending pain during the years of persecution, lit a candle; thereafter the IKG's cantor sang the El Mole Rachamim in a low voice.[31]

Ultimately, this event reflected a larger memorial structure. In a context where Austria's public sphere was occupied with the exclusionary narration of the country's victim myth, there was no space for alternative articulations. If anything, the IKG's silence dramatized this inequality.

The IKG's memorial resignation was much more than a momentary reflection of Austrian power structures. Echoing an entire history of commemorative violence, it highlighted the Jewish community's general inability to resist Austria's postwar hegemony. As such, the silence of March 1963 implicitly recalled a number of failed attempts at inserting the Jewish experience into the Second Republic's master narrative. An event in November 1948 was crucial in the exclusionary structure's originary constitution. Seeking to confront Austria's political elite with the Jewish memory of the catastrophe, the IKG staged a ceremony on the tenth anniversary of *Kristallnacht*.[32] As thousands of Jews congregated in one of Vienna's festive halls, their demand for "Peace, humanity, and justice!" would be clearly heard by the non-Jewish guests of honor.

That group was led by Chancellor Leopold Figl (ÖVP). But his speech at once performed and cemented the Jewish exclusion from postwar Austria's master narrative. For, even in the face of the victims of racial genocide, he reaffirmed the cynical notion of a common Nazi experience. "If you have invited me to speak at this ceremony of mourning and memory," he opened his remarks in metonymic representation of Austria at large, "it is because I endured the time of degradation with so many of your co-religionists."[33] Figl proceeded to elaborate on the identificatory fiction. As Austria was "raped" in front of an indifferent world, its population could not stem the "crimes and atrocities designed and organized beyond our borders." But even if all Austrians thus suffered equally, the postwar government was willing to make amends. As Figl made clear, however, this gesture would be purely symbolic. "Reconstruction and reparation need to start in the intellectual realm," he noted, effectively limiting the state's task to one of re-education. If Figl thus dashed Jewish hopes for justice and restitution, he went even further when he identified his Jewish audience as a potential hindrance in Austria's postwar path. While he praised the Jews who were willing to "regard themselves as part of the Austrian people," he admonished those "victims" who were still "closing off their hearts." Figl granted that the "rubble of the destroyed temples and the wreckage of so many destroyed lives" might weigh heavily on Austria's Jews, but that, he concluded, should not impede the quest "toward our common goal."

The constitutive exclusions transported in Figl's speech were both obvious and painful. On the one hand, Austria's victim narrative equated the Jewish experience of racial genocide with the state's political disenfranchisement — a situation that at once obscured and silenced the specificity of Jewish suffering. On the other hand, the Jewish memory of that suffering was itself figured as an obstacle in the constitution of postwar nationness — a construction that placed Jews outside the boundaries of Austria's imagined community. In staging the memorial event of November 1948, the IKG hoped to win sympathy for the plight of post-war Austria's Jews. Instead, members of the Jewish community were admonished for their persistent memories of genocide. In light of the distress brought on by such impudence, Vienna's Jews retreated into the private realm of memory. Indeed, when the IKG organized an event to commemorate the twentieth anniversary of *Kristallnacht* in 1958, official representatives of the Austrian state were not invited.[34] Much like the commemoration of March 1963, Jews could only articulate the specificity of their post-Holocaust experience in isolation from public domains of national reproduction.[35]

The constitutive exclusion of Jewish experience from the symbolic economy of postwar Austrian nationness was embodied in paradigmatic fashion by Bruno Kreisky. On the surface, the notion might seem counterintuitive. Kreisky, after all, was the scion of a Jewish family who emerged as one of the defining politicians of Austria's Second Republic, serving as the country's Socialist chancellor from 1970 to 1983. On closer inspection, however, it becomes clear that his political career retraced rather than resisted postwar Austrian hegemony. Central to that pattern was Kreisky's persistent refusal of public Jewish identification. This was not an act of opportunistic duplicity, but a reflection of deeply held cultural values. A product of the assimilationist variant of German-Jewish emancipation, Kreisky had always rejected ethnic and national conceptions of Jewishness. Instead, he understood Jews as an exclusively religious entity; and given his own secularism, he never felt a particular allegiance to a community constituted on confessional grounds.[36]

Kreisky's cultural background, of course, was shared by many postwar Jews, who had also regarded socialism and communism as vehicles of secular assimilation. For most of them, however, the Holocaust had occasioned an identification with the fellow members of a Jewish *Schicksalsgemeinschaft* (community of fate). What rendered Kreisky's position unique and uniquely acceptable to the Second Republic's body politic was his refusal to identify even with the racialized targets of genocide. Instead, he constructed his wartime experience in Swedish exile in the terms of Austria's victim narrative:

I would have been persecuted, driven into emigration, or left to succumb in a camp if German fascism had been free of antisemitism. Mussolini banished our Italian comrades to the Liparian Islands, the German Socialists went to concentration camps. I never understood my emigration as a consequence of my Jewish background: I would have been persecuted in the same manner that I had been four years prior [in the wake of the 1934 civil war]: for purely political reasons.[37]

Kreisky's sentiments were sincere. But they aided and abetted the structural exclusion of Jewish experience from postwar Austria's political field. Here, after all, was a "racial Jew" who constructed his biography in the dominant terms of political victimization. In doing so, Kreisky not only diffused vague feelings of Austrian guilt by effecting a collective exoneration, but he foreclosed the legitimacy of a distinctly Jewish Holocaust experience. That foreclosure, of course, was constitutive of postwar Austrian nationness in general; it was in that sense that Kreisky stood less for the public articulation of Jewishness than for its foundational repudiation.

Kreisky sought in fact to protect Austria from Jewish incursions. In 1975, he famously attacked Simon Wiesenthal when the latter threatened the country's postwar arrangements. Wiesenthal, who had already criticized the inclusion of former Nazis in Kreisky's cabinets, uncovered the involvement of Friedrich Peter in war crimes committed by the Waffen-SS. As the leader of the Freedom Party (FPÖ) — the successor of the Union of Independents (*Verband der Unabhängigen,* VdU), itself founded as a political haven for Austria's former NSDAP members — Peter was not an immediate political associate of Kreisky. But in the interest of political alliances and the acceptance of former Nazi sympathizers into postwar Austria's imagined community, Kreisky came to Peter's defense. In the process, he constructed Wiesenthal as a dangerous outsider who sought to undermine Austria's ongoing quest for national reconciliation. In an interview, he went so far as to suggest that "the man [Wiesenthal] must disappear."[38] In Kreisky's Austria, there was no space for Jews who articulated the specificity of Jewish suffering. Their experience would remain incompatible with the realities of postwar Austrian nationness.

Jewishness and the Mass Media

It was not just postwar Austria's political field that constructed Jews as inherent outsiders of the imagined community. The country's mass media were also complicit in the national project of structural exclusion. In the years after World War II, media outlets had represented Jews as agents of foreign demands for restitution, and when the country's press began to engage the Jewish question more substantively in the 1960s, they continued to produce the constitutive dichotomization. In the eyes of the mass media, Jews were at once separate and subordinated, a representational structure that created an Austrian Self in foundational opposition to a Jewish Other. While the state apparatus subjugated Jews through the dismissal of their Holocaust experience, the mass media thus gave cultural contours to their continued abjection.

A 1964 article in *Die Furche,* a centrist Catholic publication, provided a paradigmatic template for the mass-media representation of postwar Austria's Jews.[39] Written as a well-meaning contribution to an emerging Catholic endeavor of Christian-Jewish reconciliation, the piece was designed to examine the project's difficulties. Those were quickly located. They lay with Vienna's Jews, who, as the article proclaimed at the very beginning, were unwilling to enter into the proposed dialogue. Ultimately, the piece sought to uncover the reasons for this hesitancy, finding them not in the experience of the Holocaust or the realities of persistent antisemitism, but in the Jews' irreducible difference. Focusing exclusively on Vienna's small orthodox minority, the city's Jews were portrayed as the bearers of a strange set of beliefs and practices that were intrinsically incompatible with Austrian culture at large. Indeed, as the article proceeded to recount the author's quest into the heart of Jewish darkness, his subjects seemed like members of a clandestine cult that willfully shunned the prospect of social recognition.

The first site of Jewish sociability already sets the stage of impenetrable difference and cultural destitution. The "dilapidated" building that is home to an orthodox youth group is marked by "cool darkness."[40] It takes time to adjust to the scene; but when the author does, he beholds a "not particularly cozy room whose walls are adorned with pictures of bearded rabbis as well as some posters." Fitted with "one of those caps that orthodox Jews wear everywhere and all the time," he enters into conversations that are interrupted when the "boys are called to the afternoon prayer." "The girls stay in the room," the author informs his readers, because "among the Jews, praying and worship are men's affairs."[41] As the author waits for the boys' return, the girls start to sing, and "the metallic sound of their voices holds a strangely foreign charm for the visitor."

As the article went on to discuss the goings-on in Vienna's only kosher restaurant in similarly exoticist terms, the interpretive gist became clear. In a logic that recalled Chancellor Figl's speech of 1948, Austria — or, in this case, Catholic Austria — was constructed as a space of cultural normalization. But if the nation was thus imagined as a champion of antifascism and Christian-Jewish reconciliation, the operative logic of the victim myth prevented the identification of Austria and its citizens as the bearers of historical and social responsibility. In the absence of adequate restitution and genuine remorse, however, Jews were unable to enter into unencumbered dialogue. This refusal potentially undermined the fiction of postwar Austria as a racially and ethnically neutral space, and it was in that situation that the Jews themselves were accountable for their exclusion from the national sphere. Whereas Figl found Jewish hearts to be closed, *Die Furche* reinvented the Jews as an inherent Other on religious grounds. Jews, the publication ultimately suggested, were an intrinsically foreign entity, whose strange customs and bizarre existence prevented their ready integration into postwar Austria's national field.[42]

The mass-media construction of Jews as national outsiders was a persistent feature of postwar Austria's cultural field. But it came to a virulent climax in the spring of 1974, when the *Neue Kronen Zeitung* published a series of forty-two articles under the title "The Jews in Austria." A seminal moment in postwar Austrian-Jewish history and the history of the country's antisemitism, the series brought unparalleled attention to the "Jewish question." Written by Viktor Reimann — a journalist with a complicated Nazi past and German nationalist sympathies — and advertised on huge billboards across the country, it purported to settle age-old debates regarding the "Jewish character" and its influence on Austria and Western culture at large.[43] In this light, the series' title was hardly accidental. Juxtaposing two discrete entities, it gestured to a basic incompatibility that was never in doubt. If the framing of the series was thus highly tendentious, it assumed added significance in light of the publication venue. A tabloid with center-right leanings, the *Krone* has always been unabashedly populist and readily antisemitic. As the self-styled "voice of the small man," it had a history of "guarding" Austrian interests against Jewish demands, particularly in regard to questions of restitution. Other Austrian newspapers had followed similar agendas, but the *Krone* stood out for its sheer popular success. In a country of seven million people, the paper maintained a readership of over two million.

In the course of the series' publication in April and May of 1974, "The Jews in Austria" developed a convoluted argument about the persistence of Jewish difference. On the one hand, Jews were portrayed as obstinate bearers of a tradition that required their self-imposed isolation from the rest of society. To make the point, Reimann repeatedly discussed some religious aspects of Judaism, commenting that "no people" was more "stubborn" in the "preservation of its customs."[44] On the other hand, however, Jews were also seen as particularly adaptable. "As an eternal wanderer," "the Jew" had the ability to take on the cultural guises of different national traditions.[45] But that, too, was ultimately seen as a form of exceptionalism. While other peoples lived sedentary existences, Jews distinguished themselves by invading Europe's national spheres. In the *Krone's* racial logic, in which Karl Marx figured as the Jewish "Moses of Socialism," this constituted an intolerable imposition of foreign elements — a notion Reimann supported with numbers documenting the undue "influence" and "strength" of the Jews in pre–World War II Austria.[46]

In the framework of the *Krone* series, such arguments on Jewish difference and influence had a number of concrete implications. First and foremost, it allowed Reimann to recast the responsibility for antisemitic persecutions. Between the Jews' stubborn refusal to abandon their religious isolation and their aggressive infiltration of other peoples, they were themselves to blame for their frequent oppression. As Reimann put it repeatedly, "One of the major reasons for antisemitism can be found in the Jew himself."[47] This logic, of course, articulated perfectly with Austria's postwar arrangements. If the Jews were responsible for their own victimization, then Austria was hardly culpable.

But not even Reimann could overlook the sheer devastation of European Jewry. While he suggested that "Jewish reports of over six million dead were clearly exaggerated," he did express outrage over the Holocaust.[48] In classic accordance with Austria's victim myth, however, he went to great pains to exculpate the country and its citizens. He had identified the Jews as a cause of antisemitism; now he argued that its development into a political force of genocidal proportions had nothing to do with Austria. According to Reimann, it was a foreign import, invented by such figures as Arthur Gobineau, Houston Stewart Chamberlain, Wilhelm Marr, Eugen Dühring, and Adolf Stöcker.[49] This list conveniently omitted the Austrian pioneers of political antisemitism. But to Reimann, Schönerer and Lueger had been "unsystematic" in their Jew-hatred, which proved not only that "Austria never had fundamental thinkers of antisemitism," but that the country was truly innocent of the Holocaust.[50]

Reflecting the country's victim myth, Reimann's fiction of Austrian innocence was connected to the question of restitution. Jewish demands for compensation appeared both outlandish and fundamentally unfair in this framework. Austria, in this widely resonant reading, was the target of a predatory plot by world Jewry — a situation that not only demanded the vigorous defense of the country's integrity, but fueled Reimann's basic contention that Jewish impudence was at the heart of antisemitism. Indeed, Reimann himself performed this reversal of victims and perpetrators in response to protests by Vienna's Jewish community. In late April of 1974, the IKG had appealed to Austria's press council, pleading for a condemnation of the series in "moral support" of a "defenseless Jewish population."[51] Reimann responded with vitriol. Having established the Jewish control of America's mass media at the beginning of the series, he regarded the IKG's action not as a desperate attempt by a besieged minority, but as part of an international Jewish conspiracy.[52] "The Jews in Austria" thus readily stood in for the country at large, and Reimann threatened that the series' discontinuation would be the "beginning of a real antisemitism."[53]

But if "The Jews in Austria" thus turned on the ramifications of the country's postwar victim narrative, Reimann's series also articulated with an older logic of nationalist exclusion. That exclusion was a function of the Jews' fundamental alterity, which Reimann asserted both on cultural and racial grounds. In presenting the historical trajectory of an inherently alien entity, much of the series could in fact be read in terms of a purifying national project. Reimann's audience certainly understood the series in those terms. In a typical letter to the editor, a reader insisted that the "Jews are a foreign body in our people," while another praised Reimann's "developmental depiction of Judaism," since it showed that the "best solution of the Jewish question" was the "strengthening of one's own nationality."[54] Reimann himself seemed to advocate a similarly exclusionary solution when he closed his series with an invocation of Israel. With the state's founding, he noted, "the Jew as eternal wanderer and refugee is a thing of the past." Now, "Jews who are not comfortable in the land of their birth" need not look for a "new homeland," but can "return to their true home."[55]

In the antisemitic context of Reimann's series, the concluding remark seemed clear. Reproducing the modernist logic of Jewish abjection, it envisioned the departure of Austria's Jews as an act of national fortification. Reimann, to be sure, did not advocate a new Holocaust. But much like the postwar Austrian nation-state he championed, he regarded Jews as an obstacle and a burden. Between their imagined characteristics and real Holocaust experiences, they stood apart from the imagined community, structurally excluded from its public and publicized reproduction.

Antisemitic Lifeworlds

Jews in postwar Austria experienced structural exclusion in the form of unabated antisemitism. For some of them, it came as a terrible shock.

Many rémigrés had anticipated a warm welcome in light of their faith in Austria's future. Instead, they were greeted with the same contempt that was shown to the new arrivals from Eastern Europe, who quickly came to constitute the majority of Vienna's Jewish community.

Ignored by the public at large, the antisemitic excesses could be traced in the pages of the Jewish press. In the immediate postwar years, reports of administrative harassment and popular antipathy dominated. Bitter complaints were registered in this manner about demeaning questions by officials and outright hostility in the face of claims for restitution.[56] By the 1950s, individual cases of violent antisemitism took center stage, foremost among them a 1954 instance of police brutality against a rabbi who was detained amid shouts of "Hitler has not exterminated enough Jews."[57] Such coverage received renewed urgency in the early 1960s, when an anti-semitic wave swept over Germany and Austria. In January of 1960, *Die Gemeinde* — the official publication of the IKG — reported on the deface-ment of Vienna's main synagogue; a few months later, the paper noted that an event commemorating the last Jewish victims was disrupted by bellows of "Heil Hitler."[58] The next few years brought a litany of antise-mitic incidents. Covered with increasing despondency in *Die Gemeinde,* they ranged from repeated vandalism of Jewish cemeteries and open ridicule of Holocaust victims to public singing of Nazi songs and the per-sistent appearance of prominent antisemitic graffiti.[59]

Ethnographic realities mirrored the picture created in the Jewish press. In interviews conducted with Austrian Jews who had returned to Vienna in the immediate postwar years, experiences with antisemitism were a constant theme. Ranging from random epithets to routine deal-ings with hostile bureaucracies intent on protecting "Austrian" against "Jewish" interests, they painted a picture of permanent subordination.[60]

Covering Jewish experiences from the late 1950s onward, the ethno-graphic interviews conducted for this study reveal a similar picture. Simply put, every Austrian Jew I talked to had had foundational encoun-ters with antisemitism. Narratives of such experiences were frequently set in Vienna's schools. There Jews were subject to unique forms of surveil-lance that reinforced their identification as perennial outsiders. Recording students' religious affiliations, such official documents as transcripts and the so-called "class books," for instance, publicly marked Jews as Other.[61] Even more importantly, Jews did not sit in on Catholic religion classes. Offered during regular school hours and attended by the overwhelming majority of any school's student body, these classes segregated Jews on a regular basis, constituting microcosms of Austria's imagined community.

Produced and identified by the school apparatus as a distinct entity, Jews were thus a ready target for antisemitic excesses ranging from verbal abuse to willful exclusion from the student community — painful experiences that occupied prominent places in many postwar Austrian-Jewish narratives.[62]

If schools appeared as archetypical sites for the experience of antisemitism as a face-to-face phenomenon, the anonymity of Vienna's urban space provided a layer of collective hostility. Numerous Jewish interlocutors supplemented their accounts of specific incidents with an overall perception of antisemitism in the population at large. Antisemitic comments overheard in such public and semipublic spheres as sporting events, government offices, and restaurants were central to such narratives. To most Jews coming of age in postwar Vienna, such comments were more than incidental events; they evidenced the country's antisemitic realities and served as potent reminders of Austrian Jews' perilous existence.

Social scientific research confirms Jewish perceptions of Austrian antisemitism during the Cold War era. Setting aside for the moment the inherent problems of "representative sampling," it seems clear that the overwhelming majority of Austria's population readily adopted the postwar master narrative of Austrian victimization and its concomitant antisemitism. Surveys conducted in the 1970s and early 1980s showed that roughly 80 percent of the populace rejected Jewish claims for restitution, not least because — as the same percentage of respondents held with *Krone* series author Viktor Reimann — the Jews were at least partially responsible for their repeated persecution.[63] This antisemitic reflex went hand-in-hand with a collective construction of Jews as a numerically powerful, and hence imminently threatening, presence. In 1976, nearly 90 percent of Austrians overestimated the number of Jews living in Austria by a factor of fifty, with 50 percent missing the actual mark of less than ten thousand by a factor of more than a hundred. If these numbers hinted at the significance of antisemitism in the constitution of non-Jewish Austrian selves, its centrality was further confirmed by the responses to a range of classic survey questions. In this vein, studies in the late 1960s and 1970s indicated that only 23 percent of Austrians regarded Jews who had converted to Christianity as true Christians, while fewer than 50 percent entertained the notion that Jews could be considered genuine Austrians.

Along with the structural exclusions engendered by postwar Austria's victim myth, this persistent antisemitism had momentous repercussions for Jewish existence. As a technology of social reproduction, it not only demarcated the national sphere in constitutive abjection of a Jewish Other, but foreclosed altogether the public articulation of Jewishness. Jewish identity, in consequence, became necessarily privatized — a mode of cultural subordination that extended modernity's exclusionary project. Jews were no longer murdered, of course, but since the public sphere was still policed in the interest of national purification, they were forced into a diffident posture. In practice, this meant that Jews were effectively absent from public debate. As a collectivity, they were given no voice in Austria's official realms, and even individual Jews hardly ever appeared in the country's mass media. In the rare circumstances in which Jews did emerge into the national sphere, moreover, they tended to follow Kreisky's model, downplaying their Jewish identity in the interest of foregrounding a public image of normative Austrianness.[64]

In the ethnographic realities of everyday life, this enforced privatization took similar forms of identity management. Hoping to pass in public as unmarked citizens, Jews avoided the display of overt signs of difference. Thus it became common, for example, to give children two names. Among family and Jewish friends, an individual would be known by an identifiably Jewish appellation like "Avi" or "Shuki." Officially — on birth certificates, in school, and in professional contexts — the person would appear as "Alexander" or "Michael."

Given its overt iconography, the Star of David was seen as far too provocative for public display. Klara — a lawyer who came of age in the Vienna of the late 1950s and early 1960s — described her feelings in regard to the symbol in typical fashion:

When I was young, it would never have occurred to me to wear a *Magen David* [Star of David], not even on a necklace. Who knows what could have happened if people in the streetcar had been able to tell that I was Jewish. I was Jewish at home with my family and our friends, but outside of the house, I tried to make sure that no one would know.

Hannah, who was born in 1960, gave a similar account of her feelings during the 1970s and 1980s. "I didn't try to expose myself," she noted, so "when I would go out to shop for example, I never wore a Star of David. I was just too afraid about the reaction." In private, Vienna's Jews regarded the symbol as a sign of affirmative Jewishness, but in public, it was eschewed as a compromising icon of abject difference.[65]

Such sentiments are not idiosyncratic. Quite on the contrary, they are indicative of larger social realities characterized by the systematic retreat into a private sphere of Jewish association. Confronted with the constant threat of antisemitism, Jews turned to other Jews in an effort to consti-tute a lifeworld apart from the public sphere of Austrian nationness.[66] In building this privatized society, a number of institutions played central roles. Predictably, Vienna's main synagogue and other sites of worship were significant, but the overwhelming majority of Viennese Jews were secular, rendering religious locales a relatively minor component in the creation of Jewish lifeworlds. More important than religious sites were informal friendship networks. In interview after interview, I heard about prominent memories of birthday celebrations, dinner parties, and family outings spent in exclusively Jewish company.[67] "We just got each other's jokes," was the way one man put it, while another interlocutor empha-sized the "basic political understanding" that sustained Jewish convivial-ity. In many instances, such Jewish friendship networks persisted over a number of generations, often lasting into the twenty-first century.

More than in any other institution, however, the constitution and reproduction of postwar Jewish society occurred in Vienna's two Jewish youth organizations. Those groups — the secular, socialist HaSchomer Hazair (Young Guard) and the religiously oriented Bnei Akiba (Sons of Akiba) — achieved a remarkable level of social integration, uniting the overwhelming majority of Jews who grew up in postwar Vienna in cross-generational ties of enduring personal association. In existence since 1947 and 1949 respectively, the youth organizations functioned as a crucial alternative to the antisemitic realities of Vienna's schools. There Jewish children were excluded from the normative processes of social reproduc-tion, a situation that often translated into a persistent sense of difference. As one man who entered school in late 1960s Vienna put it, "It was there that I realized I was totally different. I didn't just look different, I was brought up differently too." Many other Jews experienced Austrian schools in similar terms; it is against such a backdrop of personal isolation and antisemitic rejection that the Jewish youth groups functioned as defining spaces of postwar Jewish socialization. Ilana, who entered the HaSchomer Hazair in the late 1960s, offered the following paradigmatic narrative:

It was incredibly difficult for me to find friends in school, because I always had the feeling that the other children saw me as an intruder. I didn't have the same clothes and I didn't speak the same language, and they always made me remem-ber that. And then my search for another situation began. One day, a girl from a higher grade came to me and said, "I'll take you to a group, and you will be com-fortable there." So when I was twelve, I went to the Schomer for the first time. That was a group of wild, lively, and funny children. There, I had the feeling I could be the way I was, I didn't have to disguise myself. For me, that was a fundamental experience. . . . I immediately felt a part of it. . . . The Schomer has been more formative for me than anything else in life.

Such sentiments were expressed to me again and again; like Ilana, a majority of postwar Jews lived from weekend to weekend, abiding their marginalization in Austria's schools in anticipation of their authenticating inclusion in Vienna's Jewish youth organizations. Against the hegemonic processes of structural exclusion that rendered Jews constitutive outsiders in Austria's national field, the HaSchomer Hazair and Bnei Akiba thus served as principal anchors of positive identification. If Vienna's schools reproduced the antisemitic lifeworld, it was the youth groups that provided and created a privatized sphere of affirmative Jewish difference.

Jewish Subjectifications

The privatized society of postwar Austrian Jewry induced modes of identification that reflected its structural configuration. In its near total separation from Austria's antisemitic lifeworld, it engendered a drastically oppositional stance — a stance that was a function of the strict dichotomy between "Austrians" and "Jews." While a minority of the latter favored the abandonment of their Jewish identity in the interest of national normalization, the overwhelming majority chose the obverse route, creating their subjectivity in constitutive opposition to a hegemonic Austrian Self. It was in this sense that most postwar Austrian Jews readily disavowed any Austrian identity. In conversation after conversation, I was told by Jews that they never "felt Austrian." They may have had Austrian citizenship, but this was rarely experienced as anything other than a formal arrangement. Jews readily noted that they "didn't really care about Austria"; they were quick to differentiate themselves from such ostensibly Austrian traits as conservatism and provincialism, which came to function as the constitutive outside of Jewish identification. Up until the twenty-first century, this dissociation with Austria was reflected in Jews' everyday discourse, where the unmarked term *Austrian* always referred to non-Jews. In a cultural field shaped by the Holocaust and the victim myth, Jews found and located themselves outside the symbolic confines of the Austrian nation-state.

The Jewish rejection of Austria's imagined community reflected the availability of a ready alternative. That alternative, of course, was Israel; for years it seemed that the Zionist state was the inevitable destiny of post-war Viennese Jews.[68] In 1948, the founding of the state of Israel was welcomed enthusiastically by all of Vienna's Jewish organizations, and from that moment on, all official ceremonies featured the Hatikwah and Israeli flag alongside their Austrian counterparts.[69] This is not to say that all political groupings within the IKG were equally committed to the Zionist project as individual practice. Some exhibited reserve about the prospect of aliya, while others championed it with great vigor.[70] Regardless of their particular stance on the question of emigration, however, all groups regarded Israel as the self-evident site of Austrian Jewry's future. After all, Vienna's Jewish community had been reestablished in 1945 to facilitate emigration to Palestine, and between the European experience of genocide and the treatment of Jews in postwar Austria, Zionism emerged as the defining mode of Jewish cultural identification.[71]

This was particularly the case for the younger generation. For Jews born in the years after the Holocaust, Israel not only held out the prospect of a viable Jewish existence, but it presented a powerful model of social autonomy in the face of Austrian subordination. Once again, HaSchomer Hazair and Bnei Akiba were the central sites of this Jewish socialization process. Both youth groups were explicitly Zionist, committed to the strengthening of Jewish national consciousness as well as the goal of eventual aliya. "Israel was the thing," one member of Bnei Akiba noted in describing the group's commitments in the late 1950s and 1960s, "the idea was to be prepared for aliya, and it was clear that everyone would move to Israel at one point." The situation was analogous in the Schomer. "For us," Ilana told me, "Israel simply was the holy land of milk and honey. We all dreamed of moving there immediately to build up the country." This feeling persisted from the late 1940s until well into the 1980s. Describing her time in the Schomer in the early 1950s, one woman commented that "Israel was simply the future" — a sentiment that was echoed by a man who attended the group in the late 1970s and who noted that "our identities were totally focused on Israel. To live in Austria or to stay there was a historical mistake." Indeed, the highlight in the calendars of Vienna's Jewish youth organizations was the annual pilgrimage to Theodor Herzl's original grave at the city's Döbling cemetery. The grave, of course, was empty; and that fact took on an obvious symbolic significance. Much like Herzl's remains, the members of HaSchomer Hazair and Bnei Akiba would leave Europe's antisemitic confines for the safe haven of the Jewish state.

While the Jewish youth groups were the principal sites of alternative national identification, they were not alone in constructing Israel as the telos of Austrian Jewry. The Jewish press also imagined Vienna's postwar community in overtly Zionist terms. Nowhere was this situation more apparent than in the pages of *Die Gemeinde*. In principle, the official newspaper of the IKG was supposed to cover a broad range of topics, including Austrian and European politics, antisemitism, and the struggle for restitution, as well as religious life and ritual affairs. In practice, however, the publication was almost exclusively concerned with Israel, particularly in the years following the Six-Day War, when a typical issue of the monthly paper rarely appeared with less than 60 percent of its coverage devoted to the Jewish state. Even more significant than the statistical dominance by Israeli affairs, however, was the identificatory thrust transported in *Die Gemeinde*. In issue after issue, the publication constructed a view of Jewish life completely centered on the state of Israel. In this manner, the front pages of *Die Gemeinde* were usually devoted to aspects of the Middle East conflict, while the bulk of the remaining articles chronicled aspects of everyday life and reported on Israel's social, cultural, scientific, and technological accomplishments.[72] As Austrian-Jewish affairs went practically unreported, the predominance of Israeli coverage constituted Vienna's Jews as part of an imagined community of Zionist affiliation. It was in this sense that *Die Gemeinde* at once reflected and engendered a situation in which Vienna's Jews came to see themselves as something akin to a temporary Israeli outpost.

However, the invocation of Israel was not the only mode of Jewish identification beyond the antisemitic realities of the postwar Austrian nation-state. A simultaneous process of Jewish subjectification had strategic recourse to a privileged moment in Austrian-Jewish history. That moment was linked to the supranational structure of the Habsburg Monarchy and anchored in the glorious image of fin de siècle Vienna. Although the monarchy had given way to exclusionary nation-states, the supranational vision of a Habsburg identity was remarkably persistent among post-Holocaust Jews. Many Jews who arrived in postwar Austria as immigrants from former Habsburg lands regarded Vienna as a symbol of successful Jewish emancipation, and it was in this sense that the mediated memory of the monarchy came to serve as a crucial reference point. Anchored in the urban topography of the imperial capital, Vienna, and bracketing the political antisemitism that characterized its last decades, the monarchy signaled the possibility of Jewish advancement according to the nineteenth-century model of German-Jewish emancipation.

The forging of links with Habsburg elements thus allowed immigrants from Eastern Europe to feel at home in Vienna; even more importantly, however, their children would be socialized into an imaginary cultural field whose coordinates were not the antisemitic lifeworld of postwar Austria, but selective narratives of Jewish greatness in the age of Francis Joseph. In many ways, this mode of affirmative subjectification was sanctioned by the Jewish community at large. *Die Gemeinde,* for instance, regularly published articles on Austrian Jewry's accomplishments during the Habsburg Monarchy.[73] In these pieces, Jews invariably figured as cultural heroes; they were not only the bearers of a distinctly Jewish tradition, but the true representatives of all that was good in Austrian history. In an article on Jewish writers, for example, the author suggested that Austrian literature as a whole was the product of Jewish genius. This was in contrast to Germany, where Jews had played a comparatively minor role in the formation of the literary canon.[74] Such arguments about Austrian-Jewish specificity were always linked to the privileged status of Jews in the supranational monarchy. While other groups vied for national autonomy, Jews were perfectly content in a structure that decoupled citizenship from ethnic and religious identity. The monarchy's pluralist design was in turn always represented by the figure of the emperor. "The Jews of his empire loved [Francis Joseph]," an article in *Die Gemeinde* extolled, because he "was no antisemite and respected accomplishments without regard to confession." His fairness brought Jews "titles and honors"; such Jewish "luminaries as Sigmund Freud and Arthur Schnitzler" praised Francis Joseph, "who had become a legend, almost a myth, in the highest tones."[75] Vienna was the spatial epitome of Habsburg's supranational vision, and it was in that sense that the "Jews of the Monarchy" saw the city as the "center of all feeling and longing, the goal which everyone espoused." Vienna was thus the place where all the "talent and genius of the Jews came together, where it was ignited, and where it unfolded."[76] While the author located this Jewish cultural efflorescence at the fin de siècle, the essay's textual economy extended it to the post-Holocaust period. To be sure, the Jews of postwar Vienna "live in difficult circumstances"; but viewed from the perspective of its glorious tradition, the "Vienna of today is a livable place for those who cannot be in Israel."

If such *Gemeinde* articles were designed to imagine a cosmopolitan Vienna beyond the exclusionary principles of the Austrian nation-state, my ethnographic interviews suggest their widespread resonance. For Jews coming of age in postwar Austria, the city functioned through a memorial economy that separated it from Austria's symbolic field. In such quintessentially urban spaces as the coffeehouse and the various institutions of high culture, postwar Jews could localize and inscribe themselves in the enduring legacy of a Jewish fin de siècle. Ilana, for example, invoked the coffeehouse when she asserted that "there are Jewish continuities in Vienna; even though Vienna was almost free of Jews (*judenrein*), there still is a continuity."[77]

For most postwar Jews, such continuities only existed in a fictional realm of transhistorical identification. As children of Eastern European survivors, they had no immediate connections to pre-Holocaust Vienna. But in the context of the city's social construction as an enduring space of supranational affiliation, it could serve as a site of Jewish subjectification beyond the confines of the Austrian nation-state. Bettina, who was born to Eastern European survivors in the mid-1950s, echoed *Die Gemeinde* when she invoked fin de siècle literature as a durable feature of Jewish identification:

To me, Vienna's Jewish connotation exists primarily in the realm of fantasy. This is how we grew up, with the literature of the turn of the century and that has stayed with me. It is a part of Vienna and it is a part of me, even though in reality there might not exist much of it. As a child, I was enamored of these great stories of turn-of-the-century Vienna, and I believe that it was that seemingly perfect, Jewish, intellectual, pristine world of bourgeois and artistic bliss that was so attractive.

For Sarah, like Bettina the child of Eastern European immigrants, the collective memory of the fin de siècle figured similarly in the constitution of a specifically Viennese-Jewish sensitivity. As she put it, "my entire history is" caught up in "those books that I feel I truly understand — that is, Schnitzler or Joseph Roth." In turn, these texts were constitutive of a fantasmatic field that allowed the constitution of a viable Jewish subject position independent of Austrian hegemonies:

I believe I started reading these things [in the late 1950s] when I was around ten. In my girlish fantasies, I wanted to live at the turn of the century. I so longed to sit in the *Kaffeehaus* with Schnitzler and all these other people, to have a salon — all these things greatly excited me. I would have loved to have the clothes of the time. I wanted to be surrounded by all these smart men — the fantasies of a young girl. I imagined that this city was a fascinating place, and that I played an important role in it.

The Jews who came of age in postwar Vienna lived in the Austrian nation-state, but few experienced it as a viable site of affirmative identification. Constituted through the structural exclusion of a Jewish Other, it not only engendered popular antisemitism, but foreclosed the very articulation of Jewish specificity. In this situation, Jews turned to sites of subjectification beyond the exclusionary logic of the Austrian nation-state. They found them in Israel and fin de siècle Vienna. The former offered the model of a nation-state where Jewishness was normalized, while the latter gestured to a supranational field in which Jewish difference could be readily integrated into the imagined community. In public, Jews endured their constitutive subordination; in private, they forged the alternative identities that would place them outside the homogenizing logic of the Austrian nation-state and its antisemitic life-world.

The Specter of Waldheim

Jews refused identification with the postwar Austrian nation-state in light of persistent antisemitism and structural exclusions. Throughout the Second Republic, these had constituted an enduring pattern of symbolic violence — a pattern that reached a virulent climax in 1986. In the so-called Waldheim affair, Austria's postwar arrangements were at once staged and heightened. But if the event thus reproduced the Jewish community's subordination, it also became a turning point, not only for Austria's Jews, but for the country at large.

In 1985, the ÖVP had nominated former U.N. Secretary-General Kurt Waldheim as the party's candidate for the upcoming election for the largely ceremonial Austrian presidency. After a rather uneventful early election campaign, the situation heated up in March of 1986, when Austrian and American media published documents that revealed Waldheim's previously unknown military involvement in the Balkans, as well as his possible membership in two National Socialist organizations.[78] At the same time, the World Jewish Congress (WJC) began to publicize its investigations into Waldheim's wartime activities. In a number of press conferences and press releases, its representatives presented additional documentary material suggesting Waldheim's extensive knowledge of prisoner interrogations, assassinations, kidnappings, and deportations.[79]

As more and more documents were issued by the WJC, the reactions of Waldheim and other Austrian politicians followed the national script of the victim myth. From the initial disclosure of his possible association with Nazi organizations, Waldheim categorically dismissed such allegations as vicious lies. In doing so, he not only avoided the substantive issues raised in the course of the investigation, but readily recast himself as the victim, in this case of a slander campaign. In reproducing postwar Austria's reversal of victim and perpetrator, the discourse of Waldheim and his supporters quickly shifted to a frantic "search" for the campaign's supposed instigators. That search was undertaken by members of the ÖVP and a substantial part of the national media, the *Krone* most vocal among them; in concert, they quickly identified a culturally intelligible culprit. Waldheim suggested that he was targeted by Jews who held him responsible for the United Nations' Middle East policies;[80] some leading ÖVP politicians eagerly seconded that assessment. To them, the "campaign" was carried out by "dishonorable cohorts of the WJC" who orchestrated a "manhunt" using "Mafia-like methods." In this manner, the "campaign" against Waldheim was readily constructed as a Jewish conspiracy — a notion further evidenced by the critical reporting of the "east coast press," which was seen as the handmaiden of an all-powerful American-Jewish lobby.[81] The ÖVP's ostensible concern that the WJC's "unreasonable attacks" might feed "emotions that none of us wanted" revealed a subtext that ascribed the origin of antisemitism to Jews rather than antisemites.[82]

In such an atmosphere, where "Jewish" allegations against a respected Austrian diplomat challenged the country's victim myth, the election campaign became a struggle to maintain postwar Austrian nationness. According to Alois Mock, the chairman of the ÖVP, the "campaign" against Waldheim was an "attack against Austria and our history. We need to be aware of that. They wanted to attack Waldheim. And they attacked Austria and its history."[83] In this situation, a vote for Waldheim became synonymous with the fortification of an Austrian Self vis-à-vis a Jewish Other. Indeed, for Michael Graff, the ÖVP's party secretary, "the election of Waldheim" was tantamount to a "patriotic deed"[84] — a notion whose instrumentalization of the Jew as alien threat became all the more evident in light of Waldheim's main campaign slogans: "We Austrians elect who we want," "Now more than ever." By casting their ballot for Waldheim, Austrians could fend off the Jewish challenge and preserve the Second Republic's status quo.

Predictably, the Waldheim affair unleashed a wave of antisemitic incidents. But even as the affair and its shocking effects caused many Austrian Jews to contemplate immediate emigration, the IKG remained essentially mute. Reproducing Jews' enforced privatization, the organization maintained the diffident posture it had assumed in a long-standing effort to garner tolerance in return for nonconfrontational behavior. Indeed, throughout the Second Republic, the IKG had aided in the protection of Austria's status quo. Tacitly accepting the position accorded Jews through the logic of the victim myth, it had failed to challenge Austrian hegemony by public articulation of Jewish specificity. Instead, the official governing body of Vienna's Jews had generally chosen an accomodationist path, centered on behind-the-scenes struggles for recognition and deferential appeals for acceptance.[85]

This dynamic engendered the official Jewish position during the Waldheim affair. Continuing its postwar policy of passive nonintervention, the IKG did not intervene in the reckless deployment of political antisemitism. Represented by the aged president Ivan Hacker, the IKG neither sponsored demonstrations nor held public protests; it failed to denounce Waldheim's campaign and refused to recommend a vote against him. But the victim's performative acquiescence went even further. Fearing the antisemitic repercussions occasioned by any breach of postwar Austria's status quo, the IKG found it prudent to defend the country against "foreign" accusations of antisemitism. In a statement published in the newspaper *Kurier* at the height of the Waldheim affair, the IKG's governing board thus noted that the "impression Austria was an antisemitic country" was wrong; "even though the small Jewish community has been the subject of much abuse and many threats in the past weeks, we say 'no' to this assessment."[86] In the final analysis, IKG's stance during the Waldheim crisis was emblematic of Jews' constitutive silencing in Austria's postwar cultural field. Given the violent logic of the Second Republic's victim myth, its hegemonic reproduction rested on the reiteration of Jewish abjection — an abjection, moreover, that engendered the victims' enforced consent at the very moment of their displacement from the imagined community.

The Waldheim affair reproduced the constitutive subordination of Jews in postwar Austria. But if the event thus extended the structural exclusions and compulsory privatizations characterizing Jewish existence throughout the Second Republic, it also ushered in a new era for the symptoms of modernity. For, as became clear over the next few years, the Waldheim affair galvanized a younger generation of Austrian Jews, who embarked on a path of political and cultural resistance that would come to anchor Jewishness in Vienna's public sphere.

CHAPTER 2

Laws and Closets

I

Outside the thick walls, life pulses
but no sound reaches the prisoners.
They barely remember that the sky turns blue
in the morning, when the yellow towers shake,

touched by a distant hand. In the courtyard,
the flowers, watched tenderly, lift their
withered leaves; weighted by day with the dew of suffering,
the night sees them pulling back to the ground.

They hear how tired misfortune speaks
when the damned make their circles.
They hear words: injustice, doubt, belief.

They see dim light in many eyes,
thoughts, wishes that escape on high:
And from the roofs, doves ascend.

II

In front of tight cells, cold and circular hallways,
the bottomless pit of their torture opens.
That is how the tower stands: roofed with dull glass,
it holds innocence in its clutches.

In the minds of his victims hang
memories, painfully inflamed

by the scorn of the prison guards. Those who have spent the night
on hard boards, who have been burnt by the irons,

who have lived in the stench of the rusty lavatories,
those know your ground:
You stand on hatred, symbol of barbarism!

But no words break through your stone.
The pale face over the rag
is chased from the window by a brutal scream.

III

A "holy of holies" in the chapel
of the Gray House. Candles of ash glimmer.
Two flowers that palely bloom toward death
are more colorful in the unaccustomed light.

In the choir a young man, on the same spot
where judges strive for truth
(and punish innocent people). Hard and bold
his look, still untainted by the light of the cell.

The blond youth sings. The high ceiling,
rusty and dirty, reflects the sound,
his pure "Blessed, by the suffering of persecution."

It is as if the entire room is startled.
The prison guards turn away their gaze in shame,
and the anointed ones stand like poor pagans.

IV

I see him bathe in the stream of the shower,
the brown boy. Hot water sprays
around his slender limbs, steams and clouds
the beautiful picture with white clouds.

He only knows a few of the many graces
our existence provides others so plentifully.
He loved a friend only once —
and pays for it, weighted by his imprisonment.

Now he is humiliated on "hard camp,"
his lunch is made bitter with hunger,
his pleadings are suffocated by the rut of the prison.

Ridicule is the answer for those who ask in fear.
And when they pray, the barbed wire fence catches
the verses and keeps them from reaching God.

V

The last of your days has started,
the light in the courtyard was extinguished in a thin stream.
The black sky turns pale in the East —
look back at your long pain:

Humiliation and hunger, endured
without complaint. The hypocritical morality
kept you (like a mangy jackal)
imprisoned in the affliction of your situation . . .

Dammed, the one who banished you into such misery;
Dammed, the one who hits and tortures his brothers,
Dammed, the hatred that screams at you!

Blessed, every hand that offered help,
Praised, the word that strengthened your resolve,
Praised be your name: humanity.

> Erich Lifka, "Provincial Courthouse Two, Vienna"

More than any other text written in postwar Vienna, Erich Lifka's discursive poem captures the violent modes of subordination that marginalized homosexuals during the first decades of Austria's Second Republic. Set in the "Gray House" — the colloquial term for Vienna's courthouse and prison — the text not only juxtaposes various levels of oppression, but exposes their devastating interarticulation. Specifically, Lifka emphasizes the operative connections that link church, state, and society in a systematically homophobic project. In this manner, the courthouse takes on the shape of a chapel, while the prison guards, stand-ins for society at large, enforce the state's project of constitutive abjection with inhuman severity. In this world of totalized oppression, there is no saving grace for homosexuals; Lifka's prisoner escapes into a secular fantasy of Catholic redemption anchored and transported through a plea for tolerance and humanity.

Lifka is a unique figure in Austria's cultural fields. Among a handful of people who lived their homosexuality with any degree of openness in the immediate postwar era, he served as the Vienna correspondent of the Swiss homophile periodical *Der Kreis* (The Circle).[1] Committed to its liberal quest for improvement through scientific enlightenment, he tirelessly monitored the "situation of Austria's homophile minority." In that context, he had criticized the Austrian state's persistent "attacks on the human rights" of that group as early as 1955, specifically bemoaning the "sadistic pleasure" the country's "primitive prison guards" derived from the "torment of convicted homosexuals."[2] Lifka's poem "Provincial Courthouse Two" continued this project of liberal protest, but this time the inspiration was more immediate than had been the case with his previous pleas for legal reform. The text, it turned out, reflected Lifka's personal experience. When *Der Kreis* published it in 1956, the subheading identified it as the product of the author's own imprisonment in 1955–56. Like "Fr. L., the companion of my confinement" to whom the poem was dedicated, Lifka had been arrested and charged with homosexual acts.[3] The result was the first of four prison sentences; by 1970, the poet, translator, and journalist had spent a total of thirty months in Austria's jails.[4]

The fact that Lifka wrote about his victimization as a homosexual was highly unusual, but the experience itself was not. On the contrary, the Austrian state actively persecuted the "homophile minority," whose same-sex sexual activities were not only criminalized but threatened with severe punishment during the first decades of the Second Republic. As such, the postwar state continued and redeployed an exclusionary project of virulent nation-building. The abject invention of homosexuals had given coherence to late-nineteenth-century nationness, and their systematic eradication had been a constitutive aspect of the Nazi quest for total national purification. The severity of persecution may have eased with the onset of the Second Republic, but the structures of exclusion remained in place. Much like during the Third Reich, Austria's postwar community was imagined in constitutive opposition to a homosexual Other whose pollution of the national sphere needed to be prevented through legal measures. The total interdiction of all homosexual acts was the judicial vehicle designed to effect this ongoing purification.

In 1971, this so-called *Totalverbot* was abolished in the context of general legal reforms. The exclusionary logic of the nation-state, however, continued to operate. While Austria's legislature did decriminalize most forms of same-sex sexual activity at that time, it also created a series of new laws that were at once designed to protect the nation's heteronormative reproduction and safeguard the public sphere from homosexual infiltration. In turn, the everyday existence of Austria's lesbians and gay men continued to retrace the contours of the state's homophobia. The former remained invisible in light of the interarticulated oppressions of sexism and homophobia, and while the latter continued to sustain the clandestine scene of gay male sociability that had developed during the time of the *Totalverbot,* it remained privatized, the liberalizations of the early 1970s notwithstanding. As symptoms of modernity, Austria's homosexuals existed in the nation's individual closets; as a collectivity, they would remain there until well into the 1990s.

State Persecution

Postwar Austria was characterized by the virulent exclusion of homosexuals from the nation's imagined community. For the Catholic Church, same-sex sexuality continued to figure under the specter of sodomy; the medical and psychiatric establishment still considered it to be a self-evident pathology; and the population at large retained old-standing prejudices that, if anything, had been heightened during the Nazi era. Most detrimental to the lives of lesbians and gay men, however, was the state and its legal apparatuses, which continued to construct homosexuals as an abject category. In this manner, the demise of the Third Reich brought no end to the systematic persecution of Austria's homosexuals. Before the country's *Anschluss* to Nazi Germany, §129 Ib of Austria's penal code had criminalized all forms of same-sex sexuality, threatening violators with imprisonment for one to five years. Formally, the statute had remained on the books between 1938 and 1945, and while its execution was adapted to the German §175, resulting in intensified persecution, countless concentration camp sentences, and numerous deaths, it was left unchanged when Austria's Second Republic was constituted.[5] Homosexuality, in other words, was still illegal — a situation that not only safeguarded the postwar nation's sexual purity but systematically obfuscated the criminality of Nazi persecution in this area. This pattern was codified in the *Opferfürsorgegesetz,* whose focus on the political victims of National Socialism mapped the contours of postwar Austria's imagined community. Homosexuals were not just ineligible for support under the law; their continued legal abjection disallowed and prevented any kind of intervention. By 1947, the *Opferfürsorgegesetz* accommodated those whose victimization on account of "race, religion, or nationality" had occurred in violation of the rule of law.[6] The persecution of homosexuals, however, had not violated the constitutional state's principles, and it was in this light that postwar Austria not only rejected the concept of compensation for homosexual victims, but effectively sanctioned Nazi Germany's project of sexual purification.

The continued subordination of Austria's homosexuals was not codified only in legal theory. In practice, too, it constituted a significant aspect of the state's social project. This affected women and men differently. While §129 Ib criminalized same-sex sexual activities regardless of gender, its execution overwhelmingly concerned men. This is not to say that the postwar state was indifferent to the specter of lesbianism; a series of measures taken by the Ministry of Justice in the early 1950s to prevent same-sex activity in women's prisons suggested as much.[7] But criminal statistics identified men as the principal victims of §129 Ib, whose ongoing application yielded thousands of convictions in the postwar era. In the years after 1945, between five hundred and seven hundred people were sentenced annually for violations of the statute; by 1971, the total number of convictions had exceeded thirteen thousand.[8] Even higher, of course, was the figure for people prosecuted in conjunction with §129 Ib. In Vienna alone, the police had records of some sixteen thousand men who had come to the authorities' attention as convicted, charged, or suspected homosexuals.[9]

These numbers hinted at the severity of the postwar state's suppression of same-sex sexuality. Indeed, throughout the 1950s and early 1960s, the legal persecution of homosexual men had a particularly high priority; and trials against entire groups of people were commonplace. In 1955–56 alone, for example, there were two large trials: one in Vienna featuring eighteen defendants, and one in the province of Vorarlberg with over 130 accused.[10] According to *Der Kreis,* which monitored the proceedings, Austria's police had not only pursued the cases with extreme vigor, but had deployed illegal tactics to bring the indictments. In Vienna, these tactics included extortion, deception, and the dissemination of false information, all used to uncover a network of homosexual men. Procedures in Vorarlberg had been similar, resulting in the manufacture of evidence against over four hundred suspects.

If the rule of law was readily suspended to protect Austria's national sphere from homosexual infiltration, the authorities could also count on the tacit cooperation of their victims. Since convictions for §129 Ib brought massive social stigmatization and certain loss of employment, homosexual suspects regularly volunteered information, either in the hope of lenient treatment by the courts or out of sheer desperation. Escalating convictions were the result, individual resignation the by-product. Both helped the state achieve its goal of safeguarding the heteronormative order. This, of course, came at the heavy expense of Austria's gay men (and lesbians). While the archives yield little information on individual fates during the postwar era, the anonymous account of an "unhappy comrade" sheds light on the tragic dynamics occasioned by the state's violent subordination of homosexuals. Published in *Der Kreis* in 1963, the piece was written by a twenty-three-year-old man who recalled the past two years of his life:

When I was twenty-one years old, I met a young man of the same age. With unending sympathy and much, much love, he helped me cope with the hardships of my life. After a few weeks, we became close sexually as well, and that gave Austria's law the right to treat us as "criminals." Alone and in deep desperation, the person who was the dearest thing to me in the world hung himself in his cell because he was not allowed to love me. To smooth over this wound I was sentenced to eight months in prison.

I lack the words to describe my emotional state at the time. But I'm not doing any better today either. I stand here, lonely, alone, and desperate. Every venture into the public brings taunts and jeers. Austria's authorities were not ashamed to demand five thousand schillings to cover the costs of my imprisonment three weeks after I was released from jail, and to collect that amount they even took my watch and electric shaver. For months I tried to get work. But here it is easier for a robber to become director of a bank than for a "fag," as they like to put it, to be hired into any position.

If I'm totally honest, I must say that I hate this country, this country where, day and night, there is talk of freedom, the golden West, and the economic miracle, but where there is no compunction to drive one man who is happy the way he is to his death and slowly get the other one to that point as well.[11]

If this narrative identifies the state and its legal system as the main agents of oppression in the postwar era, it also implicates Austria's population in the subordination of homosexuals. Not only did a person's real or suspected homosexuality provoke "taunts and jeers," but, as in the Nazi period, it occasioned denunciations.[12] During the Third Reich, lesbians and gay men had been imagined as sexual pollutants whose eradication would enhance the strength of the *Volksgemeinschaft*. In the postwar era, the rhetoric was less strident, but its cultural logic remained essentially unchanged. As a criminal assault on the social order, homosexuality still figured as a constitutive threat to the national community, which at once necessitated and justified the population's ongoing vigilance.

The continuities between Nazi and postwar constructions of homosexuality were evident across the spectrum of public discourse; however, no item exemplified it as much as the 1957 film *Anders als Du und Ich* (Different Than You and I). Produced in Germany and directed by Veit Harlan — the creator of the notorious Nazi propaganda picture *Jud*

Süß — the film starred Paula Wessely, Austria's foremost actress and herself a former Nazi sympathizer.[13] Released in Austria under the title *The Third Sex,* the movie's plot was overtly homophobic, detailing the struggles of a mother, Wessely, who attempts to save her son from the perils of homosexuality. These perils are represented through the demonic figure of Boris Winkler, an amalgam of stereotypes bundling the various perversions of the modern age. Winkler, a duplicitous lover of *entartete Kunst,* nearly seduces the son into his netherworld of dissolved gender roles and clandestine sociability, but Wessely's character successfully intervenes, coupling her son with a blond woman and thereby preserving the traditional family as the building block of society.

The plot of Harlan's film — the first he produced in the postwar era — clearly resonated with its audience. Reinforcing the figuration of homosexuality as inherently destructive of the social order, it not only legitimized the state's persecution of lesbians and gay men but figured their repression in terms of a collective project of national purification. Abject identification and isolation were central to this project; indeed, as late as 1971, a sociological survey suggested that 60 percent of Austria's population would cease all contacts with a person found to be homosexual.[14] Much like the Nazi state, postwar Austria persecuted lesbians and gay men; much like the Third Reich, its population responded by adopting, transporting, and enforcing the dominant ideology.

Legal Reform and the Protection of the National Sphere

In the summer of 1971, Austria's parliament voted for the abolition of §129 Ib. Part of the so-called "small penal code reform," the legislative act was in line with Bruno Kreisky's progressive political project, itself the reflection of a certain degree of social liberalization that occurred in the 1960s and early 1970s. More importantly, the reform addressed a long-standing concern with the volume of delinquency. Since the mid-1950s, Austria's governments had contemplated sweeping legal reforms that would reduce the number of citizens with criminal records; in that context, the *Totalverbot* emerged as an item of ongoing political and legal debate. At first the matter was turned over to a group of legal and medical experts. Constituted as an official body and appointed by the Ministry of Justice, the penal law commission recommended the abolition of §129 Ib as early as 1957.[15] But political contingencies and lack of urgency regarding the issue of homosexuality delayed serious consideration for several years. It took until 1962 for the commission's recommendation to be taken up by the Secretary of Justice, and an additional two years passed before the ministry issued an initial draft of a new penal code that no longer featured the *Totalverbot*.[16] At the time, the SPÖ controlled the Ministry of Justice, but since the party governed the country in coalition with the ÖVP, it had to enter protracted negotiations, yielding a new draft in 1966 that, while worded in less liberal tones, still provided for the abolition of §129 Ib.[17]

In general, the Christian conservative People's Party constituted the main obstacle in all legislative reforms of sexuality. Closely aligned with the Catholic Church, its representatives advocated the continued criminalization of same-sex sexuality, and when the ÖVP gained an absolute majority in the parliamentary elections of 1966, also bringing control of the Ministry of Justice, the party proposed a much more moderate legal reform. Codified in 1968 and issued as a third draft for a new penal code, that design continued to outlaw homosexuality but reduced its status from crime to misdemeanor.[18] Once again, though, the new code failed to come to a vote, this time because of resistance by the SPÖ, which not only insisted on the separation of church and state, but pointed to the fact that — following the abolition of the *Totalverbot*'s equivalent in Great Britain in 1967 — Austria was virtually alone among European democracies to criminalize all forms of same-sex sexuality.[19]

After more than a decade of legal and political wrangling, the SPÖ finally accomplished the task of penal code reform, along with the abolition of §129 Ib. In 1970, the Socialist Party won the national elections. Although it failed to win an absolute majority in parliament, the SPÖ nonetheless proceeded to form a single-party government under the leadership of Bruno Kreisky. Early elections in the fall of 1971 would bring the desired absolute majority and the beginning of twelve years of political dominance. But the vote on the "small penal code reform" took place at a moment when the SPÖ still needed some parliamentary support from the ÖVP and the FPÖ. Indeed, the small penal code reform — which addressed several areas of sexuality, among them adultery and child abuse — had the backing of the Freedom Party, as well as that of most members of the People's Party.[20] A complicated compromise ensued. Keen to base the reform of delicate sexual matters on the broadest political footing possible, the SPÖ had entered into negotiations with the Catholic Church as well as its political representative, and while neither the church nor the ÖVP wavered on its principled opposition to the legalization of homosexuality, they could support, or at least tolerate, a framework that would continue to ensure homosexuality's legal abjection. As one ÖVP parliamentarian who voted for the small penal code reform noted, it was essential that "homosexuality remain abnormal, that it continue to be seen as a form of immorality, and that we approve of it under no circumstances."[21]

Indeed, the abolition of §129 Ib hardly constituted the end of homosexuals' legal subordination. To be sure, the decriminalization of most same-sex sexual acts brought freedom from individual persecution. But this development had little effect on the state's fundamental position in regard to homosexuality as a social phenomenon. On the contrary, the small penal code reform reproduced the contours of long-standing concerns for the sexual purification of the national sphere. To this end, Austria's parliament substituted a number of new laws for §129 Ib — laws that were specifically designed to safeguard the heteronormative reproduction of the imagined community. To some degree, these statutes represented concessions to the Catholic Church and the People's Party; but ultimately they rested on a broad consensus regarding the need to shield the nation from homosexual infiltration.

The state's central project in this respect was the "protection" of Austria's youth. This goal had already served as a rationale for §129 Ib; now that the *Totalverbot* was about to be abolished, the state needed to take juridical actions that would guarantee the continued purity of the country's adolescents. Underlying this legal logic was the constitutive devaluation of same-sex sexuality. To be sure, the end of §129 Ib suggested the authorities' neutrality vis-à-vis homosexual acts between consenting adults, but as the state's discourse made clear, such acts continued to be seen as a function of pathology. They were now attributed to deviant development, however, which shifted the approach to juridical action. It was now believed that the sexual orientation of an adult was fully formed, which rendered criminal punishment ineffective. Adolescents, by contrast, were seen as highly malleable in terms of sexual orientation, and it was this situation that at once necessitated and guided the state's protective intervention. As the Ministry of Justice put it in its explication of the small penal code reform, "Persons at an age when their sexual orientation is not yet set need to be protected from same-sex sexual experiences that could fix them on homosexuality."[22] In this manner, the state would continue its long-standing project of safeguarding society's heteronormative order, and although it abandoned the attempt to reform adult homosexuals, it would ensure the reproduction of the imagined community through the heterosexualization of the nation's youth.

In terms of specific laws, the nation's heteronormative future was codified in the new §209. The statute prohibited same-sex sexual activities between adult men and their fourteen- to eighteen-year-old counterparts, threatening violators with prison sentences of six months to five years.[23] No such interdiction existed for heterosexual relations between members of these age brackets, which had long been legal at the age of fourteen. Nor did the new law pay attention to same-sex sexual activities between women. This was in contrast to §129 Ib, which had outlawed homosexual acts regardless of gender. The masculinist bias reflected a larger concern for the nation's reproduction. As early as 1957, the penal law commission had recommended the legalization of same-sex sexual activities between women on these very grounds. As one member of the commission put it, the "lesbian activities of a woman did not detract from her ability to have intercourse with a man and bear children."[24] This did not mean that experts and politicians approved of lesbian sexuality. But in a classic interarticulation of homophobia and sexism, female homosexuality was not seen as threatening to the national order. On the one hand, it was held to be an infrequent phenomenon and hence of minor social relevance;[25] on the other hand, it was construed as an eminently malleable condition. The "normalization of [a woman's] sexual orientation" could thus be "achieved readily."[26] Moreover, the state foresaw grave difficulties in the prosecution of same-sex sexual acts between women. As the Ministry of Justice put it in the first draft of a new penal code, the boundaries between "ecstatic friendship, sexual affection, and same-sex sexual activity" were blurred — a notion elaborated even further in the 1970 bill for the small penal code reform which held that the "distinction between tender gestures among friends, bodily contacts during help with personal hygiene, and the like, on the one hand, and genuine acts of same-sex sexuality, on the other hand, could hardly be established during a criminal trial."[27]

The same problems of legal determination did not apply in the case of same-sex sexual acts between men. Not only were they imagined as inherently discontinuous with normal activity, but they were also accorded a different order of significance. This reflected the state's construction of normative maturation, which sharply distinguished between the processes of male and female sexual development. The origin of this conception could be found in the debates of the penal law commission, whose members had drawn on a mixture of Freudian psychology and the *Prägungs-Theorien* of Konrad Lorenz.[28] Central to this set of ideas was the notion that male adolescents, unlike their female counterparts, could be seduced into permanent homosexuality in a process that "disaccustomed them from normal intercourse."[29] By the time Austria's government proposed §209 as a substitute for the *Totalverbot*, the board's opinion was codified in the official discourse of the state. Since "determinative experiences during adolescence evidently play a lesser role in the development of the sexual orientation of female persons than they do among men,"[30] Austria's male youths needed to be shielded from same-sex sexual activity; and a "protective age" of eighteen was instituted to safeguard their heterosexual development, as well as that of the nation.[31]

The protection of Austria's male youth through §209 was not the only legislative measure conceived to preserve the nation's heterosexual order in the face of the *Totalverbot*'s abolition in 1971. Even more indicative of the state's ongoing subordination of homosexuality were two statutes designed to ensure its total absence from the public sphere. Respectively, §220 and §221 interdicted "propaganda" for "sexual relations between persons of the same sex" and the formation of "associations" intended to "facilitate same-sex sexual relations."[32] In tandem, the two laws not only prevented the emergence of an emancipatory movement on behalf of homosexuals' rights, but also effectively disallowed any form of lesbian/gay visibility. This indeed was their explicit purpose. Throughout the debates on the small penal code reform, experts had voiced concerns about the consequences of the *Totalverbot*'s rescission, and while §209 would safeguard the nation's normative future, its heterosexual present seemed uncertain. "Penal laws," after all, had the "power to shape morality," and in that context, the decriminalization of homosexual acts between adults constituted a potential "threat to the people's natural order and conduct of life."[33] But if the legalization of same-sex sexuality was thus seen as a moral and demographic disruption, the legal reform gave rise to even greater concern about homosexuality's impact on the social body. In this regard, experts feared not only the "entry of homosexual cliques into various official institutions of culture," but a general "corruption of public life."[34] Most threatening, however, was the specter of a "general acceptance of homosexuality as a form of sexual existence that was ethically equal to normal sexual activities."[35]

Ultimately, the state concurred with these assessments, and as early as 1964, the first draft of a new penal code made provisions that anticipated the introduction of §220 and §221. In doing so, the Ministry of Justice sought to "prevent the misinterpretation" that the abolition of §129 Ib "meant the sanction" of "homosexual activity" by "the legal order."[36] On the contrary, the "dam against all forms of homosexual propaganda," in particular, exemplified the state's ongoing commitment to ensure the public sphere's heterosexual configuration.[37] For not only would it persecute people who overtly "encouraged same-sex sexual activity," but it would even intervene against anyone who "dealt with it publicly in a manner that might lead other persons to same-sex sexual activity."[38] The cultural logic enunciated by the state was clear. The abolition of the *Totalverbot* notwithstanding, the state would continue its heteronormative protection of the national sphere; by extension, it would prolong homosexuality's constitutive suppression. Indeed, in light of the statutes substituted for §129 Ib, the state was confident that "in the future, too, homosexuality would essentially be kept in the dark."[39]

The continued legal subordination of homosexuality was not associated with extreme positions on the political spectrum. On the contrary, in the form of the heteronormative "protection" of Austria's male youth and the interdiction of homosexual association and advertising, it represented a complete consensus among the state's constituencies. If anything, Austria's conservative forces pushed for greater restrictions, but they went along with the more "liberal" proposal that was realized in the small penal code reform. That proposal reflected the political design of the Socialist Party — a design, however, that was just as committed to homosexuality's structural exclusion from Austria's national sphere as the more conservative vision of the party's competitors. Indeed, even the first draft of the new penal code — completed in 1964 under the most liberal of Socialist politicians — proposed the establishment of a law to protect male youths against seduction, and its assertion that the "criminality of same-sex sexual activity with adolescents was never in dispute" was affirmed throughout the debates on penal code reform.[40] The same liberal Ministry of Justice similarly introduced the mechanisms to curb "propaganda" for homosexuality. In the final analysis, then, the Socialist project differed from the conservative approach in strategy but not in ultimate object. To be sure, the small penal code reform constituted a move away from "interdiction, punishment, and imprisonment," as one SPÖ member put it during the bill's parliamentary debate, but the same politician's insistence that §209, §220, and §221 would help in the efforts of "education, prevention, and assistance" ultimately revealed the reform's larger cultural vision.[41] Championed by the SPÖ and accepted by the conservative parties, the abolition of the *Totalverbot* yielded neither equality nor acceptance for Austria's lesbians and gay men. On the contrary, the state continued to subordinate homosexuality in the interests of the nation's normative reproduction.

In legal practice, the state's efforts at sexual purification focused on the execution of §209, which emerged as a genuine threat to Austria's gay men. Given the more limited scope of the law, the number of adjudicated cases never approached that of §129 Ib, but it was far from insignificant. In the first ten years of its existence, §209 led to more than five hundred convictions. While the number dropped off slightly in the course of the 1980s and early 1990s, it remained at the substantial level of more than thirty per year.[42] By contrast, §220 and §221 led to only a handful of court cases over the years.[43] In part, this was a function of the laws' relatively lax enforcement. Even more to the point, however, it reflected a cultural field where the public representation of homosexuality essentially conformed to the state's legal code. Indeed, throughout the 1970s and 1980s, homosexuality was mostly absent from the mass-media realm, and when it was thematized, it figured in stereotypical terms that reinforced its constitutive subordination.

Homosexuality and the Mass Media

Throughout the postwar period, the mass-media representation of homosexuality mirrored its hegemonic construction by the state. As such, it was not only rendered as an inherently deviant phenomenon but anchored in a criminal demimonde characterized by danger, treachery, and violent excess. In consequence, homosexuals appeared in the mass media only as a diffuse threat to the social order or on the occasion of individuals' criminal apprehension. Trials of real or suspected homosexuals occasioned most of the coverage in the decades following World War II.[44]

Even after the decriminalization of most forms of same-sex sexuality, the tenor of its mass-media representation remained unchanged. Throughout the 1970s and early 1980s, homosexuality continued to appear almost exclusively in the domain of criminal reporting. And while same-sex sexuality as such still figured as an illicit phenomenon, its legalization only heightened the need to construct its various contexts as inherently unlawful as well. In the process, Austria's mass media imagined the "homosexual milieu" as the intrinsically criminalized space of all same-sex sexual life.[45] There prostitution, extortion, and murder were par for the course, so much so that it functioned both as the self-evident site and explanatory framework for the incidents under question. In the case of a murder, for instance, its localization in the "homosexual milieu" not only sufficed to account for its motives but conveyed a lesson on the perils of same-sex sexual existence.[46]

A case in 1977 is paradigmatic of the discursive strategies employed by Austria's mass media to delineate and sensationalize homosexuality as an inherently criminal phenomenon.[47] In January of that year, a gay man had died of a heart attack that occurred at a friend's apartment in the wake of an altercation with two potential tricks. While the facts of the case were clear from the outset, the centrist newspaper *Kurier* ran a prominent story that speculated wildly about the possibility of murder or manslaughter.[48] Under the heading "Death of a Homosexual," the article not only insinuated the culpability of the victim's friend, but went out of its way to construct him as the likely suspect. Introduced as a shady figure — a "presumably self-appointed ballet teacher" who "does not enjoy the best reputation among his neighbors" — he emerged as a gay male stereotype on account of his ostensible "complaints" at being taken to the police station "without makeup." There his inherent dubiousness was heightened by seemingly conflicting statements and his inability to give a "plausible" explanation for the "mysterious" situation. The *Kurier* article did close with an exoneration of sorts. By the time the reader learned that the "autopsy confirmed the theory of a heart attack," however, the larger script was fully in place. Identified both by his stage and real name, the victim's friend was not only linked to a homicide but effectively exposed as a homosexual. The intended association between homosexuality and criminality, in turn, was clear. Reinforcing the construction of the "homosexual milieu" as a space of inherent criminality, it reproduced the hegemonic subordination of same-sex sexuality and rendered it intelligible on the level of mass-media discourse.

Articles that constructed homosexuality through the figure of the criminal dominated mass-media representations of lesbians and gay men until well into the 1990s. But even stories that eschewed or questioned the equation of homosexuality with illegality tended to reproduce its constitutive abjection. Such "positive" articles, which only began to appear in conjunction with the legal reforms that decriminalized same-sex sexuality, thus often espoused homosexuals' rights in a broadly liberal framework. At the same time, their language almost invariably subordinated lesbians and gay men as socially inferior and morally corrupt. An early piece in the center-right weekly *Wochenpresse* was typical of this discursive practice.[49] Published in 1967 on the occasion of the political debates on the small penal code reform, the cover story maintained an ostensibly neutral stance from which it weighed the arguments for and against the decriminalization of homosexuality. But if the article's impartiality translated into a degree of sympathy for the legal plight of the "third sex," the piece left no doubt about the group's foundational devaluation. The article was redolent with stereotypical images, ranging from the criminal case that opened the piece to the lengthy account of an unrepentant pederast. Even more importantly, the piece deployed a host of discursive figures to construct homosexuality as inherently illicit. In seemingly innocuous asides, same-sex sexuality thus figured as "tactless" and a "social abyss," while its practitioners were exoticized on account of their "love games" as well as their "shocking readiness" to discuss them in "vivid detail."[50] Disapprobation for Austria's clandestine gay male couples and speculation about the secret existence of a "homosexual 'international'" only rounded out an article whose cultural vision fully retraced the contours of homosexuality's dominant figuration.[51]

Conservative and centrist periodicals like *Kurier* and *Wochenpresse,* however, were not alone in reinforcing the state's constitutive subordination of homosexuality. Even progressive publications were complicit in the delineation of a public discourse that imagined homosexuals outside the sphere of national respectability. More than any other left-leaning periodical, the weekly *Profil* thematized same-sex sexuality in the course of the 1970s and early 1980s; it was in the magazine's coverage that homophobic structures inherent even in the most self-consciously liberal positions became apparent. This was never clearer than in the spring of 1976, when *Profil* published a lengthy cover story entitled "Homosexuals in Austria."[52] In principle, the piece — much like the magazine itself — was committed to a liberal project of social equality and justice; as such, it took central aim at the discriminatory laws instituted in the wake of the *Totalverbot*'s abolition. Moreover, the article gestured to a genuine critique of the power relations inherent in the normalized construction of heterosexuality as the privileged mode of sexual organization. In this manner, the piece opened by putting such expressions as "normal people" and "healthy majority" in quotation marks — a discursive practice that clearly exposed the mechanisms of homophobic subordination.[53] But if the opening thus critiqued the arbitrary construction of homosexuals as a "perverse minority," the article as a whole buttressed that very conception through its relentless stereotyping and sensationalizing.[54]

This strategy started with *Profil*'s cover. Displaying two naked men in a close embrace — itself a deliberately shocking image — the cover underscored a title whose obvious pun turned on the conception of male homosexuals as inherently feminized. "Man Seeks Man to Play Checkers" was readily intelligible as "Man Seeks Man to Play Woman with Him" (*"Herr sucht Herrn — um mit ihm Dame zu spielen"*). While the story's headline thus articulated a classic stereotype of same-sex sexual perversion, the article rendered its subject matter as a veritable catalogue of deviant types. In line with the story's title, *Profil*'s list commenced with the "effeminized fairy" who "swung his purse and hips," moving on to "transvestites" as another instantiation of gay male femininity.[55] These classic types were in turn contrasted with such masculine variants of homosexual deviance as "leather fetishists" and "sadomasochists."[56] In *Profil*'s discursive logic, such extreme forms of social difference were linked to intrinsically abnormal forms of sexuality; hence the article displayed a near obsessive concern with male homosexuals' perverse practices. These were not only listed with gleeful attention to detail — "fistfucking is only enjoyed by the sadomasochists: finger, fist, and possibly the entire forearm are thrust into one another's rectum: for beginners this brings soreness of the sphincter" — but also introduced as activities that made "gay men weak."[57] And to further substantiate that assertion, *Profil* dwelled on anal intercourse and anilingus as additional exemplars of gay men's sexual debilitation.[58]

Indeed, *Profil*'s analysis ultimately turned on a reification of gay male sexuality as intrinsically abject. To be sure, the article went to great lengths to critique such execrable aspects of homosexual existence as duplicity, secrecy, anonymity, and isolation.[59] But while the article gestured toward a political critique of Austria's sexual hegemonies, it ultimately explained them not as the result of structural homophobia, but as a function of gay men's inherent deviance. That condition invariably produced such undesirable phenomena as lasciviousness, promiscuity, anonymous sex, prostitution, and crime;[60] thus homosexuality necessarily remained outside a framework of normalized respectability. The state had codified the national sphere as an intrinsically heterosexual space; while *Profil* policed its purity with much less ferocity than the publications further to the right of the political spectrum, it too naturalized homosexuality as a wholly separate and constitutively subordinated form of social existence. In the final analysis, then, the entire range of Austria's mass media was complicit in a hegemonic project that demarcated and devalued same-sex sexualities in the interest of cultural homogeneity.[61]

The Homosexual Scene and Its Subjects

The multiple forms of subordination were reflected in the patterns of lesbian and gay male sociability. Without fail, such interactions occurred away from the public sphere. In the case of women, they were more or less confined to a private realm of friendship networks; while ethnographic reconstructions suggest the existence of an informal lesbian scene in Vienna, it is clear that the postwar era was marked by social pressures that allowed few individuals to escape a life of performative heterosexuality, often in the form of unhappy marriages.[62]

Gay men faced similar strictures, but much like other metropolitan locales, Vienna contained a well-developed infrastructure that provided opportunities for social and sexual encounters. If Vienna's "homosexual scene," as it was referred to by the gay men who frequented it, thus resembled that of other European cities, it was distinguished by its unusually clandestine character — a character that was essentially unaffected by the legal liberalizations of the early 1970s. The ongoing furtiveness was widely seen as a function of homosexuality's continued subordination; the gay male travel guide *Spartacus* put the situation in these very terms when it noted in its 1976 edition that "homosexual acts are still taboo for the public." In consequence, the gay male scene was much the same as before the decriminalization of homosexuality. "The few bars do not want to seem gay to the outside," *Spartacus* bemoaned. "Much activity takes place in parks and toilets."[63] This assessment was confirmed in the course of my ethnographic research. As one of my interlocutors put it, the "homosexual scene really didn't change between the 1960s and the 1980s. People breathed a sigh of relief in 1971, but the practical situation, from my vantage point at least, was no different."

Indeed, my ethnographic reconstruction of gay male association revealed a remarkable continuity from the 1950s to the early 1990s. In interview after interview, secrecy and surreptitiousness appeared as the operative modes of gay male existence; they underwrote the production and reproduction of the homosexual scene as an assemblage of sites located apart from the public sphere and its heterosexual order. This did not mean that same-sex sexuality was practiced only in private, however. On the contrary, Vienna's gay male topography was constituted within and through a careful negotiation of the city's geography, much like in other Western cities. For gay men whose personal sphere of family and living arrangements was often coded as intrinsically heterosexual, the enforced privacy of homosexuality could only be had in public; thus parks, toilets, baths, and saunas constituted central coordinates in an economy of furtive association.

The social and spatial organization of these meeting sites was extraordinarily complex. The half-dozen parks that served as cruising areas in the postwar period, for example, were differentiated by the class status of the men who frequented them, while the dozens of public toilets that functioned as tea rooms were organized according to their hours of greatest popularity. Among these venues, a number of sites in Vienna's first district occupied privileged positions. In regard to cruising areas, the park at city hall remained a favorite spot, while a chain of lavatories on the *Ringstraße* — the boulevard encircling Vienna's city center — was among the most widely attended *Logen*.[64] But while gay men congregated at the heart of Vienna's urban geography, their collective actions hardly constituted an appropriation of the city's symbolic landscape. On the contrary, the cultural logic of their association enacted their exclusion from public respectability. In parks and toilets, clandestine sex occurred in an effort to hide homosexuality from a heterosexual gaze, and the same logic was evident in regard to the baths and saunas frequented by gay men. There too they sought to forge spaces where same-sex sexuality could be localized in seclusion from the public sphere. Concretely, this meant that gay men met at sites a presumptively heterosexual public had either abandoned or avoided in the first place. The Esterhazybad in Vienna's sixth district, for example, was barely functional as a conventional bath. A holdover from the imperial period, it was described as a "horrible dump" that was "dirty as hell." These conditions had driven out the general public, thereby allowing Vienna's gay men to occupy it as a space for same-sex sexuality. Other dilapidated baths and saunas, such as the Dianabad and the Zentralbad, offered similar forms of protection against heterosexual incursion, as did the nudist areas at the more popular swimming pools. Instituted during the interwar period in the context of modernist body movements, they had come to be seen as disreputable in the Cold War era, and this enabled their appropriation as more or less exclusive sites of gay male association.

The same cultural logic governed the central sites of the homosexual scene — the gay bars. Between the 1950s and the 1980s, Vienna consistently featured between five and eight establishments that specifically catered to a gay male clientele; while individual venues went in and out of business, these establishments shared fundamental features that enacted homosexuality's enforced seclusion from the public sphere. This did not translate into an absence of internal variation. On the contrary, Vienna's gay bars were always differentiated according to their respective patrons, particularly along the axes of age and class. Regardless of their specific clientele, however, all gay male establishments placed a premium on their inconspicuousness. In the case of the only venue open during the day, the Café Quick in Vienna's first district, this meant a rigorous avoidance of overtly gay actions. "People had to behave themselves, otherwise they were thrown out," was the way one former patron described the locale, which was in operation until the early 1980s.

In contrast to the "open" Café Quick, the more typical venues provided a "closed" environment affording some opportunity for same-sex sexual interactions. However, the availability of such amenities presupposed more exacting methods of concealment. All of Vienna's gay bars thus featured bells, spy-holes, and face-checks, and most went so far as to board up their windows to ensure added protection. The Alte Lampe, Vienna's oldest gay bar and in continuous operation throughout the postwar period, is paradigmatic. Located in the fourth district, it had the outward appearance of a modest pub, but while a lamp further advertised its existence, the darkened windows obscured the goings-on inside. Other establishments went even further in their quest for seclusion. For instance, Alfi's Goldener Spiegel, a bar and restaurant that opened in the sixth district in the 1970s, was essentially unrecognizable from the outside. With its windows boarded up and its outer walls and door painted black, nothing announced the presence of the establishment, which could only be entered after a face-check. Throughout their long existence, Alte Lampe and Goldener Spiegel primarily catered to an older gay male clientele. Their seclusion from the public sphere, however, was not the result of a generational dynamic. Rather, it was paradigmatic of a general situation that constructed and enacted homosexuality as an inherently clandestine phenomenon. Even in establishments that sought to attract a younger crowd, the technologies of separation remained in full evidence for the entire postwar period. Throughout its existence in the 1970s and early 1980s, for example, the popular Domstube — later renamed Hyde Park and Jeans — had a bell; as late as the early 1990s, the discotheque Why Not featured darkened windows as well as the requisite face-check. In this way Vienna's gay male scene, marked by the constitutive connection of hidden bars and their closeted patrons, reproduced the hegemonic logic of homosexual exclusion, the decriminalization of same-sex sexuality in 1971 notwithstanding.

Much like Vienna's homosexual scene, the subjectification of lesbians and gay men followed a remarkably constant pattern throughout the postwar period. To be sure, there were vast differences between the archetypical experiences of men and women, and, naturally, individual biographies varied a great deal, inflected as they were by the variables of class, location, and generational belonging. What was notable in the course of my ethnographic research, however, was the consonance between the different narrativizations, which revealed the broader contours of postwar lesbian/gay existence. In general terms, these mirrored the cultural configuration of Vienna's gay male scene, engendering fractured identifications that compartmentalized homosexuality in the interest of performative respectability. At issue, then, were the dynamics of the Austrian closet and its hegemonic mode of operation in the individual lives of lesbians and gay men.

The central figure in my interlocutors' narrativizations of their lesbian/gay subjectification was the gradual realization both of their same-sex sexual desires and their constitutive devaluation in Austrian society. Invariably, this process was described in adversarial terms. Families appeared as hostile domains whose exertion of heteronormative hegemony rendered homosexuality either a discursive nonentity or a figure of moral revilement. While hardly exclusive to postwar Austria, both gestured to the country's Catholic tradition and its repressive approach to most forms of sexuality. Indeed, traumatic encounters with Catholicism represented a recurrent motive in my interlocutors' accounts. Even more prominent in their narratives of lesbian/gay subjectification, however, were experiences in school. Constituting an initial and defining encounter with society at large and coming during the process of sexual maturation, most lesbians and gay men identified their years in junior high school as the time when they gained an initial awareness of homosexuality as a concept, learned of its negative connotation, and began to negotiate their same-sex sexual desires accordingly. All of my interlocutors offered similar accounts in this respect. From Thomas, who told me about his educational experience in the late 1940s, to Clemens, who attended junior high school in the late 1980s, my interviewees recalled persistent tirades against homosexuals. While the vocabulary changed — the Austrian word *warm* was gradually supplanted by the German *schwul* as the colloquial designation for male homosexuality — the semantic effect remained consistent, rendering young men's realization of their same-sex sexuality concurrent with their recognition of its inherent abjection. And while female homosexuality figured as a slightly less prominent trope, many of the lesbians I interviewed also identified their time in Austria's schools as the moment when awareness of their sexual orientation and its foundational devaluation began to crystallize.

If the discourse at Austria's schools constructed homosexuality as an abject category of social organization, its intrinsically negative connotation was further reinforced by its public representation in and beyond the mass media. Indeed, in the accounts of their lesbian/gay subjectification, my interlocutors repeatedly pointed to the centrality of socially sanctioned narratives. In several interviews, lesbians and gay men recalled their readings of available encyclopedias and sex education manuals. Until well into the 1970s, such treatises were bound to render homosexuality as a psychological and moral pathology, and while the attitudes expressed in such publications gradually shifted in the later decades of the twentieth century, the texts that were accessible in homes and school libraries were usually dated. In this respect, one man recalled a typical experience when, following the realization of his same-sex sexual desires in the mid-1980s, he proceeded to consult the literature available to him: "At home we had this encyclopedia from the early '60s, and I remember how shocked I was at how it portrayed homosexuality as something negative, even a disease."

Even more prominent than the association of homosexuality with illness, however, was its figuration as inherently criminal. The prominence of this association was apparent in interview after interview, regardless of age or gender. As such, it not only reflected homosexuality's dominant construction in Austria's newspapers, but also evidenced the centrality of mass-media discourse in the delineation of lesbian/gay identities. For a woman who came of age in the late 1950s, for example, reports of homosexuals' criminal prosecution at once coalesced and problematized her inchoate feelings of sexual desire. "I really didn't understand the concept of homosexuality. But then, the newspapers wrote about this trial, and I knew that that was the way I was, and I became really scared." A man who grew up in the Vienna of the 1960s put his experience in similar terms when he recalled the arrest of a homosexual man as a formative event in his gay male subjectification: "I read about it in the papers, and so I knew that homosexuality was something that was incredibly disreputable and dangerous." While the volume of persecution lessened in the wake of the *Totalverbot*'s abolition, Austria's mass media continued to construct homosexuality in criminal terms; hence my younger interlocutors also recalled newspaper coverage as a principal site of negative information. A man who came of age in the late 1980s expressed it in typical form when he pointed to the frequent crime stories as the main reason for his reluctance to seek out the gay male world. "The homosexual scene," he told me, "was always where people got killed, so it seemed like the scariest place, and being gay itself became totally scary."

The systematic abjection of homosexuality by the Austrian state, society, and mass media had massive ramifications for the life trajectories of lesbians and gay men. For one, the severity of social and religious opprobrium brought enormous psychological pressures. In one narrative after another, the process of lesbian/gay subjectification was described in terms of fear, pain, and shame. In this regard, numerous men related their initial experiences with same-sex sexuality as positively traumatic. "I desperately wanted to do it," I was told by Karl, who had his internal coming out in the late 1970s, "but when I finally had the chance, I was totally petrified, and I ran out of the guy's house." Other men recalled similar experiences of fear and moral doubt. One man who discovered Vienna's homosexual scene in the mid-1960s related his guilt whenever he had sex in a public toilet: "As soon as I came, I just got out as fast as I could because of my bad conscience. I promised myself that that would be the last time, but then I always went back the next weekend. I just thought I was sick." While women rarely narrativized their lesbian identity formation in conjunction with sexual activity, they too experienced the realization of their same-sex sexuality as profoundly disorienting. "I knew," a Viennese woman born in 1960 told me, "that wanting to be with a woman not only went against the educational and religious principles of my parents, but it just seemed wrong in general." Another woman put it in even more general terms when she recalled her internal coming out in the late 1980s: "At fourteen or so, I realized that I'm lesbian, and I also realized that that was not accepted at all, and so I really thought that I wasn't normal."

However, the difficulty of coming out to oneself in a homophobic society was not the defining feature of same-sex sexual existence. For even when lesbians and gay men did come to terms with their individual desires, they were forced to negotiate their sexual orientation according to the cultural logic of Austria's social fields. This translated into a careful compartmentalization of people's lives — the continual form of identity management expressed through the concept of the "closet." Its operative principles necessitated a rigorous separation between performatively heterosexual and secretly homosexual Selves. And whether the enactment of normalcy was confined to such semipublic sites as the workplace and living arrangements or, as was typically the case in Vienna, extended to the more private realm of family and friends as well, it induced the double life that characterized much of modern lesbian/gay existence. In the immediate postwar period, then, Austria was hardly unusual, particularly among those European countries that criminalized all forms of homosexuality. As Thomas, who came of age in the late 1940s and early 1950s, recalled, the closet was a self-evident feature of lesbian/gay existence in the first decades of the Second Republic:

It would have been totally inconceivable to say at work that I was homosexual. There always was the sword hanging over one's head of going to prison, and so everyone had to be very careful. The only people who knew about me were my gay friends, no one else knew. And when my mother found out — I don't remember how, I think she had gone through some of my things — she was totally desperate. I don't know if she was more concerned about me going to jail or the family finding out; they were very Catholic. In any case, I was really concerned not to let on. I never spent the night at my boyfriend's apartment, for example, just to make sure that nobody could say anything.

Recalling his life in the Vienna of the 1950s and early 1960s, Thomas's narrative captured the complex dynamics of the Central European closet as well as its more specifically Austrian manifestation, defined as it was by a combination of violent state subordination, religious oppression, and such social technologies as denunciation.

In 1971, much of the legal threat disappeared, of course. But Austria's social realities remained essentially unchanged, and in light of the country's pronounced conservatism, the lifeworlds of Vienna's lesbians and gay men continued to be defined by the same self-evident closet that had organized their existence prior to the *Totalverbot*'s abolition. Here, then, lay the exceptionalism of the Austrian state. Whereas European countries with similar legal histories, such as Germany and Great Britain, witnessed marked transformations of same-sex sexual existence in the 1970s and 1980s,[65] neither Vienna's homosexual scene nor its subjects embraced the socially affirmative notion of a lesbian/gay community. In consequence, the process of lesbian/gay subjectification continued to be governed by a logic of individualized pathology, a mode of socialization that produced homosexuality as an inherently closeted identification until well into the 1990s.

Indeed, as late as 1994 — the year I commenced the ethnographic research for this project — it was clear that the overwhelming majority of Austria's lesbians and gay men concealed their sexual orientation as much as they could. Individual rationales for this social practice varied, of course, but they closely retraced the long-standing concerns of homosexuals in Austria's profoundly homophobic society. While the fear of legal persecution had subsided for the most part, conversation after conversation revealed deep-seated concerns about religious intolerance, moral indignation, and the lack of social acceptance. In this manner, many closeted men and women invoked a potentially disapproving family as the grounds for the ongoing concealment of their same-sex sexuality, while others pointed to their professional career as the main reason for their double life.

The most frequent explanation I received in the mid-1990s, however, made reference to the desire to keep one's sexuality fully private. The position was articulated paradigmatically by Herbert, a musician in his late thirties. While career considerations clearly played a role in his decision to remain in the closet, he ultimately regarded the concealment of his sexuality in terms of a quid pro quo. Feeling that his family and friends would be burdened by his homosexuality, he sought to minimize its significance. This did not mean that Herbert forwent gay male association. On the contrary, he ventured into Vienna's homosexual scene on an almost nightly basis. But the careful separation between his sexual and public persona would ensure the protection of his reputation as well as the social relationships he cherished. In a constitutive devaluation of his gay male existence, those would remain intrinsically heterosexual; thus Herbert reproduced the cultural logic of Austria's sexual hegemony. In 1971, the state had rescinded the *Totulverbot* on the implicit condition, enshrined in §220 and §221, that homosexuality continue to exist apart from the nation's public sphere. In this manner, Herbert's quid pro quo was not just with his family and friends. Much like the dozens of other lesbians and gay men who insisted to me that their sexual orientation was nothing but a personal matter and the many thousands who clearly thought the same, he ultimately enacted a social contract that decriminalized homosexuality only on condition of its continued invisibility.

Outing and Its Subordination

The cultural logic that underwrote the pervasive insistence on lesbian/gay privacy was not only codified in Austria's penal code. Even more important for the concept's social valence, it was reproduced in the mass media. The country's newspapers, of course, had a long history of same-sex sexual abjection. But while that discursive tradition turned on the construction of homosexuality as inherently criminal and pathological, the 1980s witnessed the appearance of a new type of coverage. This form of public discourse responded to the emergence of a small lesbian/gay emancipation movement;[66] and while reports on the movement's activities brought the topic of homosexuality closer to the journalistic mainstream, they ultimately functioned as yet another systemic technology of subordination. In the cultural logic of the Second Republic, the movement's public actions violated the hegemonic strictures against lesbian/gay visibility, and Austria's newspapers took it upon themselves to enforce the nation's decorum by putting the newly politicized homosexuals in their place. In practice, this meant that the efforts of the lesbian/gay movement were either ignored or held up for censure and public ridicule.[67] Not all reports were equally derisive, of course, but the few pieces that displayed genuine sympathy with lesbian/gay concerns were vastly outnumbered by reports that took the movement's activities as occasions for rebukes that doubled as checks against homosexuality's public deployment.[68]

An early article in the *Wochenpresse* was typical of the refusal to engage the movement's substantive demands, at the same time as it used a host of conventional stereotypes to mock the movement's political efforts.[69] Published in 1982, the piece portrayed activists as "jokers," who staged a "lusty fag revolt" in the interest of "uninhibited same-sex pleasure." In such a discursive context, the aims of the movement were systematically obscured. The *Wochenpresse,* in fact, put the "mechanisms of oppression" targeted by activists in quotation marks, as if to suggest that they were the figment of a capricious homosexual imagination.[70] Even more common than ridicule, however, was outright hostility against the establishment of homosexuality in the national sphere. When activists distributed information on same-sex sexuality at Austrian schools in 1988, for instance, the country's media joined an indignant campaign that demanded the containment of homosexuality. For the center-right *Presse,* it was "fine that female and male homosexuals can live without fear of persecution," but this did not mean that "society accepts their sexual behavior as normal." Therefore it was necessary to "attack" any public actions that might lead to the "acquisition" of this "'other' sexuality."[71]

Austria's mass media reproduced these discursive patterns in their coverage of lesbian/gay activism as late as 1995. Specifically, it was that year's so-called outing affair that engendered the derision of political work on behalf of lesbians and gay men as a function of individual pathology, and brought a renewed insistence on homosexuality's status as inherently nonpublic.[72] In the summer, gay activist Kurt Krickler had identified four Catholic bishops as clandestine homosexuals to protest ongoing discrimination against Austria's lesbians and gay men and to call attention to the church's role in that state of affairs; it was in the mass-media response to this scandalous event that the operative subordination of homosexuality became manifest. That response systematically evaded the political and social issues motivating Krickler's actions. To be sure, a number of liberal commentators were quick to concede the legal inequity of Austria's antihomosexual statutes;[73] none, however, showed any tangible concern for the quality of life among the country's lesbians and gay men. More than anything else, it was the failure to recognize the devastating effects of homophobia that came to define the massive coverage of the outing affair; in this context, Krickler's intervention could only be illegitimate.

Mirroring mass-media reactions to the lesbian/gay activism of the 1980s, this construction was transported through the constitutive devaluation of a publicly homosexual subject position. A cover story in *Profil* was paradigmatic in this respect.[74] Under the title "Confess That You Are Gay," *Profil* ostensibly took a stance against the "continued discrimination against homosexuals."[75] But if this position gestured to the magazine's progressive politics, the tolerance it evoked was not extended to such public homosexuals as Krickler, who quickly emerged as the article's genuine object of scrutiny. Much like other mass media, *Profil* ultimately found Krickler's illiberal and unreasonable actions — rather than the predicament he was protesting — in need of explanation. In this situation, the magazine avoided linking the outings to the social ills of homophobia, instead fixing its critical faculties on an investigation of Krickler's personal psycho-pathologies. With easy recourse to the long-standing image of homosexuality as a disease, a diagnosis was readily available. As *Profil* concluded, Krickler's "radicalism" and the resulting "deed of desperation" had their origin in his personal plight: "For ten years, [Krickler] has known that he is HIV-positive. . . . Three years ago, his long-term companion died of the disease."[76] The operationalization of the powerful chain of signification "homosexuality–disease–AIDS–death–despair–unreason" was further elaborated through remarks on Krickler's early and painful knowledge of his deviant sexuality and adult experience burdened by constant "pressure" and "fear," as well as the "suicides of numerous friends."[77] It ultimately served a clear purpose. In the hands of *Profil,* Krickler became a pitiful gay stereotype, whose outings could be readily dismissed as the act of a disgruntled, desperate, and pathological activist-loner. Much like the 1980s, when lesbian/gay activists were spurned as "jokers," *Profil* turned the outing affair into a mechanism of social surveillance; in concert with the country's other mass media, it undermined the legitimacy of a self-consciously lesbian/gay subjectivity at the very moment of its socially intelligible constitution.

The pathologization of lesbian/gay activism was in turn part of a larger social technology designed to protect the public sphere from homosexual intrusion. This project of sexual homogenization had always been at the core of the state's subordination of same-sex sexuality, of course; the mass-media response to the outing affair affirmed it through the performative relegation of homosexuality to a sphere of inherent privacy. By making the bishops' supposed same-sex inclinations a feature of public knowledge, Krickler had challenged that sphere, but unanimous outrage against this breach ultimately reasserted its boundaries. Indeed, commentators on all sides of the political spectrum vigorously denounced Krickler's violation of the "victims'" privacy. Thus, when an editorialist for the left-liberal daily *Standard* spoke of Krickler's actions as a "violation of human dignity" in light of its "invasion of the private sphere," the sentiment was not only echoed by Austria's state-run broadcasting company, which called the outings an "attack on the personal rights of human beings," but by members of the clergy, one of whom referred to Krickler's actions as a "cruel destruction of a person's basic rights."[78] Such reactions were intended as a defense of Austria's bishops, but they doubled as social acts that prescribed a proper location for homosexual difference according to the abject logic of the state.

This performative dynamic was in evidence across the mass-media spectrum, exemplified paradigmatically in a *Kurier* editorial. There Austria's embattled bishops were given empathetic advice on how to deal with the unpleasant situation most effectively: "The most reasonable reaction of those affected would be the calm insistence on their right to respect for their intimate lives . . . , establishing beyond question that homosexuality is a private matter, quite naturally among bishops as well."[79] Even though the editorial went on to assert that homosexuality should not reflect negatively on an individual's public reputation, its insistence on the private nature of same-sex sexuality remained absolute. Heterosexuality did not even need to be mentioned to substantiate the assertion; its absence actually reinforced the message. While homosexuality was to be diagnosed, circumscribed, and constituted as part of an inherently personal domain, heterosexuality required no boundary-setting intervention. Much as it was imagined in the state's penal code, it would function as the normal condition of public existence, fortified as it was by a cultural logic that assigned same-sex sexuality to a status of abject privacy.

Along with other forms of lesbian/gay activism, the Outing affair had challenged the self-evident relegation of homosexuality to a privatized sphere of abject difference. By declaring the illegality of Krickler's actions, the state would soon uphold the sexual integrity of the national sphere.[80] In the immediate aftermath of the affair, however, it was the country's mass media that most forcefully pronounced the hegemonic structuration of Austria's socio-sexual fields. In continuing a discursive practice that constructed lesbian/gay activism as an affront to the public order, publications like *Profil* and *Kurier* not only reproduced the state's project of homosexual exclusion, but articulated the cultural vision that disciplined the overwhelming majority of Vienna's lesbians and gay men into acco-modationist submission. As symptoms of modernity, the city's queers lived in the state's closets; soon, however, they would emerge into the national sphere.

PART TWO

Resistance

CHAPTER 3

Street Fairs and Demonstrations

Shalom. Some members of our community have asked me not to speak this evening because it is not appropriate for a Jew, and especially for a rabbi, to be involved in politics. I disagree with this opinion, and I am speaking today.

Chief Rabbi Paul Chaim Eisenberg on April 6, 2000

It was a chilly evening in early spring; but the cold weather could not dampen the crowd's resilient spirit. Well over five hundred people had turned out on April 6, 2000 to take part in a Jewish demonstration against the recently formed coalition government of the Christian Conservative People's Party and the right-wing Freedom Party. Under the leadership of Jörg Haider, who had taken over the party's reins in a 1986 putsch, the FPÖ had steadily gained at the polls; in the national election of October 1999, it reached almost 27 percent of the popular vote, just ahead of the ÖVP and only a few percentage points behind the Social Democrats. Haider had achieved his electoral triumphs with a peculiar mixture of German nationalism, Austrian patriotism, and xenophobia on the one hand, and a persistent critique of the country's postwar arrangements on the other. To Haider, the child of unrepentant Nazis, these arrangements meant postwar Austria's antifascist consensus had effectively divided the state apparatus between Social Democrats and Christian Conservatives. Former and seemingly reformed Nazis had been readily integrated into the two parties, of course; for those who remained publicly loyal to their erstwhile cause, however, the country's official stance did bring a certain degree of disenfranchisement. But if Haider's quest could be read as an attempt to legitimize his parents' biography, his political triumphs were ultimately enabled by the ossification of Austria's postwar system. Although a formal democracy, it produced ever-increasing lethargy among citizens who knew that their votes would merely serve to reinstantiate the status quo of *Sozialpartnerschaft* and *Proporz* — the economic and political arrangements that allowed SPÖ and ÖVP to govern Austria's course by indirect rule. Against this backdrop, Haider could style himself as a democratic "reformer" whose populism — at one point he rechristened himself the leader of a movement rather than a party — would bring about the Third Republic.[1]

Ever since 1986, Austria's Jews had monitored Haider's rise with grave concern. Coming in the wake of the Waldheim affair, it not only represented the continuation of a perilous situation, but raised the ideological stakes considerably. Waldheim, after all, had never been a committed Nazi, and while he had constructed his biography in the convenient terms of Austria's victim myth, he ultimately sought to distance himself from National Socialism. Haider, by contrast, could be regarded as a kind of neo-Nazi, or at least an apologist for Nazism — an interpretation suggested by his praise of Hitler's employment policies and his readiness to congratulate former members of the Waffen-SS on their steadfast ideology.[2] Many Jews were aware that Haider's growing popularity was not exclusively or even principally based on his national-conservative roots, but the fact that his nostalgic flirtations with Nazism did not impede his steady rise was deeply troubling.

In February of 2000, the fears of Austria's Jews were realized when Haider's FPÖ became a partner in the country's governing coalition. The Jewish reaction to this event, however, was as surprising as it was public. In contrast to 1986, when the Waldheim affair forced the Jewish community into the diffident posture characterizing its postwar existence, Vienna's Jews took to the streets to protest the Freedom Party's inclusion in the national government. Coming in the wake of several smaller events, the demonstration of April 6, 2000 showcased the newly resistive stance. Organized by the Association of Jewish University Students (VJHÖ) and rendered a de facto official event of the IKG on account of the active participation of President Ariel Muzicant and Chief Rabbi Paul Chaim Eisenberg, the protest marked the first time Vienna's Jewish community ever took to the streets to demonstrate against postwar Austria's political hegemonies.[3] To the participants, the historical nature of the

STREET FAIRS AND DEMONSTRATIONS   91

event was evident; and while Eisenberg's opening remarks made clear that some IKG members still believed Austria's Jews ought to shun the political spotlight, the largely younger crowd gestured to a sea change in Jewish self-understanding.

The new Jewish sensibility was captured in the demonstration's slogan. "Who, if not we; when, if not now!" identified Austria's Jews as the bearers of a particular responsibility. As Julia Andras, head of the VJHÖ, made clear in her speech, that responsibility was tied to the specific nature of the Jewish experience, both in the Holocaust and in the Second Republic:

We Jews have a past that will accompany us for our entire life, a past that brought the worst tragedy in the history of humanity on many of our ancestors. . . . Austria claimed that it was Hitler's first victim, but Austria was, some resistance notwithstanding, also a culprit. As long as this country refuses to clarify Austria's guilt, the impossible will always be possible again.

Andras's analysis of the Holocaust and Austria's Second Republic recalled critiques formulated in postwar Vienna's Jewish environs. What distinguished it, however, was its decisively public articulation. Offered in the context of a protest held at a prominent square in Vienna's city center, it recast the stance of Austria's Jews as openly oppositional. In so doing, Andras echoed the leaflet that had announced the demonstration in the weeks prior to the event. There Vienna's Jews were emboldened to "no longer keep our mouths shut," a sentiment Andras seconded when she told the cheering crowd that "our resistance must not cease."

In its open antagonism toward a sitting Austrian government, the Jewish demonstration of April 6, 2000 was a unique event. But it did not come out of a vacuum. The protest was engendered by a multifaceted process that occurred in the wake of the Waldheim affair. On the one hand, that process propelled individual Jews into Austria's public sphere, where they came to figure as some of the country's most persistent critics. On the other hand, it furthered developments within the IKG that resulted in the adoption of an aggressive political stance and led to the strategic deployment of Jewish difference in Vienna's cultural fields. In promoting a "new Jewish self-confidence," this process thus not only ended the enforced privatization of Viennese Jewry, but also socialized an entire generation of Jews into public defiance of Austrian hegemonies. In countering the structural exclusions that had silenced them in the postwar era, the Jewish symptoms of modernity were about to find their voice through an act of collective resistance.

Jewish Intellectuals and the Public Sphere

The emergence of Jews as critical public intellectuals was a generational phenomenon. It involved children of survivors, who began to articulate the pains and frustrations caused by postwar Austria's structural exclusions. This is not to say that the survivors themselves were unaware of the Second Republic's glaring inequities. On the contrary, they often complained bitterly about them. But such sentiments were usually reserved for private conversations; at most, they found a textual representation in the pages of the Jewish press. *Die Gemeinde,* for instance, published critiques of the victim myth as early as the 1950s, and the realities of Austrian antisemitism were a recurring topic throughout the postwar years.[4] In retracing Austrian hegemonies, however, such critical engagements with the country's status quo practically never entered the larger public sphere.[5] Individual Jews were hardly ever present in the mass-media realm; even when they were, they followed Kreisky's example of submerging the particularism of postwar Jewish experience in a newly imagined Austrian nationness. Such Jewish writers as Hans Weigel and Friedrich Torberg, for instance, readily acquiesced to the state's master narrative, avoiding all discussion of Austria's Nazi past and its effects on contemporary Jewish existence.[6]

The postwar generation began to break this silence in the late 1970s. In large part, this was a function of a radically different socialization process. To be sure, Vienna's postwar generation came of age during a period of intense antisemitism, but they were spared the ultimate trauma of genocide and cultural annihilation. As bearers of mediated Holocaust memory, they suffered from the aftereffects of the catastrophe — their parents' pained silence and fearful retreat into the private sphere.[7] These realities, however, became the occasion for intense questioning and internal critique, and by the 1970s, a number of younger Jews sought to overcome their parents' perceived "ghetto existence."[8] Rather than passive victims, they would be active champions of social justice, challenging Austrian hegemonies from a position of defiant opposition.

More than any other institution, it was the Jewish youth organizations, particularly the HaSchomer Hazair, that fostered this resistive enterprise. Since the late 1960s, the group had been a veritable hotbed of critical debate. In meeting after meeting, its members discussed questions of memory and Austria's political scene, with Kreisky serving as a favorite topic of conversation. In a global context of Jewish reethnicization, the constitutive suppression of his Jewishness along with his anti-Zionism were anathema to the group's commitment to Jewish national pride.[9] Indeed, in light of Israel's existence, Kreisky's adherence to and defense of Austria and its antisemitic realities seemed positively self-defeating. To the members of the Schomer, as well as those of Bnei Akiba, Israel was a source of collective strength that could be tapped to articulate an autonomous Jewish position. As Holocaust survivors and displaced persons, their parents had been forced into a diffident quest for tolerance; they would replace it with a proud critique of Austrian hegemonies.

The importance of Israel in the emergence of a critical Jewish position can hardly be overstated. As one interview after another made clear, the Zionist state profoundly affected the coordinates of Austrian-Jewish existence. For Viennese Jewry's Zionist majority, it engendered the alternative mode of national identification that would underwrite much of the emergent critique. "To identify with the state that fights," as one of my interlocutors put it, was the basis for postwar Jews' resistive interventions. But Israel's reach extended even beyond its immediate supporters. Non-Zionists, too, came to regard the state as a kind of safety net. Their primary allegiances may have been to communist internationalism or Austrian tradition, but, as a former communist put it, "Israel was there as a place to go in absolute need." It was in this sense that the existence of Israel enabled the gradual articulation of a public Jewish critique.

In its initial formulations, the Jewish critique was confined to a few alternative and left-leaning publications that shared in the common project of unmasking Austrian power. An early article by Elisabeth Spira, a member of Austrian Jewry's immediate postwar generation, was paradigmatic for the anger underwriting such newly public Jewish interventions.[10] Published in December 1975 in the socialist youth magazine *Trotzdem,* the piece was titled "It Is Cold in Austria"; the subtitle, "Notes on Austrian Antisemitism," struck an exceedingly aggressive tone.[11] Antisemitism, to Spira, was not only lamentable, but a veritable outrage; even worse, however, was the absence of an appropriate response to such events as the *Krone* series on the Jews in Austria.

Nobody gets up to burn the papers. Nobody gets up to clench a fist. . . . And nobody gets up, thirty years afterward, and begins to ask, to warn, to fight. Nobody gets up and closes the door to the [Nazis]. Nobody gets up and says: shame on you. It is cold in Austria.

For Spira, the apathy was directly linked to Austria's postwar arrangements. Charging the state with blatant hypocrisy, she noted the absence of *Vergangenheitsbewältigung,* the coming to terms with the past that would set the stage not only for adequate restitution, but for an acknowl-edgement of the country's persistent antisemitism. "After 1945 it was said that there was a need to gain some distance before working through the past. When they waited long enough, it was said that the past should finally be laid to rest."

If Spira's critique focused on the contours of Austrian hegemonies, other members of the postwar generation began a public exploration of the Jewish lifeworlds engendered in these antisemitic contexts. An arti-cle by Erika Wantoch, another representative of the immediate post-Holocaust generation, was easily the most powerful instantiation. Pub-lished in 1981 in the progressive weekly *Profil,* the piece presented a scathing assessment of a Jewish community whose multiple victimiza-tions left it without political autonomy or cultural agency.[12] In Wantoch's textual economy, the Jews of Vienna were a shell, a deeply disenfranchised group whose existence in the land of the perpetrators was a function of their collective resignation. To the antisemitic state, these Jews were nonetheless a potential nuisance. No one had called them back after the war, but now that a few thousand of them were here, they needed to be turned into docile subjects. The IKG was the product and emblem of this larger state apparatus, and Wantoch sought to unmask its unbearable diffidence vis-à-vis the sites of national power. "Subservience describes the condition of submission," she noted, illustrating her contention with the excessive acclamations IKG's representatives showered on Austrian politi-cians whenever they addressed Jewish audiences.[13] To Wantoch, such obsequiousness not only enabled continued Austrian hegemonies, but it also prevented the Jewish community from articulating an independent political and cultural stance. The overall assessment was deeply pes-simistic, but Wantoch had an alternative vision for Vienna's Jews grounded in just such a quest for autonomy. The Austrian state had imposed "boundaries" and "rules" that "let Jews be" only if they did not "attract attention as Jews"; it was this situation of permanent subordina-tion that needed to be countered with an anti-assimilationist "con-sciousness of oneself and one's worth."[14] Wantoch's article itself func-tioned in this manner, staging a specifically Jewish intervention in Austria's public sphere.

If the basic contours of the Jewish critique were in place by the early 1980s, its full potential was not unleashed until the Waldheim affair. Simply put, the presidential campaign of 1986 galvanized the postwar generation into action to an unprecedented degree. Socialized in the resis-itive Zionist environs of the youth organizations, Vienna's younger Jews were appalled not only by the reckless deployment of political anti-semitism, but also by the IKG's seeming inaction in the face of the crisis.

Many early Jewish responses to Waldheim were confined to the Jewish press, but the steady string of articles clearly pointed toward an aggres-sive move into the public sphere. To the authors, the Waldheim presi-dency and its concomitant circumstances were simply "unbearable," necessitating the development of a "new self-confidence among Jews."[15] Doron Rabinovici, then a student at the University of Vienna, put it most drastically. Writing in *Das jüdische Echo,* the annual publication of the Association of Jewish University Students, he reassessed the mode of postwar Austrian-Jewish existence.[16] Jews, he argued, had attempted to placate Austria's antisemites through their solidarity with the country. The Waldheim affair, however, had made it clear once more that "our actions do not influence them." In this light, Austria's Jews had a choice. They could continue to serve as "alibi Jews of Austria's national lie *[Lebenslüge]*" or they could become the "chief witnesses" of history.[17] Rabinovici, of course, advocated the latter; he reimagined the role of Vienna's Jews as historically situated critics of Austrian hegemonies.

Rabinovici articulated a widespread sentiment among younger Jewish intellectuals, and in the course of the late 1980s and 1990s, several of them came to national prominence as vigorous critics of Austria's status quo. This did not occur in an intellectual vacuum. A number of non-Jewish scholars had also been galvanized by the Waldheim affair. Within a few years, an entire library of revisionist historiography not only established the degree of Austrian complicity in the Third Reich, but scrutinized its systematic obfuscation in the course of the Second Republic.[18] But it was the Jewish intellectuals who articulated the newly critical position most powerfully, establishing it in the public sphere by linking it to Austrian Jewry's specific lifeworlds. As a result of openings created by the Waldheim affair, this process took place both in the mainstream press and on Austria's broadcast media, and it allowed such writers, filmmakers, and essayists as Robert Schindel, Ruth Beckermann, and Robert Menasse to prominently thematize the status of Austrian-Jewish existence.[19] It was Rabinovici himself, however, who became the most prominent voice of Jewish critique, emerging by the late 1990s as Austria's leading public intellectual and political activist.

In many ways, Rabinovici's trajectory was paradigmatic of Jewish intel-lectuals of the postwar generation. Born in Tel Aviv in 1961 as the child of Eastern European survivors, he arrived in Vienna at the age of three. After a childhood marked by persistent feelings of exclusion, Rabinovici found his social and intellectual home in the HaSchomer Hazair, which he joined in the late 1960s. Much like other Jews who attended the Schomer between the 1960s and 1980s, Rabinovici has noted the exhilarating atmosphere of the youth group; in his narrative, he stressed its dual attention to political and personal development. Israel was at the heart of the former, but so was a strong sense of social justice — an overall orientation that was connected to a "revolutionary" emphasis on "Jewish consciousness." In the early 1980s, Rabinovici enrolled at the University of Vienna, but a projected career as a physician was sidetracked during the Waldheim affair. "I don't want to be a well-behaved Jew," Rabinovici proclaimed in a *Profil* article written by Erika Wantoch at the height of the Waldheim controversy.[20] Indeed, he was about to shift into a career of political activism. In the wake of Waldheim's election campaign, he cofounded the Republikanischer Club Neues Österreich, a progressive organization dedicated to combating right-wing politics and raising awareness of Austria's responsibility for the Third Reich.[21] Over the following years, Rabinovici complemented his activities in the organization with frequent publication of opinion pieces, and by the mid-1990s, he had emerged as the most vocal critic not only of antisemitism and Austria's victim myth, but of racism and right-wing politics more generally.[22] Gaining added celebrity through the publication of a collection of short stories and a novel, Rabinovici emerged as a key political figure in the wake of Austria's 1999 election.[23] In response to Haider's victory at the polls, Rabinovici cofounded the Demokratische Offensive — an antiracist action group that would go on to organize the largest demonstration in the history of Austria's Second Republic. As the group's speaker, Rabinovici became not only one of the country's most widely recognized political figures, but the very embodiment of the post-Waldheim Jewish critique.

The New Jewish Politics

The public intellectuals of the post-Waldheim era were not the only agents of Jewish critique. The same dynamics that propelled figures like Doron Rabinovici and Ruth Beckermann into Austria's national sphere also shifted the political orientation and public style of the IKG. In the process, the official governing body of Viennese Jewry emerged as a highly visible organization, dedicated to the struggle for social justice in matters pertaining to Jews and non-Jews alike. Much like the case of the

Jewish intellectuals, the transformation was ultimately a generational phenomenon, further accelerated by the Waldheim affair.

For the first decades of the Second Republic, the IKG and its representatives had avoided Austria's public sphere. Reproducing the country's hegemonies, they had hoped to advance the state of Viennese Jewry through private appeals to members of the political elite.[24] Like most things in postwar Austria, this strategy followed a strict logic of political affiliation. In this logic, the IKG was allied with the Socialist Party, whose internationalist platform appealed to the postwar Jewish elite, comprised as it was of returnees whose commitment to Austria was predicated on a universalist vision. By and large, this vision was not shared by postwar immigrants from Eastern Europe. Many of them had been refugees of Stalinism, and their antisocialism combined with a more traditional approach to Jewish life. For decades, intra-Jewish politics were dominated by this split; and while the Socialists lost their absolute majority by 1976, it was not until the early 1980s that a more particularist agenda came to dominate Jewish politics.[25] For years, however, this transition failed to affect IKG's public profile. Much like Socialists of the survivor generation, their bourgeois counterparts shunned the national spotlight, hoping to safeguard Austrian-Jewish existence through measured appeals for tolerance.

For politically active members of the postwar generation, however, this accomodationist stance soon became intolerable. Especially in the wake of the Waldheim affair, which was widely seen as proof of the failure of Austrian Jewry's appeasement politics, it seemed absurd to humor the state's antisemitic apparatuses through diffident behavior.[26] The generational conflict dominated discussions of the IKG board, but it was staged most dramatically at a 1988 event organized by the Vienna chapter of B'nai B'rith, the Jewish anti-defamation league, which was run by members of the survivor generation. B'nai B'rith had invited three representatives of the *Krone* to discuss whether Austria's mass media were antisemitic. To younger Jews radicalized by the Waldheim affair, it seemed like yet another plea for tolerance. Even more, it would allow the *Krone* to whitewash the paper's antisemitism through the cynical instrumentalization of the invitation by and conversation with a Jewish group. Given this situation, the Association of Jewish University Students had tried to dissuade B'nai B'rith from holding the event; and when that proved futile, the group decided to take action. As the discussion got underway in front of an audience of several hundred, forty members of the VJHÖ stormed the stage, disrupting the proceedings and vocally demanding that Jews refrain from engaging in a dialogue with antisemites. After a few minutes of tumult and heated debate, the *Krone* representatives left the stage and the discussion was thwarted. To most members of the older generation, the incident was horrifying. Committed to a politics of appeasement, they feared that the "students' actions" would create antisemitism by providing "the opponents with ammunition."[27] To the students, however, the event was a singular triumph. Convinced that Jewish actions did not affect antisemitic sentiments, they saw their intervention as a resistive act of Jewish agency. Writing in *Die Gemeinde* a few months after the incident, the VJHÖ insisted that antisemites were not entitled to justify their resentments. Only "we Jews decide who is an antisemite. Antisemites have always had the first word. They should not have the last."[28]

The generational conflict staged at the B'nai B'rith event occurred outside the IKG's political structures, but a similar dynamic also took place within Viennese Jewry's official governing body. In the course of the early 1980s, more and more members of the postwar generation had been elected to serve on the organization's board, and when the Waldheim affair dramatized the Jewish leadership's inability to articulate a critical position, these representatives began to push for radical changes in the IKG's political style. Much like previous IKG presidents, Ivan Hacker had advocated a deliberately cautious approach centered on the performance of loyalty to the Austrian state. For the younger generation of Jewish politicians, however, such perpetual pleas for tolerance had proven inadequate. No longer wanting to aid and abet the reproduction of Austrian hegemonies, they were determined to reinvent the IKG as a site of resistance. During Waldheim's presidential campaign, the organization had failed to function in this manner, but in its immediate aftermath, the new style of Jewish politics began to take center stage.

A press conference following the election gave an early indication of the new direction. Hacker opened the event with a general statement bemoaning the antisemitic dynamics of the Waldheim affair.[29] A number of younger IKG representatives, however, found much clearer words. Ariel Muzicant, then an IKG board member in his early thirties, broke with the postwar status quo most thoroughly when he identified a number of ÖVP politicians as responsible both for the antisemitic campaign and for the concomitant rise in antisemitic incidents. Prior to this moment, the IKG had never scrutinized the self-characterization of Austria and its ruling parties as stalwarts of antifascism, and Muzicant's angry statement aroused considerable attention in Austria's mass media.[30] The provocation was deliberate, of course. For decades, the IKG had shunned the public sphere in an effort to preserve postwar Austria's arrangements. But as those arrangements became the principal target for a new generation of Jewish representatives, the aggressive move into the public sphere became both necessary and inevitable.

If the 1986 press conference gestured to a new style of Jewish politics, the following years brought its full implementation. The 1987 election of Paul Grosz as IKG president was widely seen as a pivotal event in this process. While technically a member of the survivor generation — the product of a "mixed marriage," he had survived the Holocaust in Vienna as a child — he stood for an assertive approach grounded in a critical analysis of postwar Austrian hegemonies. Indeed, Grosz's presidency had an immediate effect on the IKG's political visibility. Unlike his predecessors, Grosz aggressively sought out the public sphere, and through his continuous interventions in debates, he gradually attained a national profile. The result of this strategy was not only an unprecedented degree of media coverage, but the establishment of an official Jewish position within Austria's mainstream press. In 1989, for example, Grosz used an interview with the left-liberal daily *Standard* to address the persistent injustice occasioned by Austria's victim myth. Reminding the state and its citizens that full restitution of Jewish property was still outstanding, he pledged a continuing struggle: "It was easy to come to terms with dead Jews — but with the living, things will not be so easy."[31] The aggressive tone was typical, characterizing an approach that was concerned less with appeasement than with the articulation of a critically autonomous position.[32]

But Grosz's presidency altered the IKG's political orientation in even more far-reaching ways. Initially, his election was primarily seen in terms of a fortification of a new Jewish self-confidence, and while his term did coincide with the establishment of a distinctly Jewish cultural sphere, it also brought an unprecedented attention to political developments at large. In the process, the IKG transformed itself from the official governing body of Viennese Jewry to one of Austria's central sites of progressive politics. As early as 1992, Grosz announced that the organization needed to "speak up" whenever "democratic principles" seemed in jeopardy, and by the mid-1990s, it was centrally involved in various antiracist struggles. In 1993, the IKG underwrote the Lichtermeer (Sea of Lights), a massive demonstration organized in protest against an FPÖ referendum designed to curb immigration to Austria; two years later, IKG representatives Grosz and Rabbi Paul Chaim Eisenberg were among the featured speakers at an event commemorating the violent deaths of four Roma men who had fallen victim to a bomb planted by a neo-Nazi.[33]

If anything, the level of IKG's political engagement intensified even further when Ariel Muzicant was elected as Grosz's successor in 1998. Reiterating that Jews had an obligation to combat all forms of racism, Muzicant quickly established himself as one of Austria's most vocal proponents of human rights.[34] In 1999, he took a leading role in the commemoration and protest of the death of Marcus Omofuma — a West African asylum seeker who died under the eyes of several Austrian policemen during deportation. Speaking at the memorial event, which was co-organized by the IKG, Muzicant emphasized the "moral duty" to create a "public consciousness" that would "keep such an inhuman course of action from ever taking place."[35]

Muzicant was similarly outspoken on numerous other occasions, demanding respect rather than mere tolerance for Jews and other minorities alike. This public involvement was not lost on the members of the Jewish community; and in many of my interviews, it was a topic of conversation. Predictably, the responses had a degree of generational stratification. While some older members of the community continued to be nervous about Jews' political involvement, particularly in regard to seemingly non-Jewish issues, the overwhelming majority took great pride in IKG's progressive orientation. For some, it served as an important corrective to Austria's political climate, while others regarded it as indicating a greater Jewish presence in the country's public sphere. All of my interlocutors, however, saw it in marked contrast to the IKG's pre-Waldheim stance; they described it as the sign of a "change of consciousness." As a man in his late 40s approvingly put it, "There was no point in always being nice and good." Instead, Jews needed to "voice their opinions publicly, even if it was controversial." Under Grosz and Muzicant, the IKG did just that; and in the process, the Jewish community emerged as a principal agent of political resistance in late-twentieth-century Austria.

Schools and Sports, Festivals and Street Fairs

In the late 1980s and 1990s, Jewish intellectuals and IKG representatives forcefully emerged into Austria's public sphere. In doing so, they were driven by an oppositional vision that sought to challenge the country's inequities from a critical Jewish perspective. That vision had germinated in such environments as the Jewish youth groups, where a post-Holocaust generation negotiated Jews' enforced privatization in light of emergent designs for Jewish self-assertion. The newly politicized stance of the post-Waldheim period was a direct result of this socialization process. However, its effects extended far beyond the political realm. The same processes that propelled individual Jews into the forefront of progressive Austrian politics also had momentous repercussions for the Jewish community at large. In the last years of the twentieth century, the everyday existence of Jews expanded from a privatized realm of difference to Vienna's public and semipublic spheres. This development was the result of an aggressive cultural agenda implemented by members of the postwar generation in an effort to fortify and collectivize an autonomous Jewish consciousness. Facilitated by demographic shifts rejuvenating the Jewish community in the course of the 1980s, Austria's Jews thus followed the trajectories of IKG's representatives, gaining a new visibility that would render them a clear counterpoint to postwar Austria's cultural homogenization.

Much like the IKG's political agenda, the organization's approach to cultural work reflected generational divides; there too the decisive conflicts came to the fore in the late 1970s and 1980s. For the first decades of the Second Republic, the governing body of Vienna's Jews had simply neglected to foster Jewish cultural life. On the one hand, this was a result of the genocide, which necessitated an emphasis on the sheer struggle for individual and collective survival. On the other hand, a cluster of political considerations ran counter to a quest for cultural self-assertion. For the IKG's Socialist leadership — committed to a universalist vision of social integration — any prospect of Jewish autonomy raised the specter of separatism and disloyalty. Underlying this fear, of course, was the hope for inclusion into Austria's imagined community, which was thought to be in jeopardy whenever Jews insisted on or performed their supposed cultural difference.

Members of the postwar generation had an entirely different analysis of the matter. Often brought up with some awareness of Jewish cultural specificity and less committed to a broadly assimilationist agenda, they tended to view the cultural realm as a principal arena of Jewish reproduction. This was all the more pertinent in light of postwar Austria's hegemonies, which placed Jews in a subordinate position through the assertion of the state's neutrality. In this situation, the solution was not the reinforcement of Austrian sensibilities, but the resistive strengthening of a distinctly Jewish subject position. In the course of the 1960s and early 1970s, the IKG leadership had made a number of concessions in that direction. But the creation of a "House of Youth" (in 1966) and the hiring of an IKG youth official (in 1974) proved ineffective, in part because of severe underfunding and in part because the political constellations within the Jewish community had undermined the Socialists' credibility in cultural work.[36]

More than anything else, however, the generational debate on cultural autonomy turned on the issue of Jewish schooling. For the IKG leadership, the matter had low priority. In line with Austrian law, the organization oversaw Jewish children's religious education, but this only involved providing teachers for pooled classes held in the afternoon at designated schools. In the course of the 1970s, the IKG leadership sought to maintain this system, which was seen as the most effective balance between Jewish integration and religious preservation. By the end of the decade, however, a group of young parents articulated a much more radical vision. Without official IKG support, they founded a Jewish elementary school to provide an affirmative setting outside the antisemitic structures of Vienna's educational institutions.[37] Housed next to Vienna's main synagogue, the school opened its doors in the fall of 1980; in its initial form, it comprised a kindergarten and grades one and two.[38] The success was overwhelming. The student body quickly grew from the original fifty, and by 1983, the institution was ready to expand into a *Gymnasium*.[39] Under popular pressure, the IKG could no longer withhold its support, and when the Zwi Perez Chajes School opened in its own building in the fall of 1984, it was not only the first Jewish *Gymnasium* in the post-Holocaust German-speaking world, but the showcase of an IKG that was rapidly embracing the cultural orientation championed by the younger generation.[40]

That orientation was articulated most clearly by Ariel Muzicant, who had been the main proponent of the school. According to him, the educational institution was not only supposed to "give children profound Jewish knowledge," but was designed to "strengthen their Jewish identity." In doing so, it directly countered the abject individuation many Jewish children experienced in Vienna's schools.[41] In place of daily struggles with Austrian antisemitism, students would thrive in a vibrant social climate that fostered the creation of a "unified generation." In turn, that generation would neither "retreat into a ghetto" nor "choose assimilation."[42] Socialized into an autonomous site of Jewish subjectification, its members would instead emerge as the proud bearers of a distinctly Jewish tradition.

The school's success underscored the community's approval of this quest for Jewish autonomy. As the various grades were built up, the number of students gradually rose, and after registration increased markedly in the wake of the Waldheim affair, the school passed the mark of two hundred pupils.[43] By 1991, all grades were in operation, with attendance of some three hundred students. In relative terms, too, the success was palpable. While nearly 30 percent of Jewish *Gymnasiasten* attended the Zwi Perez Chajes School in the late 1990s, the numbers were even more staggering for elementary students, of whom a full 45 percent were enrolled in the Jewish institution.[44] Indeed, ever since its founding, parents regarded the Jewish school as a nearly ideal place for children's early education. Several of my interviewees had attended the institution as youngsters. "It was really important for me," one man in his early twenties told me in typical fashion — "I encountered Judaism not just as a religion but as a culture . . . and to this day, I'm in close contact with the people I met there."

But if the Jewish school was constructed as an enduring site of affirmative subjectification away from Austria's antisemitic lifeworlds, its existence was predicated on a fundamental demographic shift. For most of the Second Republic, Vienna's Jewish population was characterized by a very high average age and a perilously low number of younger people. In the mid-1950s, only 42 percent of Viennese Jews were under the age of fifty; and by the mid-1960s, the number had dropped as low as 37 percent.[45] With the average age reaching over sixty-five, the situation became truly dramatic in the 1970s, when informal estimates gauged the number of IKG members under the age of thirty-five at less than one thousand.[46] It was in light of such figures that Erika Wantoch had predicted the imminent demise of Vienna's Jewish community, the invocation of a new Jewish autonomy notwithstanding.[47]

Writing from the vantage point of 1981, Wantoch's assessment was essentially correct, but it was offset over the next few years, when the immigration of several thousand Jews from the then Soviet Union radically altered the demographic profile of Viennese Jewry. Given the rising death rates among members of the survivor generation, the total increase in the number of Austrian Jews was slight. But while IKG's total membership remained well below ten thousand, the ratio of those below fifty rose to 46 percent by 1985. By 1988, the number had increased to almost 50 percent; and the indicator continued to rise, reaching 56 percent by 1990 and close to 63 percent by 1993, when nearly 5,000 of the IKG's 7,500 members were under the age of fifty.[48] This demographic shift ultimately rendered the Zwi Perez Chajes School feasible, both as a viable educational institution and as the site of affirmative Jewish subjectification.[49] Before the influx from the Soviet Union, Vienna's Jewish community seemed destined for extinction; it its aftermath, it was ready to be schooled into the resistive autonomy championed by the postwar generation.

The Jewish school, however, was not the only site of affirmative Jewish subjectification. Throughout the 1980s, and particularly in the wake of the Waldheim affair, Vienna's Jewish organizations thrived in a larger context of Jewish authentification. Traditional groups like the HaSchomer Hazair and Bnei Akiba continued to work inwardly, joining the Zwi Perez Chajes School in the constitution of Jewish networks away from Austria's social realities. In contrast to the postwar era, however, this process of identificatory collectivization would no longer be restricted to a privatized realm, and by the early 1990s, new kinds of institutions began to anchor Jewish difference in the public and semipublic spheres. In structural terms, these institutions all resembled each other in the way they constructed an integrated vision of a newly expanding Jewish community in foundational opposition to an Austrian Other. Thus sports organizations, culture festivals, and street fairs became the principal vehicles for the constitution and performance of a newly resistive Jewish visibility.

More than any other institution, it was the Jewish sports clubs that came to embody and transport the Jewish community's post-Waldheim consciousness.[50] This is not to say that athletic organizations did not exist prior to the 1990s. Quite on the contrary, Jewish sports had a long tradition in Austria that dated back to the 1909 founding of Hakoah (Hebrew for "strength"), one of the country's leading athletic clubs during the interwar years.[51] Closed by the Nazis, the club was reactivated in 1945, but in light of the demographics of postwar Austria's Jewish community, it focused its efforts on social pursuits and the nostalgic cultivation of its heritage. By the early 1980s, the club's only athletic activity was swimming, which featured a dozen members in regular practice sessions and occasional club championships.

The situation changed abruptly in the late 1980s and early 1990s. The influx of Jews from the Soviet Union greatly increased the pool of potential athletes, and within a few years, Hakoah underwent a rapid expansion, augmenting its swimming section by establishing or reestablishing programs in basketball, tennis, table tennis, wrestling, and karate. Hakoah's success, however, was only part of the story. In 1995, Oskar Deutsch — a member of IKG's board in his mid-30s — founded a second Jewish sports club. Maccabi (named for the Maccabees) was a direct reflection of the quest for Jewish autonomy. Created to offer "Jewish youth the opportunity to spend their leisure time pursuing sports in a Jewish environment," the club placed quantity over quality in an effort to curb assimilationist tendencies.[52] In the resistive context of the post-Waldheim era, this design had enormous success; and within a year, Maccabi offered programs in gymnastics, squash, golf, bridge, and most importantly, soccer.[53]

Maccabi's raison d'etre resembled that of the Jewish school. Much like the educational institution, it provided a space for Jewish communalism away from the pressures of Austrian homogenization. However, this collectivizing project had an additional component. Central to Maccabi's mission was the redeployment of Jewish specificity within the semipublic sphere of athletic competition. In this sense sports occupied a privileged position in the resistive process of rendering Jews culturally visible. After all, the participation in Jewish sports engendered a performative enactment of ethnic difference — an enactment, moreover, that occurred on a culturally intelligible level of embodied interaction. To put it differently, it was the prolonged moment of athletic competition under the sign of affirmative Jewish difference that rendered the members of Maccabi, as well as those of Hakoah, legible as autonomous cultural agents. Indeed, in the late 1990s, Maccabi and Hakoah fielded dozens of competitive teams, and of the clubs' combined membership of five hundred, well over two hundred individuals regularly competed under the organizations' respective banners.[54]

For the members of Hakoah and Maccabi, the process of becoming visible as Jews in Austria's semipublic athletic sphere was multilayered. This started with the basic motivation for involvement in Jewish sports. In the many interviews I conducted among Jewish athletes in the late 1990s, I was told again and again that an individual's membership in Hakoah and Maccabi was a function of a person's athletic predilections. Hence Avner — a student of political science in his mid-twenties and a member of Hakoah's tennis team — told me that he joined the club because "I have always enjoyed sports." Similarly, Martin — a high school graduate and a member of Maccabi — remarked that he came to the team "because I just like to play soccer." When I inquired further, it turned out, however, that neither athlete had participated in organized sports prior to their respective membership in Hakoah and Maccabi. The pattern was typical. While the overwhelming majority of the Jewish athletes I spoke with professed a general interest in sports, few had ever ventured into non-Jewish clubs. Fear of antisemitism, as well as other forms of rejection, was the recurring motive for this noninvolvement, a general sense that

Jews would be neither accepted nor fully integrated into a non-Jewish organization. For example, Bela — a law student and recent immigrant from Hungary — told me that he had considered joining a non-Jewish soccer club prior to Maccabi's founding, but that he was discouraged by what he perceived as an antisemitic environment. When I asked him to elaborate, he told me:

Here at Maccabi, they don't call it a "Jew" when you kick the ball with the tip of the shoe. They always say that at other clubs. I just hate that. It really makes me feel uncomfortable.[55]

Victor — a business student and member of both Hakoah and Maccabi — expressed an analogous sentiment when he noted,

I just love sports. But it is totally clear that I would only get involved in a Jewish team. It would have been out of the question to play for a non-Jewish club. I never even tried. I just don't think I would have felt comfortable.

In contrast to such individualized fears of antisemitic rejection, Hakoah and Maccabi enjoined a distinctly collectivized sense of community. For some members of Vienna's Jewish sports clubs, the atmosphere was simply more friendly. "One just feels more comfortable here," one member of Maccabi told me. Another soccer player elaborated that "Maccabi is more of a social club than a sports team. Having fun together is more important than winning. That's how you create a real community." The situation was similar at Hakoah, where belonging to the collectivity was affirmed over and above athletic success. Erich — an engineering student in his mid-twenties and a member of Hakoah's table tennis section — explained to me:

Hakoah is very Jewish when it comes to social things. We have great cohesiveness. Everyone can come and participate in sports, even those who have no talent at all. In other clubs, people like that would never be accepted. But at Hakoah they are part of the team. Everyone contributes to the success of the club at large.

In the final analysis, it was this communalist rhetoric that not only separated Hakoah and Maccabi from other sports clubs, but rendered them a constitutive part of the Jewish community's quest for resistive autonomy. In contrast to the disempowering individuation engendered by an antisemitic social field, the sports clubs thus emerged as sites of affirmative Jewish collectivization; in this way, members of Hakoah and Maccabi came to regard the clubs as sites of Jewish pride and empowerment. As

Martin noted, "Maccabi is a place where Jewish existence is lived through sports. This is really important for the Jewish community in Vienna. People come together." Victor echoed this powerfully collectivist sentiment when he told me that "my motivation for being in Maccabi is that there are eleven Jews on one field, that we win together and that we lose together."

Such communal sentiments had a powerfully transformative effect, particularly in regard to the social iconization of Jewish difference. Nowhere was this phenomenon more evident than in the refiguration of the Star of David. Worn by members of both Hakoah and Maccabi for athletic competitions,[56] it came to signal in ways that were radically different from the postwar era. During the first decades of the Second Republic, Jews had shunned the symbol in an effort to maintain the public status of unmarked citizens. In the post-Waldheim era of Jewish authentification, however, it became a central icon in the resistive affirmation of cultural specificity. Their parents may have regarded the Star of David as an exteriorized sign of abject difference; but Jewish athletes in late 1990s Vienna came to see it as the self-evident marker of an assertively publicized identity. The comments by Victor rendered readily apparent the synecdochic relation between Jewish sports, the Star of David, and the new Jewish visibility:

I play for Hakoah, so I have a *Magen David* on my chest, and I am very proud of that. I am very proud to be part of a Jewish team, not only a team that is made up of Jews, but a team that presents its Jewishness to everyone.

For Alexander — a business student in his early twenties and member of Hakoah's tennis team — the star of David similarly stood at the heart of his involvement in Jewish sports:

I am very conscious that I am playing with a jersey that displays the *Magen David* on my chest. The others do the same. And just from the feeling you get in this situation, it is like I'm not just fighting for myself, but for the team, and ultimately for Judaism in general. Everyone can see that I'm Jewish, that I'm part of the Jewish people.

In the final analysis, Victor's and Alexander's invocations of the star of David were typical enactments of a chain of signification that linked the culturally salient iconization of Jewish difference to a publicly articulated and affirmatively figured collectivity.

It was this resistive construction of a public identity — embodied by the teams of Hakoah and Maccabi, which stood in for Judaism at large — that ultimately rendered Jewish sports a privileged site in the emergence of an intrinsically public conception of Jewish difference. As Erich put it,

The Jewishness of Hakoah allows an opportunity to reach the wider society, since the club functions like a voice of Judaism. And that's very important. In a sense, Maccabi and Hakoah have entered uncharted territory here, because what they do is totally different from what the Schomer does or what other groups do. Those are all concerned to keep Jews among each other. So I see it as a very positive aspect that Maccabi and Hakoah are Jewish organizations that go outside the community.

The relevance of Jewish sports for the newly publicized Jewish self-understanding was also evidenced in a statement offered to me by Timmy, a hotel receptionist in his mid-twenties and a member of Maccabi's soccer team:

It is important for Maccabi to exist. Maccabi has to exist, and it has to be very public, so that it becomes known that there still is Jewish life in Austria. The non-Jews need to be confronted with us. And soccer is the country's most popular sport. It is the sport that has the highest number of participants. And there, Maccabi has to become even more active and open. We need to organize events and also invite teams from across the country. If we did that, then we would get invitations, and then we could represent the community in other places as well. Not just in Vienna. After all, people only know about Maccabi in Vienna, but there should also be a Jewish presence in the rest of Austria.

As such narratives of affirmative difference suggested, the conceptual environment of Hakoah and Maccabi interpellated its members and supporters in the resistive design of Jewish subjectivity that had been articulated in the wake of the Waldheim affair. As Jewish intellectuals emerged as Austria's most vocal critics, and as the IKG became a prominent champion of progressive politics, the ordinary Jews of Hakoah and Maccabi also came to reimagine their social role. No longer passive victims of Austrian antisemitism, they claimed their place in the country's national sphere as proud members of a critically revitalized and newly assertive community.

The 1998–1999 soccer season brought the triumph of late-twentieth-century Vienna's Jewish sports movement. From its inception, Maccabi's soccer team had captivated the Jewish public. Competing in Austria's most popular sport, the club was seen as the athletic representation of Viennese Jewry at large. This identification was aided by the fact that Maccabi's team comprised roughly equal numbers of Austrian- and Soviet-born players. Thus the squad's athletic trajectory became a widely watched indicator of the new Jewish prowess.[57] Indeed, Maccabi's exploits received extensive coverage in *Die Gemeinde,* and the team's home games regularly drew a small crowd of Jewish fans. For the first few seasons, however, the club's supporters had little to cheer about. A young and inexperienced team, Maccabi failed to excel, finishing at or near the bottom of Viennese soccer's entry league in their first two years of competitive play.

All this changed with the third season. With growing experience and the arrival of a new star forward from the former Soviet Georgia, the team's fortunes turned around, and after a year of excellent play, Maccabi was in position to win its division. The decision came down to the last game of the season, which was scheduled to take place on Maccabi's home field on June 6, 1999.[58] With the team's growing success, interest in the Jewish community had increased exponentially; and by the time of the decisive game, excitement had reached a fever pitch. Indeed, when Maccabi entered the field to take on Rennbahn, nearly a thousand fans were on hand to cheer the Jewish team to victory. This support was particularly significant in light of Maccabi's previous encounters with the opposing side. Rennbahn's members had frequently used antisemitic slurs to denigrate Maccabi's athletes, and while few felt intimidated by the aspersions, they were hopeful that a noisy crowd would silence them.[59]

Indeed, when the game got underway, the cheering patterns encapsulated and expressed the cultural logic of the new Jewish visibility. Waving flags with the Star of David and loudly chanting encouragement in Hebrew and German, Maccabi's supporters demarcated the soccer field as a specifically Jewish space.[60] In the process of this territorialization, they not only constituted a pan-Jewish community in foundational contrast to Maccabi's Austrian opponents, but effectively reversed the power dynamics governing Jewish existence in the course of the Second Republic. More than anything else, it was a victory chant that signaled the resistive rearticulation of Austrian hegemonies. Throughout the game, Maccabi's supporters had chanted encouragement, but when a quick succession of goals put the game out of reach in the last fifteen minutes of the contest, the crowd switched to the triumphant slogan "Here rules the sporting club Maccabi" *(Hier regiert der S.C.M.* [Sportklub Maccabi]).[61] Appropriating a chant frequently heard on Austria's soccer fields, the line was clearly taunting the opposing team. In the context of the larger issues at stake, however, it had obvious overtones. Articulated at the constitutive intersection of athletic competition and the newly autonomous stance, it marked and performed the public display of Jewish prowess. In the postwar era, Jews had been erased from Austria's public sphere; in the late twentieth century, they would lay claim to its sites. No longer the subjects of an enforced privatization, Vienna's Jews would rule their domains in the city's urban landscape.

If Maccabi and Hakoah established the new Jewish visibility in the semipublic sphere of Vienna's athletic fields, the Jewish Culture Festival and Jewish Street Fair deployed it at the symbolic core of the city's cultural fields. Once more, the initiative had come from members of the postwar generation. Having taken charge of IKG's cultural commission in the late 1980s, they rearticulated the quest for Jewish autonomy in the dominant terms of Austrian society. Those terms emphasized the domain of high culture as the definitive site of collective identity formation — a phenomenon reflected in the country's singular valuation of such entities as the State Opera and the Vienna Philharmonic Orchestra. Prior to the Holocaust, Jews had played a pivotal role in the constitution of Austria's high cultural fields, but ever since the catastrophe, they had been essentially absent from the public sphere of artistic production.

It was in this context that the creation of a culture festival came to be seen as a crucial act in the resistive establishment of a Jewish presence in Vienna's urban landscape. Not only would it reinforce the quest for Jewish authentification, but it would be the perfect vehicle for showcasing the newly diversified community and its concomitant self-esteem. As Ellinor Haber, the chair of IKG's cultural commission, noted in *Die Gemeinde,* "We were in agreement about the need to present the cultural achievements of Vienna's Jews to a broader public."[62] For the commission, this was directly tied to the recent influx of Jews from the former Soviet Union. Their arrival had occasioned a "new self-understanding, which has in turn led to a new self-confidence." In terms consonant with the general quest for Jewish authentification, Haber proclaimed that Austria's Jews longed to display that new confidence publicly:

People want to integrate but not assimilate. They want to be part of the social and cultural life of this city, but without abandoning their identity. They know that only those who respect themselves can count on the respect of others. With increasing self-confidence, it is only a small step to wanting to present one's achievements and one's culture to the other inhabitants of the city.[63]

The Jewish Culture Festival was designed to fulfill this collective desire; when it was inaugurated in the spring of 1992, it was billed as the "most extensive [and] most important Jewish cultural event to take place in over fifty years."[64] Indeed, with its week-long sequence of performances, which strategically combined appearances by recent immigrants and shows of Austrian-born artists, the festival was a landmark moment. Designed to enable the "self-presentation of today's Jewish community," it represented a highly self-conscious attempt to break with the enforced privatization of postwar Austrian Jews; in this sense, the event could be understood as the definitive "signal for the resurgence of an Austrian-Jewish cultural symbiosis."[65]

The inaugural Jewish Culture Festival was a tremendous critical and popular success, and in the course of the 1990s, the event grew steadily. In the process, it became routinized, a highly professional affair that increasingly combined the presentation of contemporary Austrian Jewry's cultural achievements with performances by international artists representative of a wider world of Jewish cultural production. The festival also grew in length. Initially, it had been billed as a Jewish Culture Week (*Jüdische Kulturwoche*), but within a few years, it was expanded into Jewish Culture Weeks (*Jüdische Kulturwochen*), which lasted for close to a month. However, that too proved inadequate, and the mid-1990s witnessed the creation of a second set of culture weeks. Complementing the original spring event, that set was to take place every fall. In 1998, for example, three weeks in May and June were supplemented by four weeks in November, resulting in a remarkable density of public Jewish performances. Indeed, whereas the festival had been initiated in 1992 with a mere five shows, the 1998 affairs featured thirty events.[66]

This stunning development was not lost on members of the Jewish community. Not only did they flock to the performances, but they recognized the historical import of the events. In conversation after conversation, members of the postwar generation pointed to the Culture Festival to illustrate the transformation of Austrian-Jewish existence. "When I was young," I was told frequently, "we had nothing like that." Ilana, whose account of her youth in 1960s and 1970s Vienna appeared in Chapter 1, put it in particularly stark terms when she noted that "we didn't have any Jewish culture back then." "Now," she said, "Vienna has all these Jewish events, which have established a strong and independent cultural presence." The effect of this presence was palpable, leading Ilana to echo the IKG's cultural commission in explaining the ultimate meaning of the Jewish Culture Festival in the resistive terms of the new Jewish visibility: "We are part of this country, we are here, you have to reckon with us."

While the festivals have anchored the Jewish community in Vienna's high cultural fields, no institution has done more to regularize Jews' presence in the city's public sphere than the Jewish Street Fair (*Jüdisches*

Straßenfest). Initiated in 1990 and incorporated into the Jewish Culture Festival in 1992, the annual event quickly came to embody the authenticating quest for Jewish visibility.[67] Indeed, its very design was transgressive, especially when set against the structural exclusions characterizing postwar Austria. During that prolonged moment of cultural subordination, Jews were systematically erased from the public sphere, leading to their retreat into a sphere of privatized difference. There the postwar generation was reared with a persistent sense of Jewish specificity; in the openly resistive context of the post-Waldheim era, that sentiment came to be articulated through public celebration. Such institutions as the Jewish school, the Jewish sports organizations, and the Jewish Culture Festival were all engendered by the new cultural logic, but none had the social immediacy and public impact of the Jewish Street Fair. For, in its figuration of Jewish culture as integral to the city's topography, the Street Fair not only conveyed a vision of affirmative Jewish difference, but it reimagined Jewishness as inherently public.

Much of this effect was achieved through the fair's physical environs. Held in the winding streets adjacent to Vienna's main synagogue, in a prominent and historically significant area of the city's first district, the day-long event was marked by its sheer opulence. On several stages, artists featured in the Jewish Culture Festival took turns entertaining the crowds with loud music, frequently leading them in Israeli-style communal dances. At the same time, Vienna's various Jewish institutions, from youth groups and social service organizations to bookstores and community publications, advertised their activities at a series of tables surrounded in turn by the smells emanating from food stands operated by the proprietors of the city's Jewish-owned eateries. The popular success of the event was overwhelming. In its first year, the Street Fair had already drawn several thousand people; when it was incorporated into the Jewish Culture Festival, attendance rose even further. As one of my interlocutors put it, "It was like the entire Jewish community was on the street."[68]

From the organizers' point of view, this was, of course, the point. Even more than the Jewish Culture Festival, they had imagined the Street Fair both as a showcase and vehicle for the new Jewish self-understanding. The Festival's artistic performances, after all, took place in front of self-selected audiences; the Jewish Street Fair, by contrast, would effect the aggressive appropriation of Vienna's urban landscape itself. The dynamics of this process were clearly on the organizers' minds. To them, the public celebration of Jewish culture not only promised to have a definitive effect by creating a distinctly Jewish space, but it would serve as a direct antidote to Austria's antisemitic realities. The Street Fair would not change those realities, of course, but as a powerful "demonstration of self-confidence," it would "strengthen that self-confidence even further" — a process that would ultimately render antisemitism less relevant.[69]

Indeed, over the years the Jewish Street Fair came to function as the definitive site of resistive authentification. The self-evident reference point for the new Jewish visibility, it was invoked repeatedly in my ethnographic interviews. Many interlocutors recalled their fond experiences on particular occasions, while others asserted that the event was the highlight of their Jewish year. Even more importantly, the Street Fair clearly came to permeate the dominant self-image of Viennese Jewry. The event was seen as the quintessential representation of a community proudly displaying the diversity of its cultural prowess. One man in his late thirties put it in typical terms:

I always go to the Jewish Street Fair. To me, this is what being Jewish in Vienna is all about. There is dancing there and singing, and everyone is there, those who are religious and those who are not, those from Austria and those from Russia. It's a beautiful picture that has a lot to do with the new self-confidence.

However, such paradigmatic narratives only begin to suggest the cultural transformations effected by the new Jewish visibility. To be sure, such events as the Jewish Culture Festival and the Street Fair altered the postwar generation's self-perception, but they had an even greater impact on the Jews who came of age in the post-Waldheim era. This became particularly evident to me in the spring of 2000 when I interviewed Lisa, Ilana's sixteen-year-old daughter. Like other Jews of her generation, she had grown up with the emergent sites of Jewish autonomy, and while Jews of her mother's age always described them with a sense of wonder, I was struck by the degree to which they were a normalized part of Lisa's cultural reality. Her comments about the Street Fair were particularly fascinating:

The Street Fair is great, because we can dance Israeli dances there. I love to dance, and every time I do those dances, I'm happy. It is a unity, like a mutual language, but you don't even have to say anything. It's just a beautiful atmosphere.

As we continued our conversation, the importance of this unified atmosphere became evident as Lisa juxtaposed it with the threat of antisemitic rejection. During her years in an Austrian elementary school, she had felt excluded, but unlike her mother, who had had similar experiences in the late 1960s, she never compartmentalized her Jewishness. Wearing a prominent necklace with a Star of David, she invoked the Jewish Street Fair as the principal impulse for her public Jewish subjectivity:

I like to be on the street. It means freedom; and it is great that we can do it without being afraid. It's just incredible to be able to listen and dance to loud Jewish music, and to do it in the center of Vienna. Sometimes I am nervous wearing the Star of David or outing myself as Jewish, but then I think about the feeling of strength and unity, and it's just clear that I want people to know.

Lisa's sentiments were a prime instantiation of the new Jewish self-understanding. That conception of resistive difference had been pioneered by her mother's generation, but only in the post-Waldheim era was it normalized into a constitutive component of Austrian-Jewish identity. In large part, this normalization occurred in the emergent sites of Jewish authentification. There, under the sign of collective visibility, the post-Waldheim generation was constituted in terms of a publicized Jewish subjectivity. Ilana had confined her Jewishness to the privatized realms of the Schomer; her daughter Lisa would display it to all of Vienna.

The Politics of Resistance

This chapter opened with an account of the first Jewish demonstration against a sitting Austrian government. In protesting the inclusion of Jörg Haider's FPÖ in the country's ruling coalition, Vienna's Jews enacted a powerful form of resistance that stood in definitive contrast to the accomodationist stance of the postwar era. Reflecting the structural exclusions of the Second Republic, that stance had forced the IKG into public diffidence as late as 1986, when the Waldheim affair unleashed a wave of political and popular antisemitism. In 2000, the FPÖ's ascent to power promised to do the same, but this time the Jewish community took to the streets to confront the political developments in an aggressively oppositional posture. This chapter has sought to identify the processes that engendered this publicly resistive stance, locating them in intellectual, political, and cultural projects of Jewish authentification. These projects were championed by members of the postwar generation whose vision of Jewish autonomy enunciated a new Jewish self-confidence. However, these collective endeavors had an even greater impact on those Jews who grew up in the post-Waldheim era. Socialized into the cultural projects of Jewish authentification, they experienced the resistive sites of Jewish autonomy not as a break with an oppressive past, but as a normal cultural reality. That normalcy ultimately produced the publicized Jewish subjectivities that engendered the protests against Austria's government.

Indeed, while such figureheads of the postwar generation as Doron Rabinovici and Ariel Muzicant came to be seen as embodiments of Jewish opposition, people in their teens and early twenties constituted its base. Whereas members of the survivor generation experienced the coalition between FPÖ and ÖVP as an immediate threat to their safety, and whereas many of the Jews who had come of age in postwar Vienna found the situation profoundly unsettling, the post-Waldheim generation was unintimidated and eager to express its oppositional stance.[70] It was no coincidence, then, that the Association of Jewish University Students took the lead in organizing the antigovernment demonstration of April 6, 2000. Like the members of the Jewish youth organizations, the university students had taken part in many of the general protests.[71] But in line with a larger quest for Jewish autonomy, the VJHÖ sought to articulate a specifically Jewish form of resistance. The association commenced these activities on March 12, 2000, when it organized an antigovernment dance party in conjunction with the Jewish youth groups. Held in a prominent square in Vienna's city center, "Hora Dancing Against Black and Blue" attracted over a hundred people;[72] and it was that success that ultimately paved the way for the Jewish demonstration of April.[73]

Sustained by members of the post-Waldheim generation, the unprecedented Jewish opposition to Austria's government was a product of the quest for Jewish authentification. But not only did the Jewish response reflect the resistive position articulated in defiance of Austria's hegemonies, but the larger antigovernment movement also bore the imprint of the Jewish critique developed by members of the postwar generation. Indeed, as many of my Jewish interlocutors were fond of pointing out, the so-called resistance movement *(Widerstandsbewegung)* opposing Austria's right-wing government was run almost entirely by Jews. As speaker of the Demokratische Offensive, Doron Rabinovici played the most prominent role in the mobilization of the country's civil society, but other Jewish activists were centrally involved as well, not only in the Demokratische Offensive but also in such direct-action groups as the student-run gettoattack.[74]

The resistance movement did not represent itself as a Jewish project, of course. But in its amalgamation of an antiracist platform and a sustained critique of postwar Austria's dealings with its Nazi past, it closely retraced the interventions of Jewish intellectuals in the post-Waldheim era.

Along with the writings of a number of sympathetic non-Jewish critics, these interventions had defined the contours of the "other Austria" *(das andere Österreich)* — an entity imagined beyond the exclusionary boundaries of the postwar nation-state.[75] It was this other Austria that Rabinovici and his fellow activists sought to rally in opposition to the government formed by FPÖ and ÖVP. They did so in a massive demonstration held in Vienna's historic Heldenplatz on February 19, 2000. Rabinovici called for an "end to the coalition with racism," and 300,000 citizens of the other Austria joined the Jewish activist in the largest protest in the history of the Second Republic.[76]

But it was Ariel Muzicant who most forcefully represented the event's Jewish dimension. Speaking as the official representative of Austria's Jewish community and addressing thousands of Jews and hundreds of thousands of other participants, he not only articulated the post-Waldheim critique in climactic fashion, but reimagined it as the foundation for Austria's civil society. "It is a scandal," he exclaimed, "that even after the Holocaust, racism, xenophobic agitation, and antisemitism are treated in Austria as minor infractions."[77] Not only that, but they had been "legitimized" by some of the "highest positions in the state." Affirming that "we want to live in a free society that respects peoples' rights," Muzicant insisted that this situation was "unacceptable" to Austria's Jews. But while he clearly gestured to Jews' ongoing struggles against Austrian hegemonies, Muzicant made an even more general argument regarding the Jewish community's social role. Noting that for "thousands of years, we Jews have championed human rights, human dignity, and humanity," Muzicant ultimately figured Vienna's Jews as the crucial agent in the resistive constitution of the other Austria. In the post-Waldheim years, Jews had articulated an intellectual, political, and cultural critique of postwar hegemonies; now that its tenets were foundational to Austrian-Jewish subjectivity, the symptoms of modernity would become the basis of a polity imagined beyond the nation-state's exclusionary principles.

CHAPTER 4

Cafés and Parades

It is beautiful that this is possible today in Vienna, after it has been done in other cities for ten, fifteen, twenty years. . . . It is terrific that so many people came, that they showed themselves, that they showed that we are everywhere. . . . For me, this parade is a sign of resistance and protest against the narrow-mindedness in this country, against the monotony — in contrast to diversity and colorfulness — and against the vestiges of a dark past. It is a sign of the love of life and the joy of living. It is a sign that we exist and that we will no longer tolerate being pushed to the margins of society, where they want us. We are right at the center, just as we are right at the center of this city today.

Ulrike Lunacek, Federal Green Party Secretary,
on June 29, 1996

On Saturday, June 29, 1996, Vienna witnessed an epoch-making event. On a gloriously sunny day, around ten thousand marchers and twenty thousand spectators populated the city's historic Ringstraße to join Austria's first Regenbogen Parade (Rainbow Parade). The route for the event had been carefully chosen. Battles with the municipality's hostile bureaucracy notwithstanding, organizers had insisted on holding the parade at Vienna's physical and symbolic center. And indeed, when thousands of people congregated in front of the venerated Vienna State Opera in the early afternoon of June 29, they were ready to parade before Austria's most august symbols of nationness and statehood: the Hofburg (the Habsburg winter palace), the Kunsthistorisches Museum (the museum of art history, and as such the shrine of Austria's artistic heritage), the house of parliament, the Burgtheater (the state theater and another shrine to the country's cultural prowess), Vienna's city hall, and the University of Vienna.

The parade, which was made up of numerous colorful and noisy floats, lasted the entire afternoon, creating a powerful image of boisterous diversity. Much like other gay pride parades, the procession was led by "dykes on bikes," followed by a host of cars representing the constituencies of Vienna's lesbian/gay scene. Many of the city's gay bars and commercial establishments were present, as were a number of political and social institutions, ranging from activist groups to AIDS organizations. In the early evening, the event reached its official end with a rally and party in one of Vienna's historic squares. But countless smaller functions followed, many held in private homes, others organized in the city's various lesbian/gay locales.

For Austria's queers, the Regenbogen Parade was a watershed. In the course of a single day, it not only inscribed Vienna's lesbian/gay community in the city's social topography, but effectively suspended the country's postwar arrangements, which had consigned homosexuals to a self-evident closet. As such, the parade was both a massive act of resistive visibility and a crucial form of publicized identification. For individual participants, this development was simply stunning. Given their homophobic lifeworlds, many people had been reluctant to attend the parade, fearing the event's failure and their personal exposure. In light of the lesbian/gay masses, however, these fears turned into rapturous disbelief at what — only a few years prior — had seemed like an utterly inconceivable degree of queer visibility and puissance. As one gay man in his early thirties put it, "I never thought this was possible. I thought a few hundred people might show up. But this is just so incredible, I could cry." Similar sentiments were echoed throughout the day, invoked most frequently by the word *unglaublich* — "unbelievable." One lesbian in her mid-twenties put it this way:

This is the most fun I've ever had in Vienna. I just can't believe it's happening. It's like the city belongs to us. When I moved to Vienna six years ago there was nothing like that. I went out to places where other lesbians and gays would go, but it was never, like, taking over the city. I mean, look — we're walking in the middle of the Ring [Ringstraße], and there is nothing anyone can do about it.

A similar sense of empowerment was expressed to me by other participants, many of whom regarded their involvement in the Regenbogen

Parade as their definitive coming out. A gay man in his late twenties narrated his personal experience in the following terms:

I just think this is the most important thing that has ever happened to gays in Austria. And I mean that very personally. Only my good friends know that I'm gay, and I've never been involved in gay politics, but today, it's just totally different. When I saw the posters for the parade, it just seemed like it might be fun. So I came, and I just couldn't believe how many people there were — thousands and thousands; it's like all of Vienna is gay.

This sense of disbelief reflected the suddenness and magnitude with which lesbians and gay men had burst into Vienna's public sphere. But while the first Regenbogen Parade was a wholly unprecedented event in Austria's history, its resistive constitution of a public queer community did not arise out of a cultural vacuum. The parade only seemed to "come out of nothing," as one woman put it. In fact, it was the product of long-standing efforts to anchor a lesbian/gay presence in Austria's national sphere. These efforts commenced in the 1970s, when a small gay liberation movement began to articulate the political critique of the Austrian closet that would organize the activities of the Homosexuelle Initiative Wien (HOSI), the country's first lesbian/gay rights organization. Throughout the 1980s, HOSI championed the cause of homosexual emancipation; however, its political vision of lesbian/gay visibility appealed only to a tiny minority of Austria's queers. In consequence, Vienna's homosexuals remained in the closet — a situation that began to change only when the lesbian/gay scene diversified in the early 1990s. Those years witnessed the creation of organizations and institutions that rearticulated the movement's political critique into a cultural vision of lesbian/gay existence. That vision in turn produced the social realities of a queer community and instigated its reconceptualization as an inherently public entity. If the resistive groundwork for lesbian/gay visibility was thus laid in the years prior to the first Regenbogen Parade, the event enacted the process of affirmative community-building with unprecedented force. In the course of the parade's routinization in the late 1990s, it emerged as not only the principal vehicle for the public articulation of lesbian/gay existence, but as the main site of collective subjectification.

In many ways, this historical trajectory mirrored the development of queer communities across Western Europe and North America. Indeed, the path from the closet to massive lesbian/gay visibility, via phases of radical politics, grand emancipatory schemes, and the eventual commercialization of queer identities, is hardly unique.[1] Moreover, the history of

Austria's lesbian/gay movement evidences a profoundly internationalist orientation, marked by constant attempts to duplicate and introduce strategies and designs developed in such locales as Germany, France, and the United States. What made the Austrian case different, however, was the belatedness in the emergence of a publicly queer community. In her speech at the rally following the first Regenbogen Parade, Ulrike Lunacek alluded to this situation when she noted that such events were commonplace in the major cities of the Western world. If they had not happened in Austria, it was a reflection of the country's "narrow-mindedness" and the "vestiges of a dark past." Lunacek had herself struggled against these forces when she became the first openly lesbian candidate for parliament.[2] Her 1995 bid had failed when Austria's electorate affirmed the socially conservative course of the ruling SPÖ/ÖVP coalition. The population and its elected officials, it seemed, would maintain the nation-state's normalizing order. That order, however, was about to be disrupted; with the staging of the first Regenbogen Parade, "diversity" and "colorfulness" came to invade Vienna's socio-sexual landscape. In Lunacek's words, this meant that Austria's lesbians and gay men would no longer be "pushed to the margins of society." And indeed, in the course of the late 1990s, Vienna's queers claimed their place in the city's symbolic center — after decades of subordination, the symptoms of modernity emerged into the public sphere.

Political Designs for a Lesbian/Gay Movement

Much like the trajectory of queer culture in general, the institutional history of Austria's lesbian/gay movement replayed that of other Western locales. In this manner, homophile activities were succeeded by radical liberationist designs, which were followed in turn by a broadly emancipatory agenda.[3] But if Austrian efforts thus emerged as part and parcel of an international movement, they were severely undermined by the country's hegemonies. Compared to their counterparts abroad, the creation of individual organizations thus always occurred with considerable delay, and even when groups did take shape, their small size and semilegality drastically curtailed their social and political efficacy. This was certainly true of the isolated attempts to establish a homophile movement;[4] but it also characterized the activities of the post-Stonewall era.

Activities by organized groups did not commence until the 1975 founding of Coming Out. In that year, a few Viennese activists took such radical platforms as West Germany's Homosexuelle Aktion and France's Front Homosexuel d'Action Révolutionnaire as models for a leftist men's group.[5] Committed to the overthrow of bourgeois sexualities and their political and social structures, Coming Out's initial membership fluctuated between five and ten people.[6] In the course of the next two years, the informal organization grew, and at its highpoint, three sub-sections were in operation — a political group, a reading group, and a support group.[7] The group's heyday occurred after its relocation to premises in Vienna's third district. There Coming Out subleased a space from a Socialist youth organization under the innocuous name "Working Group for Cultural Initiatives." Regular meetings were attended by a few dozen men, and parties attracted close to a hundred people.[8] However, Coming Out's leaders remained primarily committed to the group's political project, which was actualized in the late spring of 1977, when Vienna served as the site of the Pentecost Meeting — the annual gathering of Germany's radical gay groups.[9] The meeting was a watershed in Austrian history, but it failed to solidify the group. On the contrary, soon after the event, Coming Out split into a radical and a more moderate faction. The former stopped its activities almost immediately, and when notice was given on the premises in the third district in 1978, the latter also disbanded.[10] During its existence, Coming Out had never attempted to become an officially registered voluntary association. In part, this reflected the group's radical attempt to evade all forms of state surveillance. Even more importantly, it was a result of Austria's legal hegemonies. To the members of Coming Out, the group's formal recognition seemed inherently impossible, especially in light of a court order to stop production of *CO-INFO,* the group's irregular publication.[11]

A year after the demise of Coming Out, a new effort was made to establish a homosexual rights movement. Under the name Homosexuelle Initiative Wien (Homosexual Initiative Vienna), the project was initially conceived as a support group for men. As such, it grew steadily in 1979, especially in the wake of a television appearance by founder Wolfgang Förster.[12] By the end of the year, HOSI — the organization's widely used acronym — encompassed three self-help groups, a theater group, and a group concerned with public relations. After meeting for several months in private homes and various sites of Vienna's alternative scene, HOSI rented its own facility in the city's second district. The organization moved there in 1980. A year later, it welcomed women through the formation of a lesbian group.[13]

Since its founding, HOSI was centrally concerned with the creation of an affirmative environment for lesbians and gay men, and the HOSI center served as the principal site where gays and lesbians could find social validation and personal authentification. For about one hundred regulars, HOSI did function in this manner, but the organization saw its mission on a much larger scale. Modeling itself after such political interest groups as New York's Gay Activist Alliance and Toronto's Body Politic, HOSI regarded itself as the emancipatory agent of an oppressed minority. Coming Out had sought to evade the authorities; HOSI, by contrast, hoped to engage the state as the political representative of Austria's homosexuals. To that end, the organization needed to attain official status as a voluntary association. In light of §221, this seemed implausible, but, showing a certain degree of liberalization, the Justice Department — controlled, like the entire government, by the SPÖ — permitted the organization's constitution with the proviso that it not create a "public nuisance."[14] To comply with this condition, HOSI reformulated its founding charter. Whereas the initial draft had called for a "change of people's consciousness in regard to homosexual life," the final version heeded the state's desire to protect the public sphere, calling instead for a "change of people's consciousness in regard to the equal rights of homosexuals."[15] In a similar manner, HOSI was quick to pledge its compliance with such laws as the *Werbeverbot* — the interdiction against propaganda for homosexuality. In its first publication, HOSI not only asserted that the group did not have the "purpose" of "facilitating same-sex sexuality," but that it even refused to "condone [it] in any way" for fear that it "might encourage such forms of lechery."[16]

Although the state did force HOSI to moderate its position, the organization's status as a legally recognized entity was still unprecedented. Not only was HOSI Austria's first official homosexual rights organization, but its existence would ensure an ongoing struggle against the country's legal inequities. Even before the group received formal recognition as a voluntary association, HOSI had commenced a letter-writing campaign to protest the penal code's discriminatory statutes, and when the organization was officially constituted in January of 1980, these efforts further intensified.[17] The fight against Austria's injurious legal code took center stage in HOSI's ongoing activities. Initially, these focused on interventions with politicians. Working as a lobbying organization, HOSI presented members of parliament with information and petitions, while also seeking direct contact with lawmakers. As early as May 1980, HOSI leaders met with a member of Austria's Socialist government; and later in the year, the group initiated communication with the

People's Party both on the federal and municipal levels. Over the next years, HOSI undertook countless such lobbying efforts, of which a 1992 visit with Chancellor Franz Vranitzky would constitute the symbolic highlight.[18] But if HOSI represented Austria's lesbians and gay men at the highest levels of state authority, the organization's efforts failed to produce tangible results. In the mid-1980s, the group resorted to legal action to repeal Austria's anti-lesbian/gay statutes. In 1986, HOSI made an initial appeal to the country's constitutional court, followed — after its rejection — by several other interventions that similarly failed to end homosexuals' legal discrimination.[19]

Throughout the 1980s, HOSI maintained the stance of a moderate interest group. For several of its members, however, this position was far too accomodationist, and by 1982, a split had become evident between a "bourgeois" and a "leftist" camp. The latter — comprised in part of former members of Coming Out — rejected the HOSI leadership's attempt to achieve homosexual emancipation through work within the state apparatus. Instead, they advocated more radical forms of lesbian/gay resistance. On a political level, this translated into a number of high-profile protests, including spectacular incidents at the Vienna Philharmonic's New Year's Concert, where two naked men stormed the podium with a banner that demanded "human rights for gays," and at the Opera Ball, where activists dropped leaflets to draw attention to discrimination against homosexuals.[20] The social dimension of this radical dissent from HOSI's quest for respectability had more enduring effects. In the context of an ongoing squatters' movement, a group of male and female activists took possession of a dilapidated building in Vienna's sixth district to claim it as a "house of lesbians and gays."[21] Named Rosa Lila Villa (Pink Lilac Villa) and painted accordingly, the building not only served as a highly visible signpost of lesbian/gay existence, but functioned as a social experiment in antipatriarchal living. In this manner, the Villa united lesbians and gay men in three communal households, which were partially sanctioned when Vienna's deputy mayor permitted the building's permanent occupation. Despite the house's desolate condition, its inhabitants quickly turned it into a focal point of activism. When the Villa officially opened in November of 1982, it featured not only Austria's first lesbian/gay counseling office, but a number of rooms that would soon become the "Warm Nest," an informal café and community center.[22]

The splintering of Austria's lesbian/gay movement was a result of political differences. Indeed, in the groups' self-perception, the agendas of Coming Out and Rosa Lila Villa, on the one hand, and HOSI, on the other, seemed diametrically opposed.[23] Reflecting their respective intellectual models, the former saw themselves as advocating a radical brand of sexual politics anchored in the revolutionary overthrow of society and its conventional gender norms; the latter, by contrast, sought to achieve the establishment and acceptance of homosexuality within existing social fields. In articulating their radical position, the members of Coming Out in particular invoked the theoretical principles of figures like Guy Hocquenghem and Michel Foucault, who had identified homosexuality's revolutionary potential on account of its construction as a threat to bourgeois society.[24] Analogous to the working class, whose systematic exploitation rendered it a revolutionary subject, homosexuals were seen as agents of social transformation. For the members of Coming Out, consciousness raising was at the center of this project, which would "create subject groups that politicize their discontent."[25] In turn, this development would go hand in hand with homosexuals' critical "reflection of their constitution and the process of their evolution" — a situation that would produce the desire for a society organized above and beyond the oppressive structures of bourgeois sexualities.[26] Much like other proponents of liberationst thought, Coming Out thus envisioned the abolition of homo- and heterosexuality, along with the establishment of a genderless society as the ultimate goal of a gay movement.

Certain strands in HOSI echoed such radical positions. In the 1980 manifesto "For a New Order of Love," for example, the group rejected the "definition of so-called 'homosexuals' as a 'minority,'" demanding the liberation of all forms of sexuality instead — a process that could take place only in "connection with societal liberation from economic and social constraints."[27] HOSI's dominant position, however, was decidedly more moderate. In the first paragraph of its publication *Warme Blätter* — soon renamed *Lambda Nachrichten* — the group articulated its political vision as a response to homosexuals' "social ostracism and legal discrimination."[28] This situation had severe psychological effects. Existing in a "hostile and scornful environment," gay men lacked "self-confidence," and HOSI vowed to "find and strengthen" their resolve at the same time as it would "represent their interests" in political terms.[29] An accurate foreshadowing of HOSI's eventual practice, the sentiments expressed a project concerned less with the subversive rearticulation of conventional gender norms than the "undisputed acceptance [of homosexuals] as citizens with equal rights."[30] Indeed, for the leading figures of HOSI, the European theorists of homosexual revolution were of secondary relevance; much more influential were the social realities of the United States. For HOSI, U.S.

social organization represented the inception and telos of their organizational efforts, as well as a model of the problem-free existence they espoused for Austria's homosexuals. Coming Out and Rosa Lila Villa also inscribed themselves in the lesbian/gay movement that originated in the Stonewall Rebellion, but their commitments to radical and alternative projects brought a certain degree of skepticism about American models. For HOSI, by contrast, they were the self-evident paragon. In particular, the gay ghettos of North America's metropolises seemed like a realization of HOSI's design for an unencumbered existence. Indeed, as early as the first issue of the *Warme Blätter,* the group extolled the accomplishments of America's lesbians and gay men.[31] In the longest article of HOSI's initial publication, the group created a seamless narrative that moved from recollection of the Stonewall riots to a detailed account of the political and social accomplishments underwriting current lesbian/gay existence. Such phenomena as gay churches, gay travel agencies, and gay political candidates were seen as products of and evidence for the self-confidence that would translate into homosexuality's cultural normalization. HOSI's construction of "America" might have been selective, but as it was articulated through regular articles in the *Lambda Nachrichten,* it provided the group's blueprint for lesbian/gay integration into mainstream society.[32]

The split in Austria's lesbian/gay movement between leftists and moderates was very real, but it tended to obscure the far more fundamental concurrence in the camps' respective positions. Indeed, it was remarkable to what degree the institutional practices of HOSI resembled that of Coming Out and Rosa Lila Villa. The congruence was particularly striking when placed in the context of Vienna's homosexual scene. In that framework, all components of the lesbian/gay movement advocated a similarly radical stance that sought to render the deeply personal both public and political. In this regard, the formal announcement of Coming Out's creation captured the general orientation in paradigmatic terms. Published in April 1976 in the left-wing monthly *Neues Forum,* it was the first tangible manifestation of a lesbian/gay movement, enunciating a project that came to be shared fully by HOSI and Rosa Lila Villa:

Coming Out!
Group Initiative Homosexuality, Vienna — Founding of a Group CO

We are tired of playing hide-and-seek!
We no longer allow for our personality to be divided into heterosexual mask and homosexual reality.
We don't just want to be tolerated!

We want to create publicity: no longer ask shyly for sympathy or tolerance, but provoke public debate. We want to show how discriminatory the very existence of homosexual laws is.[33]

The announcement of Coming Out constituted a multilayered challenge to the traditional existence of Austria's homosexuals. On the one hand, it opposed the production of an individual's same-sex sexuality as a secret; on the other hand, it sought to mobilize the political potential of a disenfranchised group. In this manner, Coming Out encouraged homosexuals to come out of the closet for the sake of personal authentification as well as social betterment — a dual agenda that came to define the activities of the entire lesbian/gay movement throughout the 1980s and into the early 1990s.

For Austria's lesbian/gay movement, the quest for personal authentification figured in direct opposition to the cultural logic of the homosexual scene. That scene, after all, was an elaborate infrastructure designed to keep gay male sexuality hidden from public view. As such, it not only constrained gay men into leading disingenuous double lives, but was a central vehicle in the perpetuation of homosexuality's subordinate position. Gay male commercial establishments were seen as particularly odious. In the anticapitalist framework of Coming Out, they appeared as part and parcel of a system of exploitation that preyed on the victims of respectable society. Capitalism had commodified all forms of sexuality in the interest of "achieving significant profits"; in the case of gay men it was further aided by a state apparatus whose abjection of homosexuality allowed the "owners of the certain discotheques and saunas" to "make money off homosexuals' feelings of social inferiority."[34] HOSI's rhetoric was less strident, but the organization was no less vocal in its opposition to the homosexual scene. Its leaders regarded the "subculture" as a "commercialized gay ghetto" whose clandestine quality not only prevented the integration of public and private identities, but thwarted any possibility for affirmative gay male association.[35] Indeed, as HOSI founder Wolfgang Förster explained during his 1979 television appearance, the group was created initially to fill this very void. In the "subculture of bars, saunas, parks, toilets, etc.," interactions were "largely standardized" on account of the "oppression that forced most gay men into secrecy." HOSI, by contrast, would break through this mode of anonymous and depersonalized association by providing a space for "regular contacts between gay men."[36]

The opposition to the cultural logic of the homosexual scene thus had two components. On the one hand, it entailed the formation of support systems and alternative environments for openly lesbian and gay people — a design realized most enduringly through the creation of the HOSI center and the Rosa Lila Villa. On the other hand and even more importantly, the project required the development of strategies that would effect the fundamental redeployment of homosexuality as a public entity. Coming Out had already identified the creation of visibility and public awareness as a crucial component of the gay movement: group members had introduced the Pink Triangle in Austria after German activists used it as a marker for "our history of oppression" as well as a "means of rendering gayness public."[37] The introduction of homosexuality into the public sphere was central to HOSI's political vision. Only such a development could accomplish the dual function of changing popular opinion and homosexuals' self-perception. Along with the public at large, lesbians and gay men had to be "enlightened" about the fact that homosexuality was not "unnatural, abnormal, sick, or inferior," nor something that "needed to be cured, hidden with embarrassment, or even persecuted." To that end, HOSI pledged to undertake a "continuous campaign" that would establish homosexuality's affirmative presence in the public sphere.[38]

The central vehicle in this project was the mobilization of the lesbian/gay population. Its emergence into the national sphere would not only constitute a powerful act of resistance against same-sex sexuality's structural exclusion, but it would also provide the kind of presence that could correct homosexuality's abject figuration, substituting a collectively articulated image of pride and self-confidence. Given this conjuncture, Austria's lesbian/gay movement aggressively sought the public eye from its very inception. The Pentecost Meeting hosted by Coming Out in 1977 featured a "gay walk" through Vienna's city center,[39] and when HOSI became an officially recognized voluntary association in 1980, the organization quickly turned to public appearances as a central focus of political activity. In April of that year, the group made its debut at an antifascist demonstration, and a few weeks later, HOSI participated in Vienna's Alternative Culture Festival, where its members staffed an information booth.[40]

Over the next few years, the public activities of the lesbian/gay movement became routinized. On the one hand, individual members engaged in a number of spectacular actions; on the other hand, the movement regularly participated in and later organized political demonstrations. The 1982 actions at the New Year's Concert and Opera Ball were followed in 1988 by the disruption of a parliamentary session on youth legislation and the occupation of the office of Austria's Secretary of Family Affairs.[41] HOSI organized another high-profile event in 1994, when it demanded registered partnerships for lesbian and gay male couples by staging mock weddings at Vienna's city hall.[42] Invariably, such spectacular actions engendered a significant amount of publicity, but in light of the homophobic backlash they produced in Austria's mass media — of which the 1995 Outing affair was the pinnacle — their efficacy was widely debated within the lesbian/gay movement.

If spectacular actions were seen as controversial, demonstrations were regarded as a more appropriate means of creating lesbian/gay visibility. Indeed, in the course of the 1980s, marches, rallies, and protests became the movement's principal forms of public articulation. In contrast to disruptive actions whose mass-media representation reproduced rather than offset stereotypes, demonstrations conveyed a sense of dignity anchored in the construction of participants and the population they represented as a political entity struggling for their legitimate rights. In consequence, the lesbian/gay movement tended to appear in public as somber and serious, emphasizing the history and social reality of homosexual victimization. This stance was not only evident in the movement's visual logic, which was dominated by political banners and slogans chanted via megaphone, but it also governed the modes of political engagement. Ever since its inception, the lesbian/gay movement sought to align itself with broader struggles for equality and justice; for this reason, HOSI and Rosa Lila Villa duplicated modes of representation that characterized such events as peace movement rallies, protests against the right wing, and May Day demonstrations.

Central to the public articulation of homosexuals as victims of injustice was the history of Nazi persecution. Since World War II, the commemoration of Nazi victimization had been a focal point of progressive politics in Austria, and when the lesbian/gay movement commenced to seek recognition for homosexuals as an oppressed minority, it turned to the Nazi past as an obvious site of critical engagement. As early as HOSI's first public appearance, the group identified itself as the representative and legatee of Nazism's victims when it carried a banner that prominently displayed the Pink Triangle along with the slogan "300,000 homosexuals murdered in Nazi concentration camps."[43] Over the following years, the organization established a permanent presence in the foremost space of antifascist collectivization — Mauthausen concentration camp in Upper Austria. From the fall of 1980 until well into the 1990s, HOSI regularly attended memorial events at the camp; in 1984, the group unveiled there the world's first memorial plaque to Nazism's homosexual victims.[44]

The recollection of Nazi victimization was a crucial vehicle in the struggle for political recognition. By itself, however, the quest for membership in a progressive alliance of antifascists fell short of achieving homosexuality's social redefinition. Hence the lesbian/gay movement sought venues for the public articulation and affirmative representation of same-sex sexuality. Christopher Street Day — the gay pride events commemorating the Stonewall Rebellion — was the obvious occasion for such a resistive display of lesbian/gay puissance. In the United States and some parts of Western Europe, Christopher Street Day had become the setting for the kind of massive visibility the lesbian/gay movement hoped to engender in Austria. As early as 1981, HOSI marked the Stonewall anniversary by setting up a centrally located information booth, and starting in 1982, Christopher Street Day became the occasion for lesbian/gay demonstrations.[45] By 1984, these events were organized in cooperation with Rosa Lila Villa, and while they were only held biannually, they represented the most prominent displays of lesbian/gay visibility in Austria's history.[46]

In light of Austria's sexual hegemonies, the political demonstrations of the 1980s and early 1990s were momentous occasions. In many ways, however, they confirmed and reinforced the constitutive marginalization of the country's homosexuals. To the great disappointment of their organizers, the events failed to function as showcases for lesbian/gay prowess. Quite the opposite: the demonstrations ultimately enshrined Austria's homosexuals as a multiply disenfranchised group. The iconography of the events focused on homosexuals' victimization by emphasizing their historical and legal subordination. To the organizers, this political self-presentation may have seemed essential in the quest for acceptance as a disenfranchised minority; in practice, it failed to convey the desired image of collective resistance. More than anything else, however, it was the persistently low turnout that undermined the intended display of lesbian/gay visibility. Indeed, in the course of the 1980s and early 1990s, Vienna's Christopher Street Day events never attracted more than a few dozen protesters; thus their marches through the city center not only reflected but performed homosexuals' constitutive absence from the public sphere.

For members of the lesbian/gay movement, the inability to mobilize the homosexual masses was a source of ongoing frustration. In 1986, for example, *Lambda Nachrichten* scolded Vienna's queers for refusing to march on an exceptionally hot day.[47] More typically, however, the movement attributed the failure to rally Austria's lesbians and gay men to the hostility it encountered in the homosexual scene and among its closeted subjects. Indeed, throughout the 1980s and early 1990s, the overwhelming majority of Vienna's gay male commercial establishments kept their distance from lesbian/gay activism. In particular, the movement's quest to render same-sex sexuality socially visible conflicted with the homosexual scene's economy of secrecy. Vienna's gay bars operated on the margins of legality, and as potential targets for police raids and administrative harassment, they not only sought to keep a low profile, but had a vested interest in avoiding any public association with homosexuality. In consequence, the city's commercial establishments regarded the activities of the lesbian/gay movement with considerable trepidation — a situation that quickly translated into an overtly antagonistic stance.[48]

While HOSI encountered open resistance in most proprietors, the opposition was even greater among the patrons of the homosexual scene. Many of them lived an existence protected by the hegemonic quid pro quo that granted a relative degree of tolerance in exchange for the public suppression of their homosexuality. To such individuals, the lesbian/gay movement not only drew undue attention to the issue of same-sex sexuality, but constituted a real threat to an inherently tenuous status quo. Fearing collective repercussions for the movement's confrontational behavior, the closeted subjects of Vienna's homosexual scene often reacted to lesbian/gay activism with anger and resentment. A HOSI veteran — one of the few active members of the movement who regularly frequented the homosexual scene — characterized the situation in the 1980s by recalling his experiences in the Alte Lampe:

Whenever we had an activity and I would go to the Lampe afterwards, people would abuse me: how could you do this? Why don't you just let things rest? You're just mobilizing the powers against us. . . . People would say that we were doing fine as it was, and by stirring things up, everything would just get worse. That was the regular reaction.

If a large contingent of Vienna's homosexuals opposed the activities of the lesbian/gay movement on categorical grounds, another cohort sympathized with the cause. However, this accord translated into concrete action only for very few individuals. In my interviews with the many persons who followed the activities of HOSI and Rosa Lila Villa but failed to get involved, several rationales were given for their distance from the movement. On the most basic level, the degree of visibility espoused and enacted by the lesbian/gay organizations impeded individuals' participation. In the context of a profoundly homophobic environment that forced most queers to conceal their same-sex sexual desires in nearly all fields of social interaction, the movement's public events simply seemed too daring. In particular, demonstrations required inordinate courage and conviction, as marchers were subject not only to police surveillance and the ridicule of passers-by, but the likely discovery of their homosexuality by friends and acquaintances. For many lesbians and gay men, this risk made any involvement in the movement inherently untenable. Thomas — discussed in Chapter 2 — put it in typical terms when he recalled his feelings about the activities of HOSI and Rosa Lila Villa:

I was really in favor of the things they were doing. And I really wanted to get involved; but I didn't know how. I knew that they were doing these demonstrations on the Kärntnerstraße. But I never had the courage to go there. It was in the center of the city; and I was just too scared that someone would see me. It was just out of the question.

For Thomas, the hegemony of the closet constituted the principal deterrent to involvement in the lesbian/gay movement. But even among those queers who were somewhat open about their sexual orientation, there often was considerable reluctance to join in the events organized by HOSI and Rosa Lila Villa. Some supported the project of making homosexuality public but found it difficult to identify with the movement's political style. In the interviews I conducted, this style was often characterized as "too radical," "too alternative," and "too left" — indicating widespread discomfort with the aggressive critique of the norms of respectability. If the lesbian/gay movement of the 1980s and early 1990s appeared as "too political," many individuals also perceived it as "too serious." Indeed, in its effort to establish homosexuals as an oppressed minority, the movement emphasized modes of representation that highlighted lesbians' and gay men's formal discrimination. But if the demonstrations in Vienna's city center functioned as solemn protests against homosexuals' legal subordination, few of the lesbians and gay men who were out of the closet actually experienced discrimination as a pressing personal concern. In their everyday lives, Austria's injurious penal code played little or no role, and while the abolition of the country's anti-lesbian/gay legislation was seen as a desirable goal, it provided insufficient motivation for participation in the demonstrations organized by HOSI and Rosa Lila Villa. Thus the movements' gay pride events not only failed to unveil the closeted masses, but fell short of mobilizing the lesbian/gay population that was at least partially out.

For members of the lesbian/gay movement, this state of affairs was profoundly frustrating, and it engendered a sustained reflection on the causes of homosexuals' inaction. This analysis focused on the invidious dynamics of the closet. On a basic level, the closet prevented the process of authentification that might produce publicly lesbian/gay subjectivities. Even more importantly, however, it was also seen as causing the hostility and indifference the lesbian/gay movement encountered in the homosexual scene. Indeed, from the vantage point of the movement, the various reasons for inaction — from violent opposition to any form of lesbian/gay visibility and the inability to achieve a personal coming out to the feeling that the movement was "too political" — appeared homologous. In social practice, they all kept the homosexual scene and its patrons apart from lesbian/gay activism, and in their enunciation of an apolitical position, they were ultimately anchored in a form of false consciousness. As Kurt Krickler explained in a 1984 article in HOSI's *Lambda Nachrichten,* the "rejection" of the "emancipatory movement" was grounded in homosexuals' misrecognition of their systematic discrimination[49] — a situation that reproduced the closet as the imaginary site of individual and collective protection:

Many, far too many, think that society has the right to treat "those of a different kind" the way it does. Homosexuals just have to accept that. They are satisfied with the small spaces they are granted. . . . To not be imprisoned, beaten, and abused already means to them that they are not discriminated against. They suggest this self-deception to themselves until they actually believe it, at which point they are no longer aware of their self-oppression. A perfect lifeboat lie. They don't care about their human dignity. . . . Many escape into a double life and into an invisibility with which they are not only content, but which they don't want to abandon under any circumstances.[50]

For the lesbian/gay movement of the 1980s and early 1990s, this conception of false consciousness ultimately delineated a course of action. More than anything else, the movement would construct its social identity in opposition to the political misrecognition of homosexuals' oppression. The result, however, was a stark dichotomization that amplified the gap between the lesbian/gay movement and the homosexual scene at large. From its inception, the movement had been defined in contrast to the various technologies of secrecy that characterized the homosexual scene, but when proprietors and patrons reacted with hostility and indifference, the distinction was no longer just marked by the concept of the closet; it was ossified along ideological lines. According to that logic, the political subjectivity enjoined by the lesbian/gay movement represented the only viable alternative to homosexuality's continued abjection.

In practice, however, this stance not only subordinated other concepts of same-sex sexual identity as insufficiently emancipatory, but effectively precluded the movement's integration into the homosexual scene. Indeed, as frustration with the political apathy of Austria's homosexuals grew, it became increasingly apparent that the movement operated in complete isolation from the lifeworlds of most of Vienna's lesbians and gay men. HOSI and Rosa Lila Villa provided affirmative spaces for emancipated queers, but they were unwilling and unable to intervene in the lives of ordinary homosexuals. Trapped by the false consciousness of the closet and its apolitical articulations, they were bound to reproduce the subordination of same-sex sexuality.

If most ordinary homosexuals were unaffected by the lesbian/gay movement, so was the homosexual scene at large. Between the resistance of the homosexual scene to the movement's emancipatory vision and the movement's oppositional retreat from Vienna's commercial establishments, the homosexual scene remained, much as it had been in the 1960s and 1970s, a site of clandestine association, protecting itself and its patrons according to a cultural logic that insisted on same-sex sexuality's inalienable privacy. In the United States and much of Western Europe, the lesbian/gay movement had made commercial establishments a cornerstone in the massive public redeployment of homosexuality; because of Austria's homophobic realities and the political commitments of the country's lesbian/gay activists, an analogous process would not be initiated in Vienna until the 1990s.

Cultural Articulations and the Imagination of a Queer Community

The reimagination of Vienna's homosexual scene as a public site was the result of diversification in the lesbian/gay movement. Until the early 1990s, all organized efforts on behalf of Austria's queers had been undertaken in terms of a larger quest for political emancipation. While the groups involved in this project differed in their methods and strategies, they were all committed to an overarching vision of an authenticating lesbian/gay existence in opposition to the lifeworlds of the homosexual scene. All this changed at the turn of the decade, when the emergence of several new organizations radically transformed Austria's lesbian/gay movement. While HOSI and Rosa Lila Villa pursued their political project, the new groups sought to overcome the separation between lesbian/gay activism and the homosexual scene. Rather than creating emancipatory spaces beyond Vienna's commercial establishments, these new organizations intended to transform the homosexual scene itself. The affirmative publicization of homosexuality remained the same, but this quest was no longer seen in the exclusively political terms of total lesbian/gay liberation. Instead, it was now seen in relation to a cultural vision that would transform existing queer lifeworlds. For HOSI and Rosa Lila Villa, homosexual authentication presupposed the abandonment of the clandestine worlds of same-sex sociability; for the new organizations, lesbian/gay visibility would be achieved through reinvention of the homosexual scene as a public site of social resistance.

The origin of this cultural agenda for lesbian/gay activism can be traced to the late 1980s, when a centrifugal process brought rapid diversification in the field of lesbian/gay activism. Until that time, HOSI and Rosa Lila Villa had managed to unite several interests under their institutional umbrellas, and the former was especially keen to retain its organizational integrity as an effective lobbying group. By the early 1990s, however, personal and ideological conflicts led to tensions that could no longer be contained, and within a short period of time, a number of HOSI activists left to found such groups as the legal organization Rechtskommittee Lambda (1990) and the safer-sex advocacy group Safeway (1991). At the same time, a number of other groups — ranging from religious organizations like Homosexualität und Kirche (Homosexuality and Church, 1990) and Re'uth (1991) to sports and leisure clubs — constituted themselves independently of the established lesbian/gay movement.

The ramifications of this institutional diversification were manifold. The new groups increased public representation. While the members of HOSI and Rosa Lila Villa had a modest presence in Austria's mass media, the creation of additional organizations brought a significant rise in the number of queers who spoke in the public sphere as openly lesbian/gay people.[51] Even more important than their impact on homosexuality's mass-media representation, however, was the new organizations' effect within the lesbian/gay scene. There the groups stood for a more or less common vision, unified by its enunciation beyond the traditional commitments of HOSI and Rosa Lila Villa. In particular, HOSI continued to adhere to a "comprehensive politics of homosexuality, national and international";[52] in contrast to such an overarching agenda of lesbian/gay emancipation, the new organizations championed a more flexible approach driven less by political ideology than by social pragmatics.

Rechtskommittee Lambda (RKL) was paradigmatic of the postideo-
logical turn in lesbian/gay activism. The legal organization was founded
by Helmut Graupner, an aspiring lawyer and active member of HOSI in
the late 1980s. Graupner had coordinated many of the group's legal initiatives, but in the process, he had found himself at ideological logger-
heads with members of the organization's founding generation. Having
come of age in a political climate dominated by new left activism and the
cultural fallout of 1968, they continued to regard HOSI as part of a larger
progressive movement for social equality and justice. Graupner, by
contrast, had come of age in the 1980s; along with a number of other
younger activists, his primary commitment was less to the transformation
of society as a whole than to the specific improvement of lesbian/gay existence. In practice, this meant a more or less exclusive focus on legal discrimination against homosexuals, the eradication of which needed to be
pursued independently of an overarching social vision. To Graupner,
HOSI's commitment to alternative politics undermined its effectiveness
as a lobbying group; for this reason, he left the association to found RKL
as a mainstream organization positioned outside of Austria's political
spectrum.[53]

If RKL stood for depoliticization of the lesbian/gay movement,
Safeway was created to overcome the separation between activism and the
homosexual scene. Like RKL, the founders of Safeway had been members of HOSI in the late 1980s. There they developed programs for HIV
prevention based on German models. Those models emphasized safer-sex
education at sites of gay male sociability. HOSI was strongly committed
to AIDS work, both in terms of lobbying and as a recurrent theme for
events at the group's headquarters, but its leaders balked at the idea of
moving the organization's activities into the homosexual scene. If
HIV/AIDS was a problem there, it was ultimately the responsibility of a
state that pushed gay and bisexual men into a closet of anonymity — an
analysis that placed the burden of HIV prevention on state-run AIDS
organizations rather than HOSI. To the founders of Safeway, this position was unacceptable. In reasserting HOSI's distance from the homosexual scene, it seemed to consign the apolitical masses of gay and bisexual men to their fate. Its creators regarded Safeway as a vital intervention
in a dire situation, and for many years, the group maintained a highly visible presence in Vienna's homosexual scene, organizing safer-sex workshops and distributing condoms and informational brochures at gay bars
and saunas. However, Safeway's impact lay primarily in its enunciation of
a new logic of lesbian/gay activism. Much like RKL, Safeway had developed an approach whose ideological flexibility transcended the closely cir-

cumscribed world of the traditional lesbian/gay movement; that break ultimately allowed the reimagination of the homosexual scene itself as the principal site of a publicly affirmative queer activism.

The new logic of lesbian/gay activism governed Safeway's endeavors in the realm of HIV prevention, but its full impact was only felt at the end of 1992, when the organization began to publish its groundbreaking periodical, *XTRA!*. Within a few months, the magazine was not only Austria's largest lesbian/gay publication but the principal vehicle in a social transformation that reimagined the homosexual scene as a publicly intelligible lesbian/gay community. *XTRA!* was not, of course, Austria's first lesbian/gay publication. However, it represented a watershed, particularly when compared with HOSI's *Lambda Nachrichten*. Published quarterly since the group's inception, *Lambda Nachrichten* was a political journal concerned with the situation of lesbians and gay men within and beyond Austria. Thus the publication mirrored HOSI's overarching commitments, and much like HOSI itself, *Lambda Nachrichten* attracted an audience that shared its basic political orientation. Beyond its base of a few hundred subscribers, however, the magazine had little impact.[54] Aside from the HOSI center, it was sold only at select kiosks and bookstores, and while a few gay bars made it available for purchase, especially in the early 1980s, the publication ultimately reproduced the division between a politicized lesbian/gay movement and a commercialized homosexual scene. Only the movement received affirmative coverage in *Lambda Nachrichten;* the homosexual scene appeared obliquely, usually in articles that lamented the defeatist stance of closeted homosexuals. In contrast to this schismatic orientation, Safeway's *XTRA!* was conceived as an integrated "magazine for communication" — a publication that would merge reporting on political "initiatives" with coverage of the "scene."[55] Prior to *XTRA!*'s inception, the lesbian/gay movement had dismissed the commercial establishments of gay male sociability as part of a larger structure of oppression; in Safeway's periodical they were integrated into an emancipatory project of affirmative publicization — a project *XTRA!* at once signaled and signified.[56]

The inspiration for Vienna's *XTRA!* was overtly transnational. The brainchild of Safeway cofounder Michael Toth, the publication was modeled on a lesbian/gay magazine of the same name in Toronto. For Toth, who had spent six months in the Canadian metropolis in 1990, it was significant that the North American publication was financed through ads for the city's commercial establishments and that it was available free of charge throughout the lesbian/gay scene. As such, Toronto's *XTRA!*

reflected and was sustained by the lesbian/gay community — a dynamic that served a dual function of integration and publicization. Upon his return to Vienna, Toth began to explore the possibility of translating the North American concept into the Austrian context; by fall 1992, Vienna's *XTRA!* was ready for publication. Like its Canadian counterpart, it would be distributed to sites of the homosexual scene and would sustain itself through advertisements. Most importantly, however, it would create a mass-media representation of Vienna's queer lifeworlds, reimagining a previously secretive homosexual scene as a socially intelligible lesbian/gay community.

In its initial form, Vienna's *XTRA!* was a cheaply produced four-page leaflet. But its extensive listings of the goings-on in the lesbian/gay scene already created an image of queer existence that was far removed from its representation in HOSI's *Lambda Nachrichten.* Organized under such categories as "events," "groups," "initiatives," "scene," and "personals," *XTRA!* publicized a vision of lesbian/gay life that was concerned less with political struggles than with the everyday choices afforded by Vienna's queer infrastructure.[57] Safeway had printed five hundred copies of the magazine's initial issue;[58] in light of the enthusiastic response, the group was emboldened to increase the print run, expand the periodical, and publish *XTRA!* on a biweekly basis. Over the next months, *XTRA!* grew continuously; after a year of publication, it had grown to between twenty and twenty-eight pages and was issued in three thousand copies.[59] The magazine's contents expanded as well. In the second issue, *XTRA!* complemented its listings with a number of articles on events within Vienna's lesbian/gay scene and the representation of homosexuality on Austrian television; in January 1993, the periodical began to feature announcements of political rallies, reviews of recent publications, and gay-themed fiction. By the end of 1993, the magazine included a section entitled "Aktuell" (Current Events), which gestured to *XTRA!*'s ambition to cover not only events in the lesbian/gay scene but political affairs and developments in AIDS research as well.

Through the 1990s, *XTRA!*'s editors adhered to the model they had created during the first year of publication. In so doing, they blurred the boundaries between lesbian/gay activism and the homosexual scene. In HOSI's *Lambda Nachrichten,* the distinction had been a political absolute; but *XTRA!* portrayed the existence of Vienna's queers as an integrated lifeworld. The lesbian/gay movement was seen as aligned with rather than opposed to commercial endeavors, and while this conception may have been less overtly political than HOSI's vision, it conveyed a structurally similar agenda centered on the affirmative publicization of lesbian/gay existence. *XTRA!* thus served as both medium and message. In its journalistic coverage, it not only enunciated a broadly emancipatory vision of lesbian/gay rights, but expressed this demand in the collective voice of the community constituted in its very pages. Thus an ever-increasing number of advertisers along with an ever-growing list of shops, organizations, and clubs at once imagined and enlisted a rapidly growing queer community in a public quest for affirmative existence. Indeed, by early 1996, about thirty commercial establishments — ranging from bars and restaurants to saunas and bookstores — supported *XTRA!*'s vision through regular placement of prominent ads, while the lists of stores, groups, and bars/restaurants had grown to about thirty, forty, and fifty, respectively.

In the wake of *XTRA!*'s success, a number of analogous publications began to appear in the latter half of the 1990s. Some, such as *Bussi,* endured over an extended period of time, while others, from *Rainbow News* to *G,* folded in short order. Specific differences notwithstanding, they all contributed to the process instigated by *XTRA!*. Along with the pioneering publication — which went to a monthly format in 1997, nearly doubling its print run to five thousand[60] — they thus effected the reimagination of an anonymous homosexual scene as a collective space of queer existence.[61] In HOSI's *Lambda Nachrichten,* Vienna's commercial establishments had figured as sites of clandestine inauthenticity; in *XTRA!* and its fellow publications, they began to appear as pillars of a culturally imagined lesbian/gay community.

If *XTRA!* and other lesbian/gay media began to reconceive Vienna's homosexual scene in terms of an affirmatively visible queer community, it was the Café Berg and the Löwenherz bookstore that pioneered its physical realization.[62] Opened in Vienna's ninth district in June of 1993, the project represented a watershed in Austria's lesbian/gay history. Owned and operated by Leo Kellermann, formerly an active member of Coming Out and HOSI, the bookstore and café constituted an unprecedented integration of the political designs of the lesbian/gay movement with a commercially structured homosexual scene. In its basic conception, the Berg/Löwenherz project was a self-conscious part of the movement designed to address "gay concerns and introduce them to a broad public." But if café and bookstore were intended to "reduce discrimination and prejudice," the institutions' strategies differed from conventional sites of lesbian/gay activism.[63] Rather than operating on an overtly political level, Berg/Löwenherz sought to make an intervention into the social dynamics of everyday life. It was in that sense that café and bookstore were centrally envisioned as "sites of gay pleasure and culture"[64] — a conjoined space that would routinize the emancipatory quest for affirmative publicization as part of Vienna's commercially defined lesbian/gay lifeworlds. To some degree, such a process was already underway, as was evident in the trajectory of the Rosa Lila Villa. For much of the 1980s, the Villa had adhered to its countercultural commitments, but by the end of the decade, its occupants sought to diminish the Villa's distance from lesbian/gay life, evidenced by the opening of a restaurant in the fall of 1988.

Berg/Löwenherz built on and accelerated this rapprochement between activism and the homosexual scene. Conceived from the beginning as a commercial space of public queerness, the project enunciated and conveyed an unprecedented vision of lesbian/gay normalization. Neither bookstore nor café was designed as an overtly oppositional site. Instead, great care was taken to create conventional instantiations of the respective forms. Therein lay the project's radical quality. Before the opening of the Löwenherz bookstore, for example, a number of Viennese stores carried lesbian/gay titles, but they were often hidden or consigned to a bashful backroom. In contrast, the Löwenherz followed North American and German models of gay bookstores, displaying the shop's queer contents rather than concealing them.

Like the Löwenherz bookstore, Café Berg was a drastic departure from previous routines of lesbian/gay existence. Connected to the store through a swing door, the café combined the sleek design of a cosmopolitan locale with the charms of a Viennese *Kaffeehaus*. Other lesbian/gay cafés had existed in the past, but at locales such as the Café Quick, which had been popular until the early 1980s, or the more conventional establishments of Vienna's homosexual scene, the site's queer nature had been carefully hidden. In direct contrast to the clandestine gay bars, Café Berg announced itself as a public space of queer sociability. It did so through a prominent selection of symbols and iconography, ranging from Pink Triangles and Rainbow Flags to homoerotic artwork and lesbian/gay posters. Just as Café Berg was publicly intelligible as a queer site, its patrons were thrust into affirmative visibility: a large window front ran along one side of the café, effectively positioning the café's patrons in a display case. For decades, the commercial establishments of Vienna's homosexual scene had been designed to shield guests from public view — in Café Berg, they would not only be visible, but would function as part of an emancipatory quest for queer normalization.

Before the opening of Berg/Löwenherz, its radical departure from conventional lesbian/gay locales cast doubt on the project's economic viability. One member of Kellermann's original staff described his shock upon seeing the design: "I just saw this huge window; and I thought — oh no — no one's going to come here; no one will come inside. Fortunately, I was wrong, of course, and people just loved it." Indeed, in the months after its opening, Berg/Löwenherz established itself as an exceedingly popular attraction. The café in particular drew a dedicated clientele. In part, this was a function of its location, as its proximity to the University of Vienna quickly rendered it a favorite lunch spot and hangout for students, both gay and straight. This development had been anticipated by Kellermann, who saw Berg/Löwenherz as a means of overcoming the "ghettoization" of lesbian/gay existence. But if the project constituted an unprecedented "dissolution of the barriers" between the "sexual orientations," it had its strongest impact within Vienna's lesbian/gay scene.[65] As Café Berg emerged as the city's most popular queer establishment, especially among the younger generation of lesbians and gay men, it heralded an era of unprecedented visibility. Indeed, within a few years, a number of other openly lesbian/gay bars and restaurants opened, while a number of older establishments ceased to conceal their queer nature.[66] For the patrons of the newly visible homosexual scene, the integration of an emancipatory quest for affirmative publicization had enormous ramifications. Before the 1990s, Vienna's lesbian/gay infrastructure had sustained the hegemonic project of homosexual subordination by reproducing docile subjects of the closet. In the wake of Berg/Löwenherz, the city's lesbian/gay scene began to disrupt the constitutive subjugation of its clientele. The result of this structural transformation was a new form of lesbian/gay subjectivity, constituted as a public entity at the intersection of political resistance and commercial culture.

By the mid-1990s, the new emancipatory framework of Vienna's homosexual scene had markedly transformed the lifeworlds of the city's lesbians and gay men. As more and more people came into contact with the new sites of queer visibility, the cultural articulations of same-sex sexuality were normalized into a constitutive aspect of homosexuality's public representation. In the process, same-sex sexuality not only ceased to appear as an inherently clandestine phenomenon, but was effectively reimagined as part of Vienna's urban topography. No event contributed more to this refiguration than the 1996 creation of the lesbian/gay culture festival Wien Ist Andersrum (Vienna Is the Other Way Around).[67] Like no other manifestation of the new lesbian/gay visibility, the festival announced the queer resignification of a dominant symbolic system — Vienna's valorized domain of high culture. Since the inception of Austria's lesbian/gay movement, activists had been attempting to occupy a high cultural realm. But while such events as lesbian/gay film weeks — first conceived by Coming Out and later organized, albeit irregularly, by HOSI[68] — gestured in that direction, Wien Ist Andersrum introduced an entirely different order of cultural appropriation. Held for nearly a month and advertised with provocative posters that queered some of Vienna's most prominent symbols, the festival was designed as a whimsical disruption of the city's sexual homogeneity.[69] In this manner, it was not only intended for the "scene," but targeted at Vienna's staid cultural field at large.[70] Wien Ist Andersrum made the daring proposition that it was lesbians and gay men who would deliver the city from its "counter-reformatory" slumber through the subversive insertion of "fun and excitement." Along with a more conventional plea for the "unhindered development and acceptance of a social minority," it pioneered a truly radical conception of queers as privileged creators of high culture.[71] In a state that defined its national character through recourse to a tradition of high culture, yet figured homosexuality as a social pathology, it was a supremely powerful vision, whose relevance only increased when Wien Ist Andersrum became an annual fixture on Vienna's cultural calendar.[72]

Vienna's Regenbogen Parade and the Actualization of a Queer Community

The cultural developments of the early 1990s had disrupted homosexuality's figuration as an individualized pathology. It was not until the Regenbogen Parade, however, that the resistive transformation of a clandestinely homosexual scene into a publicly queer community was fully accomplished. Such a public community had been imagined in the pages of XTRA!, instantiated at such locales as Café Berg, and projected into the high cultural realm of Wien Ist Andersrum. But it was not actualized until June 29, 1996, when the first Regenbogen Parade transformed Vienna's lesbians and gay men into a socially visible mass, recognizable both to itself and to the cultural field at large. For several years, the trajectory of the city's lesbian/gay scene had pointed to such a constitutive moment of collective subjectification; when it arrived, it had enormous ramifications for the queer individuals who came to recognize themselves as part of the community the Regenbogen Parade made manifest.

As an event, the Regenbogen Parade was conceived by the Kulturverein Berggasse (Berggasse Cultural Association). Based at Café Berg and run by the staff of the Löwenherz bookstore, the small group had been active in the promotion of lesbian/gay culture since the bookstore's opening in 1993. Having always stressed cultural over political programming, the association's activities mostly consisted of occasional literary readings held at Café Berg. In 1996, however, the group set itself a more ambitious agenda. They planned to cluster a series of events under the name Sichtbar '96 (Visible in '96) that would display the queer presence in Vienna's cultural fields. For the most part, these events continued the Kulturverein's emphasis on queer literature, with several readings scheduled throughout the spring.[73]

The highlight of Sichtbar '96, however, would be an unprecedented event — Austria's first gay pride parade. The members of Kulturverein Berggasse had decided to undertake the massive project during a heated meeting in January of 1996. In that meeting, opinions about the viability of such an event were sharply divided. A number of activists doubted the possibility of publicly mobilizing Vienna's lesbians and gay men, recalling HOSI's failure to do so for its gay pride demonstrations, the last of which had been held in 1991.[74] Another group, by contrast, insisted on the changed cultural climate, and their argument that a successful mass-based event was now possible eventually carried the day.

The new climate and its implications for lesbian/gay activism were captured by Andreas Brunner, a key member of Kulturverein Berggasse, in a 1997 article published in Vienna's alternative weekly, *Falter*. There he reflected on the new queer openness, attributing it to a series of factors ranging from years of effort by the lesbian/gay movement and the emergence of a publicly visible commercial scene to a breakdown in the social boundaries between homosexual and heterosexual worlds. In a context where lesbians and gay men had "countless" international "role models" and "often preferred the mixed rave over the gay disco," fewer and fewer queers experienced their sexual orientation as a source of social constraint. In particular, members of the younger generation, Brunner argued, no longer regarded their "lives as difficult" — a situation that needed to be taken into account by the lesbian/gay movement.[75]

HOSI's activism, Brunner explained, had been premised on a struggle against legal discrimination. But even if it was "sad for a political activist like myself," it was clear that "the abolition of §209 is not a concern for the majority of gays." Neither, Brunner asserted, was the quest for lesbian/gay marriage and a series of other issues that had dominated the movement's agenda. If the 1980s and early 1990s had already shown that Vienna's lesbians and gay men were largely indifferent to HOSI's political vision, it now ran the risk of "completely missing the needs and concerns of the people [the organization] purported to represent." Those people were no longer looking for a way to be "consciously lesbian or gay" — "they just were". It was the achievement of that "self-evidence that must be the goal of the movement." Rather than carry the "political banners of the 1968 protest culture," activists needed to ensure that "lesbians, gays, and transgender persons [could] dance on the street" — the very agenda Kulturverein Berggasse sought to actualize through the Regenbogen Parade.[76]

According to Brunner, the realization of this goal depended on the successful fusion of "commerce and movement." While a movement could provide the ideological framing, it was ultimately the homosexual scene that would render the parade a true event. In their embrace of Vienna's commercial scene, the members of Kulturverein Berggasse deliberately broke with HOSI's "strict conception of the political."[77] Instead of a purposive demonstration with political slogans, the Regenbogen Parade was planned as a big party — "colorful, joyous, proud, and very musical."[78] But if the event was advertised under the principal motto of "Have fun! Have fun and more fun!" the strategy reflected a powerful vision that comprehended a mass of seemingly apolitical queers having fun as a deeply resistive act against Austria's sexual hegemonies.[79] Where political efforts at lesbian/gay publicization had failed, the Regenbogen Parade would mobilize a cultural scheme for the constitution and articulation of the queer prowess imagined by the lesbian/gay movement.

The immediate models for this production of queer visibility were, of course, international. In the United States and Western Europe, annual gay pride parades had been fixtures for some time, and while many of them had started out as overtly political rallies for lesbian/gay rights, their character had shifted in the course of the 1980s, when they came to resemble ethnic festivals in the United States and large urban parties in Europe.[80] In the course of the early 1990s, the members of Kulturverein Berggasse had attended several of these events, which became blueprints for Vienna's Regenbogen Parade. Much like the United States and Western Europe, the Viennese version was imagined as an irreverent spectacle, replete with colorful floats and trucks, loud dance music, and scantily clad people.[81] Only such a format, the organizers were convinced, would generate the mass attendance of gays and straights that characterized the international occasions. By the mid-1990s, these events had become a sign of the cosmopolitan character of their host cities; and the organizers of the Regenbogen Parade speculated that it would be accepted as a sign of Vienna's metropolitan status. As one member of

Kulturverein Berggasse put it, "We believed that there was a desire for Vienna to no longer be the little sister of Europe's capitals."

If the Regenbogen Parade was conceived according to a transnational logic, the organizers were careful to give it a decisively local articulation. Only such a framing, they believed, could provide the cultural immediacy and emotional potency to make it a truly transformative experience. Central to this collectivizing project was the subversive resignification of hegemonic spaces and cultural icons. The deliberate choice of Vienna's Ringstraße as the site of the Regenbogen Parade was a result of this strategy. Also referred to as "die Straße der Republik" (the Street of the Republic), the Ringstraße — a lavish boulevard encircling Vienna's first district — always figured in metonymic relation to Austrian nationness. Created in the late 1850s, when Vienna's medieval city walls were razed, the Ringstraße's institutions and architecture embody late nineteenth-century *Gründerzeit* — the glorious fusion of liberal progressivism and Habsburg splendor.[82] In its historicist homogeneity, figured as the "Ringstraßen-Stil," the boulevard is the site not only of such democratizing institutions as the Austrian parliament and Vienna's city hall, but of numerous imperial icons, ranging from the Votivkirche (erected in commemoration of a foiled assassination attempt on Francis Joseph) to the Habsburg winter palace, Hofburg — all building blocks of Austria's imperial and late-twentieth-century national imaginary.

Given the Ringstraße's powerful valence as a symbol of Austrian nationness as well as for its sheer splendor, the boulevard has historically been the preferred site of political and social mass convergences. In this sense, the street figured prominently at such occasions as the 1927 socialist uprisings and the 1938 *Anschluss* to Nazi Germany. At these events, the appropriation of the Ringstraße functioned as a symbolic challenge to the hegemonic order, reinscribing the site of Austrian statehood from oppositional ideological vantage points. But the Ringstraße has not only been the preferred site for the spatial articulation of violent overthrow, for the very logic of appropriation that underwrote the revolutionary moments of 1927 and 1938 also made the Ringstraße the logical space for the resistive rearticulation of any number of Austrian hegemonies.

Thus the boulevard has been the privileged site for the public enactment of political and social prowess since the late nineteenth century. At that time Vienna's working class began to affirm its strength in annual labor day parades held on the Ringstraße on the first of May. Marching on the boulevard in the tens of thousands, the city's workers protested their electoral disenfranchisement and social and economic oppression, and laid symbolic claim to the state's bourgeois and imperial institutions, from which they were excluded.[83] If the May Day Parade originated as an oppositional display of working-class prowess, over the years it became the most prominent and regularized event held on Vienna's Straße der Republik. At the end of the twentieth century, thousands of people still marched every year, but the political significance had drastically shifted after nearly thirty years of social democratic governance. In this context, the May Day Parade still represented the public affirmation of the left's constituency, but it did so in the interests of maintaining power. When Social Democrats marched in front of the parliament and city hall, they celebrated the hegemonies of Austria's *Realpolitik,* anchored as they were in the *Sozialpartnerschaft* and the institutional power bases of social democracy.

By insisting on the Ringstraße as the site of the Regenbogen Parade, the parade's organizers sought to inscribe the event in the historical and social realities of the boulevard's political deployment. In contrast to HOSI, which had held its Christopher Street demonstrations in Vienna's city center, the members of Kulturverein Berggasse were intent on staging their intervention at the very site of Austrian nation-building. In 1998, Hannes Sulzenbacher explained the strategy in terms of the parade's purposefully ironic invention of a new "working class" under the queer sign of resistance against a heteronormative sexual order:

We're doing something similar to what socialists did during the monarchy and the interwar period. Marching on the Ring was really a way of questioning the status quo. . . . It revealed to the state and to the workers themselves that they were a mass to be reckoned with. . . . Today the socialist May Day Parade is just pointless. They have nothing to fight for. So I guess we're continuing the original tradition by taking possession of the Ringstraße.

Indeed, the members of Kulturverein Berggasse were confident that several thousand queerly marked people parading joyfully in front of Vienna's most venerated political and cultural institutions would have unprecedented topographical significance. Much like earlier socialist efforts, which reimagined the working class at the very center of Austrian nationness, the capital's urban landscape would be restructured — if only temporarily — as a queer-affirmative space.

However, the reterritorialization of Vienna's Ringstraße would not constitute the Regenbogen Parade's only resistive appropriation of locally hegemonic icons. In discussions regarding an appropriate finale for the event, members of Kulturverein Berggasse decided on a subversive rearticulation of Austria's national dance: the waltz. For Andreas Brunner, it was an ideal climax — a "terrifically round, harmonic dance, not at all aggressive, where it was possible to revel." And it was clear that it would be danced to Johann Strauss's famed *An der schönen blauen Donau* (Blue Danube Waltz). Since its composition in 1867, the *Donauwalzer* — the work's colloquial title — has come to signify Austria more than any other piece of music, including the national anthem. Romanticized as a remnant of imperial glory and valorized as the embodiment of Austrian sociability and *Gemütlichkeit,* the *Blue Danube Waltz* is a ritualized fixture of Austrian cultural life. Attendees have come to expect its prominent rendition at each of Vienna's frequent balls, and it traditionally closes the Vienna Philharmonic's annual New Year's Concert held on the first of January. In a similarly ritualized manner, the waltz also rings in the new year. At the stroke of midnight, Austrian radio and television broadcast the ringing of the bell at Vienna's St. Stephen's Cathedral with the opening chords of the *Donauwalzer* in the background. When the bell stops, the waltz plays for over ten minutes, during which the majority of Austrians, schooled in ballroom dancing, and waltzing in particular, dance to Johann Strauss's music — most famously on St. Stephen's Square, where hundreds of thousands traditionally gather to welcome the new year.

In a public sphere policed by heterosexual presumption, these rituals of Austrian nationness were closed off to queers, most of whom would never venture to dance openly with a same-sex partner. For this reason, the organizers of the Regenbogen Parade selected the *Blue Danube Waltz* as the logical endpoint of an event designed to move Austria's queers into the country's public sphere. More than any other feature, a *Donauwalzer* danced in the middle of Vienna by hundreds of same-sex couples would at once serve as the parade's emotional highlight and realize its agenda of oppositional visibility. For the successful appropriation of this heteronormatively gendered symbol of Austrian culture would not only disrupt a socio-sexual order that defined the waltz as the exclusive domain of opposite-sex couples, but would reimagine the realm of Austrianness itself in affirmatively queer terms.

As the first Regenbogen Parade got underway on a beautiful early summer day, it actualized the concept of its organizers to a remarkable degree. During the event, I had numerous conversations and overheard many more comments that reflected on the temporary appropriation of Vienna's Straße der Republik. Like the young woman whose sentiments I invoked at the beginning of this chapter, countless people experienced the parade as empowering. "The Ring is ours," was a phrase I heard over and over again, echoing the organizers' promise that "we will take possession of the city."[84] The symbolic potency of this collective act was evidenced by a longer conversation I had with a gay man in his mid-twenties. While walking in the middle of the boulevard, he recalled his elementary school days when a teacher took his class to see the Ringstraße: "Ever since then, the Ring has been my favorite place in the city. I just love all the history it has. Normally, of course, it's all the cars that go here, not to forget the horrible politicians [pointing at the parliament]. Not today, though — we have it just for us." Indeed, when it became necessary to reroute Vienna's traffic to accommodate the queer spectacle, the parade's success was manifest. For several hours, Vienna's lesbians and gay men had suspended the state's heterosexual order at the very site of its political and symbolic reproduction.

Participants experienced the appropriation of Vienna's Ringstraße as a powerful political act. But it was the climactic *Donauwalzer* that provided the Regenbogen Parade's emotional highlight. Unlike other features of the event, the dance had not been announced ahead of time, which rendered it particularly poignant. As the two-hour rally that followed the parade was winding down, the several thousand people in one of Vienna's beautiful squares were preparing to leave. At that moment, the event's moderator reappeared on stage to announce a surprise. Without any further ado, he uttered the words "Alles Walzer" (Everything waltz) — the ungrammatical phrase that traditionally, and famously, opens the dance floor at the annual Opernball, the State Opera Ball and Austria's most glamorous social event. Seconds later, the familiar chords of the *Donauwalzer* could be heard through the speakers. For a moment, the crowd was taken aback. But in a minute, almost everyone had found a dancing partner, and hundreds of same-sex couples, as well as a good number of opposite-sex couples, proceeded to waltz, publicly, to Austria's national tune. The atmosphere was one of collective jubilation; following the dance, people were applauding, hugging, and crying. "It was just so beautiful to dance here with my boyfriend," one man told me, close to tears, while another man reported that he had just grabbed a complete stranger and made him his dancing partner. A year later, individuals who had been at the rally still recalled the moment with vividness and affection. As one lesbian in her late twenties told me,

Last year, [my girlfriend and I] just had so much fun [dancing the *Donauwalzer*]. I have always loved dancing the waltz, but I was never able to do it with Helga, not in the city anyway. It was like New Year's — just better. Before last year, I just never thought something like that was possible, especially in Austria.

Such sentiments were expressed not only in regard to the climactic *Donauwalzer*. Indeed, in the conversations I had with lesbians and gay men in the weeks following the Regenbogen Parade, it became clear that the event had been a genuinely transformative moment. More than anything else, it was the self-recognition of queers as a public mass that galvanized the lesbian/gay scene. For the organizers of the parade, the actualization of a queer community had been a central goal. But even the members of Kulturverein Berggasse had been anxious about the level of participation, fearing that a low turnout would reinforce the figuration of homosexuality as a clandestine phenomenon. Optimists among them had hoped for a few thousand participants and onlookers, but a crowd of a few hundred seemed possible as well. Those in the homosexual scene who were familiar with earlier efforts at lesbian/gay mobilization echoed the organizers' worst fears. It was against that horizon of expectations that the mass of thirty thousand people came as a genuine shock. One gay man in his mid-forties put it in typical terms when he recalled his skepticism at the "announcements and expectations" issued by the parade's organizers. "But then," he continued, "I was just totally overwhelmed by the number of people who were actually there." A woman in her early thirties echoed the feeling when she told me that she had thought it "impossible for an event of this size to take place. That so many people would take to the street and basically say, 'Yes, I'm lesbian' or 'Yes, I'm gay' was truly unbelievable."

The recognition of queers as a public mass translated in turn into an unprecedented sense of communal belonging and prowess. For gay men, especially, this feeling contrasted sharply with their sentiments regarding traditional modes of same-sex sexual association. While several of my interlocutors professed continued enjoyment of the opportunities afforded by Vienna's homosexual scene, they singled out the Regenbogen Parade as a moment of personal transformation. "The parade was the first time I was proud to be gay," one young man put it characteristically, while another related that the event made him aware that "being gay was about more than just sex. It's about being part of a larger group." As a socially intelligible force, that group had been constituted on Vienna's Ringstraße, engendering a sense of belonging captured eloquently by a man in his mid-twenties:

The parade was really a milestone, it was truly uplifting for all those who were there. There was a genuine we-feeling *[Wir-Gefühl]*. And I felt that even though I hate mass events — it is so easy to manipulate a mass, which can be quite frightening. But that was just not at all the case. It was similar to the *Lichtermeer* from a couple of years back. There really was a common cause and it just gave me an awful lot.

In the final analysis, it was the creation of such affirmatively communal sentiments that constituted the lasting effect of the first Regenbogen Parade. As the organizers had hoped, the process of becoming visible as part of a collectivity was not easily reversed. In providing a space where previously abject sexualities were publicly anchored and valorized, the parade not only realized the lesbian/gay movement's quest for resistive publicization of homosexuality, but provided an enduring vision of queer prowess to sustain openly lesbian/gay identities.

This process of affirmative collectivization was cumulative; over the next years, the Regenbogen Parade grew steadily in size and reach. In large part, this development was a function of increasing specialization and professionalization. Following the massive success of the first parade, a number of newly energized queers joined the activists of Kulturverein Berggasse in founding a new voluntary association, the Verein Christopher Street Day (CSD), which was charged with the annual organization of the Regenbogen Parade. This institutionalization resulted in projects of ever-increasing scope. Within short order, CSD began to address such issues as public relations and the Regenbogen Parade's entertainment value for spectators. Whereas the 1997 event essentially replicated the inaugural parade, the 1998 version pioneered a much more ambitious scheme. Held on July 4, the third Regenbogen Parade was promoted in a glossy *Pride Guide,* modeled on American examples, and a citywide poster campaign. Most importantly, however, the parade's organizers sought to render the event more attractive to onlookers. To that end, they introduced vendors and concession stands, and lined the parade route with three stages presenting political, operatic, and festival events. The latter was the site of the closing rally and intended for all participants, but the first two were in operation while the parade was winding its way around the Ringstraße and were designed to entertain the crowd as it awaited the arrival of the colorful procession. Predictably, the opera stage — which featured performances by a counter-tenor along with campy fare from the classical repertoire — proved exceedingly successful.

In line with the Regenbogen Parade's ever-increasing popularity, the efforts of CSD markedly transformed the nature of the event. As the first two parades were advertised only in the lesbian/gay scene, queers had made up the overwhelming majority of onlookers. With the introduction of the additional stages and the event's concurrent promotion among the population at large, more and more heterosexuals attended the Regenbogen Parade as spectators. At the same time, many of the queers who had followed the early parades from the sidelines began to join the marchers. Recalling a typical experience in this regard, a man in his late thirties described his reaction to watching the first Regenbogen Parade as a "feeling of total awakening [*völliges Aufbruchsgefühl*] that made it clear that I would join the next parade." By the late 1990s, opportunities to do so mounted as more and more lesbian/gay groups — many of them founded since the first parade — joined the procession, along with ever-increasing numbers of commercial establishments that tempted revelers to join their respective floats. These circumstances ultimately accounted for the Regenbogen Parade's staggering development. While organizers had put the total attendance at the first two events at about thirty thousand, the figure had risen to sixty thousand by 1998. A year later, with the level of professionalization stepped up even further, the combined number of participants and spectators reached a full hundred thousand; and while such figures could only be estimates, the number of groups participating in the parade hinted at the massive increase. In 1996, the first Regenbogen Parade had featured only thirty-seven organized groups; by 1999, the number had risen to sixty-three, of which a full twenty-two featured elaborate floats or trucks.[85]

Within a few short years, the Regenbogen Parade thoroughly transformed the public face of homosexuality. Until the early 1990s, Vienna's lesbians and gay men had been more or less invisible, members of a subordinated group whose attempt to conceal their sexual orientation enacted their constitutive abjection. Earlier efforts at resisting the state's sexual hegemonies through the actualization of an openly queer community had failed. With the inception and institutionalization of the Regenbogen Parade, however, a fundamental goal of the lesbian/gay movement was finally realized. As their annual act of affirmative self-presentation emerged as one of Vienna's biggest public events, the city's queers not only came out in ever-increasing numbers, but routinized and cemented their presence in the public sphere. As one of my interlocutors put it, the "Regenbogen Parade made gayness a normality" — a process that rendered publicly queer subjectivities a matter of self-evidence.

The attainment of this self-evidence had been a central goal of the parade's organizers, and as they anticipated, it was a development that could not be reversed. This became abundantly clear at the Regenbogen Parade of 2000. Scheduled for June 17, the event took place only months after the inauguration of the coalition between the People's Party and the Freedom Party. Given the two parties' history in regard to the country's anti–lesbian/gay legislation, many queers were gravely concerned about a homophobic backlash;[86] in the weeks preceding the parade, there was speculation that Vienna's lesbians and gay men might abstain from the

Regenbogen Parade because of political intimidation. Such worries, it
turned out, were entirely unfounded, as the 2000 event produced another
record-breaking crowd of well over a hundred thousand.[87] The organizers had placed the parade under a motto of protest, "A clear sign of separation from the current Austrian government," [88] and while the event
duplicated the joyous irreverence of the previous parades, many groups
did introduce an overtly political note into their self-presentation. As the
event came to a close, Green Party politician Ulrike Lunacek articulated
the parade's defiantly oppositional stance. In 1999, she had become the
first openly lesbian or gay member of Austria's parliament, and when she
spoke at the closing rally, she captured and affirmed the resistive sentiment not only of the present moment, but of the larger process that had
propelled the queer symptoms of modernity into Vienna's public sphere:

Especially now, it is necessary to show that another Austria *[ein anderes Österreich]*
exists and that a part of it is queer *[andersrum]* — lesbian, gay, transgendered — and
that we are here on this square and that we take possession of this city, and that
we won't let them take us down. We are here to show that we exist, that we are
loud and big and strong, and that no one can take anything away from us.

PART THREE

Reproduction

CHAPTER 5

Museums and Monuments

Esteemed ladies!
Esteemed gentlemen!
Good evening!
*That you chose the Burgtheater for your anniversary celebration
is a great pleasure for me, as well as an honor and distinction for our
theater.*
*Of course, it would be even more joyous for all of us if this could
have been a two-hundred-year or three-hundred-year or even a five-
hundred-year anniversary.*
*But the self-evidence with which you celebrate your birthday on
this stage should make us happy. This would not have been possible
in all periods in the long history of Austria's national theater — in
the horrible time of the Nazis, not even thinkable.*
A heartfelt welcome!

Claus Peymann, director of the Burgtheater, June 20, 1999

On June 20, 1999, Vienna's Jewish community commemorated the 150th
anniversary of its official existence with a festive event held at the city's
Burgtheater. Obviously, the event did not recall Jews' initial arrival in
Vienna. After all, Jews had lived in the city off and on from medieval to
early modern times, their presence subject to the whims of the religious
and ruling elites.[1] At the end of the eighteenth century, the patent of toleration brought them into the orbit of the enlightened state, and the liberal quest for constitutionalism made them full citizens by the last third

of the nineteenth century.[2] In the context of this gradual liberalization, Vienna's Jews came to be organized under the official representation of an *Israelitische Kultusgemeinde*. As early as 1849, a young Emperor Francis Joseph received and addressed a Jewish delegation in those terms — an event the IKG chose to celebrate as the organization's, and hence the modern Jewish community's, originary moment.

In many ways, the anniversary gala followed a standard narrative of oppositional Jewish self-representation. Recalling the lionization of high culture and its producers, the stage was dominated by over a hundred large portraits of famous Austrian Jews, most of them associated with the glorious moment of fin-de-siècle Vienna. The program itself emphasized cultural achievement, and the first half was dominated by such Jewish icons as Sigmund Freud and Theodor Herzl. The texts chosen to represent these figures enunciated a broadly antiassimilationist agenda. The passage by Freud, for example, recalled his "clear consciousness of an inner [Jewish] identity" and spoke of his life-long commitment to B'nai B'rith, while the extract by Herzl, taken from his diary, recalled the composition of *The Jewish State*.[3] Texts by Arthur Schnitzler and Arnold Schönberg articulated a similarly defiant agenda, pairing the former's non-nationalist invocation of Jewish pride with the latter's call for Zionist mobilization in the face of imminent Nazi persecution.[4] The fate of Austria's Jews under Nazism and its legacies in the Second Republic served as the focus of the program's second half. Contributions addressed the complicity of Austrians in the dehumanization of the Jewish population and denounced the postwar state's refusal to provide adequate reparations.[5] A powerful protest against Austrian Nazism and the effects of the victim myth, the presentations recalled the critical Jewish intellectuals who had emerged into the public sphere in the post-Waldheim era. Indeed, prominent figures such as Ruth Beckermann, Robert Menasse, and Doron Rabinovici were among the event's participants. Robert Schindel most forcefully enunciated the group's collective critique of postwar Austrian hegemonies when he captured Jewish feelings of persistent disenfranchisement in a stirring poem titled "Carinthian Spring Ballad."[6]

In a Jewish context, such discourses were hardly unusual. Narratives of high cultural achievement had been foundational to postwar Viennese-Jewish identity formation, and the critical negotiation of Austria's victim myth and the country's pervasive antisemitism were central to the ongoing quest for Jewish cultural autonomy. What distinguished the anniversary celebration from such oppositional modes of Jewish subjectification, however, was the degree to which it was suffused with and engendered by the presence of the Austrian state. Indeed, the event at the Burgtheater was a remarkably official affair. The site itself gestured to that status. As Austria's national theater, the Burgtheater functions as the symbolic center of the country's literary and cultural imagination. Its appropriation by the IKG may have had a vaguely oppositional valence, but as the opening remarks by director Claus Peymann made clear, the state-owned and operated institution had readily opened its doors to the Jewish community. Nor, for that matter, was the performance a specifically Jewish act of resistive reinscription. It was planned by the Burgtheater's executive producer and performed in large part by the theater's permanent ensemble.

But the state's presence at the anniversary celebration far exceeded its mediated role as proprietor of the Burgtheater. The event was created under the auspices of an honorary committee, whose members included political luminaries ranging from Vienna's mayor, Michael Häupl, and Austria's former chancellor Franz Vranitzky (both of the SPÖ) to Federal Secretary of Education Elisabeth Gehrer and Vienna's Councilor for Cultural Affairs, Peter Marboe (both ÖVP).[7] Even more indicative of the state's presence, however, was the guest list at the actual celebration, which was a veritable who's who of public Austria. With the exception of the FPÖ, all political parties received invitations to the event; along with senior civil servants, religious representatives, cultural leaders, university personnel, and journalists, they gave the festivities the character of an official state affair — a sense that was only heightened by the presence of the country's highest elected officials, President Thomas Klestil (ÖVP) and Chancellor Viktor Klima (SPÖ). Two days after the event, the society columnist of the *Kurier* could only gush. "'Tout Autriche' celebrated with President Ariel Muzicant and Chief Rabbi Chaim Eisenberg," she wrote in a story entitled "A Sign that We Belong."[8] Other periodicals similarly praised the event as a self-assured representation of Austrian Jewry,[9] and the centrist weekly *Format* used the occasion to run a long story extolling the "self-confident generation" of young Jews, that, after transforming Vienna's Jewish society, was poised to make an impact on Austria at large.[10]

IKG's anniversary celebration and its mass-media representation stood in stark contrast to the cultural logic of the postwar era. After all, during the first decades of Austria's Second Republic, the state and its various apparatuses had gone to great lengths to bar Jews from the country's public sphere. As embodied critics of Austria's victim myth, Jews threatened to undermine the postwar nation-state, necessitating their structural exclusion from the imagined community. Austria's Jews continued to figure in opposition to the country's fiction of collective victimization, but by the late 1990s, this no longer represented an impediment to their integration into the national sphere. On the contrary: as the anniversary event made clear, the state now sought the inclusion of Jews in Austria's imagined community. As such, the IKG celebration was indicative of a larger structural transformation that had fundamentally altered the relationship between the Austrian state and its Jewish citizens. That transformation had occurred in the late 1980s and early 1990s, and it resulted in the creation of several state institutions designed to bring Jews into the country's national fields. The resistive quest for Jewish visibility was about to propel Jews into Vienna's public sphere, but it was the state that would ultimately anchor an affirmative vision of Jewish specificity. As symptoms of modernity, Jews had figured as the constitutive Other of the postwar nation-state; at the end of the century, they would be celebrated as icons of a new body politic.

Structural Transformations

The state's altered approach to the Jewish question was the result of a series of structural transformations predicated on generational, international, and geopolitical shifts and realignments. The generational dynamics were relatively straightforward, reflecting and mirroring those that had characterized the Jewish community. There the salient distinction was between survivors and those born after the Holocaust, and a similar scheme organized the generational dynamics of Austria's citizenry at large. In that scheme, the war generation (*Kriegsgeneration*) occupied an intrinsically conservative position. As likely collaborators with, yet supposed victims of, Nazi aggression, its members had a vested interest in the protection of a postwar arrangement that shielded them from individual and collective incrimination. By and large, the post-Holocaust generation was not overly troubled by this state of affairs, but given its historical distance, its members tended to be less committed to the victim myth and its concomitant exclusion of Jews from Austria's imagined community. In the 1970s, the country's political and cultural spheres were firmly controlled by the *Kriegsgeneration*. However, in the 1980s a generational shift took place, propelling into positions of power some who took seriously, and sometimes even shared, the critical positions articulated by Jewish intellectuals and the IKG.[11] For a number of these leaders, the integration of Austria's Jews into the country's imagined community became a gen-

uine concern, reflected most prominently in the self-conscious abandonment of the public designation *jüdische Mitbürger* (Jewish fellow citizens)
in favor of the more overtly inclusive *jüdische Bürger* (Jewish citizens).[12]

While generational dynamics contributed to the state's refiguration of
Austria's Jewish community, they were of somewhat minor relevance
compared to the international and geopolitical forces that came into play
in the late 1980s and early 1990s. The first international realignment was
a direct result of the Waldheim affair. Until 1986, the role of Austria and
its citizens during the Third Reich had escaped international scrutiny.
Under the intense glare of worldwide media attention, however, the
country's image as an "island of the blessed" quickly crumbled.[13] Rather
than a quaint haven of classical music and alpine charm, Austria now
seemed a country of incorrigibles, amnesiacs at best and Nazis at worst.
Austria's political elite was keenly aware of this new perception, and in
light of the country's dependency on such intrinsically international
trades as tourism, the state began to invest considerable energy in enhancing Austria's reputation in the world. In this context, the country's
Jewish community, both past and present, came to be seen as asset and
opportunity. What better way, after all, for a state to dispel allegations of
Nazism and antisemitism than by showcasing its Jewish heritage and contemporary Jewish culture.

Such a celebration contradicted the exclusionary logic of the victim
myth. As it turned out, however, its perpetuation became less and less
important, again as a result of geopolitical transformations. In many
ways, the victim myth had been a quintessential product of the Cold War
era. Instigated by the allied forces in an effort to incite anti-Nazi resistance
and foster a sense of Austrian national identity, it safeguarded the country's independence in Europe's postwar order. As the perpetrator of
World War II, Germany was occupied and divided. As a victim, Austria,
by contrast, was restored to sovereignty within its pre-1938 borders and
in 1955 was made a neutral country. With the escalation of the Cold War,
the importance of neutrality grew, a situation that aligned Austria's freedom with the fiction of victimization. All this changed in the wake of
1989. In the new geopolitical order, Austria's neutrality not only seemed
like a vestige from a bygone era, but it quickly lost its political usefulness.
The state's efforts to join the European Union, which the Soviet Union
had blocked as a breach of neutrality, was the most immediate consequence of the new situation. As the need for neutrality eased, however,
so did the necessity of retaining the victim myth as a foundational narrative of Austrian nationness. During the Cold War, Austria's supposed

suffering at the hands of Nazi Germany had secured the country's freedom and independence; but with the erosion of the postwar order,
Austria's geopolitical position was no longer contingent on the victim
myth and the neutrality it had sustained.

The de-emphasis of neutrality and the victim myth created unprecedented openings for the Austrian state's reimagination of its Jewish citizens, and nothing prompted its realization so much as the country's move
into the European Union. Negotiated in the early 1990s, voted on in the
spring of 1994, and made official on January 1, 1995, Austria's acceptance
into the new Europe occurred at a time when the EU was shifting from
its original form as an economic union of nation-states to a political fed-
eration. The new EU began to identify itself as the bearer and champion
of fundamentally liberal principles, tolerance and pluralism foremost
among them. As a supranational entity, the EU was constituted in opposition to modern forms of exclusionary nationalism, and in its codification
of "European values," it treated Nazism as a baseline of negative identification. As it was imagined in the 1990s, the EU was thus a result of and a
reaction to Europe's most painful historical lesson — a lesson whose
reception would be monitored continuously to ensure the continent's
democratic future. In this context, the Austrian state experienced new
pressures, and it responded by redoubling its efforts to offset the damage
caused by the Waldheim affair. Vienna's Jews remained at the heart of this
project. Like no other group in Austria, their existence signified the state's
commitment to European values of tolerance and pluralism. Jews were
also crucial to the country's attempts to come to terms with the darker
aspects of its history. As Austria's relationship to its Nazi past continued
to be debated in the court of European opinion, the state took unprecedented steps to acknowledge and make amends for the country's complicity — a situation that made Jews the center of a new memorial economy. In the Cold War era, Jews had been excluded from the imagined
community of the nation-state; in the integrating world of the late twentieth century, they emerged not only as objects of public celebration, but
as the veritable guardians of Austria's postnational state.

Museums for New Discourses

The structural transformations in the relationship between the Austrian
state and the country's Jews had immediate ramifications. Jews had been
essentially absent from the public sphere until the early 1980s; when they

were invoked, such as in the *Krone* series of 1974, their depiction followed the nation-state's abject logic of cultural subordination. By the late 1980s, however, the situation had changed fundamentally. In the post-Waldheim years, Jews not only emerged as a central focus of the state's representational apparatuses; they were now constructed as an integral part of Austria's history and culture. Jews began to make frequent appearances on state television and radio stations in shows invariably designed to document the accomplishments of Austrian Jewry in their past and present incarnations.[14] Beyond such relative ephemera, the late 1980s saw the institutionalization of a new discourse. In 1987, a group of prominent elected officials across the political spectrum initiated a League of the Friends of Judaism; a year later, Lower Austria, the province surrounding Vienna, created a federally supported Institute for the History of the Jews in Austria.[15]

The state's new representational logic was conveyed in numerous other initiatives of the late 1980s and early 1990s. By far the most important and enduringly visible of these efforts, however, was the founding of the Jewish Museum of the City of Vienna. More than any other Austrian institution, the municipal museum embodied and enunciated the altered relation of the state to its Jewish citizens. This was particularly evident in light of the history of a previous incarnation, which traced the contours of Jewish representation from hegemonic erasure to state-sponsored redeployment at the heart of Austria's symbolic geography.

Vienna's Jewish Museum had a long and distinguished history.[16] Originally founded in the 1890s, it was the first museum of its kind in the world. Not a state institution, but the private project of a voluntary association sustained by the Jewish community, the museum displayed thousands of ritual objects according to a cultural logic that anticipated respect through recognition of Jewish cultural accomplishments. Much like other aspects of the so-called German-Jewish symbiosis, these hopes were unrealized, and while the museum was a point of Jewish pride in late imperial and interwar Vienna, the institution attracted few non-Jewish visitors and could do little to offset the modern logic of Jewish abjection. In 1938, immediately following the *Anschluss,* Vienna's Jewish Museum was shut down and its objects confiscated, packed up in boxes and stored in the city's anthropology museum.[17]

The fate of the collection in the postwar era continued to mirror Austria's hegemonic structures. In the aftermath of the war, the ownership of the stored objects was recognized, but the state expended no effort to return them, let alone display them. It took until the 1950s for the IKG to reclaim the collection, and when the Jewish community decided to exhibit parts of it in the early 1960s, neither interest nor aid was forth-coming from the state.[18] Indeed, when the IKG Museum opened its doors in the fall of 1964, the tiny display area, a single room in a dilapi-dated building in Vienna's second district, indicated the structural exclu-sions of the Cold War period. The exhibit contained part of the prewar museum's collections and featured a "memorial corner" to commemorate the victims of national socialism, but in the absence of federal or munic-ipal funding, the institution was only open three afternoons a week, and even then, it catered to an almost exclusively Jewish audience. Ignored by the country's mass media and the public at large, the museum remained marginal to Vienna's urban landscape. If anything, it reproduced the enforced privatization of postwar Austrian Jewry; in this context, its clos-ing in 1967 was to be expected.

Another Jewish museum project also took place at the periphery of Austria's public sphere. A result of the personal initiative of Kurt Schubert — a Catholic scholar who occupied the professorship for Judaic Studies *(Judaistik)* at the University of Vienna for most of the postwar ear — the Austrian Jewish Museum of Eisenstadt was inaugurated in 1972.[19] Situated in the capital of Burgenland, the country's easternmost and smallest province, the institution was primarily committed to the realization of a scholarly agenda. Indeed, in light of the museum's mini-mal funding and marginal location, it would have been impossible to attract the public at large. Instead, the institution cultivated an audience of international specialists who regularly congregated in Eisenstadt on the occasion of the museum's scientific symposia.[20] In its basic political ori-entation, the Austrian Jewish Museum of Eisenstadt clearly opposed the country's postwar status quo. Its interventions, however, failed to make a wider impact. A 1978 exhibit on the persecution and destruction of Austrian Jewry was symptomatic. The display was initially mounted in Vienna's Old City Hall, but was not open to the public. Instead poten-tial visitors had to register with Schubert's Institute for Judaic Studies to arrange a viewing.[21] The exhibit was virtually ignored by the mass media; in tandem with the museum's reticence to display it in Vienna, its cir-cumstances corroborated that in the context of postwar hegemonies, the realities of Austrian-Jewish history could not occupy the symbolic core of the nation.

All this would change in the post-Waldheim era. In the decades after World War II, Jewish museums had existed only at the margins of the public sphere, but now that the state had a vested interest in the celebratory representation of its Jewish citizens, they became a privileged vehicle for the depiction of a newly imagined Austria. Nothing exemplified the centrality of the state and its international concerns more readily than the genealogy of Vienna's Jewish Museum. Neither the result of Jewish initiatives nor the product of scholarly ambitions, it was a personal project of Vienna's mayor, Helmut Zilk. The Social Democratic politician had conceived the institution in reaction to the Waldheim affair, and it was no coincidence that the announcement of the plan took place in New York. In July 1986, at the height of the controversy over the former U.N. secretary general, Zilk had traveled to the United States to take part in the opening of an exhibit on fin-de-siècle Vienna; it was there that he first disclosed his plans for a Jewish museum in Austria's capital city.[22]

Zilk clearly conceived of the Jewish Museum as a crucial part of his municipal agenda. Over the next few years, he made the project a priority. In 1987, he championed the creation of a temporary exhibit titled "Judaism in Vienna" which was mounted at the city's Historical Museum.[23] The first state-sponsored display to be held on the topic in postwar Vienna, the show featured the Judaica collection of Max Berger, a Holocaust survivor who had amassed ritual objects from the Habsburg lands as a commemoration of his murdered family. The municipality regarded the exhibit at the Historical Museum as the direct antecedent of the Jewish Museum; with its success, the institution was formally founded as an administrative unit in 1988. In Zilk's original vision, the museum was to be financed equally by the city of Vienna, the state of Austria, and private donors. But as the opening drew nearer, it became clear that the project would be sustained almost exclusively by the municipality. Indeed, when the institution welcomed the public in March of 1990, it was named the Jewish Museum of the City of Vienna.[24]

Zilk had hastened the museum's opening; and initially, it was housed in a provisional setting in the IKG compound that also contains Vienna's main synagogue and the Jewish community center. There, in a single room that would later be converted into the museum's library, the new institution presented a series of smaller exhibits, while most of the energies were expended on the search for a permanent home.[25] Among all parties involved, there was agreement that the eventual space needed to be centrally located, dignified, and stately; and in 1993, Zilk identified the Palais Eskeles as the ideal site for Vienna's Jewish Museum. Indeed, the urban mansion corresponded perfectly to the political design underwriting Zilk's museum project. A regal building located at the very heart of Vienna's first district, it would not only provide ample space for the museum's exhibits, but would prominently deploy a pluralizing vision of Austria's body politic at the center of the capital's urban geography.

The new museum opened its doors to the public in November of 1993. At the provisional location, only a single exhibit could be shown at any one time. The three floors of the Palais Eskeles, by contrast, allowed simultaneous presentation of several displays, and within a few years, dozens of exhibits were mounted.[26] The scope of activities reflected the generous budgetary support by the city; and when museum officials proposed a costly renovation and further adaptation, the municipality readily accommodated the financial request. When the museum reopened in March of 1996, after four months of refurbishing, it had not only expanded to four floors, but installed a number of permanent exhibits on Austrian-Jewish history and Jewish ritual life.[27] The latter incorporated the surviving objects from prewar Vienna's Jewish museum, on indefinite loan from the IKG, and merged them with Max Berger's Judaica collection, which the city had acquired in 1988. Zilk's vision of a Jewish Museum had been realized; along with the two or three temporary exhibits shown at any given time, the institution's permanent displays loudly proclaimed the new cultural logic governing the state's approach to the Jewish question.[28]

In structural terms, the cultural logic enunciated in Vienna's Jewish Museum reversed the hegemonic construction of Jews in the postwar era. That construction had followed the exclusionary model of the modern nation-state, imagining Austrianness in opposition to a collective Jewish entity. In practical terms, this meant that Jews were either viewed as inherently alien or made invisible as far as their ethnic identity. Taking Sigmund Freud as an example, the former tenet, usually enunciated by virulent nationalists, would denounce psychoanalysis as intrinsically incompatible with Germanic values and traditions; the latter approach, more closely associated with the logic of postwar Austria's victim myth, would appropriate Freud as a national genius while suppressing his Jewish identity. In either case, Austrian nationness was imagined in opposition to a Jewish component, which in turn found its social articulation in the ethnic purification of the country's public sphere.

Vienna's Jewish Museum inverted this cultural logic. Its very institutionalization ran counter to the previous eradication of Jewishness from Austria's public sphere, but more importantly, it challenged the constitution of the nation-state in relation to a Jewish Other. In contrast to the modern logic of national homogeneity, the museum thus reimagined Austrianness as the partial product and reflection of specifically Jewish contributions. In his initial vision, Mayor Zilk may have conceived the museum as a way of enhancing the international reputation of the post-war Austrian nation-state; in practice, however, the celebration of its Jewish citizens marked the pluralizing dissolution of that entity. Zilk him-self seemed to be aware of this process. On the occasion of the museum's opening in 1990, he noted that the institution was concerned with "our identity and our history."[29] Zilk, of course, meant Austria, but an Austria where Jews would be integrated into, rather than excluded from, the imagined community.

This inclusionary logic came to define Vienna's Jewish Museum. As early as 1989, an advertisement for the position of director noted that "for centuries, Jewish citizens have made an indispensable social contribution to Austria"; it was clear that this contribution should be at the core of the museum's activities.[30] Over the years, the institution's officials closely fol-lowed this precept. As the museum's first director, Daniella Luxembourg saw her task as the "presentation of the social and cultural history of Jewish life in Austria, its contribution to the country's culture and history."[31] Her successors similarly resisted the traditional approach of organizing a Jewish museum as a reflection of Judaism's religious domains. According to Julius Schoeps, who headed the museum from 1993 to 1997, such an organization ran the risk of removing Austrian Jewish culture from the larger context in which it always existed. "The museum," he noted, resis-ted "treating the history and culture of the Jews in isolation, as if it were a separate history and culture." Instead it "attempted to comprehend them as an integral part of Viennese and Austrian history and culture."[32]

Over the years, countless exhibits articulated this inclusionary pro-gram. Aside from the permanent display on Viennese-Jewish history, which sought to represent the interarticulation of Austrian and Jewish culture through a holographic approach, numerous temporary exhibits revisited and refigured the country's heritage from a specifically Jewish perspective. Predictably, such Austrian culture heroes as Freud, Joseph Roth, and Karl Kraus were central to the state project of reimagining a pluralized body politic.[33] In the process, Vienna's Jewish Museum became a veritable monument to a social order constituted beyond the exclu-sionary boundaries of the postwar nation-state. Rather than a nation of Germanic victims, the Austria imagined in the Palais Eskeles was suffused with the history, culture, and memory of its Jewish citizens. As the prominent plaque dedicating the museum proclaimed, "Without their distinguished contributions in all fields of human endeavor, Austria would not have become what it was and what it is today."[34]

In the course of the 1990s, the social impact of Vienna's Jewish Museum was palpable. Through direct and indirect means, its inclusionary logic profoundly affected the public construction of Jewishness; in this manner, the institution emerged as the most visible sign of the structural transformations taking place in the state's identity. The museum's visitors were the most immediate recipients of this new message, of course; and in light of their astonishing numbers, the effect of such immediate exposure was tangible. Especially after its move to the Palais Eskeles, the institution enjoyed considerable popularity. On opening day, over seven thousand people visited the museum, and the crowds over the next few days were so large that the museum was forced to close briefly to adjust. Within half a year, the museum had welcomed some hundred thousand visitors, and while the numbers leveled off somewhat in the course of the next few years, interest in the institution remained high, producing an average attendance of about five thousand visitors a month.[35] About half of these were foreign tourists, but Austrian visitors still accounted for several hundred thousand. Jewish museum projects of the past had languished in the obscurity of Austria's hegemonic exclusions. Vienna's Jewish Museum, by contrast, capitalized on its central location in the city's cultural landscape to communicate the state's newly inclusive vision to the public at large. Indeed, the museum's guest books are full of testimonials that echo the institution's celebratory project and invoke the "old culture that has given us so much."[36]

The museum's audience was self-selected, of course, but the institution also had a direct impact on other groups, especially Austria's youth, as a result of an ambitious program of museum pedagogy that was created in the late 1990s. Designed to accommodate all grades from elementary to high school, the program became exceedingly popular among teachers, both from Vienna and from other parts of Austria, seeking to supplement their classroom activities with field trips. Indeed, by the turn of the century, Vienna's Jewish Museum hosted a dozen classes every week.[37] At such visits, teachers and students chose between two tours, one focusing on Austrian-Jewish history and another covering Judaism's religious system.[38] Configured around the museum's permanent exhibits and conducted by the institution's pedagogical staff, both tours conveyed the museum's inclusionary logic. The presentation on religion deemphasized Jewish particularity by stressing commonalities and parallels with Christian practices, while the historical tour explained the museum's vision of a Jewish-inflected Austrian history and connected the historical persecution of Viennese Jewry to contemporary prejudice and exclusion.

With Austria's textbooks about to be rewritten from the perspective of the state's newly pluralist self-representation, Vienna's Jewish Museum served as a model for the country's postnational socialization.[39]

Thousands of Austrians encountered the state's new construction of Jews through personal visits to Vienna's Jewish Museum. But the institution also extended its influence far beyond the premises of the Palais Eskeles. These effects could be gauged in Austria's mass media, whose figuration of Jews was deeply affected by the museum and the cultural logic it articulated. In this way, Vienna's Jewish Museum exerted a profound influence on the country's public sphere, creating a new discursive pattern that broke with the mass-media construction of Jews in the postwar era. The postwar construction of Jews had been marked by Austria's victim myth and its concomitant exclusion of Jews from the national sphere. Affirmative representations were foreclosed in this context, in which Jews were neglected at best and at worst constituted as abject Other. In the wake of the Waldheim affair, mass-media discourse began to shift; and a number of progressive journalists took advantage of events such as the Jewish culture festival to create positive representations of Austrian-Jewish culture.[40] But it was not until the founding of Vienna's Jewish Museum that an inclusionary rhetoric took hold across the political spectrum of Austria's mass media.

The mass media's new discourse emerged gradually. Predictably, it originated in publications that were closely aligned with the state or committed to a broadly progressive agenda. In 1987, the federally owned and operated *Wiener Zeitung* took the exhibit in Vienna's Historical Museum as the occasion for an expansive supplement on the past, present, and everyday experience of Austria's Jews.[41] Entitled "Roots of Our Own Culture," the contributions enunciated the state's new cultural logic. When the Jewish Museum was opened at its temporary location in 1990, the inclusionary sentiment was echoed by left-leaning publications that covered the event as a successful attempt of "bridging a gap of repression."[42] As plans for the museum's permanent location developed and concretized, more and more newspapers adopted the new discourse;[43] and by the time the Palais Eskeles opened its doors, Vienna's Jewish Museum was unanimously welcomed as a crucial addition to the country's cultural sphere.[44] In the extensive coverage that accompanied the museum's temporary exhibits over the following years, the state's inclusionary logic was routinized and amplified, thereby anchoring the affirmative representation of Austria's Jews to an unprecedented degree.[45]

The enormous impact of this process can best be gleaned from the populist pages of the *Neue Kronen Zeitung*. In the course of the Second Republic, Austria's most widely read paper had echoed and magnified the state's structural exclusion of Jews to a greater and more pernicious degree than any other publication. In its merging of the country's victim myth with a residual German nationalism, displayed most prominently in the 1974 series "The Jews in Austria," it had persistently viewed Jews as the inherent Other of the nation-state's body politic. The *Krone*'s initial reporting on Vienna's Jewish Museum continued this antisemitic tradition. Putting the museum's name in quotation marks, as late as 1992 the paper had questioned the necessity of the institution, suggesting that its costly creation would hardly satisfy what it implied to be Jewish demands.[46] By the time of the museum's relocation to the Palais Eskeles, however, the *Krone*'s discourse had shifted markedly. The opening itself was hailed as a much-anticipated event and Mayor Zilk's description of the museum as a "site that would document Jews' influence on art, literature, and medicine" was quoted approvingly.[47] If the approval of Zilk's sentiments countered the paper's longstanding practice of imagining Austria's Germanic culture in constitutive opposition to a Jewish Other, the next few years brought a series of articles that effectively moved Jews to the core of the country's national identity. In 1994, for example, the *Krone* praised an exhibit of paintings by expressionist Max Oppenheimer, applauding his restoration to an Austrian art canon from which he had been excluded as a Jew.[48] A year later, the paper issued a similar assessment of Isidor Kaufmann, whose work in late imperial Austria had been unduly forgotten, especially in light of the fact that even "the emperor [Francis Joseph] had bought his paintings."[49] The *Krone* may not have completely embraced the newly inclusionary discourse—a number of overtly antisemitic pieces published in the post-Waldheim era suggested as much[50]—but the articles on Vienna's Jewish Museum constituted a watershed. They not only represented a persistent counterdiscourse to the paper's antisemitic tendencies, but effected an unprecedented break with the publication's traditional orientation. For millions of Austrians, the *Krone* remained the principal source of information and collective identity formation; for the first time, the paper's discourse would effect Jews' integration into, rather than exclusion from, the imagined community. Vienna's Jewish Museum may have originated as a cosmetic cure for Austria's tarnished reputation. In the process of its establishment, however, it emerged not only as the institutional anchor for the state's new relationship to its Jewish citizens, but as the site of a cultural rearticulation whose reverberation across Austria's mass media effected a pluralizing reimagination of the country's body politic.

The cultural effects of Vienna's Jewish Museum echoed throughout Austria's public sphere, but the institution's creation had a particularly strong impact on Vienna's Jewish community. After all, the museum not only brought Jews into the city's official purview but did so in a wholly unprecedented manner, in which their history and culture functioned as the public showcase for a new Austria. The state's strategic use of the country's Jewish heritage was readily apparent, of course, and, at first, it engendered profound skepticism about the project. The museum was seen as a decidedly non-Jewish endeavor, willfully championed by Vienna's mayor regardless of Jewish interests and concerns. Those, the IKG leadership argued vigorously, did not lie with turning Austria's Jewish citizens into museum exhibits. To some extent, fear of antisemitic representation motivated the initial hostility, but more importantly, museums had a low priority in the Jewish community's quest for social and cultural revitalization. Rather than investing in a Jewish museum, it was felt, the city should be more generous in its support of such projects as the Zwi Perez Chajes School.[51]

In the course of the museum's establishment, however, the Jewish community's initial skepticism all but disappeared. Increased municipal funding for Jewish social projects partly accounted for this development. Even more importantly, however, the museum came to be seen as a seminal part of Vienna's Jewish topography. In large part, this reflected the institution's commitment to a decisive level of Jewish representation in its governing structure. Indeed, while the museum would operate as a state institution, its carefully chosen board of seven included four IKG members.[52] As members of the post-Holocaust generation, these functionaries were committed to the resistive trajectory of Viennese Jewry, and in tandem with the museum's non-Austrian Jewish directors, they set an agenda that echoed the cultural orientation of the new Jewish visibility.[53] The state, in this manner, had provided for Jewish representation that thoroughly transcended the structural configuration engendered by the victim myth. In contrast to the systematic eradication of Jews from the public sphere, the museum both anchored a Jewish presence in Vienna's cultural landscape and created a prominent, state-sanctioned forum for the Jewish community's articulation of an affirmative subject position. As Paul Grosz put it at the institution's opening, the Jewish Museum would be a "representation of ourselves by ourselves."[54]

Indeed, the next few years witnessed the realization of numerous

exhibits that articulated with the resistive project of Jewish authentification, redeploying it in overtly public terms. In 1995, for example, the
museum created an exhibit on the history of Jewish sports — a show that
perfectly exemplified the dialectical relationship between the institution's
representational apparatus and the cultural quest for Jewish autonomy.[55]
My ethnographic research indicated that numerous members of Hakoah
and Maccabi had visited the exhibit, and their collective impressions coalesced into a deeply historicized conception of their present-day existence
as Jewish athletes. When I asked Alexander, a member of Hakoah's tennis team in his twenties, about the contemporary meaning of Jewish
sports, he mentioned the exhibit and told me that whenever opponents
inquired about the nature of Hakoah, he "explained to them that it is a
Jewish club with a great tradition that has been in existence for a very long
time." Martin also invoked the display at the museum. The Maccabi soccer player had seen the exhibit at the age of fifteen, and it had left a lasting impression. When I interviewed him in the spring of 1998, he linked
the significance of his membership to the history he had encountered at
the museum:

Well, it really is important, because there was once this great Jewish tradition in
sports. Eighty years ago, there was the Hakoah, and it was the best team in all of
Austria.[56] Of course, that's not possible today, but it's something that we can
strive for. We should set our goals high and try to achieve what we have achieved
in the past.

Such affirmative identifications were ultimately at the heart of the IKG's
project for the Jewish Museum. In contrast to the state, which had
envisaged a public reinvention of Austria's body politic, the Jewish community stressed the museum's effect on the socialization of Viennese
Jewry. As *Die Gemeinde* noted in this regard, the Jewish Museum
addressed itself directly to "Austrian Jews, particularly the Jewish youth,
for whom the depiction of the role of the Jews should be an occasion for
pride in the past and confidence in the future."[57]

If the larger quest for cultural revitalization was designed to engender
a newly resistive identity formation, the Jewish Museum would effect a
kind of identity confirmation. Indeed, in exhibit after exhibit, Vienna's
Jews encountered affirmative representations that not only articulated but
reinforced, in content and sheer existence, the tenets of the new Jewish
visibility. From socially themed exhibits on sports, the working class, and
youth movements to the celebration of established high culture heroes
and the resurrection of forgotten ones, the Jewish Museum offered a con-

sistent vision of Jewish prowess that was eagerly consumed by a population intent on public authentification. If, as the prospectus announced,
the display on Jewish sports, for example, documented a history when the
"self-confident demeanor" of Jewish athletes was the "most visible and
public expression of Jews who did not believe in assimilation or its subjugation," it functioned as the state-sponsored continuation of a project
whose critique of Austrian hegemonies was echoed in the country's postnational reinvention.[58]

The remarkable convergence between the Jewish community's resistive
quest for visibility and the state's newly pluralizing vision was most evident in an exhibit mounted in 1996. "Today in Vienna" featured 130 black
and white images by Jewish photographer Harry Weber, who sought to
document, over the course of an entire year, the city's "Jewish present."
In the context of Vienna's Jewish Museum, the result was stark. To be
sure, the institution had always emphasized its commitment to honoring
the "thousands of Austrian Jews who settled again in Vienna after 1945"
and whose "efforts were and are a decisive factor in the progress of this
city and of this country."[59] But Weber's exhibit was unique in its ethnographic immediacy, which rendered the totality of present-day Vienna's
Jewish community an object of public display.[60] The show focused on the
everyday, and in its celebration of the mundane, it constituted the most
drastic rearticulation of postwar Austrian Jewry's enforced privatization.
In its ongoing quest for autonomy, the Jewish community had taken
strategic possession of Vienna's public and semipublic sphere, but in so
doing, the zone of privacy that had been constituted as a refuge from antisemitism remained essentially untouched. Against this background,
Weber's exhibit extended and radicalized the resistive project of Jewish
visibility. In the visual logic of the display, the previously hidden sphere
of Jewish difference was abandoned by artist and models alike, and
Viennese-Jewish existence was reimagined and celebrated as an inherently
public phenomenon. Weber noted that he had sought to capture how
"fully Jews are part of this city,"[61] and his sentiment was echoed by
Doron Rabinovici, who, in a contribution to the exhibit catalogue, read
the photographs in terms of a "Jewishness free of all definitions from outside . . . , something that demands admiration" and therefore "wants to
reveal itself here and now."[62]

For the bearers of a new Jewish self-confidence, Weber's exhibit was a
crucial event, signaled not least by the unprecedented level of Jewish
attendance.[63] The state also treated it as momentous. More than any other
exhibit, it had realized the original goal of showcasing Viennese Jewry as

an integral part of Austria's imagined community. Other exhibits had projected this inclusionary vision onto the country's pre–World War II past; but "Today in Vienna" anchored it in a post-Waldheim present, where it could be used as evidence of Austria's definitive embrace of the values of liberal democracy. For a state seeking to convince a skeptical international community of the successful transcendence of its Nazi past, the exhibit was an ideal site for self-presentation. In consequence, politicians featured in unusually prominent roles in the exhibit catalogue. Normally, voices of the state were absent from the museum's catalogues; but in this case, two of the municipality's leading representatives appeared in the book, whose simultaneous publication in German and English further accentuated its political significance.[64] In this context, Michael Häupl, Helmut Zilk's successor as mayor of Vienna, articulated the state's position in axiomatic terms. For him, "Today in Vienna" was a definitive sign for the country's political normalization. "Fifty years after the fall of the National Socialist régime, [it] proved impressively that a small but vibrant Jewish population has re-established itself in Vienna and today forms an integral part of the life of this city."[65] However, the state's contented assessment of the body politic's successful pluralization was not confined to the textual economy of the exhibit's catalogue. The display itself became an international vehicle for Austrian image-making. With funds provided by the federal Ministry for Foreign Affairs, the exhibit toured extensively, especially in North America, where it was shown at the Austrian embassy in Washington, D.C. "Today in Vienna" not only became the Jewish Museum's most widely shown exhibit, but emerged as a primary representation of the newly imagined Austria.

In the context of Austria's postwar history, Weber's photographs exemplified and enacted the resistive qualities of the new Jewish visibility. However, as the state's deployment of the exhibit, and the creation of the Jewish Museum itself, made clear, the project of Jewish authentification no longer figured in opposition to hegemonic interests. On the contrary, in the postnational world of late-twentieth-century Austria, the Jewish quest for cultural autonomy colluded with the state's pluralizing vision of its body politic. The result was a multivalent dialectic in which the state created venues for the celebration of Jewish specificity, whose embodied existence in turn signified Austria's new status. To constitute Jews as full members of the imagined community, however, the state needed to be reinvented beyond the exclusionary silences of the victim myth. Indeed, in late-twentieth-century Austria, the state's celebration of its Jewish citizens would coincide with a genuine reevaluation of the country's Nazi past.

Monuments to New Memories

In October 2000, a Holocaust memorial was unveiled on Vienna's Judenplatz. Designed by British artist Rachel Whiteread, it is the size of a large room and symbolizes an inverted library.[66] On its surface, incisions represent rows of identical books, their spines turned inward; although the room includes double doors, it is inaccessible. The library's contents, the monument clearly suggests, are forever lost, its books forgotten or never written in the first place. The names of Nazi concentration camps engraved on the base account for the absence.

Vienna's memorial topography already featured a shrine to the Austrian victims of Nazi aggression, as well as a monument against war and fascism. But the structure on the Judenplatz was the state's first attempt to memorialize the 65,000 Austrian Jews who perished in the Holocaust. As such, the monument represented a transformation in the official construction of Jewish suffering. In accordance with Austria's victim myth, Jews had been subsumed in a more general story of affliction that denied the specificity of the Jewish Holocaust experience in the interests of postwar nation-building. Previous monuments had symbolized and enacted this exculpatory universalization. Erected respectively in the 1960s and 1980s, they incorporated representations of Jewish victimization that equated it with or inscribed it into a larger narrative of Austrian suffering. In the monument to Austria's victims of Nazism, Jewish casualties were acknowledged by a yellow Star of David, but the symbol's alignment with the red triangle marking Nazism's political opponents obscured and belittled the relentless logic of Jewish persecution, particularly in light of the fact that the memorial's location, the former site of the Gestapo headquarters, primarily recalled non-Jewish victims. In Alfred Hrdlicka's multipart Monument Against War and Fascism, Jewish victimization was represented through the figure of the "street-washing Jew" — an homage to the humiliations visited upon Vienna's Jewish population in the immediate aftermath of the *Anschluss*. As a piece in a larger ensemble, however, the sculpture's recollection of Jewish suffering equated it with the civilian casualties of war and inscribed it in a larger teleology that culminated in the monument's final element, which commemorated the 1945 declaration of Austrian independence. This emphasis on Austrian over Jewish history was underscored by the memorial's setting — the site of a building whose collapse during an allied air raid trapped and buried dozens of civilians. In Hrdlicka's iconography, the Monument Against War and Fascism ultimately served as their gravestone, retrospectively giving meaning to their deaths in light of Austria's national resurrection.[67]

The monument on the Judenplatz thoroughly broke with this type of representational logic. Rather than subordinating the Austrian-Jewish experience to a dominant narrative of national suffering, it acknowledged and constructed Jews as Nazism's principal victims. The memorial's location was central to this revisionist project. The Judenplatz, literally "Jews' square," had been the site of Vienna's medieval ghetto until its 1421 destruction in a pogrom that cost the lives of hundreds of Jews. As such, it signified a long indigenous history of violent anti-Judaism, of which the modern Holocaust was merely the most horrible instantiation. The setting centered Jews in the state's memorial economy and served as a critique of the victim myth. The specificity of Austrian-Jewish suffering in the Holocaust, the monument and its location suggested, was not just a function of Nazi Germany's aggression but the reflection of a deep-seated anti-Jewish tradition that had paved the way toward the active complicity and passive nonintervention of Austria's citizens.

As the unveiling ceremony made clear, the state viewed the memorial on the Judenplatz in these very terms. President Klestil referred to a "long chain of entanglement" that needed to be "accepted as part of our history." Medieval pogroms were an aspect of this "centuries-long history of shame," as was the Holocaust; it was in this light that Klestil called for the "acknowledgement of the shared responsibility many Austrians had for the crimes of the Nazi regime." Such a "working-through of the past," he concluded, had been "neglected for far too long." Klestil's sentiments were echoed by Peter Marboe, who spoke as the representative of the city. Describing the monument as a "sign that the city wants to live in truth," he called it a "reminder of one's own responsibility" and an occasion for "reflection about the ease with which one was led astray."[68]

In the context of postwar Austrian hegemonies, such comments might seem startling, especially since they were offered by two members of the ÖVP — the party that had nominated Kurt Waldheim for the country's presidency and vigorously defended him according to the logic of the victim myth. But by the end of the twentieth century, they were hardly remarkable. These routinized and essentially uncontested expressions had been engendered by the structural transformations of the post-Waldheim era. Vienna's Holocaust monument and the discourses surrounding it were indicative of Austria's self-presentation in the denationalized environment of the European Union. In that context, Austria's victim myth engendered skepticism in regard to the country's democratic credentials and signified a logic of national difference the state hoped to transcend. Thus the 1990s witnessed a series of events that signaled the rapid dismantling of the victim myth as part of a political trajectory that would culminate in the unveiling of Vienna's Holocaust monument.

The originary moment in this trajectory had occurred in the summer of 1991. Until that time, the Austrian state had maintained its official posture as Nazi Germany's first victim. With the post-Waldheim fallout and the negotiations for Austria's entry into the European Union, however, the old position was no longer tenable, and on July 8, 1991, it was supplanted by an official declaration read by Chancellor Franz Vranitzky before Austria's parliament. Speaking on behalf of the government — a coalition between Vranitzky's SPÖ and the ÖVP — the country's prime minister affirmed that in 1938 the state of Austria had become the "victim of a military aggression with terrible consequences."[69] But if the "NS-dictatorship was a calamity for our country," it had become impossible to overlook the fact that "many Austrians welcomed the *Anschluss*, backed the National Socialist regime, and sustained it on many levels of hierarchy." In previous years, these circumstances would have been dismissed as secondary at best and untrue at worst. In either case, they had no repercussions for the state's official stance. By the early 1990s, however, they had come to be seen as part of Austria's historical legacy. "We acknowledge all aspects of our history," Vranitzky noted, "the good ones as well as the bad. But just as we claim the good ones, we have to ask forgiveness for the bad ones — among the survivors and the descendents of the dead."

The position articulated by Vranitzky figured Austria's Jews in radically new ways. While postwar Austria's imagined community had been constituted by the systematic repression of their Holocaust experience, they were now identified as the principal object of a "shared moral responsibility."[70] The Austrian state, of course, had never compensated individual Jews beyond belated inclusion under the law apportioning support for war victims. In the new logic of the state, however, this would change. "Much remains to be done," Vranitzky acknowledged, to "help those who have not been sufficiently addressed by previous measures."

Indeed, in the years following Vranitzky's declaration, the Austrian state took unprecedented steps to compensate Jewish Holocaust victims. Given the rapidly aging population, time was of the essence; in 1995, a National Fund for the Victims of National Socialism was created to allow the "rapid, flexible, and unbureaucratic" compensation of all Austrians who had suffered during the Third Reich. As a "moral gesture of recognition," victims were entitled to a lump sum paid in acknowledgement of the "immeasurable suffering caused by National Socialism" and the "fact that Austrians too were involved in these crimes."[71] At the same time as the National Fund dispensed the state's symbolic tokens, negotiations commenced regarding full restitution of stolen Jewish property. In 1998, a state-sponsored Historians' Commission (*Historikerkommission*) was instituted at the suggestion of Ariel Muzicant to facilitate this task; by the year 2001, a comprehensive agreement to benefit Jewish victims and their heirs reached completion.[72]

The material compensation initiated by the Austrian state was accompanied by a series of cultural and symbolic events that anchored the new recognition of Jewish victimization in the public sphere. Many of these occurred in the state-controlled electronic media, where Austria's complicity in the Holocaust, along with the country's long refusal to accept responsibility, became frequent topics. Other events took more localized forms. The 1995 exhibit "The Power of Images" was particularly significant. Created by the Jewish Museum as an attempt to chart the long and varied history of "antisemitic stereotypes and myths," it was mounted in the highly official environs of Vienna's city hall.[73] The ambitious display, which ranged from medieval images of Jews as Christ-killers to Nazi representations of racial Otherness, depicted the state as heir to an anti-Jewish tradition that needed to be acknowledged and actively combated. Mayor Häupl put it in these very terms when, at the exhibit's opening, he called the display an "educational contribution" that would stanch the "contempt for humanity that led to the mass annihilation of nearly six million Jews."[74]

If anything, the state's efforts to recognize Jewish suffering further intensified in the years following the 1995 exhibit, and by 1998, they reached a new level. These developments were occasioned in part by the sixtieth anniversary of the *Anschluss* and the *Kristallnacht*. In previous decades, commemorations of these events had served as principal vehicles of postwar nation-building. In this regard, the *Anschluss* was constructed as the originary moment of national victimization, while the *Kristallnacht* represented Austrian powerlessness in the face of Nazi Germany's brutality. By the late 1990s, however, the anniversary took on an entirely different significance. It now recalled Austrian complicity, which rendered the commemoration of the *Anschluss* particularly ambivalent. During the Cold War era, the anniversary had occasioned the state's most ostentatious performances of nationness. With the abandonment of the victim myth, however, the date lost much of its symbolic potency; in consequence, the commemorative events of March 1998 were few and subdued.

Instead, the state foregrounded a new memorial economy centered on the recognition of Jewish victimization. Its highlight occurred in May 1998, when Austria's parliament initiated an annual memorial for the victims of National Socialism.[75] The event commemorated the 1945 liberation of Mauthausen concentration camp. It was the occasion for an expansive memorial session held at Austria's diet, which also featured the performance of an operatic version of *The Diary of Anne Frank*.[76] Later in the year, the recollection of Jewish suffering took even more prominent forms when the anniversary of *Kristallnacht* was marked by a series of events, including the rededication of the synagogue in Graz and the creation of a soundscape on Vienna's Heldenplatz commemorating the Jewish victims of the Holocaust.[77] At all these occasions, the presence of the state was palpable, its representatives continually reiterating the new contours of Austrian memory. As President Klestil put it, the recollection of *Kristallnacht* brought "anger and embarrassment." But there was no alternative, for if "we forgot and repressed everything, we would only fool and deceive ourselves."[78] Indeed, the recognition of Jewish victimization was equated with the state's restorative improvement, and by the end of the year, Klestil, the immediate successor of Kurt Waldheim, spoke of "dealing with the past" as a form of "collective therapy."[79]

As the Austrian state reimagined its past and the lessons to be learned from it, the public representation of Jews shifted completely. In the operative context of the victim myth, their embodied critique of Austrian complicity had been systematically marginalized. But now that the state viewed the negotiation of its Nazi past as crucial to its postnational reconstitution, Jews emerged as celebrated guides in that process. Nothing exemplified this shift more drastically than the trajectory of Simon Wiesenthal. In the 1960s and 1970s, he had been singular among Austria's Jews in his prominent denunciation of the country's postwar hegemonies. However, his ongoing search for Nazi war criminals came at a heavy price. In the cultural logic of the day, it was seen not as a tireless quest for accountability, but as a vindictive ploy designed to undermine Austria's integrity. As a result, Wiesenthal was vilified as an enemy of the state. Politicians and the mass media alike regularly accused him of employing Mafia-like methods and running a private police and informers' organization.[80] By the time of his 1975 conflict with Bruno Kreisky, Wiesenthal had effectively been defined as the nation's bête noire, personifying a vengeful Jewry that could never be included in the imagined community of victims. As the *Krone* proclaimed, Wiesenthal was the "embodiment of the problem"; he had "tarnished Austria's reputation" and he "should be held publicly accountable."[81]

Over the years, Wiesenthal's position remained firm, as he continued to investigate Nazi war crimes and their perpetrators. After Austria's structural transformation, however, his activities appeared in a wholly new light. In the postwar era, his search for Austrian Nazis had challenged the country's victim myth, but since the state abandoned the national fiction, Wiesenthal's career came to be reimagined as an outstandingly moral pursuit of justice. In the process, Wiesenthal was constructed in entirely new terms. For decades, he had been portrayed as a relentless "Nazi hunter"; by the late 1990s, however, he was recognized as a singularly wise man, a "moral authority," and even a "monument."[82] Even more remarkable, Wiesenthal was now seen as a quintessential Austrian. Not only was he the "consciousness of the nation," but his efforts brought honor to the country, making him "one of the most famous and respected Austrians in the world."[83]

While Austria's mass media lionized Wiesenthal as the guiding light of the country's reinvention, he also attained a new degree of political influence, which ultimately led to the creation of the state's Holocaust monument on the Judenplatz. As late as 1988, Wiesenthal's protests against Hrdlicka's Monument against War and Fascism and what he regarded as its demeaning and highly situational representation of Jewish victimization went unheard.[84] By the mid-1990s, however, Wiesenthal's objections had gained a receptive audience among Austria's politicians. In the fall of 1994, when he proposed the creation of a monument exclusively dedicated to the memory of the 65,000 Austrian Jews who lost their lives in the Holocaust, his suggestion was met with eagerness, quickly resulting in a competition that produced Rachel Whiteread's winning design.[85]

The concomitant discussion also reflected the state's structural transformation. In the mid-1980s, the proposed erection of Hrdlicka's monument had prompted a highly divisive debate among Austria's political elite and in the country's mass media that, in the immediate aftermath of the Waldheim affair, ultimately reflected the struggle over victim myth and Austrian nationness.[86] Wiesenthal's proposal, by contrast, produced no significant fissure in Austria's political field. Although a heated public discussion took place, it turned not on whether Holocaust memorialization was necessary but on its appropriate form. As such, opposition was voiced primarily from within the Jewish community, and it reflected a surprising archaeological discovery. In preparing the foundation of the monument, vestiges were found of the Judenplatz's medieval synagogue. Remnants left by the fire that destroyed the synagogue after the 1421 pogrom, they represented a testament to a long history of Jew-hatred, and several members of Vienna's Jewish community advocated that the synagogue's remains rather than Whiteread's library be turned into the city's Holocaust memorial.[87] A protracted exchange ensued, ultimately leading to a compromise solution that involved a slight repositioning of Whiteread's monument and the creation of an extensive underground viewing area displaying the remains of the medieval synagogue.[88]

Less important than the details of the compromise, however, was the ultimate configuration of the debate. As an essentially intra-Jewish discussion, it reflected and constituted a political field in which Austria's Nazi past was no longer under negotiation. In the 1980s, it was still possible to reject Hrdlicka's representation of Austrian complicity on general grounds; in the 1990s, any principled resistance to Wiesenthal's monument was effectively stifled. For decades, the Jewish memory of the Holocaust had existed on the margins of the national sphere. But when the state sanctioned and adopted it at the end of the twentieth century, it not only became the guiding light for the renegotiation of Austria's history, but moved to the uncontestable center of the country's symbolic geography; and there it was enshrined in the Holocaust memorial on Vienna's Judenplatz.

New Jewish Positions

As the state reimagined its relationship to its Jewish citizens and their foundational memories, a parallel development occurred in Austria's population. In a mutually constitutive dialectic, the state's affirmative representations of Austrian Jewry found their echo in popular constructions, at the same time as the decline of antisemitism facilitated political interventions. Indeed, in the course of the 1990s, all indicators pointed in the direction of decreasing antisemitism; by the turn of the century, the numerical shifts were quite stark. In 1999, only 14 percent of Austrians believed it would be better if there were no Jews in the country, along with 10 percent who claimed to be undecided on the issue. The combined 24 percent was a significant drop from the 53 percent who had given these answers to the same question in 1973.[89] Similar changes were measured in the responses to the classic survey question, "Would you marry a man or woman of Jewish background?" where the affirmative answer rose from 33 percent in 1973 to 53 percent in 1999. By the end of the 1990s, the proportion of Austrians who viewed Jewish converts as genuine

Christians had also increased from 23 percent in the early 1970s to twice that number.[90]

Along with greater readiness to include Jews in Austria's imagined community came a decisive increase in the population's recognition of Jewish victimization. As a constitutive component of postwar Austria's victim myth, the obfuscation of Jewish suffering had undermined any willingness to offer compensation to the country's Jews. Moreover, the very demand for restitution seemed illegitimate, as it was perceived as the attempted extortion of a fellow victim. With the abandonment of the victim myth, however, the positions of the state and the Jews were effectively reversed. In the postwar era, Jews were imagined as ruthless predators on a hapless country, but now the burden had clearly shifted to the state, not only because of Austrians' complicity in the Third Reich, but because of the state's prolonged refusal to acknowledge and act on its historical responsibility. The nature of Jewish claims did not change; if anything, they were articulated more forcefully in performative reflection of the new Jewish self-confidence.[91] But they no longer fed into an antisemitic logic. On the contrary, popular representations began to identify the state, rather than the Jews, as the cause of the problem, as in a 1998 cartoon in the centrist *Kurier* that criticized Austria's unwillingness to address the issue of restitution by depicting a succession of chancellors pronouncing a litany of broken promises.[92] In the wake of such shifts in the state's official position and its mass-media representation, the country's population also increasingly approved Jewish demands for compensation. As late as the early 1980s, a full 80 percent of Austrians had rejected the concept of reparations; although the number decreased by a mere 10 percent in the immediate aftermath of Chancellor Vranitzky's 1991 declaration, the persistent articulation of Austria's new memory in the course of the 1990s eventually had a decisive effect, dropping the percentage of opponents to less than 50 percent by the end of the twentieth century.[93]

For Austria's Jews, the marked decline in the level of antisemitism had significant ramifications. Many of my ethnographic interlocutors mentioned it as one of the most important developments of the previous years, and members of the postwar generation frequently used it as a comparative marker. Hans put it in typical terms when he recalled his youth in 1960s Vienna as a time when "Austrian society was much more antisemitic than today. There was no openness at all — everything was hush-hush. I much prefer for antisemitism to be discussed openly; that way there is a much better chance to fight it." Like Hans, many older Jews experienced the drop in antisemitism as a decisive transformation. However, its impact was even greater on members of the post-Waldheim generation. In contrast to their parents, they were socialized into a cultural field in which Jews no longer figured as constitutive outsiders. In consequence, Austrian Jews who came of age in the 1990s rarely felt marginalized in their social settings. To be sure, many Jewish children primarily inhabited the autonomous environments of the Zwi Perez Chajes School and the various Jewish youth organizations. But even those who attended Austrian institutions were likely to feel included in the larger school community. Indeed, by the late 1990s, Austria's educational system was no longer seen as a haven of antisemitism; in contrast to the postwar generation, whose members often recalled their isolation from non-Jewish students, many young Jews told me about their close friendships with Austrians.

By and large, Vienna's Jews saw the decrease in Austrian antisemitism as a sign of a larger social transformation; in reflecting on the reasons for this development, they were quick to credit the state and its recent activities in regard to Jewish issues. Many of my interlocutors were wary about the state's motives, which they often characterized as instrumental rather than genuine. But at the same time, they were keenly aware of the effects, which in the opinion of most Jews often exceeded the original intentions. Characteristically, my interlocutors pointed to the Jewish Museum to substantiate their contention. On the one hand, Vienna's Jews clearly thought of the museum as an institution of the state whose creation owed more to political expediency than to a newfound love for Austrian Jewry. On the other hand, however, they greatly appreciated its establishment. By the late 1990s, it had not only become a popular meeting point for the Jewish community, but was seen as the central and most potent site in the struggle against antisemitism. For Adam, for example, Vienna's Jewish Museum contributed more than any other institution to the "dismantling of stereotypes," while Hans went even farther in his analysis, crediting it with the unprecedented "normalization" of Jewishness because of its adoption by a "state-run public establishment."

Vienna's Jews clearly recognized the state's reorientation, and while this recognition failed to turn them into Austrian patriots, it did affect their sense of national belonging. Once again, the generational difference served as a meaningful index. Most members of the postwar generation had grown up with a deep sense of cultural alienation that had bloomed into a full-fledged rejection of Austrian national identity and made Austrianness and Jewishness seem inherently incompatible. Jews who came of age in the post-Waldheim era, by contrast, were far less likely to experience these incongruities. "I am Austrian and I am a Jew," Avi told me in a fairly typical statement, "it is not irreconcilable." Even more striking than the development of collective identification was the shift in the way life trajectories were constructed. In the postwar era, young Jews rarely saw their future in Vienna, but by the end of the twentieth century, many Jews envisioned growing old in Austria. "I do believe that I would like to stay in Vienna for the long term," Esther offered. "Of course, I want to see the rest of the world and maybe live somewhere else for a while. But in the end I think I want to come back here."

The emergence of Vienna as a viable home for Jews correlated with the displacement of Israel from the center of Austrian-Jewish subjectification. This development was momentous. In the first decades of the Second Republic, the Zionist state had served not only as the foundational site of affirmative identity formation, but as the logical destination of Viennese Jewry. A collective vision, this normative trajectory had been anchored in Vienna's Jewish youth organizations, committed as they were to eventual emigration to Israel. By the late twentieth century, however, the Zionist state had lost its status as a center of gravity. Adam put it in typical terms when he remarked, "Naturally, I have a strong affinity for Israel, but ultimately, I'm more at home here in Austria." Indeed, much as in previous decades, the overwhelming majority of Vienna's Jewish population supported the Zionist project, but the degree of personal identification with the state of Israel was waning as the viability of an Austrian Jewish existence increased. Even in the Zionist youth organizations, Israel ceased to figure as the eventual destination of Viennese Jewry. By the 1990s, neither HaSchomer Hazair nor Bnei Akiba actively prepared their members for emigration to Israel, only seeking to instill a love for the country. Ultimately, this strategy reflected the realities of Jewish children coming of age in turn-of-the-century Vienna. In the context of Austrian Jewry's quest for cultural autonomy, they were more likely than ever to belong to Jewish youth organizations but less likely than ever to identify with the traditional Zionist goals of those organizations. As one leader of the Schomer put it to me in the spring of 2000, "Most of our members no longer see their roots in Israel, but in Austria. And most of them want to stay in Vienna. I don't think those children are patriotic, but they socialize here and they have their friends here."

The abandonment of Israel as the conceptual center of Viennese Jewry shows clearly the altered landscape of Austrian nationness. In part, this identificatory development came in response to the state's celebration and attempted inclusion of its Jewish citizens. Even more importantly, however, it reflected the postnational dynamics instigated by Austria's entry into the European Union. Most Austrians saw the 1994 referendum as a crucial decision for the country's future. But for Vienna's Jewish population, the ramifications of the vote were nothing short of life-changing, promising a mode of affiliation beyond the exclusionary configuration of postwar Austria's nation-state. To some degree, the hopes for Austria's membership in a united Europe reflected the mediated memory of the Habsburg Monarchy, whose construction in postwar Viennese-Jewish discourse emphasized the advantages Jews enjoyed in a supranational environment. More importantly yet, it was seen as a vital buffer against the ever-present threat of oppression under the nation-state, whether in the form of Austria's victim myth and its antisemitic implications or in the xenophobic politics of Jörg Haider and his Freedom Party. Ilana's comments were typical when she described her feelings in the months preceding the EU referendum in these very terms. For her, the European Union was not only a "chance for peace and prosperity," but a "safeguard against racism and fascism." In turn, this meant "I could live in Austria without being scared that something horrible would happen." In the postwar era, the Zionist state had functioned as a safety net for Viennese Jewry, but now "Israel seemed quite far away," especially since the "EU offered a possibility of local identification that we simply didn't have before."

Indeed, in the years after Austria's entry into the EU, the country's Jews developed a pronounced European identity. Ethnographically, this was evident throughout the course of my fieldwork. Individual Jews repeatedly told me that "being European" was important to them. When I queried further, many claimed to have special affinities with European values; others cited their fondness for such metropolises as Paris, Amsterdam, or Berlin as evidence for their European sensibility; yet others referred to their new European Union passports as a prized possession. Most importantly, however, the political realities of a European identity allowed Vienna's Jews to reconcile and normalize their presence in Austria. For decades, they had not only lived in a land of perpetrators, but existed on the margins of a postwar nation-state that continued to constitute them in antithesis to the imagined community. This dynamic changed in the post-Waldheim years, when the state made its initial attempts to reintegrate Jews into the national sphere, but these efforts could not eradicate the genocidal memory and exclusionary history that made Austria an inherently compromised site of Jewish life. In the European Union, however, the postwar nation-state effectively ceased to exist; as the country's body politic was reimagined in European terms, Vienna's Jews were fully liberated from the Austrian hegemonies that had subordinated them in the postwar era. As a Germanic construct reconstituted on the basis of the victim myth, the Austrian nation-state could never be an uncompromised site of Jewish identification. But as a part of Europe, it allowed the construction of a Jewish subjectivity independent of the exclusionary dynamics of modern nation-building. As Adam put it, "Before the EU, I never felt Austrian. I still don't — but insofar as it made me a European citizen, it now makes sense for me to live here as a Jew."

Nothing exemplified the impact of Austrian Jewry's Europeanization as much as the response to the FPÖ's inclusion in the country's government. For years, Haider's rise had been the demon of Vienna's Jewish community, not least because of his opposition to Austria's entry into the European Union. In 1994, Haider had campaigned vigorously, urging the country's population to reject EU membership in order to preserve Austria's national sovereignty. Haider's defeat and the country's subsequent admission to the EU changed the parameters. In the pluralizing sphere of European integration, Austria's Jews were no longer in danger of suffering as the nation-state's abject Other; this development encouraged the vocal resistance of the Jewish community to a governing coalition between the ÖVP and the FPÖ. The crucial importance of European citizenship in that situation became clear in the course of numerous conversations I had in the winter and spring of 2000. In the face of a right-wing government, dozens of Jews affirmed that their sense of personal and collective security was dependent on Austria's membership in the European Union. Ilana put it in typical terms when she noted that "without the EU, I don't think I would have wanted to stay here; [the new government] would have been a reason to leave. But the EU is protection against extreme positions." As for other Austrian Jews, this sense of security translated into a readiness to take public action, and Ilana voiced her protest through demonstrations and prominent display of an antigovernment button. When the postwar Austrian nation-state had reiterated its founding myth in the course of the Waldheim affair, Ilana had remained silent, but now she joined thousands of other Viennese Jews in the resistive articulation of Europe's pluralizing principles.

To be sure, the protests of the year 2000 reflected the emergence of a new Jewish self-confidence. But by the 1990s, that self-confidence had become inextricably linked to and persistently reinforced by the Austrian state's aggressive denationalization. The celebration of Vienna's Jews as an integral part of the country's body politic was one aspect of this process, but so was Austria's move into the EU. For Vienna's Jewish population, this set of circumstances ultimately engendered a mutually constitutive dialectic in which the state had become a crucial agent for the articulation of a critically autonomous position. The role of the Jewish Museum in the immediate aftermath of the new government's installment highlighted this dynamic. Ever since its creation, the festive openings of individual exhibits had been popular social events, attended predominantly by members of Vienna's Jewish community. One such event was scheduled for February 8, 2000. It was a minor exhibit of Judaica, and museum officials anticipated a small crowd of around 150. A few days before the exhibit's opening, however, the ÖVP/FPÖ coalition took office, fundamentally shifting the tenor of the occasion. As the first public event held in Vienna's Jewish community since the government's inauguration, it became a powerful communal statement, with well over four hundred people in attendance. Not enough chairs were available, but for the overwhelmingly Jewish crowd, the curators' comments on the exhibit were of secondary interest. Instead most guests wandered through the museum with friends and acquaintances, discussing the political situation and possible responses to it. These conversations helped establish and affirm the resistive Jewish position that would be articulated in the course of the following months. Vienna's Jewish community could have congregated in a space away from the public sphere, and this did occur when a town hall meeting to discuss the new government was held in Vienna's main synagogue in late February, but it was significant that the initial articulation of Jewish resistance took place at a state-sponsored and state-run institution. Ultimately, the opening signified the constitutive convergence between the state's pluralizing agenda and the new Jewish visibility — a convergence that would remain operative and take even more prominent form in the face of potential renationalization.

More generally, the opening exemplified the dynamic that accounted for the unprecedented visibility of Jews in late-twentieth-century Vienna. Much of this visibility was a result of the resistive quest for Jewish authentification, but it was bolstered in crucial ways by the state's new relationship to its Jewish citizens. In the logic of the former, the public articulation of Jewish difference developed as an oppositional act; in the context of the latter, however, it also came to function in the hegemonic terms of a newly pluralized body politic. In consequence, individual Jews took different paths to the public articulation of their cultural difference. But whether they came from a traditional milieu that no longer lived Jewishness in enforced privatization or celebrated an identity discovered in such official environs as Vienna's Jewish Museum, they enacted a larger cultural script that established, valorized, and fixed a Jewish presence in Austria's cultural fields. As symptoms of modernity, Jews had resisted their subordination in the nation-state; in its postnational configuration, the state itself had come to ensure their affirmative reproduction.

CHAPTER 6

Offices and Balls

Good evening!

I am happy to welcome you here at Vienna's city hall.

First off: many congratulations — the twentieth birthday, a very special birthday. And I am delighted that you agreed to celebrate this birthday here with us at Vienna's city hall. It is not just because of our impressive halls; I also understand it as an expression of solidarity with and support for your work on the part of the city of Vienna.

Twenty years of HOSI means twenty years of struggle for equality, struggle against discrimination, work for tolerance and for acceptance of gays and lesbians. And twenty years of successes. But many things remain to be done; many forms of social and legal discrimination still exist. . . .

We must not give up the fight. On the contrary. I think that a celebration like the one today should, first, be fun and, second, give us courage and strength so that we can struggle together to abolish all discrimination against gays and lesbians, so that in the future, everyone can live and love how he or she wants, because that is a beautiful world.

Thank you!

Renate Brauner, Vienna city councilor, March 18, 2000

On March 18, 2000, HOSI commemorated its twentieth anniversary with a lavish celebration. Hundreds were in attendance to fete the group, including a veritable who's who of Vienna's lesbian/gay community. In the course of the long evening, revelers were treated to an elaborate buffet, as well as classical and contemporary dancing. However, most of the attention was focused on the drawn-out stage show. Moderated by a longtime HOSI activist, the lineup featured musical acts ranging from traditional Viennese folk musicians and cabaret singers to drag queens, lesbian dancers, and a gay choir. Interspersed with the musical numbers was a bevy of speeches and a detailed account of HOSI's history illustrated with a slide show. The documentation of HOSI's struggles and accomplishments clearly resonated with the organization's longtime activists, and other guests also found the event invigorating. Throughout the evening, the atmosphere was exuberant, and the festivities continued until 4:00 A.M.[1]

In format and content, HOSI's twentieth anniversary celebration was not altogether different from the countless other parties that had been staged by factions of Austria's lesbian/gay movement since its inception in the 1970s. What made it unique and historically remarkable, however, was the event's setting. HOSI's anniversary took place in Vienna's venerable Rathaus (city hall) — the symbolic heart of the city's political landscape. The celebration's location had tremendous significance for HOSI, as well as the organization's congratulators. Never before in the history of the lesbian/gay movement had a political group been allowed to stage itself at such an important site of state power. HOSI's prior anniversaries had been observed at a distance from the state; as late as the mid-1990s, the very idea of an event at the Rathaus would have seemed absurd. As one longtime HOSI activist quipped to me, "We got to know the Rathaus primarily by being thrown out of it."

The tenor of the twentieth anniversary event could not have been more different. As the evening's moderator noted with obvious satisfaction, the idea of holding HOSI's celebration at city hall had not only received "much support" from the municipal bureaucracy, but the city itself generously picked up the tab. Its status as an official occasion was reflected in the event's formal announcements and attendees' even more formal attire. However, nothing exemplified the celebration's official character more readily than the speech by Renate Brauner, the Social Democratic city councilor in charge of women's, minority, and consumer affairs. A ranking member of Vienna's municipal government, Brauner served as the event's formal host as well as the city's political representative, and her unequivocal praise for HOSI's work suggested a remarkable alignment between the lesbian/gay movement and the municipality's social agenda. Indeed, in much of her long speech, Brauner recounted recent legislation implemented by Vienna's provincial diet — legislation that provided unprecedented civil rights for the city's lesbians and gay men, responding to longstanding demands by HOSI. In the political realities of municipal power as well as in the discursive context of Brauner's speech, the lesbian/gay movement and its constituency figured in terms that were radically different from their traditional construction. That construction had imagined homosexuals as a corrosive element of the social order — a situation that necessitated their legal subordination in the interests of the body politic at large. Thus Brauner's discourse and the political agenda it reflected constituted a structural reversal. Not only had the municipal apparatus recognized and attempted to end homosexuals' discrimination, but it had accepted the lesbian/gay movement as a guide toward a more "beautiful world."

The newly pluralized stance of Vienna's municipality differed from that of the Austrian state at large, where a conservative majority continued to block the extension of equal rights to lesbians and gay men. But if the traditional agendas of the ÖVP and FPÖ resisted the legal affirmation of Austria's queers, the end of formal discrimination against homosexuals was clearly in sight. Indeed, by the turn of the century, a number of legal reforms had already been put in place, in part because of international pressure on Austria and in part because of internal critiques directed against the conservative parties' anti-lesbian/gay stance. Thus Vienna's embrace of its queer population came to function as a social and legal model for the state's new relation to homosexuality. Championed by the Social Democratic Party — itself a recent convert to antihomophobic politics — that model reversed the previous logic of same-sex sexuality's constitutive abjection. As symptoms of modernity, queers needed to be subordinated in the interest of society's sexual homogeneity; now they were about to be reinvented by the state as cornerstones of a beautifully diversified world.

Toward Federal Recognition

The treatment of Nazism's homosexual victims was paradigmatic of the Austrian state's trajectory in regard to lesbian/gay issues. That this domain should serve as an indicator for the political climate at large was a result of Austria's longstanding refusal to acknowledge the distinct experience of lesbians and gay men during the Third Reich. In the eyes of Austria's postwar legislature, homosexuals had been ordinary criminals both before and during World War II; since that status had not changed after the country's liberation, lesbian and gay victims of National Socialism were not eligible for support or compensation. Cynically, the state even refused to consider internment in Nazi concentration camps as a form of undue hardship. While other survivors of the camps were allowed to figure their imprisonment in the calculation of their state-sponsored retirement plans, homosexual inmates had no such rights. Even with the abolition of the *Totalverbot* in 1971, this rule remained in force, as the postwar state continued to punish Nazism's homosexual victims.[2]

The redress of this continued injustice was one of HOSI's earliest and most persistent demands. But even in the late 1980s, when the Green Party took up the issue in Austria's parliament, the government categorically refused to alter its position. As the secretary of social affairs — a Social Democratic appointee — noted in September 1988, the persecution of homosexuals during the Third Reich had not been a "specific" result of "National Socialist ideology" — a fact that continued to render moot the question of compensation.[3] A few weeks after this statement, the state demonstrated its disregard for the lesbian/gay victims of National Socialism with brute force. On November 24, HOSI and Rosa Lila Villa decided to take the unveiling of Alfred Hrdlicka's Monument against War and Fascism as the occasion for a peaceful protest against Austria's long-standing policy. At earlier events commemorating the fiftieth anniversary of the *Anschluss,* the organization had carried a banner demanding justice for the "Thousands of homosexual concentration camp victims waiting for rehabilitation." However, when a small group of activists unfurled the poster at the Hrdlicka monument's unveiling, the situation escalated. At the apparent behest of municipal representatives, police demanded the banner's removal, and when the demonstrators asked for a reason for the request, a large group of policemen snatched the banner from them, prompting a scuffle that injured two activists.[4] No justification for the police action was ever given, but in a subsequent letter to HOSI, Mayor Helmut Zilk made clear that the authorities regarded the demand for compensation of homosexual Nazi victims a provocation. "I find it inappropriate to the highest degree," he wrote, "that your group took it upon itself to 'appropriate' a large event for its own purposes." Political victims and their descendants had not demonstrated, even though "that would have made a lot more sense to me than your banner."[5] Over the next months, the state upheld Zilk's assessment of the incident. In the weeks after the event, authorities rejected a number of HOSI complaints, and when the organization turned to Austria's highest court to demand its right to assembly and free expression, its members learned that their peaceful protest had constituted a disruption of a "solemn commemoration," which justified the police action against them.[6] Until the late 1980s, the demand for recognition of homosexuals' suffering under the Nazis had no place in Austria's political field.

Within a few years, however, the situation changed markedly. In the context of the state's intensified *Vergangenheitsbewältigung* (dealing with the past) — a result of perceived international pressure — the fate of homosexual Nazi victims received renewed attention. At the same time, HOSI continued its lobbying on behalf of lesbian/gay survivors; in 1992, the efforts yielded the first tangible results. That year, Austria's state pension system for the first time granted a request to consider years of concentration camp internment in the calculation of retirement benefits. In financial terms, the ruling had only minor implications. On a symbolic level, however, it marked a drastic departure, effectively eradicating the construction of homosexuals' imprisonment as an appropriate punishment for criminal activity.[7] A few years later, the Austrian state made its new stance explicit when it included lesbians and gay men as potential benefactors of the National Fund for the Victims of National Socialism.[8] Following the fund's 1995 creation, the state and its representatives put the new position into practice. In addition to the compensation for individual victims of Nazi persecution, which commenced in 1997, the late 1990s witnessed such events as a 1998 speech by Austria's parliamentary president at the memorial plaque to National Socialism's homosexual victims at Mauthausen and the 1999 appointment of a scholar to research the fate of lesbians and gay men under Nazism for the state-sponsored Historians' Commission.[9] As early as 1994, HOSI had welcomed the "acknowledgment and restitution of homosexual Nazi victims" as a "great success" for the lesbian/gay movement.[10] Indeed, the developments of the following years signaled an unprecedented recognition of homosexuals by the Austrian state. Rather than figuring as a criminal fringe outside the boundaries of the national community, lesbians and gay men were now imagined as a group whose history of suffering needed to be integrated and redressed in the process of Austria's postnational reinvention.[11]

A similar trajectory characterized the development of the anti-lesbian/gay statutes in Austria's penal code. There too, the logic of legal abjection was only challenged effectively in the final decade of the twentieth century, when the country's homophobic legislation came into conflict with European standards. HOSI, of course, had lobbied for the abolition of the discriminatory paragraphs since its founding in 1980, but for years the organization's efforts were rebuffed, even by the Austrian left. Whereas the Green Party had campaigned on an antihomophobic platform since its inception in 1983,[12] the Social Democratic Party backed the preservation of the status quo until the end of the 1980s. In 1989, the SPÖ gave its support to HOSI's demand for the abolition of the country's anti-lesbian/gay laws.[13] At that point, however, the party was no longer in a position to push a reform through parliament. Until 1983, Social Democrats had enjoyed an absolute majority in parliament, and even during the subsequent coalition with the FPÖ — which, in the years prior to Jörg Haider's 1986 takeover, was committed to a broadly liberal agenda — the party could have abolished Austria's homophobic legislation. In 1989, however, the party was in a coalition with the ÖVP, and while Social Democrats promoted a number of reform initiatives in the early 1990s, the Christian Social Party ensured that §§209, 220, and 221 remained on the books.[14]

It was not until Austria joined the Eurpean Union that the pressure for legislative reform began to translate into legal changes. In many ways, European pressure had been mounting for over a decade. As early as 1981, the Parliamentary Assembly of the European Council issued a recommendation designed to curb homosexuals' legal subordination, and in 1984, the European Community championed an antihomophobic agenda when the European Parliament voted for a resolution designed to fight discrimination against lesbians and gay men at the workplace.[15] Numerous other initiatives followed as the organization transformed itself into the European Union; in 1994, these efforts resulted in an affirmative vote on a wide-ranging declaration that demanded full equality for lesbians and gay men in all areas of criminal and civil law. In this vote, the European Parliament acted on a report compiled by the EU Committee for Basic Freedoms and Inner Affairs, and while the resolution was not binding for individual member states, it clearly signaled the Union's pluralizing trajectory toward lesbian/gay equality. The declaration not only envisioned anti-discrimination legislation and the possibility of registered partnerships, but specifically criticized those countries that had a different age of consent for heterosexuals and homosexuals or inhibited the social visibility of lesbians and gay men.[16]

Austria joined the EU at the very moment the organization intensified its efforts on behalf of lesbians and gay men. In that context, the country's overtly homophobic legislation not only appeared as an obstruction of the European quest for lesbian/gay equality, but came to be seen as an embarrassing blemish on a state desperately seeking to demonstrate its *Europareife* (maturity for Europe). This conjuncture put unprecedented pressure on Austria's legislature, and within a few months of the country's entry into the European Union, renewed efforts were underway to repeal Austria's anti-lesbian/gay laws. After much deliberation in committees, the proposed abolition of §§209, 220, and 221 came to a parliamentary vote in the fall of 1996. In the process, the latter two statutes were eliminated, while the vote on the former produced a tie that kept Austria's unequal age of consent on the books.[17]

In many ways, the decision reflected Austria's juridical custom. In practice, neither the interdiction of propaganda for same-sex sexual relations nor the prohibition of lesbian/gay organizations was enforced, although a few cases had been prosecuted as late as the early 1990s. As early as 1979, the toleration of HOSI signaled the state's reluctance to police the sexual purity of Austria's national sphere; and by the time the lesbian/gay presence exploded into the Regenbogen Parade, it was clear that Vienna's social realities had exceeded the law's reach. If the formal elimination of §§220 and 221 thus constituted a symbolic realignment, the situation was quite different in regard to §209. There the longstanding project of ensuring the nation's heteronormative reproduction continued to be enforced, in fact remaining central to the social vision championed by Austria's conservative parties. Indeed, when the ÖVP and FPÖ blocked the abolition of §209 in the 1996 vote, showing near unanimity, they acted in the interests of protecting Austria's body politic. As Maria Fekter, the Christian social chair of the Parliament's Judicial Committee put it in a discussion following the vote, "For us, heterosexual love is the desirable state." The "most liberal countries also have [the] greatest number of homosexuals. . . . That is not desirable . . . [and] I don't accept that society is given an orientation that is undesirable."[18] In the same debate, Martin Graf, an FPÖ member of the judicial committee, seconded the sentiment when he opposed "talk of an open, pluralistic society" with his insistence that "human rights can be curtailed — if the matter is justified and if it is accepted by the population."[19]

The ÖVP and FPÖ may have sought to safeguard Austria's body politic, but in a rapidly integrating Europe, the legal autonomy of individual states was waning. In this context, international pressure to abolish §209 was mounting, especially given that the EU was dedicated to championing the very open and pluralistic society Austria's conservative parties opposed on nationalist and religious grounds. More than any other document, the Amsterdam Treaty signaled the EU's commitment to fight the legal subordination of lesbians and gay men. Negotiated in 1996–97 and ratified in 1999, the treaty expanded the founding charter of the European Union, paying particular attention to the question of human rights. Article Thirteen of the document professed a commitment to oppose discrimination on the basis of gender, race, ethnicity, religion, disability, age, and sexual orientation. The inclusion of the latter was an unprecedented recognition of lesbians and gay men as a group whose basic rights needed special protection, and although the treaty of Amsterdam enunciated fundamental principles rather than binding laws, its acceptance by the fifteen member states — Austria among them — was widely seen as a milestone on the path toward a European future of lesbian/gay equality.[20] Furthermore, the Amsterdam Treaty was backed up by the full might of the European Union. With the EU's growing commitment to the protection of lesbian/gay rights, Austria became a target of the European Parliament. On five occasions between 1997 and 2000, the country was "urgently called upon" to "abolish the laws against homosexuals."[21]

With pressure from the European Union mounting steadily, the elimination of §209 had become a virtual certainty by the turn of the century. By that time, other international agencies, ranging from the European Human Rights Commission to the United Nations Committee for Human Rights had condemned Austria for its legal enforcement of unequal ages of consent,[22] and within Austria, the front of vocal opponents expanded rapidly. Social Democrats and Greens had embraced antihomophobic platforms years before, but as mass-media discourse shifted toward a persistent critique of Austria's legal isolation, they were joined by new political allies. By the end of the 1990s, several FPÖ members came out in opposition of §209. Shortly thereafter, a debate on §209 took place within the ÖVP. As a Christian social party closely allied with Austria's Catholic Church, the ÖVP had always been uncompromising in regard to lesbian/gay issues. And while the party's official position had not changed in 2001, the public defenders of the country's homophobic legislation had grown increasingly silent. At the same time, a number of prominent ÖVP members began to respond to the ever-increasing pressure on Austria by calling for the elimination of the remaining homophobic statute in the country's penal code. As Bernhard Görg, chairman of the Vienna ÖVP, put it, it simply "won't be possible to hold on" to §209.[23]

Given this national and international constellation, it was exceedingly likely that Austria would abandon its discriminatory age of consent law in the near future. With the battle over the consent law nearly won, the debate shifted to civil law. By the turn of the century, the quest for registered partnerships for same-sex couples came to occupy the lesbian/gay movement and its supporters. Once more, the transnational domain of the European Union provided the immediate impulse for this model of

legal recognition. The Amsterdam Treaty provided a basis for the institutionalization of "gay marriage" as the only viable means to combat discrimination against lesbians and gay men in regard to such statutes as
inheritance law, tax law, and immigration law. And registered partnerships
were, in fact, becoming exceedingly common in other EU countries.

The demand for registered partnerships had been advanced by Austria's lesbian/gay movement for well over a decade, but in the European
context the issue gained wider political currency. A 1998 initiative spear-
headed by an ad hoc activist group on the occasion of Austria's temporary
EU presidency exemplified this dynamic. Under the motto "E(u)quality
now," it comprised a series of events designed to highlight the disjunc-
tures between European principles of nondiscrimination and Austria's
legal realities. To "render Austria fit for Europe," the campaign suggested, the country needed to overcome its position as "tail end in
human rights for lesbians and gay men." The "securing of [same-sex] partnerships" would do much to alleviate the situation. Whereas similar arguments had been made in the past, their rearticulation in a European
framework resulted in an unprecedented level of political support.[24]
Indeed, by 1999, the introduction of registered partnerships was championed not only by the Green Party, but also by the SPÖ, which officially
adopted the cause as part of its program for legal reform.[25] Neither
Greens nor Social Democrats were in Austria's government after the
national elections of 1999, but a future change of government would
almost certainly bring legal recognition of same-sex couples. Even without a change in government, the extension of civil rights to lesbians and
gay men was a possibility. As with §209, the first years of the new century
brought extensive debates within Austria's conservative parties; by 2001,
a number of their members openly advocated the "legal acceptance of
same-sex life partnerships."[26] Much of this support for lesbian/gay concerns was a result of European pressure; and it was in that sense that the
Styrian ÖVP politician Gerhard Hirschmann predicted the imminent
recognition of homosexual couples by rendering the development in a
distinctly Catholic idiom: Registered partnerships would "come to
Austria too, just like the 'Amen' in prayer."[27]

Municipal Affirmations

By the turn of the twenty-first century, the federal recognition of les-
bian/gay rights was clearly underway. Given the country's conservative
majority, however, it was a slow process that received much of its impe-

tus from Austria's membership in the supranational structure of the European Union. If international pressure was working on the state, Vienna provided a model of lesbian/gay recognition. There the affirmative anchoring of queers in the city's public sphere had become official policy, and by the turn of the century, the municipality figured not only as the organizer and patron of numerous lesbian/gay cultural events, but as the country's foremost champion of political rights for queers. As the Austrian state moved toward toleration, the city of Vienna pioneered the far more radical agenda of lesbian/gay advancement. In doing so, the municipality was guided by the political recognition of ever-growing lesbian/gay visibility, as well as a desire to reimagine Vienna in the terms of a contemporary cosmopolitanism that was associated, at least in part, with the presence of a vibrant queer community.

Vienna's Life Ball — an annual AIDS charity event held since 1993 — pioneered and exemplified the municipality's emergent affirmation of the city's queers. Such an event could take place several years prior to the Regenbogen Parade because of the Life Ball's constituency as well as its cause. Because it was for AIDS victims, the event could be figured in ambiguous terms: it was not officially marked as a gay event on account of the other groups stricken by the epidemic. The Life Ball could be presented as a municipal effort in the realm of social medicine.

In this manner, the charity event continued the seemingly paradoxical development brought on by the onset of AIDS in the early 1980s. While the disease engendered panic and caused dozens of lost lives in Vienna's gay male scene, it also led to a new kind of attention by the state apparatus. Prior to the 1980s, official Austria's interactions with homosexuals had only served to subordinate them in the interests of national homogenization. In the context of AIDS and the impending health crisis, however, the state recognized male homosexuals as a target group for social medicine — an unprecedented construction that produced the state's first affirmative intervention into gay male lives. Even more importantly, AIDS fundamentally altered the state's position vis-à-vis Austria's lesbian/gay organizations. Drawing on the country's long tradition of social welfare policies, groups like HOSI now became allies in a common fight against a disease whose epidemiological pattern indicated a progression from gay men to other groups in the general population. As early as March of 1983, this new configuration had led to an unprecedented collaboration between HOSI and Vienna's city councilor for health issues, resulting in the production of Europe's first AIDS education brochure.[28] Two years later, the new coalition between lesbian/gay organizations and the state enabled the founding of the Österreichische AIDS-Hilfe (Austrian AIDS-Help), a national organization headed by HOSI chairman Reinhardt Brandstätter and generously funded by the federal Ministry of Health.[29] The organization foundered by the late 1980s, in part because of the difficulty associated with conducting AIDS work at the federal level. The health-based alliance between lesbian/gay organizations and state agencies continued, however, and when municipal organizations like the AIDS-Hilfe Wien were founded in the early 1990s, they came to anchor the state's ongoing commitment not only to the fight against the disease but to the affirmative inclusion of lesbian/gay organizations in the struggle.[30] Indeed, the 1990s witnessed numerous initiatives, including the 1994 AIDS Information Weeks at Vienna's city hall and the 1997 opening of the AIDS-Hilfe Haus, a spacious headquarters for the municipally funded organization.[31]

Vienna's Life Ball originated in this context. The brainchild of Gery Keszler, an openly gay member of Austria's fashion industry, it seized the state's history of AIDS work as a vehicle for queer legitimation. When approaching the municipality with the plan for a charity event, Keszler emphasized the universal quality of the struggle against AIDS. The fundraiser would be part of a wide array of state-supported efforts to combat the disease, thereby functioning as a logical extension of the city's social welfare policies. While Keszler stressed the generality of the event in his dealings with the mainstream media, his appeal to the lesbian/gay scene was more specific. In large advertisements in the lesbian/gay press, he promoted an explicitly queer event to be held at the heart of Vienna's symbolic geography.[32] Keszler had managed to secure the lavish banquet rooms of Vienna's city hall, and his multipage announcements featured prominent photos of the famous halls where Vienna's queers would soon be dancing for a good cause. The caption further reinforced the promise of lesbian/gay appropriation: the ball would be a "spectacle of extravagance" whose success depended on queers' willingness to "come and be fabulous!" In this spirit, Keszler encouraged participants to "be romantic, hysterical, extravagant, shrill, and beautiful. Against the clichés the public imprints upon us." The event would take place at the center of municipal power, but, as Keszler reminded his lesbian/gay readers, "It is your ball."

Held May 29, 1993, Vienna's first Life Ball was a considerable success. Incorporating such features as fashion shows and costume competitions, it expanded on the traditional format of Viennese balls, and with 1,800 visitors, it raised a substantial amount of money for a number of AIDS

organizations. The event was even more successful, however, in its promotion of queer culture. Widely covered in Austria's mainstream media,
it normalized and magnified the queer presence at Vienna's symbolic center to an unprecedented degree.[33] The daring costumes and stunning displays of skin dominated the reporting; while some media outlets were
squeamish about identifying participants as members of the lesbian/gay
scene, the event's queer nature was self-evident.

With the success of the first Life Ball, Keszler was emboldened to turn
the charity event into an annual occasion. Over the years, the festivities at
city hall steadily grew, not only in terms of attendance and financial out-
put, but also in its social standing and coverage in Austria's mass media.
By 1994, the Life Ball already admitted 3,500 visitors; in 1995, it became
part of the Wiener Festwochen, the city's annual high culture festival held
in the spring.[34] In the process, the Life Ball became an increasingly official
occasion. While Vienna's queers continued to give the event its character
and color, it became a required stop for the country's political and cultural
elite. Indeed, by the mid-1990s, neither the chancellor nor the mayor of
Vienna would miss a Life Ball; by the end of the decade, only the traditional Opernball rivaled it as the country's most popular social event.[35]

The institutionalization of the Life Ball hinted at the city's reorientation regarding lesbian/gay issues. But it was the municipality's response
to the Regenbogen Parade that fully exemplified the shift from a modern
logic of legal abjection to a pluralizing project of cultural celebration.
After all, the parade was not only conceived as an explicitly queer event,
but centered on the symbolic appropriation of Vienna's public space. As
such, it constituted an overt challenge to queers' national exclusion — a
situation that made the municipality's approach to the parade a principal
gauge for the state's trajectory on the question of homosexuality.

That trajectory, it turned out, was dramatic. In 1996, the year of the
first Regenbogen Parade, the city of Vienna had enacted a traditional
script of homosexual subordination. Although the event was protected by
the constitutional right of collective self-expression, the municipality
went out of its way to hinder the parade's realization. Hostile adminis-
trators deployed Austria's arcane bureaucracy to derail organizers' plans
for the parade route, and as late as May, the June event had still not
received the proper authorization.[36] Even when the permits were finally
granted, authorities remained cool, particularly the police, who accompanied the first Regenbogen Parade in near riot gear. Financially, too, the
city was unresponsive; parade organizers had to rely on donations and the
backing of Vienna's lesbian/gay commercial scene to finance the event.

At the turn of the century, the situation could not have been more different. By 1998, the city had discovered the Regenbogen Parade to be an effective vehicle for the performance and advertisement of Vienna's cosmopolitanism. In consequence, the municipality decided to support the parade financially, while using it to promote city tourism. The result could be gleaned in the pages of the *Pride Guide*. The state had been essentially absent from the 1996 and 1997 editions,[37] but in the glossy 1998 version, the first page displayed the logo of Vienna's municipal tourism agency. "Wien ist anders" (Vienna is different), the ad proclaimed, using a famous slogan whose early 1990s coinage had inspired the name for the queer culture festival Wien Ist Andersrum.[38] Over the next few years, the municipality's presence further increased. In 1999, Vienna's financial and institutional support was signaled by a full-page ad entitled "City of My Dreams . . . ," illustrated by photos of a flamboyant drag queen and a dyke on a bike, both taken at previous Regenbogen Parades, as well as a gay male couple pictured in a close embrace. In 2000, the city represented itself on the *Pride Guide*'s back cover with the pun "Wien 2000–Event findet Stadt" (Vienna 2000 — An Event Finds a City/Takes Place).[39]

However, nothing exemplified the state's emerging support for the Regenbogen Parade and its project of publicly affirmative queer representation more than the remarks by Vienna's politicians included in the *Pride Guide*. In 1996, the parade organizers failed to secure a statement of support from the city's Social Democratic mayor, Michael Häupl. Instead, Vienna's deputy mayor, Grete Lasker, offered a short and tepid note in which she sought to assuage the "dear gay people" with the assurance of her ongoing struggle against all forms of "intolerance and hate."[40] By 1999, the tone had changed markedly. Mayor Häupl himself was now identified as the author of city hall's greeting. More importantly, the text identified the Regenbogen Parade as an "event for tolerance and cosmopolitanism" and hence a vital component of Vienna's urban landscape:

The Regenbogen Parade stands for a diversity of lifestyles, for the cooperation of all against all forms of discrimination. It is a beautiful expression of the atmosphere of our city, which is characterized by liberalism, freedom, solidarity, and dynamism.[41]

Häupl's words in 1999 were just a prelude to his comments in 2001. That year witnessed a wholly unprecedented level of municipal support for the Regenbogen Parade and its pluralizing agenda. In 1998, parade backers had secured the right to host the 2001 installment of Europride, a rotating festival that bestowed the designation of European lesbian/gay capital on a different city each year. Vienna's Europride was conceived as an ambitious month-long series of cultural and political events, culminating in the largest Regenbogen Parade yet. Given Vienna's emerging commitment to sexual pluralism and the growing sense of lesbian/gay tourism's economic potential, Europride was assured the support of city hall. With the inauguration in 2000 of an ÖVP/FPÖ federal administration, however, the festival took on even greater importance. For the Social Democrats controlling Vienna's political field, it was an opportunity to showcase the city as a model for a Europeanized Austria — a space where the affirmation of previously abject groups signaled a commitment to the standards of political liberalism espoused by the European Union. Thus Häupl expressed his "very special pleasure" that "this year's Europride was held in Vienna." Not only would "representatives from all over Europe take part in the many events," but they would help "make Vienna even more colorful."[42] But the city's support extended far beyond such words of encouragement. Multiplying the sponsorship of previous years, the municipality emerged as the principal backer not only of the Regenbogen Parade but of the many events — ranging from film series to exhibits — that were staged under the aegis of Europride.[43] Even Vienna's cityscape reflected the municipality's commitment to queer affirmation. An enormous Rainbow Flag was hoisted from the city's tallest building, the Donauturm (Danube Tower), and Vienna's streetcars were similarly adorned with the international symbol of lesbian/gay pride. In 1988, the city's advertisement and transit authorities had categorically refused to mount posters designed by a coalition of lesbian/gay and women's organizations that carried the slogan "Lesbians are always and everywhere."[44] In 2001, Vienna's entire public transportation system constructed the city as a positively queer space.

By the turn of the century, Vienna's municipal authorities were among the principal backers of queer cultural initiatives. Even more enduring and tangible, however, was the city's political support for lesbian/gay concerns. That support was institutionalized in the Wiener Antidiskriminierungsstelle für Gleichgeschlechtliche Lebensweisen (Vienna Office for Nondiscrimination Against Same-Sex Lifestyles). In general terms, the Wiener Antidiskriminierungsstelle (WA) followed German, Scandinavian, and British models of municipal offices for lesbian/gay affairs. However, in the context of Austria's political field, its creation was a function of the SPÖ's shift toward an explicitly antihomophobic position. Given the conservative majority, that shift generated only limited reform at the federal level, but in Vienna, which maintained a left-of-center majority throughout the Second Republic, it engendered concrete measures, not least because of the additional pressure for progressive reform exerted by the left-wing Green Party. That constellation produced the political agenda for the creation of a municipal office for lesbian/gay affairs, and ÖVP concerns notwithstanding, the section was created in October 1998, officially as a branch of the Department of Women's, Minority, and Consumer Affairs.[45]

In political and judicial terms, the WA was principally charged with a review of Viennese law. The explicit goal was to identify and end all forms of municipal discrimination, a goal that was quickly achieved when executive orders guaranteed queers visitation rights at Vienna's hospitals, allowed lesbian/gay municipal employees time off to take care of significant others, and strengthened provisions giving same-sex partners the right to sign leases for city-owned apartments.[46] Most aspects of queer discrimination, however, were grounded in federal law. While the WA was conceived as a model institution for Austria at large, the office had its main impact in Vienna's social field, where it enacted and embodied the state's changing relation to homosexuality.

In that regard, it was crucial that city authorities chose two prominent lesbian/gay activists — a long-term member of the Rosa Lila Villa and an accomplished AIDS worker in Vienna's gay male scene — to staff the WA, and that the institution's office was located inside city hall. As a large Rainbow Flag in the WA windows announced the queering of Vienna's municipality, the office's concrete practices fused lesbian/gay activism and municipal politics. Much like HOSI and Rosa Lila Villa, the WA offered free anonymous counseling and advice, helped organize political events and workshops, and joined the effort of educating the larger public about homosexuality. The state had joined the movement. Not only would the WA serve as a liaison between the city and its lesbian/gay groups, but it would itself take part in the longstanding struggle for queer rights.[47]

Nothing exemplified the municipality's new orientation more drastically, visibly, and enduringly than the WA web page, which went online in 2000.[48] Prominently located on the city's official web page, "Wien-online," the vast site immediately became Austria's most comprehensive electronic resource on issues of same-sex sexuality. Even more importantly, it transported an unequivocally proqueer message. Written entirely by WA staff, it not only conveyed an explicitly antipathologizing discourse on questions of homosexuality's etiology, but constructed the subordination of queers as a form of social disease.[49] In so doing, the web

page closely followed the traditional rhetoric of the lesbian/gay movement, including strong condemnations of Austria's antigay penal code
and discriminatory civil law.[50] However, the web page was not dominated
by such critiques. Instead, the WA focused most of its attention on the
explication of queer lifeworlds. To that end, the authors not only
addressed the concept of sexual orientation and its attendant stereotypes,
but offered an explanation of the salient terms and symbols of queer existence.[51] In conjunction with links addressed to those who were questioning their sexuality ("I believe I am lesbian"), these explications functioned as a veritable coming-out guide, replete with practical advice on
"how do I tell my parents?"[52] Comprehensive listings and explanations of
Vienna's queer infrastructure, from the city's lesbian/gay organizations to
its commercial scene, reinforced the web page's broadly affirmative
stance.[53] In 1988, Vienna's municipally controlled school board had successfully sued HOSI's youth group to halt dissemination of material pertaining to lesbian/gay concerns at the city's educational institutions.[54]
Twelve years later, the municipality had not only abandoned its efforts to
safeguard Vienna's sexual homogeneity but, through the office of the WA,
had emerged as the city's most effective and powerful proponent of a plu-
ralizingly queer future.

Mass-Media Echoes

The state's late-twentieth-century shift toward an affirmative construction
of same-sex sexuality did not take place in a discursive vacuum. Rather,
it was accompanied and partially engendered by a transformation in
Austria's mass-media discourse. Much like the positions of federal and
municipal authorities, the media's transformation occurred quite sud-
denly in the mid-1990s, reflecting the political and cultural dynamics of
the period, from the increasing legal pressures exerted on Austria in the
wake of the country's EU membership and international trends in the
construction of queers to the forceful emergence of Vienna's lesbians and
gay men into the city's public sphere. In conjunction with the state's new
position, whose mass-media representation itself accounted for part of the
discursive transformation, these dynamics produced a form of coverage
that radically broke with previous depictions of homosexuality as an
inherently deviant phenomenon.

Predictably, the new mass-media discourse on homosexuality was
pioneered in Austria's left-leaning and alternative press. Such publications

as *Profil* were responsible for much of the country's coverage of lesbian/
gay issues from the 1970s through the early 1990s. But while the representation of homosexuality itself had a counterhegemonic effect, the periodical's tone reproduced the dominant discourse, particularly in its mock-
ing construction of the lesbian/gay movement and its concomitant
indifference to the plight it was protesting. *Profil*'s coverage continued to
display these characteristics as late as the Outing affair of summer 1995.
By the fall of that same year, however, the publication's stance had
markedly changed; the resulting three-part series on "Homosexuality in
Austria" initiated a new era in the representation of the country's queers.[55]
A publishing project of unprecedented breadth and depth, the series not
only recalled the suffering of homosexuals at the hands of the Nazis and
postwar Austria's refusal to grant lesbians and gay men official victim status, but took a strong stance against ongoing discrimination.[56] Where
Profil broke truly new ground, however, was in the series' final installment, which attempted an affirmative representation of lesbian/gay lifeworlds.[57] In previous decades, reports from the "scene" were inevitably
framed in terms of criminality and shame; while *Profil* did note the
oppressive secrecy of much of lesbian/gay life, the magazine went out of
its way to chronicle and extol recent developments that had given
Vienna's queers unprecedented visibility. In particular, *Profil* commented
on the city's burgeoning nightlife, which owed much to the ingenuity of
openly gay promoters.

   Both in the United States and Western Europe, the early and mid-
1990s had seen the emergence of "lesbian and gay chic" — a late capital-
ist construction of queers as stylish trendsetters and performative experts
on urban consumption. In its invocation of Vienna's flourishing club
scene, *Profil*'s series gestured to this image. But it was the mainstream
magazine *News* — the country's most widely read weekly publication —
that fully imported it into the Austrian context. The occasion for the path-
breaking representation was the approaching Life Ball of 1996. Over the
years, the event had given rise to repeated media coverage, much of it
devoted to the suffering brought on by AIDS. *News,* by contrast, ignored
the ball's cause and glossed over homophobia and its various articulations.
Instead, the magazine devoted an eight-page spread in the May 1996 issue
to the celebration of gay male culture, which it identified as the principal
motor of fashion and style.[58] Under the title "In Gay Company," the article opened with a double-page photo of seven good-looking Austrian
men, smiling and offering tidbits on the ease of an openly gay male existence. "All people who know me accept me," read one, while another

noted, "We gays no longer want to hide — why should we?" Indeed, in the world conjured up by *News,* (male) homosexuality bestowed a decidedly positive distinction, enhancing social life in general. "Gays are more creative and sensitive than heterosexual men," yet another quote sanctioned by *News* stated, which is why "gays bring zip into the life of heteros." If anything, the article's subsequent text magnified the theme of Austrian culture's indebtedness to its gay male representatives. As such, queers were not only identified as purveyors of taste ("Gays as trendsetters"), but their pleasure-affirming "gay lifestyle" was held up as a model for late-twentieth-century existence.[59]

Although *News*'s celebration of gay male culture as the quintessence of consumer capitalism was not common in Austria's mass media, it was part of a larger trajectory that replaced a set of criminalizing and pathologizing stereotypes with the assemblage of affirmative representations that came to characterize constructions of homosexuality in the late 1990s. Nothing exemplified this development more clearly than the mass media's coverage of the Regenbogen Parade. In its first year, the parade was described by the press with the same indifference that had defined coverage of the lesbian/gay movement since its inception. Most newspapers ignored the 1996 event entirely; the few outlets that devoted some coverage to the parade constructed it in the traditional logic of homosexual abjection. A short piece published in the centrist *Kurier,* for example, mixed deliberately partial information with spiteful cynicism.[60] Quoting the police's attendance estimate instead of the organizers', the paper lampooned the Regenbogen Parade for its inability to mobilize more than 2,500 participants, which meant that the "demonstrating gays, lesbians, and transsexuals were in the minority" vis-à-vis the 8,000 spectators who had dared a "peak onto the 'other side of the shore.'" In the remaining text, *Kurier* failed to note the event's political dimension, attributing it instead to a "desire to make a public nuisance," giving added weight to the paper's complaint about the severe disruption of traffic.

Only a year later, the discourse had shifted entirely. As coverage of the Regenbogen Parade increased, so did the media's sympathy for the cause. Most telling, perhaps, was the article in *Kurier.*[61] A year after dismissing the initial parade, the paper opened its piece with a headline announcing the participation of thirty thousand people at the second Regenbogen Parade. This time, the number came from the organizers; the police estimate was mocked for its implausibility ("The police prefers to count only five thousand"). Moreover, the 1997 article recognized the worth of the parade's demand for the "equality of homosexuals in our society"; as a consequence, the participants were no longer a public nuisance but "colorful and smart," appropriate to the event's "exuberant atmosphere." At the end of the 1990s, such phrases characterized the parade's coverage across the mass-media spectrum; by the year 2000, even the right-wing *Neue Kronen Zeitung* celebrated Vienna's queers for their ability to turn the city's Ringstraße into a "colorful and shiny dance floor."[62]

Indeed, by the turn of the century, the old images of homosexual abjection had all but disappeared from Austria's mass media. As more and more coverage was devoted to lesbian/gay issues in the print media and queers became commonplace on Austrian television — as subjects of sympathetic reports, talk show guests, participants in reality shows, and characters in television movies — public homophobia seemed increasingly inappropriate.[63] Instead, the normative position came to be defined in terms of explicit, or at least implicit, support for lesbian/gay concerns — a situation that characterized the unprecedented media coverage generated by Europride in June of 2001. From such left-leaning publications as the daily *Standard* and the weekly *Falter,* whose extensive reporting of the "rainbow over the city" extolled Vienna's ascent to "capital of gay Europe," to the state newspaper *Wiener Zeitung,* which echoed the organizers' call for the "breakdown of borders [and] the demand for European standards," the more conservative *Kurier,* which celebrated Vienna's queers' "self-confidence and lust for life," and *Die Presse,* the principal newspaper of Austria's right, where critical articles on the country's lackluster record on lesbian/gay rights were paired with lavish praise for Europride's film festival, Austria's mass media had adopted the emerging rhetoric of queer affirmation.[64] Within little more than five years, the country's public discourse had shifted from a hegemonic project of national purification to a postnational project of sexual heterogenization.

New Queer Subjects

It is difficult to ascertain whether lesbian/gay initiatives or the shifting positions of the state were primarily responsible for the late-twentieth-century transformations in Vienna's queer environs. As mutually reinforcing sets of factors, they both contributed to the ethnographic realities I observed in the course of fieldwork. But while a causal explanation would oscillate between lesbian/gay resistance and dominant modes of reproduction, the ethnographic realities themselves are beyond doubt.

Simply put, in the years of my research, Vienna's queer infrastructure came to be marked by an unprecedented degree of openness. Whereas the homosexual scene had remained clandestine for most of the Second Republic, the conjunction of resistive visibility and legal, political, and discursive liberalization engendered a publicly queer lifeworld that took shape in the middle of the city's urban topography.

The momentous shift could be traced in the pages of *Spartacus*. In the 1970s, the gay male travel guide had painted a bleak picture of a completely hidden gay scene with bars that sought to disguise the nature of their clientele.[65] By the late 1990s, the guide's entries for Vienna presented an altogether different image, and in 2000, the authors recommended the city without reservation to the discerning gay male traveler:

In the last years much has changed, the legal regulations were loosened. The change in climate had its greatest effect in Vienna, the (gay) capital of Austria. With its colorful and lively scene, it now occupies a leading position in the German-speaking world.[66]

The *Spartacus* staff was right, of course. In the second half of the 1990s, numerous entrepreneurs had followed the model of the Café Berg by opening proudly lesbian/gay-identified bars and restaurants; by the turn of the century, around ten such businesses had been established. But the new openness also affected Vienna's traditional gay male locales. Until the early 1990s, these bars had sought to shield themselves and their patrons from suspicion through such features as doorbells, peepholes, and darkened windows. At the end of the decade, some of these features could still be found, but, with the exception of one or two bars, they were no longer in operation. At the Alte Lampe, Vienna's oldest gay bar, use of the doorbell was abandoned in the late 1990s. Instead, the bar left the door open, except in cold weather, when the door was closed but unlocked. By 2001, the bar's proprietor had gone even further in integrating his establishment into Vienna's newly visible lesbian/gay scene. When a Rainbow Flag was installed on the bar's facade next to the lamp that gave the establishment its name, the Alte Lampe announced itself as a gay bar for the first time in its long existence.

The opening of Vienna's queer community correlated with significant transformations in the process of lesbian/gay subjectification. Whereas the clandestine nature of the postwar period's homosexual scene had kept homosexuals in the closet, the new situation presented a radically different alternative. This is not to say that the changes of the late twentieth century abolished traditional modes of homosexual being. On the contrary, as a putative majority of Austria's lesbians and gay men remained in the closet, the legacy of subordination continued to operate. Indeed, I conducted numerous interviews with men and women who, although often aware of the social transformations going on around them, either feared disclosure of their sexual orientation or considered their closeted existence a comfortable situation.

However, the widespread persistence of the closet should not obscure the momentous shifts that took place in the lives of Vienna's lesbians and gay men. Predictably, these shifts were most apparent among the members of the younger generation, who emerged as the principal bearers of a new queer subjectivity. Precise quantification would be impossible, but it is clear that people born in the late 1970s and early 1980s had an altogether different approach to the question of homosexuality than those who had come of age before them. Socialized into a lesbian/gay scene marked by the openness of the Café Berg and the Regenbogen Parade and witnessing the receding disapprobation by the state's hegemonic apparatuses, a definite majority of that generation experienced the realization of their same-sex sexual proclivities not as the traumatic entrance into an abject existence, but as part of an affirmative lifecourse. In that context, the issue of disclosure no longer posed itself in the inherently political terms of the early lesbian/gay movement. Rather it became associated with the kind of naturalness espoused by the organizers of the Regenbogen Parade. Queerness neither required concealment nor functioned as a resistive act. Instead it could be incorporated into a public persona that took it for granted.

During my fieldwork, I conducted countless formal and informal interviews that documented the newly public subjectivity engendered in the environs of Vienna's open lesbian/gay scene. The narrative of Clemens, whose experience of homophobia in junior high school was briefly mentioned in Chapter 2, was paradigmatic. Born in 1975, he came of age at the very moment Vienna's lesbian/gay scene emerged into the city's public sphere. "I encountered gayness as a totally natural thing," he told me in 2000:

The [Rosa Lila] Villa was totally important, and I remember when the [Café] Berg was opened. It was just great that there were all these men who were into other men — that was exciting and beautiful. And it was just so normal, just like you would go into any other bar. There was this kind of naturalness about it all, and I just felt right at home. It was just ok, and I realized that this was a very important part of me — homosexuality was this central part of me — and therefore it was important for me to tell other people.

The lesbian/gay scene was described to me in similarly affirmative terms by numerous young queers. "I experienced the scene extremely positively," one man born in the early 1980s told me. "The [Café] Berg was such a cool place to hang out, and everyone there was just really relaxed about being gay. I sort of had my coming-out just by being there." A woman born in the late 1970s echoed these sentiments when she described her experiences in conjunction with the third Regenbogen Parade.

I had just joined the student group [at the University of Vienna], and when I was on their truck at the parade, I realized that there were all these places lesbians went to. I checked them out with a friend and it was just so cool. Then the Orlando [a restaurant under lesbian ownership] opened, and I totally felt at home there — it's this real community.

While such narratives attest to the lesbian/gay scene's constitutive role in the creation of openly queer subjects, other interviews revealed the importance of shifts in the wider cultural context. Indeed, by the late 1990s, it was commonplace to encounter people whose sense of an affirmative queer identity had developed prior to their encounter with the lesbian/gay scene. While earlier generations had to negotiate their same-sex sexual feelings in light of hegemonic discourses of homosexuality qua pathology and criminality, those who came of age in the late twentieth century frequently described exposure to radically different constructions of queerness. Thus I was told by a man in his late teens that "watching TV made it pretty clear to me that being gay was normal," while a woman born in 1982 noted that, growing up, she read "interesting things about homosexuality in the newspapers all the time."

For queers growing up in Vienna and its vicinity, shifts in the larger cultural field facilitated their discovery of an affirmative lesbian/gay scene. The transformation was even more momentous in Austria's provinces, where Catholicism and social conservatism had made the experience of homosexuality exceedingly complicated and painful. By the turn of twenty-first century, that pressure had eased considerably, and during my fieldwork, I encountered numerous queers whose move to Vienna was no longer motivated by a desperate attempt to escape the strictures of small-town or village life. Hans, a twenty-three-year-old insurance broker from Styria, gave me a typical account:

I figured out that I was gay when I was about sixteen. I lived in our village and there was nothing I could really do there, which was pretty frustrating. But I never thought that being gay was wrong or a problem. I just knew that there would be places to go in the city, and I did find them when I went to Graz [the capital of Styria] and then to Vienna, where the scene is just great.

With few exceptions, the stories of young queers were all characterized by a remarkable ease, both in the process of sexual self-discovery and the entrance into an openly lesbian/gay world. What is most striking, however, is the younger generation's readiness to be "out" in all spheres of existence. Indeed, of the dozens of young lesbians and gay men I interviewed, a good 80 percent shared their sexual orientation with all the people in their lives, including their families. Coming-out stories, in fact, were a central part of the narratives I collected; as in the case of Clemens, they usually turned on the experience of one's sexuality as inseparable from the rest of one's personality — a situation that rendered the concealment of homosexuality not an insistence on personal privacy, but a form of misrepresentation, even outright deceit. As Clemens put it,

Being gay is just too much of what I am to not tell my parents. I just couldn't lie about that. So after going out in the gay scene for a month or so — I was eighteen and a half — I decided I must tell them. I was very theatrical about it. I called and said: in the evening, all of you have to be at home, my sister too. I have to tell you something. So I announced it, and at first they were a bit shocked. But they came around pretty quickly. When we had the celebration for my high school graduation a few weeks later, my dad got up and told everyone how proud he was of me whether I was gay or hetero. Everyone was there, even my relatives from Germany.

Among my interlocutors, such reactions were not typical. But as a result of shifting discourses on homosexuality and a parental generation socialized in the more permissive 1960s and 1970s, reports of lasting hostility and rejection were exceedingly rare. More often I was told that reactions were essentially favorable, ranging from sympathetic understanding to pride and support, particularly after the initial surprise had worn off. Even more significant than the specific reaction, however, was the social reality produced by these widespread acts of sexual disclosure. Having grown up at a moment when the integration of homosexuality into one's public persona became at once possible and desirable, the new generation of lesbians and gay men became the bearers of an open queer subjectivity.

Having come of age during the prolonged period of homosexuality's constitutive subordination, older generations of queers had been denied access to a lesbian/gay trajectory that figured the coming-out process in affirmatively public terms. But if their socialization into an inherently clandestine homosexual scene had made their same-sex inclination a carefully guarded matter, their existence was also affected by the new queer subjectivity. To be sure, an overwhelming majority of older queers continued to negotiate their sexual orientation in the traditional manner, but as my fieldwork also made clear, the dynamics of the closet were rapidly changing, often producing hybrid states of "outness" in place of total privatization. In many instances, this meant that the 1990s brought decisive departures from previous ways of life, resulting in selective disclosures while keeping certain domains of the closet in place.

The case of Siegfried is paradigmatic. Born in 1952, he had lived a typical existence for much of his adult life. The veteran of a doomed, short-lived marriage and occasional forays into Vienna's homosexual scene, he was the archetype of a closeted gay man; when I interviewed him in 2000, he offered a typical rational for the concealment of his homosexuality to his family:

That is a part of my personality that has nothing to do with them — that is my private sphere. For my mother, this is just not a relevant topic. Nobody in my family would think to ask me about my sexual orientation. I suppose that I might address the issue if my mother asked me when I would finally get married again. But she has never asked anything like that, perhaps because she suspects the answer, perhaps because she doesn't want to hear it.

A quintessential expression of traditional attitudes, Siegfried's statement echoed other narratives offered to me by older queers. Like some others, however, it was no longer indicative of a fully closeted existence. While Siegfried had relied on the clandestine quality of the gay male scene to shield his sexual orientation from the 1970s through the early 1990s, he became a public figure in Vienna's emerging queer community in 1997, when he took over a leadership role in the city's lesbian/gay choir. In that capacity, he not only performed frequently in Vienna's lesbian/gay locales, but appeared at such public occasions as the Regenbogen Parade.

Siegfried's situation was by no means unusual. I talked to many older men and women who continued to veil their sexual orientation in some contexts while becoming highly visible as queers in others. From political activists who failed to confront their parents to a growing number of lesbians and gay men who were out to their families but passed for straight at work, the new queer visibility engendered complex subjectivities that fused traditional patterns of homosexual existence with the emerging lesbian/gay openness.

In a few cases, however, older queers themselves became exemplars of homosexuality's newly public face. Most famously, this happened in the mid-1990s, when two middle-aged celebrities — television personality Günter Tolar and actor Alfons Haider — came out of the closet to overwhelmingly positive reactions.[67] In the context of my fieldwork, however, it was Thomas who was most powerfully indicative of the radical transformations in lesbian/gay existence. Born in 1933, Thomas had been my main informant on homosexual life in the Vienna of the 1950s and 1960s — a period he described in the bleak terms rendered in Chapter 2. When I interviewed him in 2000, however, the emphasis of his narrative was not on past suffering. Rather, he focused his exuberant statement on his present situation as an active member of Vienna's recently founded bear club:[68]

When I came to the bears two years ago, I started to go out again, and so I got back into the scene [after being less involved in the 1980s and early 1990s]. And I just found it marvelous how freely people are moving and how open people are. Back then [in the 1950s and 1960s], you would only be like that with your very best gay friends. That led me so far that last year I outed myself to my closest relatives. My cousin said she was hardly surprised, and the others had no problem with it either. It is totally accepted and that's a good thing, because now I can talk more openly. In the old days, I never even had the idea that one could out oneself. You had to crawl around the place in secrecy. I was also able to do it [come out] because the bear club gave me a sense of security, so I was no longer isolated. And the reactions were just so positive; people just cheered me on.

Thomas's experience was unusual for an older gay man. Nonetheless, his ability to benefit from the newly affirmative construction of queerness typified a general development, one that had brought a sea change during his own lifetime. As symptoms of modernity, homosexuals had been violently subordinated in the interest of the national collectivity; by the turn of the twenty-first century, they were able to come out, cheered on by a state and its subjects who had come to think of queerness as part of a beautiful world.

CONCLUSION

Symptoms of Postmodernity

The chapters in this book charted parallel histories. They were designed to document that Jews and queers shared a common trajectory that organized their collective existence in late-twentieth-century Vienna. I glossed this trajectory under the headings of "Subordination," "Resistance," and "Reproduction" — a roughly chronological sequence that highlights a set of structural convergences. In the postwar era, Jews and homosexuals were subject to analogous regimes of inequity. In different ways, these took the form of legal misrecognition and outright persecution, aided by the powerful vehicles of mass-media discourse and public opinion. Explicitly or implicitly, the state deployed these technologies of abjection to effect the systematic exclusion of Jews and homosexuals from the nation's public sphere. It was not until the 1970s that a younger generation of Jews and queers began to contest their marginalization; when they did, they employed remarkably similar strategies of opposition that led from the development of political critiques to the creation of resistive cultural formations. Over time, these acts of defiance were met with less and less antagonism, and by the late 1990s, the ever-increasing presence of Jews and queers in Vienna's public sphere was not only abided but actively fostered by the state and its apparatuses.

In the introduction to this book, I argued that Jews and homosexuals functioned as the constitutive Others of a nationalist imaginary that

213

sought to fix its subject through coarticulated fictions of ethnic and sexual purity. The simultaneous production and subordination of these groups should be seen as the symptom of an exclusionary modernity. In the course of the twentieth century in Central Europe, this modern project found its most enduring expression in the nation-state; in this way, the trajectory of Jews and homosexuals doubles as a history of modernity, from the nation's late-nineteenth-century invention through its catastrophic telos to its post-Holocaust détente.

One of the main contentions of this book emerges in this conceptual context. If the postwar subordination of Jews and homosexuals continued the project of safeguarding the nation's imagined boundaries, then the groups' late-twentieth-century emergence into the public sphere points to structural transformations that undermined the very integrity of the nation-state. Such an assessment is clearly supported by various supranational factors engendering specific acts of resistance and reproduction that brought forth the Jewish and queer presence. In the case of Vienna's Jews, these included the postwar creation of the state of Israel, the global phenomenon of Jewish ethnicization of the 1960s and 1970s, as well as the mass emigration of Jews from the former Soviet Union in the 1980s and early 1990s. In the case of the city's queers, similarly transnational factors were in evidence, foremost the emergence in the late 1960s and early 1970s of an international lesbian/gay emancipation movement, which effected the gradual establishment of a publicly queer culture centered around such rituals as gay pride parades.

By the late 1980s, the forces of Jewish and lesbian/gay internationalism were joined by supranational forces operating on the Austrian state. The dominant reimagination of the country's Jews began with attempts to restore Austria's reputation following the Waldheim affair and intensified in the wake of the geopolitical transformations brought on by the end of the Cold War. With the demise of the Soviet Union, Austria's neutrality lost its political raison d'etre, relieving the pressure to maintain the country's victim myth. Membership in the European Union's supranational community, conceived as a direct antithesis to the Nazi state, brought added incentive to foreground Austria's ethnic pluralism. The EU also came to function as the principal motivation for reforming the country's legislation of same-sex sexuality, and "Europe" itself began to serve as a cipher for the sexual cosmopolitanism espoused by Vienna.

European developments notwithstanding, Austria's queers were still subject to a number of formal discriminations at the turn of the twenty-first century. However, if this book's interpretation of the trajectory of

Central European modernity is accurate, these legal residues of national homogenization will disappear in the next few years. That such a scenario is quite likely is suggested by the obvious comparison with Germany. Indeed, it is remarkable how similar the Austrian developments charted in this study are to those that took place in postwar Germany. While the absence of a victim myth engendered a less severe form of Jewish subordination, the basic periodization is identical, with a postwar era marked by the essential absence of Jews and homosexuals from the national realm, followed in the 1970s and 1980s by their resistive emergence, and in the 1980s and 1990s by their reproductive presence in the public sphere. Beyond that, the specific manifestations of German Jews' and queers' public existence were strikingly similar, from the emergence of a critical Jewish literary and intellectual scene in the late 1970s to the establishment of such state-sponsored institutions as Jewish museums, Jewish studies centers, and sites of Holocaust commemoration, and from the rise of a radical gay liberation movement in the early 1970s to the spread, starting in the late 1980s, of lesbian/gay offices in Germany's municipalities.[1] That Germany abolished the last vestiges of an antihomosexual penal code by the mid-1990s, established civil unions for lesbians and gay male couples in 2001, and in the same year saw its capital elect an openly gay mayor merely suggests that the country was superseding the exclusionary strictures of the nation-state at a quicker pace than its southern neighbor.

Furthermore, these phenomena were not restricted to the German-speaking world. In other states of the European Union, Jews and queers were similarly present in the public sphere; as in Central Europe, their ascent to collective prominence was, generally speaking, a phenomenon of the late twentieth century. Different countries had radically different histories, of course, but while these had produced varying forms and degrees of legal and cultural subordination, there was no doubt that the realm of a unifying Europe engendered more rather than less Jewish and queer visibility and accounted for advances rather than setbacks in the groups' civil rights.[2]

Austria fit this pattern too, of course. But the country continued to lag behind, particularly when it came to the legal situation of lesbians and gay men. By the year 2001, it was one of only five remaining EU states that neither provided nor worked toward providing homosexuals access to civil unions, and it was the only country that singled out gay men for persecution in its penal code.[3] However, it is the context of Austrian conservatism that gives a case study of the country wider European relevance. Simply put, Austria came to Europe's postnational pluralism late and with considerable reluctance; as such, it functions as a gauge of the power of the historical trajectory identified in the present analysis. If, as the empirical material in this study documents, even Austria embraced the vision of a polity constituted beyond the homogenizing logic of the nation-state, it might well indicate the passing of (Central) European modernity more generally.

Modernity/Postmodernity

This, in fact, is the central argument advanced in this book. Jews and queers, I have proposed, were the principal indices of a European modernity characterized by the homogenizing forces of nationalism and the nation-state. Created through the twin discourses of antisemitism and homophobia, their modern configuration occurred on the nation's constitutive margins. They were thus symptoms of modernity, the abject products of the nation's reification as a fantasized space of ethnic and sexual purity, as well as the signposts of its historical trajectory. It is this conception that allows us to grasp the late twentieth century in terms of an epochal shift. For if we understand the abject creation and constitutive silencing of Jews and homosexuals as a specifically modern phenomenon for which the Holocaust served as the catastrophic telos, and if we understand the groups' continued subordination in the postwar era as a function and indicator of late modernity, then we can comprehend the developments of the late twentieth century in terms of a social and cultural transition to a kind of postmodernity.

This postmodernity was characterized by a constitutive pluralism. As symptoms of modernity, Jews and homosexuals had been subordinated in the interests of national homogenization. By the late twentieth century, however, this exclusionary project had outlived its usefulness. On the contrary, Jews and queers were now celebrated as markers of an affirmatively diversified polity, and states expanded significant efforts to effect their inclusion in the public sphere. This postmodern emergence of modernity's symptoms was ultimately predicated on a structural transformation of the nation-state. By the late twentieth century, the process of European integration had weakened the nation's integrity; and as communities were no longer imagined according to nationalism's formative principles, groups like Jews and queers not only ceased to function as constitutive Others, but came to symbolize a European community constructed beyond the exclusionary strictures of the nation-state. The postnational imaginary thus entailed a hegemonic shift from homogenizing subordination to heterogeneous reproduction; it was this development that ultimately distinguished the postmodern moment from its modern antecedent.

Theorizing the postmodern in this manner articulates with the dominant formulations that have been offered to describe the phenomenon. Indeed, conceptualizations in aesthetic as well as social terms have emphasized postmodernity's pluralizing logic, its celebration of difference over sameness, and its antihierarchical and antitotalizing qualities.[4] This book offers ample evidence of just such a process in the empirical realm of Central European social life. In a cultural space where the modern metanarrative of the nation occasioned a violent regime of exclusionary homogenization, the late twentieth century brought not only the narrative's structural disintegration, but the affirmation of its abject symptoms.

This process, however, was not without echoes of modern coercion; here the present analysis of the postmodern condition points to a level of continuity with the modern that usually goes unremarked. To be sure, the affirmative integration of Jews and queers constituted a radical break with their previous subordination. But what remained unchanged in this shift from a modern to a postmodern regime was the contours of the groups themselves. In the late nineteenth century, Jews and homosexuals had emerged in their modern configuration as the constitutive Others of an imagined space of ethnic and sexual homogeneity. While the late twentieth century witnessed the celebratory reevaluation of modernity's abject symptoms, the postmodern order failed to intercede in the process of subjectification that produced the groups in the first place. Jews and queers no longer sustained the exclusionary project of nationalism; yet, even with that project's *Aufhebung* by a supranational design, the groups' ontological reality never came under active challenge. Instead, the former symptoms of modernity became party to an essentialist collusion that reproduced Jews and queers at the intersection of resistive and reproductive technologies. This analysis is not meant as a critique either of a pluralizing state or of the subjects within its new framework, but it does point to the crucial fact that the postmodern regime brought Jews and queers emancipation *within* rather then *from* modernity's exclusionary categories. Whether this situation is figured in terms of postmodern irony or contingency, it suggests a powerful continuity between modernity and postmodernity and the disciplinary apparatuses that produce and sustain their subjects.

Accordingly, I disagree with recent assessments of the European prospects for Jews and queers. Fueled by traditional fears regarding the end of Judaism on the one side, and hopes, common in many queer studies circles, for the supersession of the modern homo/hetero dyad on the other, it has been argued that neither group is likely to have much of a future on the continent. Jews are thus expected to go away in a "vanishing diaspora," while queers are thought to face the "disappearance of the modern homosexual."[5] Regardless of political sympathies for either position, the present book offers considerable evidence to suggest that neither scenario is at hand. On the contrary, the postmodern regime described here is characterized by an affirmation of alterity that fortifies rather than deconstructs Jewishness and queerness as categories of subjectification. Indeed, as this book's final chapters suggest, it is this hegemonic fortification that, along with the resistive quest for cultural autonomy, engenders the kinds of public identifications that rendered Jews and queers so visible in late-twentieth-century Europe. To put the argument in even more generative terms, the refiguration of Jews and queers as celebrated icons of a postnational pluralism has become the occasion for production of Jewish and queer subjects. After all, the vagaries of descent, the possibility of conversion, the pressures of the closet, and the continuums of sexual experience all militate against clear-cut ascriptions of identity categories; thus the dominant system of valuation ultimately engenders both public and private identifications. The affirmative alterity with which Jews and queers are constructed in Europe's postmodern moment means that the continent's Jews and queers are "coming out" not just to an increasingly receptive public, but, in a process of collectively structured individual subjectification, to themselves as well.

Haider and the New Europe

On an ethnographic level, this dynamic of celebratory ethnic and sexual identification could be seen as a form of "Americanization." After all, it was in the United States that a postmodern sensibility of minority politics was pioneered by the civil rights and new social movements of the 1960s and 1970s.[6] In their wake, an ethic of particularity all but supplanted an older ideology of unmarked citizenship in a development that has led to a proliferation and fortification of identity categories. In the context of everyday life, this has meant that more and more people, Jews and queers prominently among them, have embraced their supposed difference and begun to imagine their existence in terms of its foundational distance from a hypostatized mainstream.

From an American perspective and in an American context, I sympathize with recent critics of this constellation.[7] With a skepticism I share, they are wary of the celebratory recuperation of previously abject identities, pointing instead to American multiculturalism's ironic reproduction of hegemonic regimes and their logics of classification. In the analysis I offered above, in fact, I made an analogous argument in regard to the postmodern fortification of Europe's Jews and queers. But my suspicion of European modernity's symptomatic reproduction is of a primarily intellectual nature.

In political terms, I am much less ambivalent about the pluralizing moment, reflecting my sense that the postmodern regime is vastly preferable to its modern antecedent. To be specific, from a European perspective and in a European context, I cannot help but view the hegemonic heterogenization of the public sphere as a vital antidote to the continent's violently homogenizing past. That past was structured by the exclusionary logic of the nation-state — a logic whose fate is at the very heart of Europe's ongoing political struggles. In the United States, a basic pluralism is enshrined in the country's constitutional principles. In Europe, however, a common constitution is still being forged; its character may or may not transcend the strictures of (supra)national exclusion.

Here, it is imperative to return to Jörg Haider and the politics of Austria's Freedom Party. As Europe's most successful right-wing movement at the turn of the twenty-first century, the party not only governed Austria in coalition with the Christian Social People's Party, but served as an avowed model for other groups, ranging from Belgium's Vlams' Block to Italy's Lega Nord. In this light, Haider was generally seen as a trendsetter in European right-wing politics — a situation that fueled much of the journalistic and scholarly interest in his personal and political trajectory. The literature on Haider has become quite vast, in fact, even though a basic analysis tends to be reiterated from one treatise to the next.[8] That analysis figures Haider as a more or less traditional nationalist, either hoping to restore, or at least exonerate, the Germanic dreams of his Nazi parents or seeking to ensure the ethnic purity of the Austrian nation-state.

There are good historical reasons for this widespread interpretation. Haider's political socialization occurred in the context of Austria's fraternities' virulent German nationalism, and that ideological framework propelled him to the leadership of the FPÖ in 1986.[9] For a few years thereafter, the party pursued a resolutely Germanic course, replete with persistent exaltations of Austria's German heritage and tacit demands for the country's *Anschluss* to the motherland.[10] By the early 1990s, Haider's

German nationalism gave way to a distinctly Austrian variant. Forged in the context of the FPÖ's opposition to Austria's membership in the European Union, Haider's new rhetoric focused on the need to safeguard the integrity of the nation-state in the face of its supranational dissolution.[11] While the identificatory subject of Haider's nationalism shifted between the late 1980s and the early 1990s, his stance retained a number of central components. Aside from the relativization of the Holocaust and a persistent critique of postwar Austria's political system, these included the strategic invocation of Jews and homosexuals as constitutive Others of the imagined national entity. Members of the FPÖ were fond of portraying Jews as inherent outsiders whose claims on the national body represented an ongoing threat to the collectivity, while they routinely figured lesbians and gay men as corrosive elements in the *Volk*'s communal health.[12]

Predictably, the FPÖ's antisemitism, and to a lesser extent the party's homophobia, have always been at the heart of observers' critical commentary. More than anything else, they are seen as indices of Haider's "true colors" — proof of his enduring commitment to the ethnically homogeneous vision of a virulently exclusionary nationalism. This interpretation had not changed by the late 1990s; if anything, it was offered with even greater urgency in the wake of the electoral triumphs that propelled the FPÖ into Austria's government.[13] The party's ascendance to federal power in the winter of 2000 was thus seen as an imminent threat to minorities such as Jews and queers — a situation that partly accounted for the massive protests staged against Haider by the "other Austria."

The protests may have revitalized Austria's left, but much like Haider's critics, they were mistaken in targeting an exclusionary logic of ethnic and sexual homogenization. Ever since Austria's 1995 entry into the EU, Haider and the FPÖ had effectively abandoned the traditional nationalism of the previous decade. In a development that resonated with the analysis offered in this book, the shifting position found its symptomatic articulation in the party's refiguration of Jews and queers. Simply put, the groups ceased to function as relevant Others of Haider's project. Instead, the FPÖ went to some lengths to incorporate them into the party's collective imaginary. Haider's personal quest for Jewish association could be interpreted along those lines, as could the rise to an FPÖ leadership position of Peter Sichrovsky, the son of Holocaust survivors and a member of Vienna's Jewish community.[14] After the party's acceptance into Austria's governing coalition, and in the wake of Haider's signing of an official "Preamble" that admitted Austria's "responsibility" for the "horrendous crimes of the National Socialist regime," the FPÖ acceded to the compensation of Nazi slave laborers, and Haider himself helped negotiate the restitution for Austria's Jewish community.[15] At the same time, Susanne Riess-Passer, the vice chancellor in the ÖVP/FPÖ coalition and Haider's nominal successor as party leader following his spring 2000 resignation, retained her position on the advisory board of the Rechtskommittee Lambda, which she joined in the late 1990s. Although she failed to usher in legal reform immediately upon her arrival in government, this was ultimately the result of the unusual power of the Catholic Church and its political stranglehold on the ÖVP. For its part, the FPÖ had embraced a more inclusive agenda that no longer figured homosexuals as self-evident Others.[16]

To be sure, such developments invited charges of political opportunism. But whatever their sincerity, they constituted fundamental transformations in the FPÖ's basic political position. In its traditional nationalist mode, Jewish participation or any support for lesbian/gay causes was not merely unacceptable but utterly implausible. By the turn of the twenty-first century, however, they were commonplace features of a political movement that no longer constituted itself in opposition to Jews and homosexuals.

This is not to say, of course, that the FPÖ of the turn of the century had abandoned exclusionary politics. On the contrary, Haider's party in fact intensified its segregationist efforts. By the late 1990s, however, that discourse was practically never directed at the symptoms of modernity. Instead, the FPÖ targeted a new set of Others, East and Southeast Europeans, Africans, and Muslims foremost among them. The rhetoric of Haider and his party in this respect was vicious, seeking to safeguard against such damaging incursions as the "Slavic way of thinking," the massive arrival of "bush negroes," and Turks' abuse of the "generosity of the Austrian welfare state."[17] By 1999, the new position found its paradigmatic expression in the campaign slogan "Stopp der Überfremdung" (Stop Foreign Encroachment), which was paired with a placard diplaying Haider and another FPÖ politician under the heading "Zwei echte Österreicher" (Two Real Austrians). The latter slogan echoed a campaign poster from 1970 which had advertised the ÖVP candidate Josef Klaus as "ein echter Österreicher" (a real Austrian). In the modern logic of the postwar era, the slogan had been immediately intelligible as an antisemitic invective, directed as it was against opposing candidate Bruno Kreisky, whose Jewish background made him a suspect member of the imagined national community. By 1999, the FPÖ poster had no such connotations.

While the message was similarly strident, Jews were not the object of its postmodern exclusion. On the contrary, the FPÖ had incorporated the symptoms of modernity, running them for political office in fact; now they were mobilized in the strategic constitution of newly imagined Others. "Among my Jewish friends," a prominent FPÖ politician announced in November 1999, "there is outrage about the high degree of Islamic presence." In the modern era, the FPÖ shared citizens' concerns about Jewish influence; in the postmodern era, Jews' "justified fear" was paraded to safeguard the body politic from "Islamic circles."[18]

Critics have remarked on the shifting targets of Haider's exclusionary politics. However, beyond an oft-repeated assertion that what used to be antisemitism (or homophobia) now manifests itself in the form of xeno-phobia against Africans and Muslims, little has been offered in terms of explanation. And even that assessment misses the larger historical context underwriting the FPÖ's political transformation. Quintessentially modern phenomena, antisemitism and homophobia were mobilized to con-stitute and protect the imagined community of the nation. The xeno-phobia of the postmodern age, by contrast, invents the collective Self as an altogether different entity. Having integrated the symptoms of moder-nity into the new imaginary, the politics of exclusion no longer define the ideal social body in terms of ethnic and sexual purity. Instead, politicians like Haider are demarcating a supranational entity constructed in oppo-sition to spaces whose distance from a supposed core of Western civi-lization renders them progressively unassimilable: East and Southeast Europeans whose economic and democratic capabilities are put in doubt, Africans whose cultural (and racial) makeup is questioned, and Muslims, who are figured as the invariant Others of a valorized Judeo-Christian tradition.

Haider, much like Europe's other right-wing politicians, has no difficulty in naming the entity constituted through such acts of hemi-spheric exclusion. To him, it is "Europe," and its constitution is ultimately at the heart of the postmodern political struggle. With the inclusion of Jews and queers into the political realm of even a right-wing party like the FPÖ, the historical transcendence of the modern nation-state is becom-ing a reality. At that very moment, however, its European successor might be constituted along structurally analogous lines of exclusion. If Austria is any indication, Haider's success in forcing Social Democrats and Christian Socials to severely tighten immigration laws in the late 1990s suggests the political potency of a supranational vision that integrates groups like Jews and queers, while setting strict boundaries for those considered wholly un-European.[19] Predictably, the FPÖ continued to pursue its exclusionary agenda in Austria's government; what is more compelling and troublesome, however, is that many of Europe's left-liberal and centrist cabinets began to move in similar directions, implementing new barriers in the hope of ensuring Europe's successful integration. Such measures were designed to appease a far right that had once sought to protect the integrity of the nation-state. But as parties like the FPÖ reinvented themselves as the guardians of a new "fortress Europe," the continent's governments were in danger of doing the far right's bidding in the interests of an internally pluralistic but tightly bounded Europe.

In the United States, conservative forces continue to deploy strident rhetoric and reactionary policies to effect the country's cultural homogenization. But even the enormity of American racism, the country's unparalleled religiosity, and its questionable level of democracy cannot offset a fundamentally pluralist constitution whose creation beyond the exclusionary principles of the European nation-state ensures universal access to full citizenship. Any critic of the Unites States would rightly interject that comprehensive civil rights are not a reality for all people; and America's queers, for one, continue to suffer discrimination as a result of the policies championed by fundamentalist Christians. In regard to lesbian/gay rights, a supranational Europe may thus be at the forefront of civil liberties. But such pluralism should not detract from the larger struggle in the postmodern polity. In light of the U.S. constitution, most lesbian/gay activists are rightly convinced of the movements' eventual success, decades of possible delays notwithstanding. In the New Europe, a viable constitution is still being forged, and while such a document will be fully inclusive of Jews and queers, it is up to the continent's progressive forces to prevent the creation of an entity that reiterates the nation-state's exclusions on a supranational level. If that effort fails, a new set of Others will emerge as the abject symptoms of European postmodernity.

Notes

Introduction

1. On the history of Vienna's Jewish community under National Socialism, see Doron Rabinovici, *Instanzen der Ohnmacht — Wien 1938–1945: Der Weg zum Judenrat* (Frankfurt: Suhrkamp, 2000); Herbert Rosenkranz, *Verfolgung und Selbstbehauptung: Die Juden in Österreich 1938–1945* (Vienna: Herold, 1978).

2. On the history of homosexuals' persecution by the Nazis, see Richard Plant, *The Pink Triangle: The Nazi War Against Homosexuals* (New York: Henry Holt, 1986). See also Burkhard Jellonnek, *Homosexuelle unter dem Hakenkreuz* (Paderborn: Schöningh, 1990); Günter Grau, ed., *Homosexualität in der NS-Zeit: Dokumente einer Diskriminierung und Verfolgung* (Frankfurt: Fischer, 1993).

3. On the enduring cultural logic of Austria's Socialist and Social Democratic Party, see esp. Helmut Gruber, *Red Vienna: Experiment in Working-Class Culture, 1919–1934* (New York: Oxford University Press, 1991). A good source on postwar Austria's political and social field is Günter Bischof, Anton Pelinka, and Rolf Steininger, eds., *Austria in the Nineteen Fifties* (New Brunswick, N.J.: Transaction Publishers, 1995).

4. The cultural world of postwar Vienna has received little attention. An important exception that begins to study the city's conventionality and conservatism in the face of European upheavals is Robert Rotenberg, *Time and Order in Metropolitan Vienna: A Seizure of Schedules* (Washington: Smithsonian Institution Press, 1992).

5. The *Sozialpartnerschaft* united members of the Social Democratic–dominated unions with the Christian conservative representatives of Austrian industry. In tandem, they organized a kind of "shadow government" that diverted political debate and decision-making away from the formal sites of participatory democracy. An attempt to amend the fissures underlying the 1934 civil war,

the *Sozialpartnerschaft* was a uniquely successful institution that changed the former enemies into mutually dependent partners in Austria's post–World War II reconstruction. On the history of the *Sozialpartnerschaft,* see Anton Pelinka, *Austria: Out of the Shadow of the Past* (Boulder, Colo.: Westview, 1998), esp. ch. 7.

6. Named for the Bermuda Triangle because of the propensity to "get lost there," the *Bermudadreieck* in Vienna's first district boasts a bevy of trendy and internationally oriented bars and nightclubs. Its emergence in the 1980s was widely seen as a decisive break with the city's nostalgic provincialism.

7. The designation "Second Republic" reflects the Austrian polity's reconstitution after World War II, the "First Republic" serving as the designation for the interwar state that commenced with the dissolution of the Habsburg Monarchy and ended with the 1938 *Anschluss* to Nazi Germany. The literature on twentieth-century Austrian history is extensive. An effective synthesis was published recently by Ernst Hanisch, *Der lange Schatten des Staates: Österreichische Gesellschaftsgeschichte im 20. Jahrhundert* (Vienna: Ueberreuter, 1994).

8. This situation has been chronicled in a remarkable text by Ruth Beckermann combining the strategies of a memoir with some historical research. See Beckermann, *Unzugehörig: Österreicher und Juden nach 1945* (Vienna: Löcker Verlag, 1989).

9. See the editors' historical sketch, "Donauwalzer — Herrenwahl: Schwule Geschichte der Donaumetropole vom Mittelalter bis zur Gegenwart," in Andreas Brunner and Hannes Sulzenbacher, eds., *Schwules Wien: Reiseführer durch die Donaumetropole* (Vienna: Promedia, 1998), pp. 91–96.

10. Virginia Dominguez, "Questioning Jews." *American Ethnologist* 20, no. 3 (1993), pp. 618–24.

11. This research ranged from exploration of the social structures engendered in *kibbutzim* to investigation of the linguistic and social imaginaries of the Jewish nation-state. See, for example, Melford Spiro, *Kibbutz: Venture in Utopia* (New York: Schocken Books, 1956); Alex Weingrod, *Israel: Group Relations in a New Society* (London: Pall Mall, 1965); Hervey Goldberg, *Greentown's Youth: Disadvantaged Youth in a Development Town in Israel* (Assen: Van Gorcum, 1984); Tamar Katriel, *Talking Straight: Dugri Speech in Israeli Sabra Culture* (Cambridge: Cambridge University Press, 1986); Virginia Dominguez, *People As Subject, People As Object: Selfhood and Peoplehood in Contemporary Israel* (Madison: University of Wisconsin Press, 1989); Susan Sered, *What Makes Women Sick? Maternity, Modesty, and Militarism in Israeli Society* (Hanover, N.H.: Brandeis University Press, 2000); Susan Kahn, *Reproducing Jews: A Cultural Account of Assisted Conception in Israel* (Durham, N.C.: Duke University Press, 2000).

12. S. N. Eisenstadt, *The Absorption of Immigrants* (London: Routledge and Kegan Paul, 1954); Moshe Shokeid, *The Dual Heritage: Immigrants from the Atlas Mountains in an Israeli Village* (Manchester: Manchester University Press, 1971); Harvey Goldberg, *Cave Dwellers and Citrus Growers: A Jewish Community in Libya and Israel* (Cambridge: Cambridge University Press, 1972); Michael Ashkenazi and Alex Weingrod, *Ethiopian Immigrants in Beersheva: An Anthropological Study of the Absorption Process* (Highland Park, Ill.: American Association for Ethiopian Jews, 1984).

13. An important ethnographic account in this vein is Philip Bohlman, *"The Land Where Two Streams Flow": Music in the German-Jewish Community of Israel* (Urbana: University of Illinois Press, 1989).

14. Dominguez, "Questioning Jews," p. 623.

15. Barbara Myerhoff, *Number Our Days* (New York: Simon & Schuster, 1978); Jack Kugelmass, *The Miracle on Intervale Avenue: The Story of a Jewish Congregation in the South Bronx* (New York: Columbia University Press, 1986).

16. Riv-Ellen Prell, *Prayer and Community: The Havurah in American Judaism* (Detroit, Mich.: Wayne State University Press. 1989); Moshe Shokeid, *A Gay Synagogue in New York* (New York: Columbia University Press, 1995); Henry Goldschmidt, "Peoples Apart: Constructing Jewish Identities and Differences in Crown Heights," Ph.D. diss., University of California, Santa Cruz, 2000; Ayala Fader, "Learning to be Bobover: Language Socialization and Maintenance in a Hasidic Community," Ph.D. diss., New York University, 2000.

17. Jonathan Boyarin, *Polish Jews in Paris: The Ethnography of Memory* (Bloomington: Indiana University Press, 1991), p. 5. For works of historical ethnography conceived in a similar vein, see Mark Zborowski and Elizabeth Herzog, *Life Is with People: The Jewish Little-Town of Eastern Europe* (New York: International Universities Press, 1952); Lucjan Dobroszycki and Barbara Kirschenblatt-Gimblett, *Image Before My Eyes: A Photographic History of Jewish Life in Poland, 1864–1939* (New York: Schocken Books, 1977).

18. Jonathan Boyarin, *Storm from Paradise: The Politics of Jewish Memory* (Minneapolis: University of Minnesota Press, 1992), p. xv.

19. As John Borneman puts it, "Unfortunately, very few German Jews remain who can give voice to this identity in both its pre- and postwar forms. The vast majority of Jews living in Germany are Polish, Hungarian, or Russian Jews, along with a sizable number of American Jews." John Borneman and Jeffrey Peck, *Sojourners: The Return of German Jews and the Question of Identity* (Lincoln: University of Nebraska Press, 1995), p. 18.

20. An important exception is the recent work by Sascha Goluboff on Jews in Moscow. See Goluboff, "Jewish Multi-Ethnicities in Post-Soviet Russia: An Eventful Ethnography of the Moscow Choral Synagogue," Ph.D. diss., University of Illinois at Urbana-Champaign, 1999.

21. On the history of the anthropology of same-sex sexuality, see Rudy Bleys, *The Geography of Perversion: Male-to-Male Sexual Behaviour Outside the West and the Ethnographic Imagination 1750–1918* (New York: Cassell, 1996).

22. See Ruth Benedict, *Patterns of Culture* (Boston: Houghton & Mifflin, 1934); Margaret Mead, *Sex and Temperament in Three Primitive Societies* (New York: William Morrow, 1935); Alfred Kroeber, "Psychosis or Social Sanction?" *Character and Personality* 8 (1940), pp. 204–15.

23. This development was exemplified and propelled by the founding in 1974 of the Anthropological Research Group on Homosexuality (ARGOH), an unofficial AAA organization that doubled as a lesbian/gay support group and institutional anchor for the ethnographic study of same-sex sexualities. Renamed the Society of Lesbian and Gay Anthropologists (SOLGA) in 1987, the group has continued its umbrella activities, both in regard to the establishment

of lesbian/ gay studies within the discipline and as a bulwark against institutional homophobia. In 1998, the organization was accorded full AAA section status.

24. Kath Weston, "Lesbian/Gay Studies in the House of Anthropology," *Annual Review of Anthropology* 22 (1993), p. 341.

25. See esp. Gilbert Herdt, *Guardians of the Flute: Idioms of Masculinity* (New York: McGraw-Hill, 1984); *id.,* ed., *Ritualized Homosexuality in Melanesia* (Berkeley: University of California Press, 1984); Walter Williams, *The Spirit and the Flesh: Sexual Diversity in American Indian Culture* (Boston: Beacon Press, 1986); Will Roscoe, *The Zuni Man/Woman* (Albuquerque: University of New Mexico Press, 1991).

26. The seminal text of the constructionist critique was of course Michel Foucault, *The History of Sexuality: Volume 1 — An Introduction* (New York: Vantage Books, 1978). In the following years, Foucault's postulates were explicated by numerous scholars, most influentially perhaps in David Halperin, *One Hundred Years of Homosexuality* (New York: Routledge, 1990).

27. See esp. Gilbert Herdt, *Same Sex, Different Cultures: Gays and Lesbians Across Cultures* (Boulder: Westview Press, 1997), which revisits Herdt's earlier work in light of the constructionist critique. For an analogous rethinking of the berdache category, see Roscoe, "How to Become a Berdache: Toward a Unified Analysis of Gender Diversity," in *Third Sex, Third Gender: Beyond Sexual Dimorphism in Culture and History,* ed. Gilbert Herdt (New York: Zone Books, 1993), pp. 329-72.

28. See, for example, Annick Prieur, *Mema's House, Mexico City: On Transvestites, Queens, and Machos* (Chicago: University of Chicago Press, 1998); Don Kulick, *Travesti* (Chicago: University of Chicago Press, 1998); Lawrence Cohen, "Holi in Banaras and the Mahaland of Modernity," *GLQ* 2, no. 4 (1998), pp. 399-424; Jennifer Robertson, *Takarazuka: Sexual Politics and Popular Culture in Modern Japan* (Berkeley: University of California Press, 1998); Rosalind Morris, "Educating Desire: Thailand, Transnationalism and Transgression," *Social Text* 52-53 (1998), pp. 53-79.

29. Seminal historical research was presented in George Chauncey, *Gay New York: Gender, Urban Culture and the Gay Male World, 1890-1940* (New York: Basic Books, 1994); Elizabeth Kennedy and Madeline Davis, *Boots of Leather, Slippers of Gold: The History of a Lesbian Community* (New York: Routledge, 1993); Esther Newton, *Cherry Grove, Fire Island: Sixty Years in America's First Gay and Lesbian Town* (Boston: Beacon Press, 1993).

30. Ethnographic work on lesbian/gay existence includes such important studies as Kath Weston, *Families We Choose: Lesbians, Gays, Kinship* (New York: Columbia University Press, 1991); Gilbert Herdt, ed., *Gay Culture in America: Essays from the Field* (Boston: Beacon Press, 1992); Gilbert Herdt and Andrew Boxer, *Children of Horizons: How Gay and Lesbian Youths Are Forging a New Way Out of the Closet* (Boston: Beacon Press, 1996); Ellen Lewin, *Lesbian Mothers: Accounts of Gender in American Culture* (Ithaca, N.Y.: Cornell University Press, 1993); *id., Recognizing Ourselves: Ceremonies of Lesbian and Gay Commitment* (New York: Columbia University Press, 1998); William Leap, *Word's Out: Gay*

Men's English (Minneapolis: University of Minnesota Press, 1996); Stephen Murray, *American Gay* (Chicago: University of Chicago Press, 1996); Martin Manalansan, "Remapping Frontiers: The Lives of Gay Filipino Men in New York City," Ph.D. diss., University of Rochester, 1997.

31. Weston, *Families We Choose*, pp. 122–29.

32. Practitioners of other disciplines, especially sociology and political science, have recently begun to pay some attention to "Western" homosexualities outside the United States. Aside from longstanding work on Britain (see, for example, work by Jeffrey Weeks), a body of comparative work on the trajectory of the lesbian/gay movement now addresses aspects of the situation on the European continent. See esp. Barry Adam, Jan Willem Duyvendak, and André Krouwel, eds., *The Global Emergence of Gay and Lesbian Politics* (Philadelphia: Temple University Press, 1999). See also Frédéric Martel, *The Pink and the Black: Homosexuals in France Since 1968* (Stanford, Calif.: Stanford University Press, 1999).

33. Written in different disciplinary and theoretical registers, that literature includes work on lesbians and gay men in Israel (Tracy Moore, ed., *Lesbiot: Israeli Lesbians Talk About Sexuality, Feminism, Judaism and Their Lives* [London: Cassell, 1995]; Amir Sumakai Fink and Jacob Press, eds., *Independence Park: The Lives of Gay Men in Israel* [Stanford, Calif.: Stanford University Press, 1999]), research on lesbian/gay Jews in the United States (Shokeid, *A Gay Synagogue in New York*), and an emerging body of scholarship on the role of (homo)sexuality in the construction of modern Jewish identities. See, for example, Daniel Boyarin, *Unheroic Conduct: The Rise of Heterosexuality and the Invention of the Jewish Man* (Berkeley: University of California Press, 1997); Ann Pellegrini, *Performance Anxieties: Staging Psychoanalysis, Staging Race* (New York: Routledge, 1997); Daniel Itzkowitz, "Secret Temples," in *Jews and Other Differences: The New Jewish Cultural Studies,* ed. Jonathan Boyarin and Daniel Boyarin (Minneapolis: University of Minnesota Press, 1997), pp. 176–202.

34. Early articulations of this theoretical orientation include Johannes Fabian, "Language, History and Anthropology," *Philosophy of the Social Sciences* 1 (1971), pp. 19–47; Bob Scholte, "Toward a Self-Reflective Anthropology." *Critical Anthropology* 1, no. 1 (fall 1970), pp. 3–33; *id.,* "Discontents in Anthropology," *Social Research* 38 (1971), pp. 777–807; Dell Hymes, ed., *Reinventing Anthropology* (New York: Pantheon Books, 1972).

35. For the backlash against critical anthropology, see Ian Jarvie, "Epistle to the Anthropologists," *American Anthropologist* 77 (1975), pp. 253–65. A key publication in the establishment of an interpretive paradigm was Paul Rabinow and William Sullivan, eds., *Interpretive Social Science: A Reader* (Berkeley: University of California Press, 1979).

36. These terms are the operative tropes in the wildly influential James Clifford and George Marcus, eds., *Writing Culture: The Poetics and Politics of Ethnography* (Berkeley: University of California Press, 1986); and George Marcus and Michael Fischer, *Anthropology As Cultural Critique: An Experimental Moment in the Human Sciences* (Chicago: University of Chicago Press, 1986).

37. This position was pioneered in such studies as Vincent Crapanzano, *Tuhami: Portrait of a Moroccan* (Chicago: University of Chicago Press, 1980); Kevin Dwyer, *Moroccan Dialogues: Anthropology in Question* (Baltimore: Johns Hopkins University Press, 1982); James Clifford, *The Predicament of Culture: Twentieth-Century Ethnography, Literature, and Art* (Cambridge: Harvard University Press, 1988).

38. See Clifford Geertz, *The Interpretation of Cultures: Selected Essays* (New York: Basic Books, 1973); *id.*, *Local Knowledge: Further Essays in Interpretive Anthropology* (New York: Basic Books, 1983).

39. Clifford Geertz, *The Religion of Java* (New York: Free Press, 1960), which compares religious variants found on the island; *id.*, *Islam Observed: Religious Development in Morocco and Indonesia* (Chicago: University of Chicago Press, 1968), which compares one religion across two culture areas; *id.*, *After the Fact: Two Countries, Four Decades, One Anthropologist* (Cambridge: Harvard University Press, 1995), which affirms the comparative orientation of Geertz's career in retrospective analysis.

40. Fred Eggan, "Social Anthropology and the Method of Controlled Comparison," *American Anthropologist* 56 (1954), pp. 743–63; Clyde Kluckhohn, *Culture and Behavior* (New York: Free Press, 1962); Mead, *Sex and Temperament in Three Primitive Societies;* Benedict, *Patterns of Culture.*

41. See Matti Bunzl, "Franz Boas and the Humboldtian Tradition: From *Volksgeist* and *Nationalcharakter* to an Anthropological Concept of Culture," in *Volksgeist As Method and Ethic: Essays on Boasian Ethnography and the German Anthropological Tradition*, vol. 8, *History of Anthropology*, ed. George Stocking (Madison: University of Wisconsin Press, 1996), pp. 17–78.

42. On Boas's debate with Otis Mason, see George Stocking, "From Physics to Ethnology," in *Race, Culture, and Evolution: Essays in the History of Anthropology* (Chicago: University of Chicago Press, 1968), pp. 133–60.

43. Franz Boas, "The Occurrence of Similar Inventions in Areas Widely Apart [and] Museums of Ethnology and Their Classification," in *The Shaping of American Anthropology 1883–1911: A Franz Boas Reader*, ed. George Stocking (Chicago: University of Chicago Press, 1974), p. 62.

44. Franz Boas, "The Limitations of the Comparative Method of Anthropology," in *Race, Language and Culture* (New York: Macmillan, 1940), p. 275.

45. Benedict, *Patterns of Culture;* Mead, *Sex and Temperament in Three Primitive Societies.*

46. Geertz, *Islam Observed.*

47. A similar Weberian logic governed Geertz's *Religion of Java,* where the location was held constant in order to trace different religions' impact on economic development.

48. Boas, "The Limitations of the Comparative Method," p. 276.

49. Ibid., p. 277.

50. On the history of German-Jewish emancipation and the entry of Jews into German culture, see Jacob Katz, *Out of the Ghetto: The Social Background of Jewish Emancipation, 1770–1870* (Cambridge: Harvard University Press, 1973);

David Sorkin, *The Transformation of German Jewry, 1780–1840* (Oxford: Oxford University Press, 1987); Michael Meyer and Michael Brenner, eds., *German-Jewish History in Modern Times,* 4 vols. (New York: Columbia University Press, 1996–98).

51. The best account of this cultural process is the remarkable study by Marion Kaplan, *The Making of the Jewish Middle Class: Women, Family, and Identity in Imperial Germany* (New York: Oxford University Press, 1991).

52. On the history of the modern antisemitic movement, see Peter Pulzer, *The Rise of Political Anti-Semitism in Germany and Austria* (New York: John Wiley & Sons, 1964); and Albert Lichtblau, *Antisemitismus und soziale Spannung in Berlin und Wien, 1867–1914* (Berlin: Metropol, 1994).

53. On the long history of anti-Judaism, see esp. Leon Poliakof, *The History of Anti-Semitism,* 4 vols. (New York: Vanguard Press, 1965–85).

54. This argument has been advanced most powerfully in George Mosse, *Toward the Final Solution: A History of European Racism* (Madison: University of Wisconsin Press, 1978).

55. Hannah Arendt, *The Origins of Totalitarianism* (London: Allen & Unwin, 1951), p. 87.

56. The Jewish body constituted in antisemitic discourse has been examined most influentially in Sander Gilman, *The Jew's Body* (New York: Routledge, 1991). See also Klaus Hödl, *Die Pathologisierung des jüdischen Körpers: Antisemitismus, Gechlecht und Medizin im Fin de Siècle* (Vienna: Picus, 1997).

57. Mosse, *Toward the Final Solution.*

58. Foucault, *The History of Sexuality;* Halperin, *One Hundred Years of Homosexuality;* S. Long and John Borneman, "Power, Objectivity and the Other: The Creation of Sexual Species in Modernist Discourse," *Dialectical Anthropology* 15 (1990), pp. 285–314; Klaus Müller, *Aber in meinem Herzen sprach eine Stimme so laut: Homosexuelle Autobiographien und medizinische Pathographien im neunzehnten Jahrhundert* (Berlin: Verlag Rosa Winkel. 1991); Ed Cohen, *Talk on the Wilde Side: Toward a Genealogy of a Discourse on Male Sexuality* (New York: Routledge, 1993); Harry Oosterhuis, *Stepchildren of Nature: Krafft-Ebing, Psychiatry, and the Making of Sexual Identity* (Chicago: University of Chicago Press, 2000).

59. Foucault, *The History of Sexuality,* p. 43.

60. On the dissemination of the modern concept of sexual identity, see esp. Müller, *Aber in meinem Herzen sprach eine Stimme so laut;* and Oosterhuis, *Stepchildren of Nature.*

61. George Mosse, *Nationalism and Sexuality: Middle-Class Morality and Sexual Norms in Modern Europe* (Madison: University of Wisconsin Press, 1985).

62. Ibid., pp. 23–40.

63. Ibid., p. 29.

64. Ibid., ch. 7. In this analytic light, it also becomes clear why the symptomatics of Jewishness and homosexuality fitted together with such seamlessness. Scholars like Sander Gilman and Daniel Boyarin have explored this phenomenon, which rendered such Jewish icons as Sigmund Freud defenders of Jewish masculinity. See Gilman, *Freud, Race and Gender* (Princeton, N.J.: Princeton

University Press, 1993) and Boyarin, *Unheroic Conduct*. Like other modern Jews, Freud confronted a cultural field that constructed Jews and homosexuals through analogous stereotypes of male effeminacy and female dominance. In treating this phenomenon as a form of antisemitic projection, Gilman has implied that these images had no basis in social reality. Boyarin, by contrast, has suggested that they refracted the gender configuration of premodern Ashkenazic Jewry, centered as it was on the valorization of the meek and studious man whose quest for religious education would be sustained by a strong and practical woman.

65. The codification of German nationness in opposition to Jews and homosexuals did not dissuade members of the groups from imagining their existence as coterminous with the nation. As representatives of the bourgeoisie, most Jews and homosexuals were in fact broadly nationalistic; the late nineteenth and early twentieth century witnessed numerous initiatives designed to convince the larger public of that fact. With tragic irony, such attempts to hide one's "true" nature merely fueled instrumentalist attacks.

66. The interarticulation of antisemitism and homophobia as operative elements of German nationalism found early expression in the circles of Adolf Stöcker. The leader of the antisemitic movement in imperial Germany, Stöcker not only demanded the restriction of Jewish immigration from Eastern Europe and the containment of Jewish participation in the professions; he was also a central figure in the moral purity movement, which sought to identify and eradicate such vices as homosexuality. On Stöcker's antisemitism, see Pulzer, *The Rise of Political Anti-Semitism*. On the moral purity movement, see John Fout, "Sexual Politics in Wilhelmine Germany: The Male Gender Crisis, Moral Purity, and Homophobia," in *Forbidden History: The State, Society, and the Regulation of Sexuality in Modern Europe,* ed. John Fout (Chicago: University of Chicago Press, 1992), pp. 259–92. Much like other early proponents of virulent German nationalism, Stöcker remained relatively ineffective politically. But in tandem with such other late-nineteenth-century figures as Wilhelm Marr, who coined the term "antisemitism," and Eugen Dühring, a widely read antisemitic publicist, he articulated the fatally exclusionary vision of nationness at the heart of National Socialism's genocidal quest for a perfect society. On Marr, see Moshe Zimmermann, *Wilhelm Marr, the Patriarch of Antisemitism* (New York: Oxford University Press, 1986). On Dühring, see the standard histories of German antisemitism.

67. Zygmunt Bauman, *Modernity and the Holocaust* (Ithaca, N.Y.: Cornell University Press, 1989).

68. Max Horkheimer and Theodor Adorno, *Dialectic of Enlightenment* (New York: Continuum, 1944).

69. Bauman, *Modernity and the Holocaust,* p. viii.

70. Ibid., p. 65.

71. Ibid., p. 70.

72. Similar arguments could be advanced in regard to the persecution of gypsies and the mentally handicapped. By the late nineteenth century, these groups were also imagined as obstacles to the nation's normative reproduction.

Given their more or less ready visibility, however, they represented much less of a threat than Jews and homosexuals, who had the corrosive ability to undermine the social order through unrecognized infiltration. See also George Mosse, *The Image of Man: The Creation of Modern Masculinity* (New York: Oxford University Press, 1996), pp. 70–71.

73. The process of modern nation-building has been theorized most influentially in Eric Hobsbawm, *Nations and Nationalism since 1780: Programme, Myth, Reality* (Cambridge: Cambridge University Press, 1990); Ernest Gellner, *Nations and Nationalism* (Ithaca, N.Y.: Cornell University Press, 1983); and Benedict Anderson, *Imagined Communities: Reflections on the Origin and Spread of Nationalism* (London: Verso, 1983). The influence of these works pervades the analysis offered in the present book.

74. In the wake of the Habsburg Monarchy's military defeat by Prussia in 1866, the German-speaking part of the empire was excluded from the political process of German unification that subsequently took place under Prussian rather than Habsburg hegemony. See Robert Kann, *A History of the Habsburg Empire, 1526–1918* (Berkeley: University of California Press, 1974).

75. Pieter Judson, "Inventing Germans: Class, Nationality and Colonial Fantasy at the Margins of the Habsburg Monarchy," *Social Analysis* 33 (1993); *id.,* "Frontiers, Islands, Forests, Stones: Mapping the Geography of a German Identity in the Habsburg Monarchy, 1848–1900," in *The Geography of Identity,* ed. Patricia Yaeger (Ann Arbor: University of Michigan Press, 1996).

76. Pieter Judson, *Exclusive Revolutionaries: Liberal Politics, Social Experience, and National Identity in the Austrian Empire, 1848–1914* (Ann Arbor: University of Michigan Press, 1996).

77. The phrase is from the seminal study of the period, Carl Schorske, *Fin-de-Siècle Vienna: Politics and Culture* (New York: Vintage, 1981). On Schönerer, see also Andrew Whiteside, *The Socialism of Fools: Georg Ritter von Schönerer and Austrian Pan-Germanism* (Berkeley: University of California Press, 1975).

78. Quoted in Pulzer, *The Rise of Political Anti-Semitism,* p. 147.

79. On Karl Lueger and the Christian Social movement, see John Boyer, *Political Radicalism in Late Imperial Vienna: Origins of the Christian Social Movement, 1848–1897* (Chicago: University of Chicago Press, 1981); *id., Culture and Political Crisis in Vienna: Christian Socialism in Power, 1897–1918* (Chicago: University of Chicago Press, 1995).

80. Quoted in Robert Wistrich, *The Jews of Vienna in the Age of Franz Joseph* (Oxford: Oxford University Press, 1990), p. 229.

81. Brunner and Sulzenbacher, "Donauwalzer — Herrenwahl," pp. 29–30. The earlier code against sodomy had been more lenient, threatening imprisonment of six months to one year.

82. On Krafft-Ebing, see Oosterhuis, *Stepchildren of Nature.*

83. The Austrian scandals around Karl Forstner and Theodor Beer are discussed in Brunner and Sulzenbacher, "Donauwalzer — Herrenwahl," pp. 37–38 and 53–54. International scandals that were widely reported in the Austrian media included the German Eulenburg affair (see James Steakley, "Iconography

of a Scandal: Political Cartoons and the Eulenburg Affair in Wilhelmin Germany," in *Hidden from History: Reclaiming the Gay and Lesbian Past,* ed. Martin Duberman, Martha Vicinus, and George Chauncey [New York: Meridian, 1990], pp. 233–63) and the trial of Oscar Wilde in Great Britain (see Cohen, *Talk on the Wilde Side*). Much work remains to be done to elucidate the same-sex sexual dimensions of fin-de-siècle Vienna. An early collection of work is Neda Bei et al., *Das lila Wien um 1900: Zur Ästhetik der Homosexualitäten* (Vienna: Promedia, 1986); and some material can be found in the pioneering study by Hanna Hacker, *Frauen und Freundinnen: Studien zur "weiblichen Sexualität" am Beispiel Österreich* (Weinheim: Beltz, 1987). More recently, a number of essays have been published in Wolfgang Förster, Tobias Natter, and Ines Rieder, eds., *Der Andere Blick: Lesbischwules Leben in Österreich* (Vienna: Eigenverlag, 2001).

84. Oscar Jásci, *The Dissolution of the Habsburg Monarchy* (Chicago: University of Chicago Press, 1929); Robert Kann, *A History of the Habsburg Empire.*

85. Ernst Hanisch, *Der lange Schatten des Staates.*

86. The dynamics of Jewish identity formation in the context of the Habsburg Monarchy's demise is elucidated in an important recent study by Marsha Rozenblit, *Reconstituting a National Identity: The Jews of Habsburg Austria During World War I* (Oxford: Oxford University Press, 2001).

87. Even the rather small and politically marginal Zionist movement in the Habsburg Monarchy advocated loyalty to the throne. On Zionism in the monarchy, see Adolf Gaisbauer, *Davidstern und Doppeladler: Zionismus und jüdischer Nationalismus in Österreich, 1882–1918* (Vienna: Böhlau, 1988).

88. Marsha Rozenblit, "The Jews of the Dual Monarchy," *Austrian History Yearbook* 23 (1992), 164.

89. The paradigmatic articulation of this position was offered by Rabbi Josef Samuel Bloch, the editor of the influential *Österreichische Wochenschrift.* On Bloch, see Wistrich, *The Jews of Vienna in the Age of Franz Joseph,* ch. 9.

90. On the trajectory of antisemitism in twentieth-century Austria, see Bruce Pauley, *From Prejudice to Persecution: A History of Austrian Anti-Semitism* (Chapel Hill: University of North Carolina Press, 1992); and John Bunzl and Bernd Marin, *Antisemitismus in Österreich: Sozialhistorische und soziologische Studien* (Innsbruck: Inn-Verlag, 1983).

91. Bruce Pauley, "Political Antisemitism in Interwar Vienna," in *Jews, Antisemitism, and Culture in Vienna,* ed. Ivar Oxaal, Michael Pollack, and Gerhard Botz (London: Routledge & Kegan Paul, 1987), p. 152. The antisemitism of the Social Democratic Party was predominantly economic in nature. To some degree, this was true also in the Christian Social camp. There, however, a religious and cultural form of antisemitism predominated. Among German nationalists, racial antisemitism was the dominant mode.

92. Some remarks on the situation during the interwar years can be found in Brunner and Sulzenbacher, "Donauwalzer — Herrenwahl," as well as in Hanna Hacker, *Frauen und Freundinnen.* On interwar Berlin, see *ElDorado: Homosexuelle Frauen und Männer in Berlin, 1850–1950: Geschichte, Alltag und Kultur* (Berlin: Verlag Rosa Winkel, 1984).

93. Albert Müller and Christian Fleck, "'Unzucht wider der Natur': Gerichtliche Verfolgung der 'Unzucht mit Personen gleichen Geschlechts' in Österreich von den 1930er bis zu den 1950er Jahren," *Österreichische Zeitschrift für Geschichtswissenschaften* 9, no. 3 (1998), pp. 400–22.

94. The level of NSDAP membership in the "Ostmark" was greater than anywhere else in the Third Reich. Judging exclusively by statistics, the numbers suggest that at least one forth of adult male Austrians were Nazis. Gerhard Botz, "Österreich und die NS-Vergangenheit," in *Ist der Nationalsozialismus Geschichte? Zu Historisierung und Historikerstreit,* ed. Dan Diner (Frankfurt: Fischer, 1987), p. 148.

95. On the level of support for Nazism among Austria's population, see Evan Bukey, *Hitler's Austria: Popular Sentiment in the Nazi Era, 1938–1945* (Chapel Hill: University of North Carolina Press, 2000). On the postwar period, see Robert Knight, "Kalter Krieg, Entnazifizierung und Österreich," in *Verdrängte Schuld, verfehlte Sühne: Entnazifizierung in Österreich 1945–1955,* ed. Sebastian Meissl, Klaus-Dieter Mulley, and Oliver Rathkolb (Vienna: Verlag für Geschichte und Politik, 1986).

96. Especially notorious were the scrubbing squads, where Jews were forced to clean the streets of Vienna with brushes and toothbrushes to the loud cheers of the city's inhabitants. On the situation following the *Anschluss,* see Doron Rabinovici, *Instanzen der Ohnmacht; Der Novemberpogrom 1938: Die "Reichskristallnacht in Wien* — Begleitband zur 116. Sonderausstellung des Historischen Museums der Stadt Wien (Vienna: Eigenverlag der Museen der Stadt Wien, 1988); Gerhard Botz, "The Dynamics of Persecution in Austria, 1938–45," in *Austrians and Jews in the Twentieth Century: From Franz Joseph to Waldheim,* ed. Robert Wistrich (New York: St. Martin's Press, 1992).

97. Rabinovici, *Instanzen der Ohnmacht.*

98. Only 5,700 Jews survived World War II in Vienna, while another 2,000 survived the extermination camps. Only 200 Jews were hidden by Viennese non-Jews and thereby saved. The persecution of Vienna's Jews occurred with the knowledge and complicity of large parts of the Viennese population. In fact, the gradual removal of Vienna's Jews relieved an acute housing shortage in the city and generated enormous revenue. Botz, "The Dynamics of Persecution in Austria, 1938–45," pp. 204–13.

99. Historical research on the history of Austria's homosexuals under National Socialism is only now commencing. Important initial findings have been published in Hannes Sulzenbacher and Nikolaus Wahl, eds., *Aus dem Leben: Begleitpublikation zur Ausstellung über die nationalsozialistische Verfolgung der Homosexuellen in Wien 1938–1945* (Vienna: Sonderheft of the *Lambda Nachrichten,* 2001). See also Sulzenbacher, "'Homosexual' men in Vienna, 1938," in *Opposing Fascism: Community, Authority and Resistance in Europe,* ed. Tim Kirk and Anthony McElligot (Cambridge: Cambridge University Press, 1999), pp. 150–62; *id.,* "Keine Opfer Hitlers: Die Verfolgung von Lesben und Schwulen in der NS-Zeit und ihre Legitimierung in der Zweiten Republik," in *Der andere Blick,* pp. 207–12; Wahl, "'Dame wünscht Freundin zwecks Kino und Theater':

Verfolgung gleichgeschlechtlich liebender Frauen im Wien der Nazizeit," in *Der andere Blick,* pp. 181–88.

100. See esp. the firsthand account by a gay male Austrian, Heinz Heger, *Die Männer mit dem Rosa Winkel: Der Bericht eines Homosexuellen über seine KZ-Haft von 1939–1945* (Hamburg: Merlin-Verlag, 1972); and the figures given by Müller and Fleck in "Unzucht wider der Natur."

101. Brigitte Hamann, *Hitler's Vienna: A Dictator's Apprenticeship* (New York: Oxford University Press, 1999).

102. Throughout this book, there is a certain tension in the space under consideration. Both Vienna and Austria thus appear as sites of investigation, even though they are far from identical. In fact, a reasonable case could be made that Vienna and Austria function antithetically, with the former standing for metropolitan imaginaries and the latter signifying provincial realities. I ultimately take a different position, viewing Vienna and Austria in a more overtly metonymic relationship. Austria may not quite be Vienna writ large, but the city's historical, political, social, and cultural centrality, along with its sheer size — nearly a third of Austria's population live in or around Vienna — make it the foremost site of Austrianness. The analytic motive for reading Austria through Vienna becomes all the more pertinent in the book's empirical contexts. Simply put, the populations in question have an indisputable association with Vienna. Although some Jews and queers live outside the city, the figures are overwhelming, with around 99 percent of postwar Austria's Jews residing in Vienna and little more than a tiny presence of openly lesbian/gay people found in the provinces. The Jewish and queer organizations outside the capital have always been rudimentary, and while their trajectory in the 1990s reflected Viennese developments, they remained marginal and secondary in regard to the goings-on in the capital. A book on Jews and queers in Austria thus has to be a study of Vienna, at the same time as such a study doubles as an analysis of the country at large.

Chapter 1: Myths and Silences

1. Erich Fried, *Nicht verdrängen, nicht gewöhnen: Texte zum Thema Österreich* (Vienna: Europa, 1987), pp. 60–61.

2. Hanisch, *Der Lange Schatten des Staates* contains a good synthetic account of the political tensions of the interwar period.

3. Scholars did not start to systematically investigate Austria's victim myth until the 1980s. Since then, there has been a steady stream of publications on Austrians' role during the Third Reich, as well as on the ways that role has been represented and negotiated in the Second Republic. See, e.g., Anton Pelinka and Erika Weinzierl, eds., *Das große Tabu: Österreichs Umgang mit seiner Vergangenheit* (Vienna: Edition S, 1987); Meissl, Mulley, and Rathkolb, eds., *Verdrängte Schuld, verfehlte Sühne: Entnazifizierung in Österreich 1945–1955;* Ruth Wodak et al., *"Wir sind alle unschuldige Täter": Diskurshistorische Studien zum Nachkriegsantisemitismus* (Frankfurt: Suhrkamp, 1990); Heidemarie Uhl, *Zwischen Versöhn-*

ung und Verstörung: Eine Kontroverse um Österreichs historische Identität fünfzig Jahre nach dem "Anschluß" (Vienna: Böhlau, 1992); Meinrad Ziegler and Waltraud Kannonier-Finster, *Österreichisches Gedächtnis: Über Erinnern und Vergessen der NS-Vergangenheit* (Vienna: Böhlau, 1993); Brigitte Bailer, *Wiedergutmachung kein Thema: Österreich und die Opfer des Nationalsozialismus* (Vienna: Löcker, 1993). An excellent overview of post–World War II Austrian history that pays particular attention to the dynamics of the country's recent *Vergangenheitsbewältigung* is Pelinka, *Austria.*

4. John Bunzl, "Austrian Identity and Antisemitism," *Patterns of Prejudice* 21 (spring 1987), p. 4. See also Robert Knight, *"Ich bin dafür, die Sache in die Länge zu ziehen": Die Wortprotokolle der österreichischen Bundesregierung von 1945 bis 1952 über die Entschädigung der Juden* (Frankfurt: Athenäum, 1988), pp. 25–33.

5. Anton Pelinka, "Der verdrängte Bürgerkrieg," in *Das große Tabu,* ed. Pelinka and Weinzierl, p. 145.

6. *Rot-Weiss-Rot-Buch–Gerechtigkeit für Österreich: Darstellungen, Dokumente und Nachweise zur Vorgeschichte und Geschichte der Okkupation Österreichs* (Vienna: Verlag der Österreichischen Staatsdruckerei, 1946), pp. 6–8.

7. Bukey, *Hitler's Austria.*

8. A similar strategy of integration was adopted by the SPÖ and the ÖVP vis-à-vis each other. As an answer to the fragmentation of Austrian society between Marxist and Catholic camps, which had led to the civil war of 1934 and the establishment of the authoritarian Christian conservative *Ständestaat,* the political strategy of the Second Republic was from its earliest moments one of compromise, exemplified primarily in the institution of the *Sozialpartnerschaft.* See Pelinka, "Der verdrängte Bürgerkrieg," pp. 146–47. On the "de-Nazification" of Austria, see *Verdrängte Schuld, verfehlte Sühne,* esp. the contributions by Dieter Stiefel, Robert Knight, Oliver Rathkolb, and Klaus-Dieter Mulley.

9. Two of the most notorious cases were the leading National Socialists Anton Reinthaller and Taras Borodaykewycz. In 1956, the former became the first chairperson of the FPÖ (when the party changed its name from VdU), and the latter quickly assumed a professorship at the Viennese Business Academy *(Hochschule für Welthandel).* Pelinka, "Der verdrängte Bürgerkrieg," p. 148.

10. The SPÖ and ÖVP had different strategies in dealing with former Nazis. Hoping to claim the majority of these presumably conservative voters, the ÖVP supported candidates whose stance appealed to National Socialist voters. The SPÖ, while also hoping for votes from former members of the NSDAP, lobbied for the founding of the VdU (Verband der Unabhängigen) in 1949. Serving as a political haven for the former Nazis, the SPÖ hoped to divert votes away from the ÖVP. Oliver Rathkolb, "NS-Problem und politische Restauration: Vorgeschichte und Etablierung des VdU," in *Verdrängte Schuld, verfehlte Sühne,* ed. Meissl, Mulley, and Rathkolb. On the VdU, see also Max E. Riedlesperger, *The Lingering Shadow of Nazism: The Austrian Independent Party Movement Since 1945* (New York: Columbia University Press, 1978). On the election campaigns of 1945 and 1949, see Norbert Hölzel, *Propagandaschlachten: Die österreichischen Wahlkämpfe 1945–1971* (Vienna: Verlag für Geschichte und Politik, 1974).

11. John Bunzl, "Austrian Identity and Antisemitism," pp. 4–5. On the day before the signing of Austria's State Treaty in 1955, a clause on the country's core-sponsibility for Hitler's war was eliminated.

12. For qualitative and historical analyses of Austrian patterns of memory of the Third Reich, see Ziegler and Kannonier-Finster, *Österreichisches Gedächtnis*. For quantitative data on Austrians' attitudes on the Holocaust, see John Bunzl and Bernd Marin, *Antisemitismus in Österreich*, esp. pp. 225ff.

13. On the centrality of neutrality in the constitution of postwar Austrian nationness, see Ruth Wodak et al., *Zur diskursiven Konstruktion nationaler Identität* (Frankfurt: Suhrkamp, 1998).

14. On the political logic of the Cold War era, see Knight, *"Ich bin dafür, die Sache in die Länge zu ziehen,"* pp. 48–54.

15. Beckermann, *Unzugehörig*, pp. 77–79. These incidents were reported in Jewish publications, particularly the postwar periodical *Der neue Weg*, as well as in the international press. According to a U.S. survey conducted in 1947–48, 44 percent of Austrians agreed that even though the "Nazis had gone too far in their treatment of Jews, something had to be done to contain them." Christoph Reinprecht, *Zurückgekehrt: Identität und Bruch in der Biographie österreichischer Juden* (Vienna: Braumüller, 1992), p. 31.

16. Cited in Reinprecht, *Zurückgekehrt*, p. 31. For a similar discourse, see Leopold Figl in *Neues Österreich*, Sept. 12, 1946.

17. Cited in Knight, "'Neutrality,' not Sympathy: Jews in Post-war Austria," in Wistrich, *Austrians and Jews in the Twentieth Century*, p. 223.

18. Bailer, *Wiedergutmachung kein Thema*, p. 135.

19. Helmer is cited in Knight, *"Ich bin dafür, die Sache in die Länge zu ziehen,"* p 107. Renner is cited in Knight, "'Neutrality,' not Sympathy," p. 222.

20. For a paradigmatic example, see "Jewish Crossfire," *Tagespost*, Nov. 25, 1954. See also "Jewish Demands," *Neuer Kurier*, Feb. 1, 1955; and "Once Again: The Jewish Demands," *Die Presse*, Feb. 12, 1955.

21. Knight, *"Ich bin dafür, die Sache in die Länge zu ziehen,"* p. 197. This pro-grammatic statement on the government's attempt to defer Jewish restitution indefinitely was made on November 9, 1948, the tenth anniversary of *Kristall-nacht*. The next day, Leopold Figl joined the Jewish community in a memorial service. *Die Gemeinde*, Nov. 1948.

22. Gustav Jellinek, "Die Geschichte der österreichischen Wiedergut-machung," in *The Jews of Austria: Essays on Their Life, History and Destruction*, ed. Josef Fraenkel (London: Valentine, 1967), p. 398. See also Beckermann, *Unzuge-hörig*, pp. 86–91, which also addresses Jewish frustrations after negotiations began.

23. Bailer, *Wiedergutmachung kein Thema*, pp. 23–27.

24. Beckermann, *Unzugehörig*, p. 72; Bailer, *Wiedergutmachung kein Thema*, p 139.

25. Bailer, *Wiedergutmachung kein Thema*, pp. 139–41.

26. Ibid., p. 142.

27. The following account of 1963 draws heavily on the superb work of

Alexander Joskowicz. See Joskowicz, "Identität, Macht, Erzählung: Der Nationalsozialismus in österreischischen Erinnerungsdiskursen der fünfziger und sechziger Jahre," master's thesis, University of Vienna, 2000. For other scholarship that has proposed similar analyses of Austrian memory, see Matti Bunzl, "On the Politics and Semantics of Austrian Memory: Vienna's Monument against War and Fascism," *History and Memory* 7, no. 2 (1995), pp. 7–40.

28. Joskowicz, "Identität, Macht, Erzählung," pp. 17, 18.

29. Ibid., pp. 18–22.

30. The Austrian system of religious administration requires the existence of a central institution organizing all Jews into one body, regardless of differences in religious observation. In this light, the IKG is sometimes thought of as an *Einheitsgemeinde,* a unified community.

31. The *El Mole Rachamim* is the prayer for the dead. The description of the event is taken from *Die Tätigkeit der Israelitischen Kultusgemeinde Wien, 1960–1964* (Vienna: Eigenverlag, 1964), p. 44. See also Joskowicz, "Identität, Macht, Erzählung," pp. 67–72.

32. The announcement for the event was made on the cover of *Die Gemeinde,* Nov. 1948.

33. Figl's speech was published in *Die Gemeinde,* Dec. 1948, p. 10.

34. On the memorial event of 1958, see *Die Gemeinde,* Nov. 28, 1958.

35. A somewhat different logic existed for Jewish commemorative rituals that did not challenge Austria's victim myth. As such, the Jewish community could commemorate the Warsaw ghetto uprising and celebrate the anniversaries of the state of Israel openly and with some degree of state support.

36. On Kreisky's refusal of the category Jewish *Volk,* see *Arbeiter-Zeitung,* Oct. 25, 1975. See also *Wochenpresse,* Nov. 15, 1975; and Wistrich, "The Kreisky Phenomenon: A Reassessment," in *Austrians and Jews in the Twentieth Century.*

37. The citation is from "Ich und die Judenfrage," *Kurier,* Sept. 9, 1978, p. 5. See also Bruno Kreisky, *Die Zeit in der wir leben: Betrachtungen zur internationalen Politik* (Vienna: Molden, 1978).

38. Cited in Wistrich, "The Kreisky Phenomenon," p. 243.

39. Helmut Bertl, "Wiens Judenschaft 1964," *Die Furche,* May 1964.

40. Ibid.

41. Ibid.

42. Similar notions were advanced by other media, such as the state radio broadcast system. See, e.g., a 1967 broadcast in which Jews were blamed for Jesus' death. *Die Gemeinde,* Apr. 27, 1967.

43. Viktor Reimann was a self-proclaimed nationalist. In his youth, he had sympathized with National Socialism, but during the war, he disavowed Nazism and briefly joined the resistance. In the postwar era, he served as a representative of the VdU. To emphasize his objectivity on the matter, the *Krone* advertised him as a "non-Jew," *Profil,* May 2, 1974. For an analysis of the *Krone* series from a different theoretical perspective, see John Bunzl and Bernd Marin, *Antisemitismus in Österreich,* ch. 2.

44. *Neue Kronen Zeitung,* Apr. 12, 1974, p. 7.

45. *Neue Kronen Zeitung,* Apr. 8, 1974, p. 6.

46. *Neue Kronen Zeitung,* Apr. 8, 1974, p. 7; *Neue Kronen Zeitung,* Apr. 7, 1974, p. 12.

47. *Neue Kronen Zeitung,* Apr. 7, 1974, p. 13; *Neue Kronen Zeitung,* Apr. 8, 1974, p. 6.

48. *Neue Kronen Zeitung,* Apr. 7, 1974, p. 12.

49. *Neue Kronen Zeitung,* May 3, 1974; *Neue Kronen Zeitung,* May 4, 1974, p. 4

50. *Neue Kronen Zeitung,* May 3, 1974.

51. *Arbeiter-Zeitung,* Apr. 27, 1974.

52. *Neue Kronen Zeitung,* Apr. 7, 1974, p. 13.

53. *Neue Kronen Zeitung,* May 5, 1974.

54. *Neue Kronen Zeitung,* May 11, 1974; *Neue Kronen Zeitung,* Apr. 22, 1974, p. 4.

55. *Neue Kronen Zeitung,* May 19, 1974, p. 9.

56. *Der Neue Weg,* Dec. 15, 1945, p. 2; *Der Neue Weg,* Jul. 1, 1946, p. 7; *Der Neue Weg,* Nov. 1, 1946, p. 5.

57. *Neues Österreich,* Nov. 17, 1954; *Der Abend,* Nov. 17, 1954; *Wiener Zeitung,* Nov. 19, 1954.

58. *Die Gemeinde,* Jan. 29, 1960; *Die Gemeinde,* Apr. 29, 1960.

59. *Die Gemeinde,* Nov. 30, 1961; *Die Gemeinde,* Mar. 29, 1963; *Die Tätigkeit der Israelitischen Kultusgemeinde Wien,* pp. 57, 60, 62. In 1965, a scandal erupted over Taras Borodajkewycz, a professor at Vienna's commerce university whose lectures were overtly racist and antisemitic. The ensuing protests caused violent incidents, resulting in the death of one antifascist demonstrator. *Die Gemeinde,* Apr. 30, 1965; *Die Gemeinde,* Jul. 9, 1965; *Die Gemeinde,* May 31, 1966. The acquittals in several trials of former Nazis in the 1960s caused further consternation. *Die Gemeinde,* Nov. 30, 1961; *Die Gemeinde,* June 28, 1963; *Die Gemeinde,* Nov. 17, 1966.

60. Reinprecht, *Zurückgekehrt,* pp. 63–65, 70, 72.

61. The *Klassenbuch* is the main tool of surveillance in Austria's schools. Identifying every member of a class and containing meticulous records of their attendance, they are kept in public view of teachers and students at all times. A student's Jewishness, which is prominently recorded in the *Klassenbuch,* is thus common knowledge.

62. One man who attended high school in the early 1980s told me, "During my school years, I was constantly confronted with antisemitism. Expressions like *Saujud* [Jew Pig] were common and people would scrawl *Jud* [the pejorative variant of Jew] into my notebook." A woman who was in school in the 1970s recalled how a school groundskeeper once refused her entrance, "For you, I won't unlock the door, for Jews I don't unlock the doors."

63. John Bunzl and Bernd Marin, *Antisemitismus in Österreich,* pp. 227ff.

64. Some examples of this practice are writers Hans Weigel and Elfriede Jelinek, music critic Marcel Prawy, and painters Friedensreich Hundertwasser, Ernst Fuchs, and Arik Brauer. In some ways, Friedrich Torberg was an excep-

tion, largely on account of his humorous writings on Jewish themes. These, however, were resolutely apolitical, so they too were an accommodation to Austrian hegemonies.

65. In religious education classes, students were counseled by Vienna's chief rabbi not to wear skullcaps in public.

66. A 1974 survey conducted in Vienna's Jewish community suggested that Jews hardly had contact with non-Jews, mostly for fear of antisemitic rejection. *Die Gemeinde,* Jan. 11, 1974; see also *Journal für angewandte Sozialforschung,* no. 3 (1975), pp. 21–23.

67. Ruth Beckermann has written of the postwar years: "We lived in Vienna, but we were in contact almost exclusively with Jews. With them we celebrated birthdays and Jewish holidays, with them we spent Sundays and vacations." Beckermann, *Unzugehörig,* p. 117.

68. The discussion of postwar Austrian Zionism draws on material originally presented in Matti Bunzl, "Austrian Zionism and the Jews of the New Europe," *Jewish Social Studies* 9 (2003).

69. Helga Embacher, *Neubeginn ohne Illusionen: Juden in Österreich nach 1945* (Vienna: Picus, 1995), p. 87. Embacher's important monograph mainly treats the IKG's internal political debates during the immediate postwar era. Its analysis usefully stands alongside the argument presented in this chapter.

70. *Aliya,* literally "going up," is the Zionist term for immigration to Israel.

71. This is a theme stressed in Evelyn Adunka, *Die vierte Gemeinde: Die Wiener Juden in der Zeit von 1945 bis heute* (Berlin: Philo, 2000), a monumental assemblage of sources chronicling the institutional history of Vienna's postwar Jewish community.

72. Articles about new buildings at Tel Aviv University could stand side by side with a story of Japanese visitors to a kibbuz; Israeli advances in the field of gerontology were likely to be complemented by reports of the booming floral industry and accounts of Israel's international leadership in swimwear design. *Die Gemeinde,* June 12, 1974, pp. 10, 11; *Die Gemeinde,* Jul. 10, 1974, pp. 10, 11; *Die Gemeinde,* Feb. 5, 1975, p. 9.

73. Topics covered in these articles included the Jewish culture of Vienna's second district, Leopoldstadt (*Die Gemeinde,* June 27, 1958), the Jewish influence on Austrian operetta (*Die Gemeinde,* June 27, 1961), the Jewish restaurant tradition (*Die Gemeinde,* Jan. 31, 1968), general Austrian-Jewish history (*Die Gemeinde,* Dec. 31, 1968), the Jewish contributions to Austrian literature (*Die Gemeinde,* Oct. 22, 1969), the Jewish dimensions of Austria's operatic tradition (*Die Gemeinde,* Mar. 25, 1970), the relationship between Francis Joseph and the Jews (*Die Gemeinde,* Jan. 13, 1971), the enduring legacy of Jewish Vienna (*Die Gemeinde,* Oct. 10, 1971), and individual Austrian-Jewish culture heroes, like Richard Beer Hofmann (*Die Gemeinde,* May 31, 1964), Joseph Roth (*Die Gemeinde,* Dec. 30, 1969), and Arthur Schnitzler (*Die Gemeinde,* Oct. 6, 1971).

74. *Die Gemeinde,* Oct. 22, 1969.

75. *Die Gemeinde,* Jan. 13, 1971.

76. *Die Gemeinde,* Nov. 10, 1971.

77. This comment, as well as a number of narratives presented in the following section, was initially published in Matti Bunzl, "The City and the Self: Narratives of Spatial Belonging Among Austrian Jews," *City and Society* (1996), pp. 50–81.

78. Ruth Wodak et al., *"Wir sind alle unschuldige Täter,"* pp. 61–69. See also Richard Mitten, "Reflections on the 'Waldheim Affair,' " in *Austrians and Jews in the Twentieth Century,* ed. Wistrich, p. 252.

79. Wodak et al., *"Wir sind alle unschuldige Täter,"* pp. 69–81. The WJC is a private organization founded in 1936 to promote common interests of Jewish communities around the world.

80. Cited in ibid., pp. 97, 119, 187.

81. Ibid., p. 162. See also Mitten, "Reflections on the 'Waldheim Affair,' " pp. 256–57. At one point, Waldheim himself stated that the international press was "dominated" by the WJC. Waldheim in *Le Monde,* May 3, 1986. Cited in John Bunzl, *Der Lange Arm der Erinnerung: Jüdisches Bewußtsein heute* (Vienna: Böhlau, 1987), p. 107. In the discourse of the Waldheim defenders, the term *WJC* repeatedly served to denote an associative chain of referents ranging from "a private special interest group located in New York" to "the Jews" in general, thus adding to the notion of a diffuse Jewish threat. Wodak et al., *"Wir sind alle unschuldige Täter,"* p. 140.

82. Cited in ibid., pp. 104, 187, 331.

83. Cited in ibid., p. 190

84. Cited in ibid., pp. 187, 190.

85. For the most part, the IKG tried to deploy this strategy in the struggle for restitution. See *Bericht des Präsidiums der Israelitischen Kultusgemeinde Wien über die Tätigkeit in den Jahren 1945 bis 1948* (Vienna: Eigenverlag, 1948); *Die Tätigkeit der Israelitischen Kultusgemeinde Wien in den Jahren 1952 bis 1954* (Vienna: Eigenverlag, 1955); as well as numerous articles in *Die Gemeinde.* In regard to the threat of antisemitism, the IKG mainly sought political alliances with the Social Democratic Party. In consequence, the fight against antisemitism mostly consisted of lobbying efforts among the party's leaders. See, for example, *Die Tätigkeit der Israelitischen Kultusgemeinde Wien, 1960–1964,* pp. 53, 55, 58, 61. On the political strategies of the IKG in the postwar years, see also Embacher, *Neubeginn ohne Illusionen;* and Adunka, *Die vierte Gemeinde.*

86. The statement is reprinted in *Die Gemeinde,* June 6, 1996, p. 6. The IKG also issued two press releases taking a similarly accommodationst position. They are reprinted in *Die Gemeinde,* Apr. 11, 1986 and May 9, 1986.

Chapter 2: Laws and Closets

1. On the history of *Der Kreis,* Europe's seminal homophile publication of the postwar period, see Hubert Kennedy, *The Ideal Gay Man: The Story of 'Der Kreis'* (New York: Harrington Park Press, 1999).

2. *Der Kreis,* 1955, no. 4: 2–4.

3. *Der Kreis,* 1956, no. 3: pp. 26–27.

4. *Profil*, Sept. 11, 1995, p. 59.

5. On the legal alignment between Germany's §175 and Austria's §129, see Sulzenbacher and Brunner, "Donauwalzer — Herrenwahl."

6. Bailer, *Wiedergutmachung kein Thema*, p. 142.

7. See the exchange of letters from the early 1950s between the women's prison at Lankowitz and the Ministry of Justice. Private collection on Austrian lesbian/gay history of Hannes Sulzenbacher.

8. The highest number of convictions in a single year was 815 in 1955. *Profil*, May 18, 1976. The total number for the period of 1950–60 was 7,480; the number for 1960–71 was 5,566. *Profil*, Sept. 11, 1995.

9. This was the number in 1971, the year when the so-called *Schwulen-Kartei* (gay lists) were supposedly destroyed. *Profil*, May 18, 1976, p. 42. Very few women were prosecuted for same-sex sexual acts in the course of the Second Republic, the total number being 314. *Profil*, Sept. 11, 1995, p. 63.

10. On the trial in Vienna, see *Der Kreis*, 1955, no. 4. On the trial in Vorarlberg, see *Der Kreis*, 1956, no. 3; *Der Kreis*, 1956, no. 7.

11. *Der Kreis*, 1963, no. 10: 7. *Warmer*, here translated as *fag*, is the most common colloquial expression for the pejorative designation of a gay man. In the early 1960s, five thousand schillings was more than the average monthly salary.

12. See also *Profil*, Sept. 11, 1995, esp. p. 60.

13. Sulzenbacher and Brunner, "Donauwalzer — Herrenwahl," pp. 89–90.

14. *Profil*, May 16, 1976, p. 42.

15. *Der Kreis*, 1957, no. 11. See also Hannes Sulzenbacher, "Die Diskussion über die Strafrechtsreform 1957" (unpublished manuscript).

16. Bundesministerium für Justiz, *Entwurf eines Strafgesetzbuches samt Erläuterungen* (Vienna: Eigenverlag, 1964). See also Bundesministerium für Justiz, *Entwurf* (1964). See also *Wochenpresse*, Aug. 16, 1967.

17. Bundesministerium für Justiz, *Entwurf eines Strafgesetzbuches samt Erläuternden Bemerkungen* (Vienna: Eigenverlag, 1966).

18. Bundesministerium für Justiz, *Regierungsvorlage eines Strafgesetzbuches samt Erläuternden Bemerkungen* (Vienna: Eigenverlag, 1968), pp. 374–75.

19. At the time, only the Soviet Union, Romania, Yugoslavia, and Finland had a total interdiction of all same-sex sexual activities. *Wochenpresse*, Aug. 16, 1967.

20. *Kurier*, Jul. 9, 1971.

21. Otto Kranzlmayr, cited in *Neues Forum*, Apr. 1976, p. 47.

22. *Profil*, May 18, 1976, p. 45.

23. The exact text of §209 is as follows: "Same-sex lechery with persons under the age of eighteen: A male person over the age of nineteen who conducts same-sex lechery with a person who has finished the fourteenth but not yet completed the eighteenth year is to be punished with a prison sentence of six months to five years."

24. Stransky, cited in Bundesministerium für Justiz, *Protokoll über die siebzehnte Arbeitssitzung der Kommission zur Ausarbeitung eines Strafgesetzbuches im Jahre 1957* (Vienna: Eigenverlag, 1957), p. 1272.

25. Rittler, cited in ibid., p. 1489.

26. Bundesministerium für Justiz, *Entwurf* (1964), p. 190.

27. Ibid.; Bundesministerium für Justiz, *Regierungsvorlage* (Vienna: Eigenverlag, 1970), p. 15.

28. Freudian ideas also came into play, but Lorenzian notions ultimately dominated, starting with the initial debates of 1957. See, for example, Hoff, cited in Bundesministerium für Justiz, *Protokoll*, p. 1272, 1279.

29. Stransky, cited in ibid., p. 1272.

30. Bundesministerium für Justiz, *Regierungsvorlage* (1970), p. 15.

31. While relations between adult men and adolescents were forbidden because of their capacity to inflict permanent damage, "experimentation" among youths was seen as a harmless diversion on the path to normal adult sexuality and were not persecuted.

32. The exact text of §220 was as follows: "Advertisement for lechery among persons of the same sex or with animals: Whoever incites or even sanctions in print, film, or any other public media same-sex lechery in a form that might suggest such acts, and if he is not subject to harsher penalties for being himself involved in acts of lechery, then he is subject to a prison sentence of up to six months or a fine of 360 times his daily income." §221 had the following text: "Organizations that enable same-sex lechery: Whoever founds an organization with a large number of members whose even partial purpose it is to enable same-sex lechery and which is hence capable of disturbing the public peace, or whoever belongs to such an organization or tries to recruit members for it, is subject to a prison sentence of up to six months or a fine of 360 times his daily income."

33. Bundesministerium für Justiz, *Entwurf* (1964), p. 191.

34. Ibid., p. 190.

35. Ibid.

36. Ibid., p. 191.

37. Ibid., p. 190.

38. Ibid.

39. Ibid., p. 191. With the exception of Liechtenstein, Austria was the only country in Europe that introduced a law forbidding the founding of lesbian/gay organizations. Laws forbidding the advertisement of same-sex sexuality were more common. In 1971, a fourth law was introduced, outlawing male prostitution. It was lifted in 1989. *Lambda Nachrichten*, 1989, no. 3: 23–24.

40. Bundesministerium für Justiz, *Entwurf* (1964), p. 191.

41. Peter Schieder, cited in *Kurier*, Jul. 9, 1971.

42. *Profil*, Sept. 11, 1995. See also Gudrun Hauer, "Lesben- und Schwulengeschichte: Diskriminierung und Widerstand," in *Homosexualität in Österreich*, ed. Michael Handl et al. (Vienna: Junius, 1989), p. 67; *Lambda Nachrichten*, 1996, no. 1: 40.

43. Between 1987 and 1990, twenty-seven charges were brought, one of which led to a conviction. Helmut Graupner, *Homosexualität und Strafrecht in Österreich: Eine Übersicht* (Vienna: Eigenverlag, 1992), p. 11. See also *Lambda Nachrichten*, 1990, no. 4: 19; *Profil*, Sept. 25, 1995.

44. See esp. the many references to the coverage of homosexuality as a crime in *Der Kreis*.

45. Wolfgang Förster, "Männliche Homosexualität in den österreichischen Printmedien — Zur Tradierung eines Vorurteils," in *Homosexualität in Österreich,* ed. Handl et al., p. 93.

46. Ibid., p. 94.

47. On the case, see *Kurier,* Jan. 11, 1977, *Kurier,* Jan. 21, 1977, *Arbeiter-Zeitung,* Jan. 11, 1977, and *CO-INFO* 4 (1977), pp. 24–27.

48. *Kurier,* Jan. 11, 1977.

49. *Wochenpresse,* Aug. 16, 1967, pp. 1, 5–6.

50. Ibid., p. 5.

51. Ibid., p. 6.

52. *Profil,* May 18, 1976, pp. 40–46.

53. Ibid., p. 40.

54. Ibid.

55. Ibid., pp. 40–41.

56. Ibid., p. 41.

57. Ibid., p. 45.

58. Ibid.

59. Ibid., pp. 40–41.

60. Ibid., pp. 40–45.

61. The mass-media coverage of homosexuality in the 1970s and early 1980s focused almost exclusively on males. Women were essentially absent; neither did they appear in conjunction with stories on crime nor were they mentioned in descriptions of the homosexual scene. Among the sources accessible to me, I found a single article that mentioned homosexual women (*Arbeiter-Zeitung,* Jul. 14, 1979), and there too it was in passing in a discussion of gay men.

62. There is a terrible paucity of historical and ethnographic work on Central European lesbians. Next to no material is available for the postwar period. For the years before World War II, we have some information thanks in large part to Hanna Hacker's groundbreaking research. See Hacker, *Frauen und Freundinnen.*

63. Cited in *Profil,* May 18, 1976, p. 42.

64. The term *Loge,* literally theater box, is the most widely used colloquialism for public toilets among Austrian gay men. The German equivalent is *Klappe.*

65. On Germany, see Hans-Gerog Stümke, *Homosexuelle in Deutschland: Eine politische Geschichte* (Munich: Beck, 1989). On England, see Jeffrey Weeks, *Homosexual Politics in Britain, from the Nineteenth Century to the Present* (London: Quartet Books, 1979).

66. The history of Austrian's lesbian/gay emancipation movement is discussed in Chapter 4.

67. Only one Austrian mass medium, for example, reported the founding of Homosexuelle Initiative, the country's first official lesbian/gay organization. In the following years, the group often complained about being ignored by the press. *Lambda Nachrichten,* 1984, no. 2: 12.

68. Two rare articles sympathetic to the demands of the lesbian/gay movement appeared in *Profil.* See *Profil,* Jul. 18, 1983, which featured a piece on the

injustice of legal discrimination, and *Profil*, Oct. 5, 1992, which addressed the issue of lesbian/gay marriage.

69. *Wochenpresse*, Mar. 2, 1982, p. 23.

70. For another article with a similar tenor, see *Wochenpresse*, Nov. 9, 1982.

71. *Die Presse*, Mar. 4, 1988. For a similar piece written on the same occasion, see *Kurier*, Mar. 4, 1988.

72. For a more detailed analysis of the 1995 Outing affair, see Matti Bunzl, "Outing As Performance/Outing As Resistance: A Queer Reading of Austrian (Homo)Sexualities," *Cultural Anthropology* 12, no. 1 (1977), pp. 129–51.

73. Hans Rauscher in *Kurier*, Jul. 28, 1995, p. 2; Herbert Geyer in *Wochenpresse*, Aug. 3, 1995, p. 15; Michael Maier in *Die Presse*, Jul. 29, 1995, p. 2.

74. Robert Buchacher and Christian Seiler, "Gestehe, dass du schwul bist: Das Zwangs-"Outing" Prominenter hat der Homosexuellen-Bewegung bisher wenig genützt — allenfalls den Boulvardmedien," *Profil*, Jul. 31, 1995, pp. 26–29.

75. Ibid., p. 26.

76. Ibid.

77. Ibid., p. 29.

78. *Der Standard*, Jul. 28, 1995, p. 28; *Österreichischer Rundfunk (ORF), News Report. Mittagsjournal*, Aug. 1, 1995; the clergy quoted in *Die Presse*, Jul. 28, 1995, p. 3.

79. Peter Rabl in *Kurier*, Aug. 2, 1995, p. 2.

80. In the wake of the scandal, Krickler was sued by outed clergy, and over the next few years, a series of court cases led to repeated convictions. See *Lambda Nachrichten*, 1995, no. 4: 19–22; *Lambda Nachrichten*, 1996, no. 2: 25–27; *Lambda Nachrichten*, 1996, no. 3: 24–26. *Lambda Nachrichten*, 1995, no. 4: 19–22.

Chapter 3: Street Fairs and Demonstrations

1. Haider has presented his political vision in two books. Jörg Haider, *Die Freiheit, die ich meine* (Frankfurt: Ullstein, 1994); id., *Befreite Zukunft jenseits von links und rechts: Menschliche Alternativen für eine Brücke ins neue Jahrtausend* (Vienna: Iberia & Molden, 1997).

2. Hubertus Czernin, *Wofür ich mich meinetwegen entschuldige: Haider, beim Wort genommen* (Vienna: Czernin Verlag, 2000), pp. 31, 46–48.

3. In *Die vierte Gemeinde*, Evelyn Adunka chronicles a number of Jewish demonstrations, e.g., against the persecution of the Jews in the Islamic Middle East. None of these events, however, was ever directed against the Austrian state.

4. See, e.g., *Die Gemeinde*, Mar. 28, 1958 (which contains a bitter complaint about Austria's victim myth), as well as some of the sources mentioned in Chapter 1.

5. I found a single exception to this trend, a 1970 article by socialist Zionist Josef Toch, in which he diagnosed and critiqued Austria's contemporary anti-semitism. Toch, "Antisemitismus heute?" *Die Furche*, June 20, 1970.

6. On the essential silence of Austrian-Jewish writers who returned to Vien-

na after the war, see Matti Bunzl, "From Silence to Defiance: Jews and Queers in Contemporary Vienna," Ph.D. diss., University of Chicago, 1998, ch. 7.

7. Beckermann, *Unzugehörig*, pp. 117–29.

8. Ibid., p. 119.

9. In the American context, this process has been brilliantly described and analyzed by Peter Novick, *The Holocaust in American Life* (Boston: Houghton Mifflin, 1999).

10. As the daughter of Leopold Spira, a leading Austrian-Jewish communist intellectual, Elisabeth Spira continued a tradition of radical opposition to antisemitism as part of a larger emancipatory project. Leopold Spira's postwar work, which received little attention beyond the small world of Austrian communism, is exemplified by his book *Feindbild "Jud": 100 Jahre politischer Antisemitismus in Österreich* (Vienna: Löcker, 1981).

11. Elisabeth Spira, "Es ist kalt in Österreich: Notizen zum österreichischen Antisemitismus," *Trotzdem*, Dec. 20, 1975.

12. Erika Wantoch, "Die Überlebenden: Eine Bilanz," *Profil*, June 15, 1981, pp. 39–43. See also the special issue of *Arbeiter-Zeitung* titled "Juden in Wien: Gegenwart, von Geschichte bestimmt," which was mostly written by young Austrian Jews. *Arbeiter-Zeitung*, Dec. 10, 1982.

13. Wantoch, "Die Überlebenden," p. 39.

14. Ibid., pp. 41, 43.

15. Georg Haber, "Nach der Wahl," *Die Gemeinde*, Jul. 11, 1986. See also Martin Engelberg, "Unerträglich," *Die Gemeinde*, Jul. 8, 1987.

16. Doron Rabinovici, "War Moses ein Zionist?" *Das jüdische Echo* (1987).

17. Ibid., p. 161.

18. Some of this work had been done before the Waldheim affair. But as the list in ch. 1, n. 3 suggests, most of it was produced in the years after Waldheim's election as president.

19. Robert Schindel's widely acclaimed books include such volumes of poetry as *Ohneland: Gedichte vom Holz der Paradeiserbäume* (Frankfurt: Suhrkamp, 1986); *Geier sind pünktliche Tiere* (Frankfurt: Suhrkamp, 1987); *Im Herzen der Krätze* (Frankfurt: Suhrkamp, 1988); and *Ein Feuerchen im Hintennach* (Frankfurt: Suhrkamp, 1992); along with the celebrated novel *Gebürtig* (Frankfurt: Suhrkamp, 1992). Ruth Beckermann, the author of *Unzugehörig*, is most widely known for her award-winning films on Jewish and antifascist topics, including *Wien Retour* (1983), *Die papierene Brücke* (1990), *Jenseits des Krieges* (1996), and *Homemad(e)* (2001). Robert Menasse, an accomplished essayist whose book *Das Land ohne Eigenschaften: Essay zur österreichischen Identität* (Vienna: Sonderzahl, 1992) constituted the most devastating critique of Austrianness published in the 1990s, is also the author of such novels as *Selige Zeiten, brüchige Welt* (Frankfurt: Suhrkamp, 1997) and *Die Vertreibung aus der Hölle* (Frankfurt: Suhrkamp, 2001). Other Jewish artists and intellectuals who came to some prominence in the late 1980s and 1990s include philosopher Isolde Charim, linguist Ruth Wodak, authors Anna Mitgutsch and Vladimir Vertlieb, and political scientist John Bunzl.

20. *Profil*, Apr. 7, 1986.

21. The name *Neues Österreich* was an allusion to the antifascist newspaper of the same name published in the postwar era.

22. A highly incomplete list of Doron Rabinovici's prominently placed pieces includes critiques of sculptor Alfred Hrdlicka (*Der Standard,* Dec. 19, 1994), Jewish writer and FPÖ politician Peter Sichrovsky (*Die Presse,* Aug. 4, 1996), and Haider himself (*Der Standard,* Mar. 20–21, 1999), as well as essays on Austria's EU policy (*Der Standard,* Oct. 19, 1998), the 150th anniversary of the IKG (*Format,* 1999, no. 14), and Austria's political situation in the wake of the ÖVP/FPÖ coalition (*Kleine Zeitung,* Feb. 20, 2000; *Der Falter,* 2000, no. 17).

23. Doron Rabinovici, *Papirnik: Stories* (Frankfurt: Suhrkamp, 1994); *id., Suche nach M.* (Frankfurt: Suhrkamp, 1997). For reviews of the latter, see *Die Presse,* Mar. 8, 1997, *Der Falter,* Oct. 1997. In the late 1990s, Rabinovici turned to history, completing the previously cited *Instanzen der Ohnmacht,* which chronicled the experience of Vienna's Jews under National Socialism.

24. See Embacher, *Neubeginn ohne Illusionen,* and Adunka, *Die vierte Gemeinde,* both of which chronicle the brief period of communist rule in the IKG, which was followed by decades of socialist dominance

25. The first major shift occurred in 1976, when the socialist Bund Werktätiger Juden lost its absolute majority within the IKG. The Bund held on to the presidency, but the growing strength of the East European–dominated Vereinigter Jüdischer Block under Simon Wiesenthal signaled the beginning of a political transition. In 1981, this transition was completed when, upon further losses of the Bund, Ivan Hacker was elected IKG president as the Block's candidate. *Profil,* June 15, 1981; *Profil,* Dec. 7, 1981.

26. Central to these interventions was the sense — captured by Ruth Beckermann — that the "feeling of not belonging" had "opened the eyes" of younger Jews to the specificity of their situation. While the survivors of the Holocaust had sought to accommodate Austrian hegemonies by way of nonconfrontational appeasement, Beckermann's generation was no longer "willing to engage in discussions with antisemites in order to beg for understanding." Beckermann, *Unzugehörig,* p. 11.

27. *Die Gemeinde,* Feb. 3, 1989, p. 10.

28. Ibid.

29. The statement was reprinted in *Die Gemeinde,* Aug. 11, 1986, p. 5.

30. See, for example, *Arbeiter-Zeitung,* June 19, 1986; *Neues Volksblatt,* June 19, 1986; *Wiener Zeitung,* June 19, 1986.

31. *Der Standard,* June 3, 1989.

32. For other interviews with Grosz that presented a similar challenge to Austrian hegemonies, see *Die Furche,* Mar. 26, 1992; *Der Standard,* Oct. 2, 1992.

33. *Die Gemeinde,* Mar. 6, 1995.

34. See, for example, Muzicant's radio interview in the show "Von Tag zu Tag" on May 13, 1998, where he voiced his dislike for the "word tolerance" in regard to Austrians' treatment of Jews, suggesting its "replacement with the word respect." The new style associated with the first IKG president of the post-Holocaust generation was also reflected in an article in *Der Standard* on Apr. 23,

1998, as well as in Muzicant's first official communication as president in *Die Gemeinde,* May 1998.

35. *Die Gemeinde,* June 1999, p. 13.

36. On the "Haus der Jugend," see *Die Gemeinde,* Apr. 29, 1966; *Die Gemeinde,* Dec. 14, 1966; *Die Gemeinde,* Mar. 27, 1968, as well as a series of articles in 1971. The hiring of a youth official is chronicled in *Die Gemeinde* on Oct. 7, 1974, and the resulting emphasis on youth work can be gleaned from the issues of *Die Gemeinde* starting with Nov. 6, 1974, each of which devoted a special page to youth concerns.

37. The 1979 initiative, which involved ten Jewish families, is chronicled in *Die Gemeinde,* May 5, 1989, p. i. Prior to the initiative that led to the founding of the Jewish school, there was only one Jewish educational institution, a tiny ultra-orthodox Talmud-Thora school in Vienna's second district. *Kurier,* Nov. 21, 1977; *Die Gemeinde,* May 5, 1989, p. i.

38. *Die Gemeinde,* Nov. 1, 1985.

39. The *Gymnasium* is the preparatory school for Central European higher education. The product of the humanistic impulses of the German enlightenment, it emphasizes a liberal arts education over vocational training.

40. *Die Gemeinde,* Dec. 19, 1983, pp. 16–17; *Die Gemeinde,* May 5, 1989, p. i.

41. To avoid the antisemitic environment of Austria's schools, many Jewish families sent their children to Vienna's international schools prior to the founding of the Zwi Perez Chajes School. Vienna's international schools are the Lycée Français, the American International School, and the Vienna International School (the last run on the British model).

42. *Die Gemeinde,* May 5, 1989, p. iv.

43. *Die Gemeinde,* Nov. 1, 1985; *Die Gemeinde,* Oct. 1, 1987.

44. *Die Gemeinde,* Dec. 1999, p. 27.

45. *Die Gemeinde,* Aug. 22, 1958; *Die Gemeinde,* Jan. 27, 1966.

46. *Die Presse,* Sept. 11, 1976.

47. Wantoch, "Die Überlebenden."

48. IKG Matrikelamt, Jan. 27, 1987; IKG Amtsdirektion, Jan. 9, 1989; IKG Amtsdirektion, Jan. 9, 1991; *Die Gemeinde,* Mar. 15, 1994.

49. *Die Gemeinde,* May 5, 1989, p. ii.

50. The following analysis of Jewish sports draws on some of the material initially presented in Matti Bunzl, "Resistive Play: Sports and the Emergence of Jewish Visibility in Contemporary Vienna," *Journal of Sport and Social Issues* 24, no. 3 (2000), pp. 232–50.

51. The history of Hakoah is chronicled in John Bunzl, *Hoppauf Hakoah: Jüdischer Sport in Österreich von den Anfängen bis in die Gegenwart* (Vienna: Junius, 1987). See also Fritz Baar, *50 Jahre Hakoah, 1909–1959* (Tel Aviv: Verlagskommitte Hakoah, 1959).

52. *Die Gemeinde,* Dec. 1995, p. 9. A Maccabi soccer club was founded in 1972. After two years, however, it was no longer able to field a team of Jewish players, and when the addition of non-Jewish players did not ameliorate the situation, the club was dissolved. *Die Gemeinde,* Nov. 6, 1974.

53. To prevent competition for members, Maccabi and Hakoah have agreed not to offer the same sports.

54. *Die Gemeinde,* Dec. 1999, p. 54.

55. In Austrian soccer parlance, the term *Jud* — the derogatory appellation for a Jew — is occasionally used to describe a ball improperly struck by the toes rather than the side of the foot. The more common term for the phenomenon is *Spitz* (tip).

56. Members of Hakoah always display the Star of David. Among members of Maccabi, the display of the Star is contingent on the specific set of jerseys worn for any given game.

57. The success of Hakoah and Maccabi also had social ramifications within Vienna's Jewish community. There it helped to ease longstanding tensions between the Schomer and the Bnei Akiba. As one member of Bnei Akiba put it to me, "I know that there used to be problems between the Schomer and the Be'a [Bnei Akiba]. But I don't see that. I don't have any problems with the people from the Schomer. Lots of my friends from the basketball team are there, and they are totally okay." Even more importantly, the sports clubs were a crucial site for the integration of recent immigrants from the former Soviet Union. In the context of considerable tensions brought on by economic and cultural differences between longstanding residents and recent arrivals, they, more than any other institution, modeled the possibility of a vibrantly unified Jewish community — a sense that was conveyed to me in numerous interviews. On the situation of Jewish immigrants from the former Soviet Union, see Alexander Friedmann, Maria Hofstätter, and Ilan Knapp, eds., *Eine neue Heimat? Jüdische Emigrantinnen und Emigranten aus der Sowjetunion* (Vienna: Verlag für Gesellschaftskritik, 1993); Grigori Galibov, *Geschichte der bucharischen Juden in Wien* (Vienna: Österreichischer Kunst- und Kulturverlag, 2001).

58. Maccabi's home field, the so-called STAW-Platz, is located in the heart of Vienna's second district, the area with the most extensive Jewish tradition, reaching back to the mass immigration of Galician Jews in the late imperial era. See Klaus Hödl, *Als Bettler in die Leopoldstadt: Galizische Juden auf dem Weg nach Wien* (Vienna: Böhlau, 1994); Ruth Beckermann, *Die Mazzesinsel: Juden in der Wiener Leopoldstadt, 1918–1938* (Vienna: Löcker, 1984).

59. The use of antisemitic invectives occurred frequently but, as I was told by Maccabi players, only when the team played against "Austrian" opponents. In contests with squads drawn from other ethnic groups, no antisemitic remarks were reported.

60. Most vocal among the supporters were members of the HaSchomer Hazair, who had brought banners and loudspeakers to cheer on Maccabi.

61. The final score was 5 to 1. For a long period, the contest was extremely close. At fifteen minutes before the end, Maccabi only led by 2 to 1, but then three quick goals put the game out of reach.

62. *Die Gemeinde,* Aug. 2, 1992, p. 19.

63. Ibid.

64. *Die Gemeinde,* May 6, 1992, p. 12.

65. *Die Gemeinde,* Aug. 2, 1992, p. 19; *Die Gemeinde,* May 6, 1992, p. 12.

66. The growth of the festival can be gauged from the reports published in *Die Gemeinde.* See *Die Gemeinde* May 5, 1992; Aug. 2, 1992; Mar. 15, 1993; Nov. 1, 1996; Apr. 1997; Nov. 1998; Apr. 1999; Nov. 1999.

67. The announcement for the first Jewish Street Fair, which was held June 23, 1990, can be found in *Die Gemeinde,* May 14, 1990. For reports of the event, see *Die Gemeinde,* June 22, 1990, and *Der Standard,* May 26, 1990, which emphasized that Vienna's main synagogue, usually closed to non-Jews, was open during the street fair and "the public appeared in ever greater numbers as time went on. . . . By 7:00, the square next to the main stage on Judengasse was completely packed, [and] the culinary attractions in the form of falafel — flat bread with salad and chickpeas, according to a member of the Jewish community a typical fast food comparable to a Viennese sausage — long finished."

68. For an account of the 1992 event, see *Die Gemeinde,* May 6, 1992, which emphasized the simultaneous presence of different Jewish musical and cultural styles, including those from Georgia, Uzbekistan, Eastern Europe, and Israel. For descriptions of subsequent street fairs that continued the multicultural Jewish tradition, see *Die Gemeinde,* June 11, 1993; *Die Gemeinde,* June 30, 1996; *Die Gemeinde,* Apr. 1997; *Die Gemeinde,* June 1999.

69. Ellinor Haber in *Die Gemeinde,* Aug. 2, 1992, p. 19.

70. On February 24, 2000, I attended a town hall meeting called by the IKG to allow members to discuss the new political situation with the community's leadership. About four hundred people came to the synagogue where the meeting was held. The audience was overwhelmingly drawn from an older generation, many individuals having experienced the *Anschluss* of 1938. Several members of that older generation expressed their fear about the FPÖ's rise to political power. As one older woman put it, "I am scared. Recently, I saw a bunch of fraternity men [in Austria, fraternities are associated with German nationalist politics]. Some of them were greeting each other with 'Heil Hitler.' I'm scared that I'll have to flee again. What should I do?" While members of the immediate postwar generation were less concerned about their personal safety, I did learn of fears, especially regarding the children. As one woman born in the early 1950s put it, "I would be scared to run around like my son, wearing a necklace with a Star of David, especially today. Maybe there is more of a need for discretion again."

71. The VJHÖ, for example, changed its regular meeting time from Thursday evening to allow members to participate in the weekly demonstrations that were held on that day.

72. The colors black and blue represent the Christian Social People's Party (black) and the Freedom Party (blue), respectively. Some attendees at the dance party wore yellow stars with a crossed-out circle of black and blue. The dance party, which was held on the square adjacent to the Jewish community center, was dominated by Israeli music, which presented many occasions for Hora-style dancing.

73. At the dance party, I overheard one woman in her late forties comment

that "we never used to have things like that. It's just great." After the events, several interviews with members of the postwar generation confirmed a widespread sense of satisfaction that the Jewish community no longer hides but takes to the streets instead. As one man in his early forties noted, "Today, we have demonstrations by the Jewish community. This had never happened. They never would have sanctioned a demonstration."

74. The Demokratische Offensive was founded and run by Doron Rabinovici, Jewish philosopher Isolde Charim, and non-Jewish journalist Robert Misik. Rabinovici served as the group's official speaker. Gettoattack brought together a large group of university students, several key members of which were Jewish.

75. *Das andere Österreich* (the other Austria) is a widely invoked term to designate the progressive faction of the country. It is in direct opposition to a vision of Austria as a space for National Socialist nostalgia.

76. The event lasted the entire afternoon and evening. At its beginning were four separate rallies held simultaneously at such central sites as Austria's Parliament and the University of Vienna. From these initial rallies, which addressed different political constituencies, participants proceeded to the Heldenplatz for the prolonged final event.

77. *Die Gemeinde,* Apr. 2000, p. 3.

Chapter 4: Cafés and Parades

1. Most of the literature addresses the United States. See Suzanna Danuta Walters, *All the Rage: The Story of Gay Visibility in America* (Chicago: University of Chicago Press, 2001); Herdt, ed., *Gay Culture in America;* Murray, *American Gay;* and Leo Bersani, *Homos* (Cambridge: Harvard University Press, 1995), among many others. Much less of this kind of sociological and ethnographic work is available on Europe. On France, see Martel, *The Pink and the Black.* The essays in Adam et al., *The Global Emergence of Gay and Lesbian Politics* tend to be limited to the institutional histories of the national lesbian/gay movements, but they do provide some context.

2. On Ulrike Lunacek's first bid for a parliamentary seat, see *Lambda Nachrichten,* 1996, no. 1: 15–16. In 1996, Lunacek was elected federal secretary of the Green Party. *Lambda Nachrichten,* 1996, no. 2: 30. Prior to its constitution as the Greens, the party's predecessor, the "Alternative Liste," had run the openly gay Rudi Katzer for Austria's parliament in 1983. At the time, the group had no chance of securing seats in parliament. On Katzer's bid, see *Lambda Nachrichten,* 1983, no. 1: 16–19; *Lambda Nachrichten,* 1983, no. 2–3: 26–27.

3. Written in the immediate context of this development, Dennis Altman's *Homosexual* remains the best source on that history, especially the new edition, which includes an afterword by Altman and an introduction by Jeffrey Weeks. Dennis Altman, *Homosexual: Oppression and Liberation* (New York: New York University Press, 1993 [1971]). See also Jeffrey Weeks, *Coming Out.*

4. In his articles in *Der Kreis,* Erich Lifka discussed informal attempts to create a homophile movement in Austria. *Der Kreis,* 1955, no. 4: 5. One initiative called on homosexuals in the late 1950s to protest their legal subordination by refusing to check their election ballot, instead demanding the abolition of §129. The anonymous author assured the readers of *Der Kreis* that the action, as a completely anonymous form of protest, would have no personal ramifications. *Der Kreis,* 1959, no. 4: 2. In 1963, a Union for Voluntary Motherhood and Sexual Equality was founded in Vienna. A local branch of the homophile movement, it advocated liberalization of Austria's legislation of homosexuality. The group's specific activities are not known and appear to have been inconspicuous and few in number. *Lambda Nachrichten,* 1998, no. 3: 34–35.

5. On the Homosexuel d'Action Révolutionnaire and the French radical scene, see Martel, *The Pink and the Black.* The radical aspects of the German gay movement are treated in the institutional histories: Manfred Baumgardt, *Goodbye to Berlin? 100 Jahre Schwulenbewegung–Ausstellungskatalog* (Berlin: Verlag Rosa Winkel, 1997); and Florian Mildenberger, *Die Münchner Schwulenbewegung 1969 bis 1996: Eine Fallstudie über die zweite deutsche Schwulenbewegung* (Bochum: Winkler, 1999). At roughly the same time that Coming Out was formed in Vienna, the informal institutionalization of a small lesbian movement took place in the context of Vienna's autonomous women's movement. See Ulrike Repnik, "Lesben in Bewegung(en): Die Lesbenbewegung in Österreich seit den 70er Jahren," in *Der andere Blick,* ed. Förster et al., pp. 225–26.

6. *CO-INFO* 1 (June 1976). See also *Sozialistische Aktion* 1979, nos. 17–18.

7. *CO-INFO* 2 (Sept. 1976), p. 18.

8. *CO-INFO* 4 (June 1977), pp. 15–16. See also *Sozialistische Aktion,* 1979, nos. 17–18; *Lambda Nachrichten,* 1987, no. 2: 25–27.

9. The Pentecost Meeting was attended by some two hundred gay men, the overwhelming majority from Germany. The event featured five days of discussions, workshops, music, and entertainment. *Sozialistische Aktion,* 1979, nos. 17–18. See also Michael Handl, "Von Rosa Villen und Wirbeln und Homosexuellen Initiativen — Die österreischische Homosexuellenbewegung nach Stonewall," in *Homosexualität in Österreich,* ed. Handl et al., pp. 120–22.

10. *CO-INFO* 5/6 (spring 1978), p. 10; *Lambda Nachrichten,* 1987, no. 2: 25–27; *Sozialistische Aktion,* 1979, nos. 17–18.

11. All in all, *CO-INFO* appeared five times between spring 1976 and spring 1978. It was economically produced — typewritten and xeroxed — comprising anywhere between ten and eighty pages. In 1979, *CO-INFO* was found to be in violation of Austria's §220, the law forbidding the advertisement of homosexuality.

12. Förster appeared on the discussion program "Club 2" in a debate on the topic of homosexuality (only the second such event in Austrian television history, the first having come in 1977). In the course of the discussion, Förster held a piece of paper up to the camera that contained the contact information for the Homosexuelle Initiative. This act provoked a minor scandal, since the conservative parties accused the state-run television station of aiding the violation of §220 and §221. See esp. Förster's recollection of the incident in Förster, "Zwi-

schen Provokation und Integration — ein Viertljahrhundert Schwulenbewegung in Österreich," in *Der andere Blick,* ed. Förster et al., pp. 216–17.

13. *Warme Blätter* 1, no. 1 (1979), p. 1; *Lambda Nachrichten,* 1980, nos. 3–4: 2; *Lambda Nachrichten,* 1981, nos. 3–4: 3–4. Ironically, Vienna's first openly gay space was quite hidden from the outside and located on the margins of the city's social geography.

14. *Profil,* 1980, no. 1. The founding of HOSI rested on the question of whether or not a lesbian/gay rights organization would "disturb the public peace." The wording of §221 suggested that any such group would do so, but the Ministry of Justice effectively decoupled them, creating the legal space for a lesbian/gay group, provided that it was not a public nuisance.

15. *Lambda Nachrichten,* 1980, no. 1: 3. See also *Profil,* 1980, no. 1.

16. *Warme Blätter* 1, no. 1 (1979), p. 7; *Warme Blätter* 1, no. 2 (1979), p. 1; *Lambda Nachrichten,* 1980, no. 1: 3; *Profil,* 1980, no. 1. Such assertions did not deter the conservative parties' opposition to HOSI. Given the SPÖ's absolute majority, however, they were in no position to thwart it. *Lambda Nachrichten,* 1980, no. 1: 5.

17. *Lambda Nachrichten,* 1980, no. 1: 3. For the beginning of HOSI's political campaign, see *Warme Blätter* 1, no. 1 (1979), p. 4–5.

18. In 1980, HOSI issued the "First Pink Manifesto against the Ignorance of Politicians," which was sent to all members of parliament. *Lambda Nachrichten,* 1980, no. 1: 11–12. The first visit to a politician — Johanna Dohnal, the SPÖ secretary for women's affairs — took place in May of that same year. *Lambda Nachrichten,* 1980, no. 2: 22. For the visit with Chancellor Vranitzky, see HOSI, *. . . Und sie bewegt sich doch . . . : 15 Jahre Homosexuelle Initiative* (Vienna: Eigenverlag, 1994), p. 16.

19. For the progression of HOSI's legal initiatives, *Lambda Nachrichten,* 1986, no. 4: 17; *Lambda Nachrichten,* 1987, no. 1: 14–15; Handl et al., *Homosexualität in Österreich,* p. 220; *Lambda Nachrichten,* 1990, no. 2: 10–14. Another area of HOSI activism concerned Austria's representation in international lesbian/gay organizations, particularly the International Gay Association (IGA, later ILGA) — activities that included the hosting of a number of conferences in Vienna. *Lambda Nachrichten,* 1980, no. 1: 13; *Lambda Nachrichten,* 1983, nos. 2–3: 11; *Lambda Nachrichten,* 1983, no. 4: 3–13; *Die Presse,* Jul. 12, 1983; *Arbeiter-Zeitung,* Jul. 12, 1983; *Lambda Nachrichten,* 1989, no. 4: 20–27.

20. *Lambda Nachrichten,* 1982, no. 1: 5–10.

21. Doris Hauberger and Helga Pankratz, "Prähistorische Erinnerungen: Von der Belle Etage zur *Villa,*" in *Rosa Lila Villa: 10 Jahre Lesben und Schwulenhaus,* ed. Rosa Lila Tip (Vienna: Eigenverlag, 1992); Rudolf Kratzer, "Wie alles begann," in *Rosa Lila Villa,* ed. Rosa Lila Tip.

22. *Wochenpresse,* Nov. 9, 1982; *Arbeiter-Zeitung,* Nov. 20, 1982; *Arbeiter-Zeitung,* Nov. 17, 1983; *Lambda Nachrichten,* 1982, nos. 2–3: 23–26; *Lambda Nachrichten,* 1984, no. 1: 12–14.

23. *Sozialistische Aktion,* 1979, nos. 17–18. This sense was also corroborated by the many interviews I conducted with members of the lesbian/gay movement active at the time.

24. *CO-INFO* 2 (1976), p.6

25. Ibid., p. 7

26. Ibid.

27. *Lambda Nachrichten*, 1980, no. 2: 15–16. The group's discussions about S/M practices and other "perversions" also reflected this more radical strand and its commitment to fight "hetero norms and ideals" and the "fascism of the nuclear family." *Lambda Nachrichten*, 1982, no. 1: 21–31.

28. Ibid.

29. Ibid.

30. Ibid.

31. Ibid., pp. 7–9.

32. In 1981, for example, an article titled "Macho USA" praised the "effective politics of the American gay movement," particularly its ability to "integrate itself into the image of the nation, which allows the creation of a [public] gay identity." *Lambda Nachrichten*, 1981, nos. 3–4: 23–26. A few years later, an article on the occasion of the fifteenth anniversary of the Stonewall rebellion similarly constructed the U.S. gay liberation movement as a model in the struggle against Austrian secrecy. *Lambda Nachrichten*, 1984, no. 3: 24–29.

33. *Neues Forum*, Apr. 1976, p. 67.

34. *CO-INFO* 2 (Sept. 1976), p. 15. See also *Sozialistische Aktion*, 1979, nos. 17–18. As *CO-INFO* put it in a pithy slogan on the cover of one issue, "Subkultur verdirbt die Buben nur" (The subculture only spoils the boys). *CO-INFO* 3 (Jan. 1977).

35. *Profil*, 1980, no. 1.

36. Wolfgang Förster speaking at the Club 2 discussion of Sept. 25, 1979 (transcript of videotape).

37. *CO-INFO* 1 (June 1976).

38. *Warme Blätter* 1, no. 1 (1979), p. 1.

39. The event was not an official demonstration, so it did not need to be coordinated with city authorities. True to its conception as a "walk," the event did not feature any banners, posters, or slogans. *Profil*, 1977, no. 23: 36.

40. On HOSI's participation in the antifascist demonstration, see *Lambda Nachrichten*, 1980, no. 2: 22. The group's participation at the alternative culture festival, which provoked a scandal when its booth was forcibly removed, is chronicled in *Lambda Nachrichten*, 1980, no. 1: 17; *Lambda Nachrichten*, 1980, no. 2: 4–6.

41. The various actions are chronicled in *Lambda Nachrichten*, 1982, no. 1: 5–10; *Lambda Nachrichten*, 1982, no. 2: 11–14; *Lambda Nachrichten*, 1982, no. 3: 15; *Lambda Nachrichten*, 1989, no. 1: 9–18.

42. *Lambda Nachrichten*, 1995, no. 1: 10–11.

43. *Lambda Nachrichten*, 1980, no. 2: 22.

44. The text of HOSI's plaque at Mauthausen reads: "Totgeschlagen, Totgeschwiegen — Den homosexuellen Opfern des Nationalsozialismus" (Struck dead and silenced — to the homosexual victims of National Socialism). In seeking to commemorate and represent the lesbian/gay victims of Nazism, HOSI always encountered resistance from other victim groups, for example at the

annual memorial events at the former concentration camp. *Lambda Nachrichten,* 1980, nos. 3–4: 6; *Lambda Nachrichten,* 1985, no. 1: 6–10; *Lambda Nachrichten,* 1985, no. 3: 9–10; *Lambda Nachrichten,* 1990, no. 3: 14–15; *Lambda Nachrichten,* 1995, no. 2: 17.

45. *Lambda Nachrichten,* 1981, nos. 3–4: 13; *Lambda Nachrichten,* 1982, no. 3: 14; *Lambda Nachrichten,* 1982, no. 4: 12–13.

46. *Lambda Nachrichten,* 1984, no. 3: 8–9; *Lambda Nachrichten,* 1986, no. 3: 8; *Lambda Nachrichten,* 1986, no. 4: 11–12; *Lambda Nachrichten,* 1989, no. 3: 7–8; *Lambda Nachrichten,* 1991, no. 3: 31–34.

47. *Lambda Nachrichten,* 1986, no. 4: 11–12.

48. As one HOSI member described the situation: "Not all bars behaved the same. But among many of them, there was pretty strong resistance to us. They were worried that if they seemed political, their normality and existence would be threatened. After all, they too were on the border of illegality."

49. *Lambda Nachrichten,* 1984, no. 4: 17.

50. Ibid., 19.

51. See, for example, *Der Standard,* June 19, 1991; *Der Standard,* Feb. 27, 1993; *Profil,* Jul. 31, 1995; *Der Standard,* Jan. 15, 1996, *Der Falter,* 1997, no. 36 — all of which discuss the organizations founded in the early 1990s. One of them, Österreischisches Lesben- und Schwulenforum (ÖLSF), was created in 1994 as a national lesbian/gay rights organization (in contrast to HOSI, which technically was local, as it was based on chapters in the provinces). For a few years, ÖLSF had a relatively large public presence, and when the outing affair tainted HOSI's reputation, the organization briefly emerged as the country's leading political group. By the late 1990s, however, the organization was significantly weakened by difficulties in the recruitment of leadership; when HOSI fully recovered at the turn of the century, ÖLSF became largely dormant.

52. HOSI, . . . *Und sie bewegt sich doch . . .* , p. 10.

53. *Der Standard,* Feb. 27, 1993.

54. In 1982, for example, *Lambda Nachrichten* had fewer than three hundred subscribers. *Lambda Nachrichten,* 1982, no. 3: 2.

55. *XTRA!* 1992, no. 00.

56. In late 1989, a group of activists based at Rosa Lila Villa conceived a magazine whose orientation was between the *Lambda Nachrichten* and *XTRA!* Titled *Tamtam,* it would serve as a medium for communication between lesbians and gay men, as well as between homosexuals and heterosexuals. The project was political, and envisaged an affirmative representation of lesbian/gay culture. Sold at a price and facing difficulties of staffing, the magazine produced a dozen issues over the next three years before its discontinuation in early 1993. See Andreas Brunner, "Eine kurze Geschichte von *tamtam,*" in *Rosa Lila Villa,* ed. Rosa Lila Tip.

57. *XTRA!* 1992, no. 00.

58. *XTRA!* 1997, no. 6: 20.

59. Ibid., 21.

60. Ibid., 22.

61. See, for example, the typical narrative of a young man who came out in the mid 1990s: "I realized that I was gay, and I was looking around to figure out what to do next. Then I found *XTRA!* and it had all this information and a ton of listings. I learned about the "Schwung" [the gay male youth group run at the time at Rosa Lila Villa], and I immediately met this great group of twenty people who made me feel like I belonged somewhere."

62. Although it carries some material pertaining to lesbian issues, the Löwenherz is primarily a gay male bookstore. As such, it functions as a kind of supplement to the longstanding Frauenbuchhandlung in Vienna's eight district, which has its roots in the autonomous women's movement of the 1970s. While the Löwenherz caters primarily to a gay male clientele, the Café Berg has been mixed from the beginning, both in terms of gender and in terms of sexual orientation.

63. *Lambda Nachrichten,* 1993, no. 3: 40.

64. Ibid.

65. Ibid., p. 39.

66. Examples of newly established and openly lesbian/gay venues include: Orlando, Living Room, and Santo Spirito. The Café Savoy, in turn, is an example of a longstanding gay male locale that is now more open.

67. The full name of the festival is: "Wien ist andersrum: Das Festival der Verlockungen vom anderen Ufer" (Vienna is the other way around: The festival of temptations from the other shore). The name is a play on a popular Vienna tourism slogan that advertises the city with the phrase "Wien ist anders" (Vienna is different).

68. *Coming Out* planned a film festival that failed to materialize. *CO-INFO* 3 (Jan. 1977); *CO-INFO* 4 (June 1977): 16–17. HOSI's efforts, which included small festivals in 1982, 1987–1990, and 1993–1994, are chronicled in *Lambda Nachrichten.*

69. One of the posters depicted Vienna's venerated St. Stephen's Cathedral covered by a condom. Another showed the male statue on top of city hall with a giant erection, while yet another presented Empress Sisi in the act of self-gratification.

70. Wien ist andersrum, program brochure for 1996.

71. Ibid.

72. In establishing the festival, the organizers continued their quest for cultural and political provocation. In 1998, for example, they advertised the event with stylized images of Austria's presidential candidates, depicting them in same-sex sexual contexts. A year later, the advertisement centered on an image recalling Leonardo da Vinci's *Last Supper* with drag queens as apostles and a drag king as Jesus.

73. *Lambda Nachrichten,* 1996, no. 3: 36–38.

74. At the final demonstration, HOSI unveiled the world's largest pink triangle in Vienna's central square. A few dozen protesters were in attendance for the action. *Lambda Nachrichten,* 1991, no. 3.

75. Andreas Brunner, "So schlimm ist es gar nicht," *Der Falter,* 1997, no. 43: 8–9.

76. Ibid.

77. Ibid.

78. Christian Michelides, "1000 Jahre ohne Parade sind genug," *Connect– Sonderausgabe* (June 1996), p. 4

79. Wien Ist Andersrum, program brochure for 1996. As Andreas Brunner put it in an interview, "We organize and finance the skeleton. But people need to bring the specific messages and opinions to give the whole thing real political content. I actually think, though, that the sheer visibility is the main political message."

80. On the American situation, see esp. Richard Harrell, "The Symbolic Strategies of Chicago's Gay and Lesbian Pride Day Parade," in *Gay Culture in America,* ed. Herdt, pp. 225–52. The European dynamic is discussed from a French vantage point in Martell, *The Pink and the Black.*

81. Organizers published instructions on what to wear and how to wear it. See *Lambda Nachrichten,* 1996, no. 3: 36–38; *Connect–Sonderausgabe* (June 1996).

82. Carl Schorske has analyzed the political and architectural dynamics of the *Ringstraßen-Stil* in unparalleled fashion in his *Fin-de-Siècle Vienna,* ch. 2.

83. On Vienna's May Day parade, see Robert Rotenberg, "May Day Parades in Prague and Vienna: A Comparison of Socialist Ritual," *Anthropological Quarterly* 56, no. 2 (1983), pp. 62–68. On the political culture of Austrian socialism, see Gruber, *Red Vienna.*

84. Michelides, "1000 Jahre ohne Parade sind genug," *Connect–Sonderausgabe* (June 1996), p. 4

85. Organizers showed increasing participation in the parade: 1996: 25,000; 1997: 35,000; 1998: 60,000; 1999: 100,000. The estimates by the police are consistently lower, but they too document a remarkable rise in popularity (1996: 2,500; 1997: 30,000; 1998: 50,000; 1999: 70,000). *Lambda Nachrichten Special,* 1999, no. 3: v.

86. HOSI, for example, organized a number of discussions that addressed the fallout from the political developments. I attended one of these events on February 15, 2000.

87. *Kurier,* June 18, 2000.

88. Connie Lichtenegger and Veit Georg Schmidt, "Zeigt Flagge!" in CSD Wien, *Regenbogen Parade 2000* (Vienna: Eigenverlag, 2000), p. 1.

Chapter 5: Museums and Monuments

1. Until recently, the standard account of the complete history of Vienna's Jews was Hans Tietze, *Die Juden Wiens: Geschichte, Wirtschaft, Kultur* (Vienna: Edition Atelier, 1987 [1933]). In the last few years, St. Pölten's Institute for the History of the Jews in Austria has commenced publication of its projected six-volume history of Vienna's Jews. To date, two volumes have appeared: Klaus Lohrmann, *Die Wiener Juden im Mittelalter* (Berlin: Philo, 2000); and Evelyn Adunka, *Die vierte Die Gemeinde.*

2. The standard accounts of this development are William McCagg, *A History of Habsburg Jews, 1670–1918* (Bloomington: Indiana University Press, 1989); Marsha Rozenblit, *The Jews of Vienna 1867–1914: Assimilation and Identity* (Albany: State University of New York Press, 1983); Steven Beller, *Vienna and the Jews, 1867–1938: A Cultural History* (Cambridge: Cambridge University Press, 1989); Robert Wistrich, *The Jews of Vienna in the Age of Franz Joseph.*

3. Israelitische Kultusgemeinde Wien and Burgtheater Wien, *Ein Fest zum 150jährigen Bestehen* (Vienna: Eigenverlag, 1999). For Freud's text, see pp. 31–33; Herzl's text appears on pp. 23–24.

4. Ibid., pp. 29–30, 37–40.

5. Ibid., pp. 41–44, 47–50.

6. Schindel's poem is reprinted in ibid., pp. 51–54. Beckermann read from a text by Günter Anders (ibid., pp. 47–50); Menasse read a text about his father and the mental scars left on him by the Holocaust (ibid., pp. 47–50); Rabinovici read an abstract story about Austrian complicity in the Holocaust and the subsequent refusal to accept responsibility (ibid., pp. 58–60).

7. Ibid., p. 3.

8. *Kurier,* June 22, 1999.

9. See, for example, *Der Standard,* June 21, 1999; *Wiener Zeitung,* June 22, 1999; *Die Presse,* June 22, 1999; *Die Furche,* June 24, 1999.

10. *Format,* 1999, no. 14: 56–65.

11. A prominent example is Ferdinand Lacina, a central figure in the antifascist student movement of the 1960s, who became a Social Democratic secretary of finance.

12. This point was made prominently and repeatedly, for example, by Franz Vranitzky, the Social Democratic chancellor of the late 1980s and 1990s.

13. The famous reference to Austria as an island of the blessed was made by Pope John XXIII. The negative impact of the Waldheim affair on Austria's international reputation can be traced in Richard Mitten, *The Politics of Antisemitic Prejudice: The Waldheim Phenomenon in Austria* (Boulder: Westview Press, 1992).

14. An early example was the television documentary "Juden heute in Wien" (Jews in Vienna today), which originally aired on October 29, 1986. Prior to the Waldheim affair, a program like this would have been well-nigh impossible on the state-run television network.

15. *Profil,* Nov. 2, 1987; *Neues Volksblatt,* June 10, 1988.

16. *Die Gemeinde,* June 1949; Leon Kolb, "The Vienna Jewish Museum," in *The Jews of Austria,* ed. Josef Fraenkel; Bernhard Purin, *Beschlagnahmt: Die Sammlung des Wiener Jüdischen Museums nach 1938*–Ausstellungskatalog (Vienna: Jewish Museum, 1995).

17. Some of the confiscated objects were also displayed in Nazi progaganda exhibits. Purin, *Beschlagnahmt.*

18. *Die Gemeinde,* Dec. 16, 1964 and Dec. 31, 1964.

19. Kurt Schubert, "Österreich, das Land jüdischer Museen," *David: Jüdische Kulturzeitschrift,* June–Jul. 1994; *Die Gemeinde,* June 1997.

20. The symposia were usually linked to specific exhibits. For a list of symposia and exhibits, see Schubert, "Österreich, das Land jüdischer Museen."

21. *Volksstimme,* Nov. 19, 1977. The exhibit catalogue is published as *Der gelbe Stern in Österreich–Studia Judaica Austriaca V* (Eisenstadt: Edition Roetzer, 1977).

22. The exhibit at the Museum of Modern Art was titled "Vienna 1900: Art, Architecture, and Design." It opened on July 3, 1986. *Arbeiter-Zeitung,* Oct. 24, 1986; *Profil,* Mar. 15, 1993.

23. The exhibit opened November 10, 1987.

24. *Der Standard,* Mar. 8, 1990; *Profil,* Mar. 11–12, 1990.

25. Early exhibits included a display of Max Berger's Judaica collection, a show on Kafka's Prague, and an exhibit on the Jews of China.

26. These exhibits included a show of ceramics, an exhibit on Jewish working-class history, and a display on the theme of memory in the Jewish tradition.

27. The permanent exhibits are the product of innovative museum design. In place of a conventional historical exhibit, the museum displays a series of holograms on Austrian-Jewish themes. Judaism's ritual domain is shown in an installation by artist Nancy Spero, as well as by the visible storage area displaying surviving artifacts from the prewar museum. On the logic of the permanent exhibit, see *Jüdisches Museum Wien* (Vienna: Eigenverlag, 1996).

28. The list of exhibits that were mounted after the renovation is lengthy. It includes several art shows, historical exhibits, and a number of innovative displays on select themes of Jewish culture and history.

29. Zilk, cited in *Die Gemeinde,* Apr. 3, 1990, p. 48.

30. The advertisement is cited in *Profil,* Jul. 24, 1989, p. 58.

31. Interview in *Der Standard,* Aug. 6, 1991.

32. Julius Schoeps, "Aufklären, Gedenken und Erinnern: Zur Eröffnung des jüdischen Museums in Wien," *Die Gemeinde,* Dec. 1, 1993, p. 33. In 1997, Head Curator Karl Albrecht-Weinberger succeeded Schoeps as director of the museum. *Die Gemeinde,* Dec. 1997.

33. Freud material was exhibited from November 1993 to February 1994; the Joseph Roth exhibit took place between October 1994 and February 1995; the show on Karl Kraus was mounted between June and November 1999. Additional exhibits on Austrian-Jewish "culture heroes" included shows on journalist Egon Erwin Kisch (May–September 1998), writer Richard Beer-Hofmann (February–April 1999), and painters Max Oppenheimer (June–September 1994) and Tina Blau (June–October 1996).

34. The plaque is displayed in the entrance hall, next to the ticket counter.

35. *Wiener Zeitung,* Jul 13, 1994; *Die Presse,* Aug. 20–21, 1994; *Die Presse,* Feb. 9, 2000.

36. Entry in the guest book of the Jewish Museum dated Dec. 28, 1993. Such sentiments recur throughout the many volumes of guest books.

37. I observed these museum activities for several weeks in the winter of 2000. On the museum's pedagogical design, see also *Die Gemeinde,* Dec. 1999, p. 53.

38. The choice usually depended on the subject matter of the class. History teachers took their students to see the historical exhibit, while religion classes,

taught as part of public school curriculum, preferred the tour emphasizing religion and ritual.

39. On the history of Austrian textbooks, see Peter Utgaard, "Forgetting the Nazis: Schools, Identity, and the 'Austria-as-Victim' Myth since 1945," Ph.D. diss., Washington State University, 1997.

40. See, for example, *Wochenpresse*, Dec. 18, 1987; *Wirtschaftswoche*, May 21, 1992; *Wirtschaftswoche*, May 28, 1992; *Wochenpresse*, Nov. 4, 1993.

41. The supplement was titled "Juden in Österreich: Geschichte — Gegenwart — Alltag," Sonderbeilage *Wiener Zeitung*, Nov. 10, 1987.

42. The quote is from *Der Standard*, Mar. 8, 1990. See also *Profil*, Mar. 11–12, 1990.

43. See, for example, *Der Standard*, June 8, 1991; *Die Presse*, Oct. 10, 1991; *Die Presse*, Dec. 14–15, 1991; *Kurier*, Feb. 25, 1992; *Die Presse*, Nov. 3, 1992; *Profil*, Mar. 15, 1993; *Kurier*, Apr. 25, 1993.

44. *Profil*, Nov. 15, 1993, pp. 94–95; *Die Presse*-Schaufenster, Nov. 12, 1993, pp. 2–3; *Der Falter*, 1993, no. 46; *Der Standard*, Nov. 17, 1993; *Kurier*, Nov. 18, 1993; *News*, Nov. 18, 1993; *Wiener Zeitung*, Nov. 19, 1993.

45. See, for example, reviews of the Chagall exhibit (*Die Presse*, Mar. 11, 1994; *Kurier*, June 21, 1994), the Oppenheimer exhibit (*Kurier*, June 23, 1994; *Der Standard*, June 25, 1994), and the Roth exhibit (*Profil*, Aug. 29, 1994; *Die Presse*, Oct. 7, 1994; *Der Standard*, Oct. 7, 1994).

46. *Neue Kronen Zeitung*, Nov. 25, 1992.

47. Ibid., Nov. 19, 1993.

48. Ibid., June 24, 1994.

49. Ibid., Mar. 2, 1995. In 1996, the *Krone* was jubilant about the museum's reopening following the renovation: "Vienna's Jewish Museum is glistening with new splendor. After only seven months of construction and well within the budget of thirty million schillings, the award-winning project . . . has been realized. Finally, the museum can display its own collection." *Neue Kronen Zeitung*, Mar. 1, 1996. The text recalled earlier raves that included the *Krone's* praise for the "sensational" Chagall show, which closed with the sad recognition that the artist had last been displayed in Vienna as part of a Nazi show on "entartete Kunst." *Neue Kronen Zeitung*, Mar. 10, 1994.

50. See, for example, Helmut Gruber and Ruth Wodak, *Ein Fall für den Staatsanwalt: Diskursanalyse der Kronenzeitungsberichterstattung zu Neonazismus und Novellierung des österreichischen Verbotsgesetzes im Frühjahr 1992* (Vienna: Institut für Sprachwissenschaft, 1992).

51. *Die Gemeinde*, Feb. 3, 1989, p. 29; *Die Gemeinde*, Mar. 4, 1990, p. 48; *Profil*, Mar. 11–12, 1990.

52. Of the seven board members, three were official appointees by the Jewish community. Along with the carefully chosen chair of the board, IKG member Thomas Lachs, the community was assured a majority.

53. Danielle Luxembourg's background is in the Israeli art scene. Julius Schoeps is a German-Jewish professor of German-Jewish history. With the 1997 appointment of Karl Albrecht-Weinberger, the museum appointed its first non-

Jewish director. Albrecht-Weinberger's longstanding association with the museum made him a widely accepted choice for the position.

54. *Profil,* Mar. 11–12, 1990.

55. The show, titled "Hoppauf Hakoah: Ein jüdischer Sportverein in Wien" (Go Hakoah: A Jewish sports club in Vienna), was mounted from May to July 1995.

56. The reference is to the soccer season of 1924–25, when Hakoah won the Austrian league championship.

57. *Die Gemeinde,* Feb. 3, 1989, p. 29.

58. See, for example, the way the state-run Hakoah exhibit was integrated into a vision of Jewish puissance by the Jewish periodical *Illustrierte Neue Welt:* "It is inspiration for those who are active today, for it cannot be forgotten that the glorious club emerged like a phoenix from the ashes and that it is committed to uphold the old traditions." *Illustrierte Neue Welt,* May 1995.

59. The text is from the dedication plaque mounted in the museum's entrance hall.

60. The arresting black-and-white images, many of which depict Jews in the context of religious activities, were published in Harry Weber, *Vienna Today: Photographs of Contemporary Jewish Life* (Vienna: Böhlau, 1996).

61. Jüdisches Museum Wien Newsletter, Aug.–Sept. 1996.

62. Doron Rabinovici, "Transparencies and Silhouettes, or The Visible and the Invisible in Jewish Life," in *Vienna Today,* ed. Weber, p. 13.

63. As the show's curator, Werner Hanak, told me, the exhibit brought more Jewish visitors to the museum than any other display.

64. The German edition was published, like the English version, by the state-owned Böhlau Press. The only other exhibition catalogue featuring municipal officials is "Hier hat Teitelbaum gewohnt," which was not translated into English.

65. Weber, *Vienna Today,* p. 6.

66. The monument measures 12 feet high, 24 feet wide, and 33 feet long.

67. For a full analysis along these lines, see Matti Bunzl, "On the Politics and Semantics of Austrian Memory."

68. *Der Standard,* Oct. 26, 2000.

69. The text of Vranitzky's speech was rendered in full in *Die Gemeinde,* Aug. 22, 1991.

70. Ibid.

71. *Die Gemeinde –Sondernummer zur Frage der Restitution,* Mar. 2001, p. 14. Individuals were eligible for a one-time payment of 70,000 schillings (approx. $5,000). Statistics on payments can be found in *Die Gemeinde,* Apr. 1997; *Die Gemeinde,* Jul. 1999, p. 14. On the history of the fund, see *Die Gemeinde,* May 12, 1995; *Die Gemeinde,* Mar. 29, 1996.

72. *Die Gemeinde–Sondernummer,* Mar. 2001; *Die Gemeinde,* Dec. 2001. The successful completion of the restitution negotiations in part reflects the intensification of American efforts, along with the threat of legal action in the United States. In this manner, the United States represented yet another layer of transnational pressure on the Austrian nation-state.

73. The exhibit was mounted from April to July 1995.

74. *Wiener Rathauskorrespondenz,* Apr. 27, 1995. On the exhibit, see also *Kurier,* Apr. 27, 1995; *Wiener Zeitung,* May 19, 1995; *Der Falter,* 1995, no. 19.

75. *Der Standard,* May 6, 1998.

76. The performance was staged by the venerated state-owned *Staatsoper.*

77. *Der Standard,* Nov. 9, 1998.

78. Klestil, cited in *Die Presse,* Nov. 10, 1998.

79. Klestil, cited in *Der Standard,* Dec. 19, 1998.

80. See Wistrich, "The Kreisky Phenomenon: A Reassessment."

81. *Neue Kronen Zeitung,* Nov. 27, 1975.

82. *Format,* Oct. 12, 1998; *News,* Dec. 17, 1998.

83. *Profil,* Aug. 12, 1996; *News,* Dec. 17, 1998.

84. Wiesenthal expressed the feelings of a large majority of Viennese Jews who felt that the street-washing Jew was a highly demeaning representation that recalled rather than ameliorated past suffering. He also noted that the monument's representation of a short-lived episode in the wake of the *Anschluss* belittled the enormity of the Holocaust. See Matti Bunzl, "On the Politics and Semantics of Austrian Memory."

85. *Kurier,* Dec. 22, 1994; *Die Presse,* Jul. 27, 1995; *Kurier,* Aug. 5, 1995; *Die Gemeinde,* Feb. 29, 1996; *Kurier,* May 4, 1996; *Falter,* May 10, 1996.

86. The heated debate between the monument's supporters (SPÖ, victims organizations, the Jewish community) and its detractors (ÖVP, FPÖ, and *Krone)* is chronicled in Matti Bunzl, "On the Politics and Semantics of Austrian Memory."

87. The intra-Jewish debate on the monument took place from the summer of 1996 to the spring of 1997. Wiesenthal's defense of the original design was echoed by IKG president Grosz (*Profil,* Aug. 5, 1996), while the initial call for a new design was issued by prominent Holocaust survivor Leon Zelman and picked up by the director of the Institute for the History of the Jews in Austria, Klaus Lohrmann, and Vienna's city archaeologist, Ortolf Harl. *Profil,* Aug. 5, 1996, p. 78–79; *Die Presse,* Jul. 6, 1996; *Der Standard,* Apr. 11, 1997; *Die Presse,* June 25, 1996; *Profil,* Mar. 29, 1997, p. 110. In turn, further opposition to the original design was voiced by IKG members across the political spectrum. See *Der Standard,* June 10, 1996; *Der Standard,* Jul. 26, 1996; *Der Standard,* Jul. 31, 1996; *Die Gemeinde,* Aug. 21, 1996.

88. The eventual solution — to integrate the excavations of the medieval synagogue into the monument design — was first proposed in the summer of 1996. *Der Standard,* Aug. 23, 1996; *Die Presse,* Sept. 13, 1996. The plan was formally adopted in March 1998 (*Kurier,* Mar. 3, 1998; *Die Presse,* Mar. 4, 1998), allowing the commencement of construction in September 1998. *Der Standard,* Sept. 25, 1998 and Sept. 29, 1998. The combined project of museum and monument delayed completion of the project. In the original conception, the unveiling was planned for November 1996; in the end, however, it took until October 2000 for the project to be completed and turned over to the public.

89. *Format,* 1999, no. 14.

90. Ibid.

91. *Die Gemeinde,* Dec. 1998; *Kurier,* Jan. 26, 2000; *Der Standard,* May 13, 2000; *Der Standard,* Jul. 1, 2000. See also *Die Gemeinde — Sondernummer,* Mar. 2001.

92. *Kurier,* Sept. 4, 1998.

93. *Die Gemeinde,* Dec. 2, 1991; *Format,* 1999, no. 14.

Chapter 6: Offices and Balls

1. See also *Lambda Nachrichten,* special issue, 2000, no. 2.

2. *Profil,* July 18, 1983.

3. Beantwortung der Anfrage des Abgeordneten SRB und Freunde an den Bundesminister für Arbeit und Soziales betreffend die homosexuellen Opfer des Nationalsozialismus, no. 2474/J., Sept. 12, 1988.

4. *Lambda Nachrichten,* 1989, no. 1: 18–21.

5. Ibid., 20–21.

6. *Lambda Nachrichten,* 1991, no. 1: 11–12.

7. *Lambda Nachrichten,* 1993, no. 1: 8–9.

8. *Lambda Nachrichten,* 1994, no. 4: 20–22.

9. On the compensation of individual victims, see *Lambda Nachrichten,* 1997, no. 3: 17. On the speech by Parliamentary President Heinz Fischer at Mauthausen, see *Lambda Nachrichten,* 1998, no. 3: 26. On the Historians' Commission and its attention to lesbian/gay victims of National Socialism, see Niko Wahl, "Forschungsgegenstand Homosexuellenverfolgung — Research Topic: Persecution of Homosexuals," in CSD Wien, *Europride Guide* (Vienna: Eigenverlag, 2001), p. 20.

10. *Lambda Nachrichten,* 1994, no. 4: 20.

11. As of this writing, lesbian and gay male victims of National Socialism are still not formally recognized under the *Opferfürsorgegesetz.* That might change soon, but given the advancing age of Nazism's homosexual victims, it may well be a purely symbolic gesture.

12. As mentioned in ch. 4, n. 2, the party originally appeared under the name Alternative Liste. In 1983, it failed to win any seats in parliament. After changing its name to the Green Party, it entered parliament for the first time in 1986.

13. *Arbeiter-Zeitung,* Oct. 31, 1989.

14. The ÖVP blocked attempts at abolishing Austria's anti-lesbian/gay laws in 1992 and 1995. *Profil,* Mar. 9, 1992, p. 28; *Kurier,* Oct. 10, 1995 and Oct. 11, 1995. See also *Lambda Nachrichten,* 1997, no. 1: 8–14.

15. *Lambda Nachrichten,* 1981, nos. 3–4: 3, 6; *Lambda Nachrichten,* 1982, no. 1: 19; *Lambda Nachrichten,* 1984, no. 2: 30; ILGA-Europa, *Gleichstellung von Lesben und Schwulen: Eine relevante Frage im zivilen und sozialen Dialog* (Vienna: Eigenverlag, 1998), p. 7.

16. *Lambda Nachrichten,* 1994, no. 2: 51–53.

17. At the 1996 vote, the abolition of §221 was backed by a solid majority made up of representatives of the SPÖ, the Green Party, the Liberal Party, and

the Freedom Party. The vote on §220, by contrast, was extremely close, and the abolition went through with a one-vote majority (with most of the FPÖ voting for the statute's preservation). The vote on §209 was tied at 91 to 91 — a situation that left the paragraph on the books (against the recommendations of their respective parties , one member of each ÖVP and FPÖ voted for the law's abolition, resulting in the tie). Regarding §209, the FPÖ also proposed a bill that would have modified §209 by raising the age of consent from fourteen to sixteen. That bill, however, did not receive a majority. *Kurier,* Nov. 28, 1996, p. 3; *Profil,* Dec. 2, 1996; *Lambda Nachrichten,* 1997, no. 1: 8–14.

18. *Profil,* Dec. 2, 1996, pp. 42–45.

19. Ibid.

20. *Lambda Nachrichten,* 1997, no. 3: 42–44; *Lambda Nachrichten,* 1999, no. 2: 49–51; ILGA-Europa, *Gleichstellung von Lesben und Schwulen,* p. 7.

21. *Lambda Nachrichten,* 1997, no. 3: 12. See also *Lambda Nachrichten,* 1998, no. 2: 13–14; *Lambda Nachrichten,* 1999, no. 1: 8–9; *Lambda Nachrichten,* 2000, no. 2: 20–22.

22. *Lambda Nachrichten,* 1999, no. 1: 7.

23. Görg, cited in *Kurier,* June 29, 2001. The ÖVP's provincial organizations in both Vienna and Styria have officially broken away from the party's anti-lesbian/gay platform. By the summer of 2001, this development was further aided by the emergence of a gay interest group within the party, a result of the widely reported coming-out of a number of low-ranking party members. *Die Presse,* June 1, 2001.

24. For the activism undertaken under the initiative of "E(u)quality now!" see *Lambda Nachrichten,* 1998, no. 4: 42–43. The quoted ad was published in *Lambda Nachrichten,* 1998, no. 4: 46–47.

25. *Lambda Nachrichten,* 1999, no. 2: 7. Under the leadership of Heide Schmidt, the socially progressive Liberales Forum (LiF) also came out in strong support of same-sex partnerships and lesbian/gay equality. Founded when a number of parliamentarians split from the FPÖ in 1994 in an effort to resurrect the liberal tradition of Austria's third camp, the new party managed to secure a number of seats in the general elections of 1994 and 1995. In 1999, the LiF lost its bid for parliamentary representation, leading to the party's effective dissolution.

26. The quote is from Görg. Cited in *Kurier,* June 29, 2001. Other prominent ÖVP members who have come out in support of lesbian/gay rights are Waltraud Klasnic and Gerhard Hirschmann. In the FPÖ, Harald Ofner and Susanne Riess-Passer have been in open support of legal reform. *Kurier,* Aug. 12, 2001; *Profil,* Aug. 6, 2001; *Profil,* Aug. 21, 2001.

27. *Kurier,* Aug. 12, 2001; *Der Standard,* Aug. 13, 2001.

28. *Lambda Nachrichten,* 1983, nos. 2–3: 15.

29. *Lambda Nachrichten,* 1985, no. 4: 5–6.

30. *Lambda Nachrichten,* 1991, no. 3: 23.

31. *Lambda Nachrichten,* 1994, no. 2: 27; *Lambda Nachrichten,* 1998, no. 1: 28–29. Austria's record on AIDS is not entirely free of controversy. At times, such organizations as the AIDS-Hilfe were underfunded, and the policy in

Vienna's hospitals to administer HIV tests without prior consent before all surgical procedures has been severely criticized. See, for example, *Lambda Nachrichten*, 1991, no. 3: 13.

32. *Lambda Nachrichten*, 1993, no. 2: 74–75.

33. *Lambda Nachrichten*, 1993, no. 3: 29.

34. *Lambda Nachrichten*, 1994, no. 2: 25; *Lambda Nachrichten*, 1995, no. 2: 27.

35. *Lambda Nachrichten*, special issue, 1999, no. 3: xii; *News*, May 14, 1998; *News*, May 11, 2000; *Kurier*, May 14, 2000, *Neue Kronen Zeitung*, May 14, 2000; *Neue Kronen Zeitung*, May 15, 2000; *Der Standard*, May 15, 2000. If anything, the Life Ball was blessed with too much popular success. By 1997, HOSI and other constituencies of the lesbian/gay movement were saying that the event had become too mainstream and "straight" and that it had lost its political efficacy in the process. *Lambda Nachrichten*, 1997, no. 3: 31.

36. *Der Standard*, May 25–27, 1996, p. 8.

37. *Connect–Sonderausgabe* (June 1996); *Rainbow News–Regenbogenparade '97*.

38. CSD Wien, *Regenbogen Parade–Pride Guide Vienna 98* (Vienna: Eigenverlag, 1988), p. 2.

39. CSD Wien, *Pride Guide 99* (Vienna: Eigenverlag, 1999), p. 51; CSD Wien, *Regenbogen Parade 2000* (Vienna: Eigenverlag, 2000).

40. *Connect–Sonderausgabe* (June 1996), p. 1.

41. CSD Wien, *Pride Guide 99*, p. 15.

42. CSD Wien, *Europride Guide*, p. 7.

43. CSD Wien, *Europride Guide*.

44. *Lambda Nachrichten*, 1989, no. 4: 50–51; *Der Standard*, Feb. 10, 1990; Handl et al., *Homosexualität in Österreich*, p. 219.

45. *Der Standard*, Nov. 6, 1998; *Salzburger Nachrichten*, Nov. 6, 1998; *Die Presse*, Nov. 6, 1998.

46. In his contribution to the *Europride Guide*, Mayor Michael Häupl stressed these very achievements. CSD Wien, *Europride Guide*, p. 7.

47. See, for example, the agendas and minutes of the "Koordinierungstreffen" — events organized by the employees of the WA to bring together the various constituents of the lesbian/gay movement. Magistrat der Stadt Wien, Wiener Antidiskriminierungsstelle für gleichgeschlechtliche Lebensweisen, "1. Koordinierungstreffen 5.12.1998"; *id.*, "2. Koordinierungstreffen — Protokoll."

48. Stadt Wien, *Wien Online*, available from Queerwien (May 15, 2000) <http://www.wien.gv.at/queerwien>.

49. Ibid. <http://www.wien.gv.at/queerwien/theor.htm> <http://www.wien.gv.at/queerwien/defhomo.htm> <http://www.wien.gv.at/queerwien/krank.htm> <http://www.wien.gv.at/queerwien/diskr.htm> <http://www.wien.gv.at/queerwien/phob.htm> <http://www.wien.gv.at/queerwien/hetero.htm>

50. Ibid. <http://www.wien.gv.at/queerwien/para.htm>

51. Ibid. <http://www.wien.gv.at/queerwien/sexo.htm> <http://www.wien.gv.at/queerwien/bezieh.htm> <http://www.wien.gv.at/queerwien/klisch.htm> <http://www.wien.gv.at/queerwien/klischees.htm> <http://www.wien.gv.at/queerwien/homo.htm> <http://www.wien.gv.at/queerwien/symb.htm>

52. Ibid. <http://www.wien.gv.at/queerwien/como.htm <http://www.wien.gv.at/queerwien/eltern.htm> <http://www.wien.gv.at/queerwien/glauba.htm> <http://www.wien.gv.at/queerwien/glaubb.htm> <http://www.wien.gv.at/queerwien/glaubc.htm>

53. Ibid. <http://www.wien.gv.at/queerwien/wien.htm> <http://www.wien.gv.at/queerwien/szene.htm> <http://www.wien.gv.at/queerwien/sub.htm> <http://www.wien.gv.at/queerwien/beratls.htm> <http://www.wien.gv.at/queerwien/freizeit.htm> <http://www.wien.gv.at/queerwien/medien.htm> <http://www.wien.gv.at/queerwien/vereine.htm>

54. *Lambda Nachrichten,* 1988, no. 4: 9; *Lambda Nachrichten,* 1990, no. 2: 15–17; Handl et al., *Homosexualität in Österreich,* p. 219.

55. *Profil,* Sept. 11, 1995, Sept. 18, 1995, Sept. 25, 1995.

56. *Profil,* Sept. 11, 1995 and Sept. 18, 1995.

57. *Profil,* Sept. 25, 1995.

58. *News,* Feb. 5, 1996, pp. 190–200.

59. *News* continued this theme over years. See, e.g., *News,* May 11, 2000.

60. *Kurier,* June 30, 1996, p. 10.

61. *Kurier,* June 29, 1997, p. 11.

62. *Neue Kronen Zeitung,* June 18, 2000, p. 15.

63. In recent years, affirmative representations of same-sex sexuality have been in frequent evidence on such shows as "Report" (covering social and political issues in Austria and abroad), the "Barbara Karlich Show" (Austria's most widely watched afternoon talk show), "Taxi Orange" (an Austrian variant of reality shows focusing on a group of randomly assembled people who have to run a cab company), and such television films as "Ach Baby, eine Baby" (a state-produced television movie whose central narrative revolves around a lesbian relationship). Beyond that, a number of overtly gay German films, such as "Echte Kerle," have recently been shown on Austrian television, along with such American lesbian/gay-themed shows as "Ellen" and "Will & Grace."

64. See, e.g., *Der Standard,* June 5, 2001, p. 10; *Der Falter,* 2001, no. 22; *Wiener Zeitung,* June 29–30, 2001, p. 8; *Kurier,* Jul. 1, 2001; *Die Presse,* June 1, 2001; *Die Presse,* June 9, 2001.

65. *Profil,* May 18, 1976, p. 42.

66. *Spartacus: International Gay Guide 2000/2001* (Berlin: Bruno Gmünder Verlag, 2000), p. 42.

67. *Der Falter,* Apr. 30, 1993; *Profil,* Dec. 1, 1997; *Lambda Nachrichten,* 1998, no. 1: 11–12.

68. The bear group, called "Wiener Runde," was founded in late 1996 on the model of American and Western European organizations seeking to champion fellowship among bearded, hirsute, and hefty men.

Conclusion: Symptoms of Postmodernity

1. On recent developments in German Jewry, much of it produced by scholars of literature, see Sander Gilman and Karen Remmler, eds., *Reemerging Jewish*

Culture in Germany: Life and Literature Since 1989 (New York: New York University Press, 1994); Sander Gilman, *Jews in Today's German Culture* (Bloomington: Indiana University Press, 1995); Y. Michal Bodemann, ed., *Jews, Germans, Memory: Reconstructions of Jewish Life in Germany* (Ann Arbor: University of Michigan Press, 1996); Sabine Offe, "Sites of Remembrance? Jewish Museums in Contemporary Germany," *Jewish Social Studies* 3, no. 2 (1997), pp. 77–89. Most of the work on homosexuals, by contrast, has been written from a legal or institutional perspective. See Stümke, *Homosexuelle in Deutschland;* Mildenberger, *Die Münchner Schwulenbewegung.*

2. On the situation of Jews in the new Europe, see esp. Jonathan Webber, ed., *Jewish Identities in the New Europe* (London: Littman Library of Jewish Civilization, 1994). See also Ruth Ellen Gruber, *Virtually Jewish: Reinventing Jewish Culture in Europe* (Berkeley: University of California Press, 2002), as well as the work of Diana Pinto. See her booklet *A New Jewish Identity for Post-1989 Europe* (London: Institute for Jewish Policy Research, 1996). As yet, there is little scholarly literature on the situation of queers in the new Europe, and the work that is available tends to be written from a legal or activist perspective. See Mark Bell, "Sexual Orientation and Anti-Discrimination Policy: The European Community," in *The Politics of Sexuality,* ed. Terrell Carver & Véronique Mottier (London: Routledge, 1998); ILGA-Europa, *Nach Amsterdam: Sexuelle Orientierung und die Europäische Union–Ein Leitfaden* (Vienna: Eigenverlag, 1999). Implicitly, some of the relevant questions are addressed in the comparative literature on the lesbian/gay movement. See Adam et al., *The Global Emergence of Gay and Lesbian Politics;* Martel, *The Pink and the Black.*

3. By the summer of 2001, Belgium, Denmark, Germany, France, Great Britain, the Netherlands, and Sweden had some form of registered partnership on the books, while Finland, Portugal, and Spain were moving toward establishing one. Only Greece, Ireland, Italy, and Luxembourg maintained the status quo. *Profil,* Aug. 6, 2001, p. 32. For a legal analysis of the possibilities and ramifications of registered partnerships in Austria, see Karin Pirolt, Hans-Peter Weingand, and Kurt Zernig, *Was wäre wenn? Eingetragene Partnerschaften von Lesben und Schwulen in Österreich* (Graz: Eigenverlag, 2000).

4. Among the more influential theorizations of postmodernity in the aesthetic realm are Fredric Jameson, *Postmodernism, or, the Cultural Logic of Late Capitalism* (Durham, N.C.: Duke University Press, 1991); Linda Hutcheon, *A Poetics of Postmodernism: History, Theory, Fiction* (New York: Routledge, 1988); Ihab Hassan, *The Postmodern Turn: Essays in Postmodern Theory and Culture* (Columbus: Ohio State University Press, 1987); Andreas Huyssen, *After the Great Divide: Modernism, Mass Culture, Postmodernism* (Bloomington: Indiana University Press, 1986). The social and political dimensions of postmodernity have been addressed with particular influence in Jean-François Lyotard, *The Postmodern Condition: A Report on Knowledge* (Minneapolis: University of Minnesota Press, 1984); Zygmunt Bauman, *Intimations of Postmodernity* (London: Routledge, 1992); *id., Postmodern Ethics* (Oxford: Blackwell, 1992); *id., Life in Fragments: Essays on Postmodern Morality* (Cambridge: Blackwell, 1995); *id., Post-*

modernity and Its Discontents (New York: New York University Press, 1997); David Harvey, *The Condition of Postmodernity* (Cambridge: Blackwell, 1990).

5. Respectively, the phrases are from Bernard Wasserstein, *Vanishing Diaspora: The Jews in Europe Since 1945* (Cambridge: Harvard University Press, 1996); and Henning Bech, *When Men Meet: Homosexuality and Modernity* (Chicago: University of Chicago Press, 1997). "The Disappearance of the Modern Homosexual" is the programmatic title of the book's final chapter.

6. See esp. Steven Seidman, *Difference Troubles: Queering Social Theory and Sexual Politics* (Cambridge: Cambridge University Press, 1997).

7. In the Jewish realm, by far the most trenchant critique is offered in Peter Novick, *The Holocaust in American Life*. In the lesbian/gay context, a number of queer theorists have challenged the cultural logic of conventional identity politics. See, e.g., Michael Warner, ed., *Fear of a Queer Planet: Queer Politics and Social Theory* (Minneapolis: University of Minnesota Press, 1993); *id., The Trouble with Normal: Sex, Politics, and the Ethics of Queer Life* (New York: Free Press, 1999); David Halperin, *Saint Foucault: Towards a Gay Hagiography* (New York: Oxford University Press, 1995). A powerful and theoretically compelling critique along the lines gestured to here has recently been advanced in the context of African-American studies in Paul Gilroy, *Against Race: Imagining Political Culture Beyond the Color Line* (Cambridge: Harvard University Press, 2000).

8. The critical literature on Haider includes Hans Henning Scharsach, *Haiders Kampf* (Munich: Heyne, 1992); *id., Haiders Clan: Wie Gewalt entsteht* (Vienna: Orac, 1995); *id., Haider: Österreich und die rechte Versuchung* (Reinbeck: Rowohlt, 2000); Hans Henning Scharsach and Kurt Kuch, *Haider: Schatten über Europa* (Cologne: Kiepenheuer & Witsch, 2000); Hubertus Czernin, *Der Haider-Macher: Franz Vranitzky und das Ende der alten Republik* (Vienna: Ibera & Molden, 1997); Christa Zöchling, *Haider: Licht und Schatten einer Karriere* (Vienna: Molden, 1999); Ruth Wodak and Anton Pelinka, eds., *The Haider Phenomenon in Austria* (Atlantic Highlands, Ill.: Transaction Publishers, 2002). Beyond this literature, several volumes of Haider quotes and citations have been published by his critics. See Gudmund Tributsch, ed., *Schlagwort Haider: Ein politisches Lexikon seiner Aussprüche von 1986 bis heute* (Vienna: Falter, 1994); Brigitte Bailer-Galanda, *Haider wörtlich: Führer in die Dritte Republik* (Vienna: Löcker, 1995); Hubertus Czernin, *Wofür ich mich meinetwegen entschuldige.*

9. At the time, the FPÖ was under the leadership of the party's liberal wing, which had secured its 1983 entry into Austria's governing coalition (as the junior partner of the SPÖ). Haider vehemently opposed the coalition, and for several years he attacked the FPÖ leadership from an explicitly German nationalist perspective. Certain of his steadily growing popularity among the party's overwhelmingly nationalist base, he challenged the FPÖ chair and vice chancellor, Norbert Steger, for the party leadership in 1986, emerging victorious at a heated convention held in Innsbruck.

10. See the Haider quotes collected in Czernin, *Wofür ich mich meinetwegen entschuldige,* esp. pp. 13–31. Most famously, Haider referred to the "Austrian nation" as an "ideological miscarriage" since it decoupled *Volkszugehörigkeit*

(belonging to the *Volk*) from *Staatszugehörigkeit* (belonging to the state). Ibid., p. 20. This statement, which challenged the very basis of Austrian nationness, caused a political scandal when it was uttered on Austrian television in 1988.

11. Czernin, *Wofür ich mich meinetwegen entschuldige,* esp. pp. 57–64. When Haider came to power in the FPÖ, he was a strong advocate of Austria's entry into the European Community. In part, this reflected the EC's structure as an economic confederation of strictly delimited nation-states. In part, it was seen as an attempt to move Austria closer to Germany, in line with Haider's German nationalist project.

12. For a statement by Haider along those lines, see Czernin, *Wofür ich mich meinetwegen entschuldige,* p. 58. Overtly homophobic comments by leading members of the FPÖ are reported in *Lambda Nachrichten,* 1994, no. 1: 52; *Lambda Nachrichten,* 1994, no. 2: 23; *Lambda Nachrichten,* 1995, no. 2: 21.

13. See, for example, the *Profil* cover story by Christa Zöchling, "Haider und die Juden: Eine verhängnisvolle Affäre," *Profil,* Mar. 13, 2000, pp. 32–41. For a discussion of Haider's attitude toward homosexuality and the reported rumors about his sexual orientation, see *Lambda Nachrichten,* 2000, no. 2: 13–17.

14. Many commentators have noted Haider's persistent attempts to associate himself with Jews. An early example is his highly publicized acquaintance with therapist Viktor Frankl, and numerous other instances have been documented (see Zöchling, "Haider und die Juden."). Haider's most widely discussed Jewish association is with Peter Sichrovsky, a member of the postwar generation and early critic of Austrian *Vergangenheitsbewältigung* (as well as the author of the acclaimed book *Schuldig geboren: Kinder aus Nazifamilien* [Cologne: Kiepenheuer & Witsch, 1987]). Haider and Sichrovsky met in the early 1990s, and their friendship, which took hold in the context of the latter's political transformation, resulted in Sichrovsky's remarkable career, which brought him into the FPÖ's inner circle by the turn of the century.

15. The preamble is quoted from an Austrian government advertisement placed in the *International Herald Tribune,* Feb. 8, 2000. On the settlement of the question of Jewish restitution, see *Die Gemeinde,* Dec. 2001, pp. 3–6.

16. The turning point in the party's position had come in 1996, when it voted for the abolition of §221 and introduced a failed amendment that would have raised the legal age in §209 to sixteen. Since then, the party has repeatedly signaled its willingness to eradicate legal discrimination against homosexuals, especially in contacts with such "assimilationist" groups as the RKL.

17. Haider, quoted in Czernin, *Wofür ich mich meinetwegen entschuldige,* pp. 93, 91, 92.

18. The quote is from Harald Ofner, who made the comment November 14 during a discussion program on Austrian television. Ofner's statement is cited in *Die Gemeinde,* Dec. 1999, p. 8.

19. The immediate political context of this development is presented and analyzed in Pelinka, *Austria,* ch. 10.

Bibliography

Newspapers and Periodicals

THE JEWISH PRESS

David: Jüdische Kulturzeitschrift
Die Gemeinde
Das Jüdische Echo
Neue Illustrierte Welt
Der Neue Weg
Nu

THE LESBIAN/GAY PRESS

Bussi
CO-INFO
Connect
G
Der Kreis (Switzerland)
Lambda Nachrichten
Rainbow News
Tamtam
Warme Blätter
XTRA!

AUSTRIAN DAILIES

Der Abend
Arbeiter-Zeitung

Kleine Zeitung
Kurier
Neue Kronen Zeitung
Neues Österreich
Neues Volksblatt
Die Presse
Der Standard
Tagespost
Volksstimme
Wiener Zeitung

AUSTRIAN WEEKLIES AND MONTHLIES

Der Falter
Format
Die Furche
Neues Forum
News
Profil
Sozialistische Aktion
Trotzdem
Wiener Rathauskorrespondenz
Wirtschaftswoche
Wochenpresse

References

Adam, Barry, Jan Willem Duyvendak, and André Krouwel, eds. *The Global Emergence of Gay and Lesbian Politics.* Philadelphia: Temple University Press, 1999.

Adunka, Evelyn. *Die vierte Gemeinde: Die Wiener Juden in der Zeit von 1945 bis heute.* Berlin: Philo, 2000.

Altman, Dennis. *Homosexual: Oppression and Liberation.* New York: New York University Press, 1993 [1971].

Anderson, Benedict. *Imagined Communities: Reflections on the Origin and Spread of Nationalism.* London: Verso, 1983.

Arendt, Hannah. *The Origins of Totalitarianism.* London: Allen & Unwin, 1951.

Ashkenazi, Michael, and Alex Weingrod. *Ethiopian Immigrants in Beersheva: An Anthropological Study of the Absorption Process.* Highland Park, Ill.: American Association for Ethiopian Jews, 1984.

Baar, Fritz. *50 Jahre Hakoah, 1909–1959.* Tel Aviv: Verlagskommitte Hakoah, 1959.

Bailer, Brigitte. *Wiedergutmachung kein Thema: Österreich und die Opfer des Nationalsozialismus.* Vienna: Löcker, 1993.

———. *Haider wörtlich: Führer in die Dritte Republik.* Vienna: Löcker, 1995.

Bauman, Zygmut. *Modernity and the Holocaust.* Ithaca, N.Y.: Cornell University Press, 1989.

——. *Intimations of Postmodernity.* London: Routledge, 1992.

——. *Postmodern Ethics.* Oxford: Blackwell, 1992.

——. *Life in Fragments: Essays on Postmodern Morality.* Cambridge: Blackwell, 1995.

——. *Postmodernity and Its Discontents.* New York: New York University Press, 1997.

Baumgardt, Manfred. *Goodbye to Berlin? 100 Jahre Schwulenbewegung – Ausstellungskatalog.* Berlin: Verlag Rosa Winkel, 1997.

Bech, Henning. *When Men Meet: Homosexuality and Modernity.* Chicago: University of Chicago Press, 1997.

Beckermann, Ruth. *Die Mazzesinsel: Juden in der Wiener Leopoldstadt, 1918–1938.* Vienna: Löcker, 1984.

——. *Unzugehörig: Österreicher und Juden nach 1945.* Vienna: Löcker Verlag, 1989.

Bei, Neda, Wolfgang Förster, Hanna Hacker, and Manfred Lang, eds. *Das lila Wien um 1900: Zur Ästhetik der Homosexualitäten.* Vienna: Promedia, 1986.

Bell, Mark. "Sexual Orientation and Anti-Discrimination Policy: The European Community." In *Politics of Sexuality,* edited by Terrell Carver & Véronique Mottier. London: Routledge, 1998.

Beller, Steven. *Vienna and the Jews, 1867–1938: A Cultural History.* Cambridge: Cambridge University Press, 1989.

Benedict, Ruth. *Patterns of Culture.* Boston: Houghton & Mifflin, 1934.

Bersani, Leo. *Homos.* Cambridge: Harvard University Press, 1995.

Bischof, Günter, Anton Pelinka, and Rolf Steininger, eds. *Austria in the Nineteen Fifties.* New Brunswick, N.J.: Transaction Publishers, 1995.

Bleys, Rudy. *The Geography of Perversion: Male-to-Male Sexual Behaviour Outside the West and the Ethnographic Imagination 1750–1918.* New York: Cassell, 1996.

Boas, Franz. "The Limitations of the Comparative Method of Anthropology." In *Race, Language and Culture.* New York: Macmillan, 1940.

——. "The Occurrence of Similar Inventions in Areas Widely Apart [and] Museums of Ethnology and their Classification." In *The Shaping of American Anthropology 1883–1911: A Franz Boas Reader,* edited by George Stocking. Chicago: University of Chicago Press, 1974.

Bodemann, Y. Michael, ed. *Jews, Germans, Memory: Reconstructions of Jewish Life in Germany.* Ann Arbor: University of Michigan Press, 1996.

Bohlman, Philip. *"The Land Where Two Streams Flow": Music in the German-Jewish Community of Israel.* Urbana: University of Illinois Press, 1989.

Borneman, John, and Jeffrey Peck. *Sojourners: The Return of German Jews and the Question of Identity.* Lincoln: University of Nebraska Press, 1995.

Botz, Gerhard. "Österreich und die NS-Vergangenheit." In *Ist der Nationalsozialismus Geschichte? Zu Historisierung und Historikerstreit,* edited by Dan Diner. Frankfurt: Fischer, 1987.

———. "The Dynamics of Persecution in Austria, 1938–45." In *Austrians and Jews in the Twentieth Century: From Franz Joseph to Waldheim,* edited by Robert Wistrich. New York: St. Martin's Press, 1992.

Boyarin, Daniel. *Unheroic Conduct: The Rise of Heterosexuality and the Invention of the Jewish Man.* Berkeley: University of California Press, 1997.

Boyarin, Jonathan. *Polish Jews in Paris: The Ethnography of Memory.* Bloomington: Indiana University Press, 1991.

———. *Storm from Paradise: The Politics of Jewish Memory.* Minneapolis: University of Minnesota Press, 1992.

Boyer, John. *Political Radicalism in Late Imperial Vienna: Origins of the Christian Social Movement, 1848–1897.* Chicago: University of Chicago Press, 1981.

———. *Culture and Political Crisis in Vienna: Christian Socialism in Power, 1897–1918.* Chicago: University of Chicago Press, 1995.

Brunner, Andreas. "Eine kurze Geschichte von *tamtam.*" In *Rosa Lila Villa: 10 Jahre Lesben und Schwulenhaus,* edited by Rosa Lila Tip. Vienna: Eigenverlag, 1992.

Brunner, Andreas, and Hannes Sulzenbaacher. "Donauwalzer — Herrenwahl: Schwule Geschichte der Donaumetropole vom Mittelalter bis zur Gegenwart." In *Schwules Wien: Reiseführer durch die Donaumetropole,* edited by Andreas Brunner and Hannes Sulzenbacher. Vienna: Promedia, 1998.

Bukey, Evan. *Hitler's Austria: Popular Sentiment in the Nazi Era, 1938–1945.* Chapel Hill: University of North Carolina Press, 2000.

Bundesministerium für Justiz. *Protokoll über die siebzehnte Arbeitssitzung der Kommission zur Ausarbeitung eines Strafgesetzbuches im Jahre 1957.* Vienna: Eigenverlag, 1957.

———. *Entwurf eines Strafgesetzbuches samt Erläuterungen.* Vienna: Eigenverlag, 1964.

———. *Entwurf eines Strafgesetzbuches samt Erläuternden Bemerkungen.* Vienna: Eigenverlag, 1966.

———. *Regierungsvorlage eines Strafgesetzbuches samt Erläuternden Bemerkungen.* Vienna: Eigenverlag, 1968.

———. *Regierungsvorlage.* Vienna: Eigenverlag, 1970

Bunzl, John. "Austrian Identity and Antisemitism." *Patterns of Prejudice* 21 (spring 1987), pp. 4–8.

———. *Der Lange Arm der Erinnerung: Jüdisches Bewußtsein heute.* Vienna: Böhlau, 1987.

———. *Hoppauf Hakoah: Jüdischer Sport in Österreich von den Anfängen bis in die Gegenwart.* Vienna: Junius, 1987.

Bunzl, John, and Bernd Marin, *Antisemitismus in Österreich: Sozialhistorische und soziologische Studien.* Innsbruck: Inn-Verlag, 1983.

Bunzl, Matti. "On the Politics and Semantics of Austrian Memory: Vienna's Monument Against War and Fascism." *History and Memory* 7, no. 2 (1995), pp. 7–40.

———. "The City and the Self: Narratives of Spatial Belonging Among Austrian Jews." *City and Society* (1996), pp. 50–81.

——. "Franz Boas and the Humboldtian Tradition: From *Volksgeist* and *Nationalcharakter* to an Anthropological Concept of Culture." In *History of Anthropology*. Vol. 8 of *Volksgeist as Method and Ethic: Essays on Boasian Ethnography and the German Anthropological Tradition,* edited by George Stocking, pp. 17–78. Madison: University of Wisconsin Press, 1996.

——. "Outing as Performance/Outing as Resistance: A Queer Reading of Austrian (Homo)Sexualities." *Cultural Anthropology* 12, no. 1 (1997), pp. 129–51.

——. "From Silence to Defiance: Jews and Queers in Contemporary Vienna." Ph.D. diss., University of Chicago, 1998.

——. "Resistive Play: Sports and the Emergence of Jewish Visibility in Contemporary Vienna." *Journal of Sport and Social Issues* 24, no. 3 (2000), pp. 232–50.

——. "Austrian Zionism and the Jews of the New Europe." *Jewish Social Studies* 9 (2003).

Chauncey, George. *Gay New York: Gender, Urban Culture and the Gay Male World, 1890–1940.* New York: Basic Books, 1994

Clifford, James. *The Predicament of Culture: Twentieth-Century Ethnography, Literature, and Art.* Cambridge: Harvard University Press, 1988.

Clifford, James, and George Marcus, eds. *Writing Culture: The Poetics and Politics of Ethnography.* Berkeley: University of California Press, 1986.

Cohen, Ed. *Talk on the Wilde Side: Toward a Genealogy of a Discourse on Male Sexuality.* New York: Routledge, 1993.

Cohen, Lawrence. "Holi in Banaras and the Mahaland of Modernity." *GLQ* 2, no. 4 (1996), pp. 399–424.

Crapanzano, Vincent. *Tuhami: Portrait of a Moroccan.* Chicago: University of Chicago Press, 1980.

Czernin, Hubertus. *Der Haider-Macher: Franz Vranitzky und das Ende der alten Republik.* Vienna: Ibera & Molden, 1997.

——, ed. *Wofür ich mich meinetwegen entschuldige: Haider, beim Wort genommen.* Vienna: Czernin Verlag, 2000.

Dobroszycki, Lucjan, and Barbara Kirschenblatt-Gimblett. *Image Before My Eyes: A Photographic History of Jewish Life in Poland, 1864–1939.* New York: Schocken Books, 1977.

Dominguez, Virginia. *People As Subject, People As Object: Selfhood and Peoplehood in Contemporary Israel.* Madison: University of Wisconsin Press, 1989.

——. "Questioning Jews." *American Ethnologist* 20, no. 3 (1993), pp. 618–24.

Dwyer, Kevin. *Moroccan Dialogues: Anthropology in Question.* Baltimore, Md.: Johns Hopkins University Press, 1982.

Eggan, Fred. "Social Anthropology and the Method of Controlled Comparison." *American Anthropologist* 56 (1954), pp. 743–63.

Eisenstadt, S.N. *The Absorption of Immigrants.* London: Routledge and Kegan Paul, 1954.

ElDorado: Homosexuelle Frauen und Männer in Berlin, 1850–1950: Geschichte, Alltag und Kultur. Berlin: Verlag Rosa Winkel, 1984.

Embacher, Helga. *Neubeginn ohne Illusionen: Juden in Österreich nach 1945.* Vienna: Picus, 1995.

Fabian, Johannes. "Language, History and Anthropology." *Philosophy of the Social Sciences* 1 (1971), pp. 19–47.

Fader, Ayala. "Learning to Be Bobover: Language Socialization and Maintenance in a Hasidic Community." Ph.D. diss., New York University, 2000.

Fink, Amir Sumakai, and Jacob Press, eds. *Independence Park: The Lives of Gay Men in Israel.* Stanford, Calif.: Stanford University Press, 1999.

Förster, Wolfgang. "Männliche Homosexualität in den österreichischen Printmedien — Zur Tradierung eines Vorurteils." In *Homosexualität in Österreich.* Edited by Michael Handl. Vienna: Junius, 1989.

——. "Zwischen Provokation und Integration — ein Viertljahrhundert Schwulenbewegung in Österreich." In *Der Andere Blick: Lesbischwules Leben in Österreich,* edited by Wolfgang Förster, Tobias Natter, and Ines Rieder. Vienna: Eigenverlag, 2001.

Förster, Wolfgang, Tobias Natter, and Ines Rieder, eds. *Der Andere Blick: Lesbischwules Leben in Österreich.* Vienna: Eigenverlag, 2001.

Foucault, Michel. *The History of Sexuality: Volume 1 — An Introduction.* New York: Vantage Books, 1978.

Fout, John. "Sexual Politics in Wilhelmine Germany: The Male Gender Crisis, Moral Purity, and Homophobia." In *Forbidden History: The State, Society, and the Regulation of Sexuality in Modern Europe,* edited by John Fout, pp. 259–92. Chicago: University of Chicago Press, 1992.

Fried, Erich. *Nicht verdrängen, nicht gewöhnen: Texte zum Thema Österreich.* Vienna: Europa, 1987.

Friedmann, Alexander, Maria Hofstätter, and Ilan Knapp, eds. *Eine neue Heimat?: Jüdische Emigrantinnen und Emigranten aus der Sowjetunion.* Vienna: Verlag für Gesellschaftskritik, 1993.

Gaisbauer, Adolf. *Davidstern und Doppeladler: Zionismus und jüdischer Nationalismus in Österreich, 1882–1918.* Vienna: Böhlau, 1988.

Galibov, Grigori. *Geschichte der bucharischen Juden in Wien.* Vienna: Österreichischer Kunst- und Kulturverlag, 2001.

Geertz, Clifford. *The Religion of Java.* New York: Free Press, 1960.

——. *Islam Observed: Religious Development in Morocco and Indonesia.* Chicago: University of Chicago Press, 1968

——. *The Interpretation of Cultures: Selected Essays.* New York: Basic Books, 1973

——. *Local Knowledge: Further Essays in Interpretive Anthropology.* New York: Basic Books, 1983.

——. *After the Fact: Two Countries, Four Decades, One Anthropologist.* Cambridge: Harvard University Press, 1995

Der gelbe Stern in Österreich – Studia Judaica Austriaca V. Eisenstadt: Edition Roetzer, 1977.

Gellner, Ernest. *Nations and Nationalism.* Ithaca, N.Y.: Cornell University Press, 1983.

Gilman, Sander. *The Jew's Body*. New York: Routledge, 1991.

——. *Freud, Race and Gender*. Princeton, N.J.: Princeton University Press, 1993.

——. *Jews in Today's German Culture*. Bloomington: Indiana University Press, 1995.

Gilman, Sander and Karen Remmler, eds. *Reemerging Jewish Culture in Germany: Life and Literature Since 1989*. New York: New York University Press, 1994.

Gilroy, Paul. *Against Race: Imagining Political Culture Beyond the Color Line*. Cambridge: Harvard University Press, 2000.

Goldberg, Harvey. *Cave Dwellers and Citrus Growers: A Jewish Community in Libya and Israel*. Cambridge: Cambridge University Press, 1972.

——. *Greentown's Youth: Disadvantaged Youth in a Development Town in Israel*. Assen: Van Gorcum, 1984.

Goldschmidt, Henry. "Peoples Apart: Constructing Jewish Identities and Differences in Crown Heights." Ph.D. diss., University of California, Santa Cruz, 2000.

Goluboff, Sascha. "Jewish Multi-Ethnicities in Post-Soviet Russia: An Eventful Ethnography of the Moscow Choral Synagogue." Ph.D. diss., University of Illinois at Urbana-Champaign, 1999.

Grau, Günter, ed. *Homosexualität in der NS-Zeit: Dokumente einer Diskriminierung und Verfolgung*. Frankfurt: Fischer, 1993.

Graupner, Helmut. *Homosexualität und Strafrecht in Österreich: Eine Übersicht*. Vienna: Eigenverlag, 1992.

Gruber, Helmut. *Red Vienna: Experiment in Working-Class Culture, 1919–1934*. New York: Oxford University Press, 1991.

Gruber, Helmut, and Ruth Wodak. *Ein Fall für den Staatsanwalt: Diskursanalyse der Kronenzeitungsberichterstattung zu Neonazismus und Novellierung des österreichischen Verbotsgesetzes im Frühjahr 1992*. Vienna: Institut für Sprachwissenschaft, 1992.

Gruber, Ruth Ellen. *Virtually Jewish: Reinventing Jewish Culture in Europe*. Berkeley: University of California Press, 2002.

Hacker, Hanna. *Frauen und Freundinnen: Studien zur "weiblichen Sexualität" am Beispiel Österreich*. Weinheim: Beltz, 1987.

Haider, Jörg. *Die Freiheit, die ich meine*. Frankfurt: Ullstein, 1994.

——. *Befreite Zukunft jenseits von links und rechts: Menschliche Alternativen für eine Brücke ins neue Jahrtausend*. Vienna: Iberia & Molden, 1997.

Halperin, David. *One Hundred Years of Homosexuality*. New York: Routledge, 1990.

——. *Saint Foucault: Towards a Gay Hagiography*. New York: Oxford University Press, 1995.

Hamann, Brigitte. *Hitler's Vienna: A Dictator's Apprenticeship*. New York: Oxford University Press, 1999.

Handl, Michael. "Von Rosa Villen und Wirbeln und Homosexuellen Initiativen — Die österreichische Homosexuellenbewegung nach Stonewall." In

Homosexualität in Österreich, edited by Michael Handl et al. Vienna: Junius, 1989.

Hanisch, Ernst. *Der lange Schatten des Staates: Österreichische Gesellschafts-geschichte im 20. Jahrhundert.* Vienna: Ueberreuter, 1994.

Harrell, Richard. "The Symbolic Strategies of Chicago's Gay and Lesbian Pride Day Parade." In *Gay Culture in America: Essays from the Field,* edited by Gilbert Herdt, pp. 225–52. Boston: Beacon Press, 1992.

Harvey, David. *The Condition of Postmodernity.* Cambridge: Blackwell, 1990.

Hassan, Ihab. *The Postmodern Turn: Essays in Postmodern Theory and Culture.* Columbus: Ohio State University Press, 1987.

Hauberger, Doris, and Helga Pankratz. "Prähistorische Erinnerungen: Von der Belle Etage zur *Villa.*" In *Rosa Lila Villa: 10 Jahre Lesben und Schwulen-haus,* edited by Rosa Lila Tip. Vienna: Eigenverlag, 1992.

Hauer, Gudrun. "Lesben- und Schwulengeschichte: Diskriminierung und Widerstand." In *Homosexualität in Österreich,* edited by Michael Handl et al. Vienna: Junius, 1989.

Heger, Heinz. *Die Männer mit dem Rosa Winkel: Der Bericht eines Homosex-uellen über seine KZ-Haft von 1939–1945.* Hamburg: Merlin-Verlag, 1972.

Herdt, Gilbert. *Guardians of the Flute: Idioms of Masculinity.* New York: McGraw-Hill, 1981.

———. *Same Sex, Different Cultures: Gays and Lesbians Across Cultures.* Boulder: Westview Press, 1997.

———, ed. *Ritualized Homosexuality in Melanesia.* Berkeley: University of California Press, 1984.

———, ed. *Gay Culture in America: Essays from the Field.* Boston: Beacon Press, 1992.

Herdt, Gilbert, and Andrew Boxer. *Children of Horizons: How Gay and Lesbian Youths Are Forging a New Way Out of the Closet.* Boston: Beacon Press, 1996.

Hobsbawm, Eric. *Nations and Nationalism since 1780: Programme, Myth, Reality.* Cambridge: Cambridge University Press, 1990.

Hödl, Klaus. *Als Bettler in die Leopoldstadt: Galizische Juden auf dem Weg nach Wien.* Vienna: Böhlau, 1994.

———. *Die Pathologisierung des jüdischen Körpers: Antisemitismus, Gechlecht und Medizin im Fin de Siècle.* Vienna: Picus, 1997.

Hölzel, Norbert. *Propagandaschlachten: Die österreichischen Wahlkämpfe 1945–1971.* Vienna: Verlag für Geschichte und Politik, 1974.

Horkheimer, Max, and Theodor Adorno. *Dialectic of Enlightenment.* New York: Continuum, 1944.

HOSI. *. . . Und sie bewegt sich doch . . . : 15 Jahre Homosexuelle Initiative.* Vienna: Eigenverlag, 1994.

Hutcheon, Linda. *A Poetics of Postmodernism: History, Theory, Fiction.* New York: Routledge, 1988.

Huyssen, Andreas. *After the Great Divide: Modernism, Mass Culture, Postmod-ernism.* Bloomington: Indiana University Press, 1986.

IKG. *Bericht des Präsidiums der Israelitischen Kultusgemeinde Wien über die Tätigkeit in den Jahren 1945 bis 1948.* Vienna: Eigenverlag, 1948.

———. *Die Tätigkeit der Israelitischen Kultusgemeinde Wien in den Jahren 1952 bis 1954.* Vienna: Eigenverlag, 1955.

———. *Die Tätigkeit der Israelitischen Kultusgemeinde Wien, 1960–1964.* Vienna: Eigenverlag, 1964.

IKG and Burgtheater Wien. *Ein Fest zum 150jährigen Bestehen.* Vienna: Eigenverlag, 1999.

ILGA-Europa. *Gleichstellung von Lesben und Schwulen: Eine relevante Frage im zivilen und sozialen Dialog.* Vienna: Eigenverlag, 1998.

———. *Nach Amsterdam: Sexuelle Orientierung und die Europäische Union – Ein Leitfaden.* Vienna: Eigenverlag, 1999.

Itzkowitz, Daniel. "Secret Temples." In *Jews and Other Differences: The New Jewish Cultural Studies,* edited by Jonathan Boyarin and Daniel Boyarin, pp. 176–202. Minneapolis: University of Minnesota Press, 1997.

Jameson, Fredric. *Postmodernism, or, the Cultural Logic of Late Capitalism.* Durham, N.C.: Duke University Press, 1991.

Jarvie, Ian. "Epistle to the Anthropologists." *American Anthropologist* 77 (1975), pp. 253–65.

Jásci, Oscar. *The Dissolution of the Habsburg Monarchy.* Chicago: University of Chicago Press, 1929.

Jellinek, Gustav. "Die Geschichte der österreichischen Wiedergutmachung." In *The Jews of Austria: Essays on their Life, History and Destruction,* edited by Josef Fraenkel. London: Valentine, 1967.

Jellonnek, Burkhard. *Homosexuelle unter dem Hakenkreuz.* Paderborn: Schöningh, 1990.

Joskowicz, Alexander. "Identität, Macht, Erzählung: Der Nationalsozialismus in österreichischen Erinnerungsdiskursen der fünfziger und sechziger Jahre." Master's thesis, University of Vienna, 2000.

Jüdisches Museum Wien. Vienna: Eigenverlag, 1996.

Judson, Pieter. "Inventing Germans: Class, Nationality and Colonial Fantasy at the Margins of the Habsburg Monarchy." *Social Analysis* 33 (1993).

———. *Exclusive Revolutionaries: Liberal Politics, Social Experience, and National Identity in the Austrian Empire, 1848–1914.* Ann Arbor: University of Michigan Press, 1996.

———. "Frontiers, Islands, Forests, Stones: Mapping the Geography of a German Identity in the Habsburg Monarchy, 1848–1900." In *The Geography of Identity,* edited by Patricia Yaeger. Ann Arbor: University of Michigan Press, 1996.

Kahn, Susan. *Reproducing Jews: A Cultural Account of Assisted Conception in Israel.* Durham, N.C.: Duke University Press, 2000.

Kann, Robert. *A History of the Habsburg Empire, 1526–1918.* Berkeley: University of California Press, 1974.

Kaplan, Marion. *The Making of the Jewish Middle Class: Women, Family, and Identity in Imperial Germany.* New York: Oxford University Press, 1991.

Katriel, Tamar. *Talking Straight: Dugri Speech in Israeli Sabra Culture.* Cambridge: Cambridge University Press, 1986.

Katz, Jacob. *Out of the Ghetto: The Social Background of Jewish Emancipation, 1770–1870.* Cambridge: Harvard University Press, 1973.

Kennedy, Elizabeth, and Madeline Davis. *Boots of Leather, Slippers of Gold: The History of a Lesbian Community.* New York: Routledge, 1993.

Kennedy, Hubert. *The Ideal Gay Man: The Story of Der Kreis.* New York: Harrington Park Press, 1999.

Kluckhohn, Clyde. *Culture and Behavior.* New York: Free Press, 1962.

Knight, Robert. "Kalter Krieg, Entnazifizierung und Österreich." In *Verdrängte Schuld, verfehlte Sühne: Entnazifizierung in Österreich 1945 – 1955,* edited by Sebastian Meissl, Klaus-Dieter Mulley, and Oliver Rathkolb. Wien: Verlag für Geschichte und Politik, 1986.

———. *"Ich bin dafür, die Sache in die Länge zu ziehen": Die Wortprotokolle der österreichischen Bundesregierung von 1945 bis 1952 über die Entschädigung der Juden.* Frankfurt: Athenäum, 1988.

Kolb, Leon. "The Vienna Jewish Museum." In *The Jews of Austria: Essays on their Life, History and Destruction,* edited by Josef Fraenkel. London: Valentine, 1967.

Kratzer, Rudolf. "Wie alles begann." In *Rosa Lila Villa: 10 Jahre Lesben und Schwulenhaus,* edited by Rosa Lila Tip. Vienna: Eigenverlag, 1992.

Kreisky, Bruno. *Die Zeit in der wir leben: Betrachtungen zur internationalen Politik.* Vienna: Molden, 1978.

Kroeber, Alfred. "Psychosis or Social Sanction?" *Character and Personality* 8 (1940), pp. 204–15.

Kugelmass, Jack. *The Miracle on Intervale Avenue: The Story of a Jewish Congregation in the South Bronx.* New York: Columbia University Press, 1986.

Kulick, Don. *Travesti.* Chicago: University of Chicago Press, 1998.

Leap, William. *Word's Out: Gay Men's English.* Minneapolis: University of Minnesota Press, 1996.

Lewin, Ellen. *Lesbian Mothers: Accounts of Gender in American Culture.* Ithaca, N.Y.: Cornell University Press, 1993.

———. *Recognizing Oursleves: Ceremonies of Lesbian and Gay Commitment.* New York: Columbia University Press, 1998.

Lichtblau, Albert. *Antisemitismus und soziale Spannung in Berlin und Wien, 1867–1914.* Berlin: Metropol, 1994.

Lohrmann, Klaus. *Die Wiener Juden im Mittelalter.* Berlin: Philo, 2000.

Long, Scott, and John Borneman. "Power, Objectivity and the Other: The Creation of Sexual Species in Modernist Discourse." *Dialectical Anthropology* 15 (1990), pp. 285–314.

Lorenz, Dagmar, ed. *Contemporary Jewish Writing in Austria: An Anthology.* Lincoln: University of Nebraska Press, 1999.

Lyotard, Jean-François. *The Postmodern Condition: A Report on Knowledge.* Minneapolis: University of Minnesota Press, 1984.

Manalansan, Martin. "Remapping Frontiers: The Lives of Gay Filipino Men in New York City." Ph.D. diss., University of Rochester, 1997.

Marcus, George, and Michael Fischer. *Anthropology as Cultural Critique: An Experimental Moment in the Human Sciences.* Chicago: University of Chicago Press, 1986.

Martel, Frédéric. *The Pink and the Black: Homosexuals in France Since 1968.* Stanford, Calif.: Stanford University Press, 1999.

McCagg, William. *A History of Habsburg Jews, 1670–1918.* Bloomington: Indiana University Press, 1989.

Mead, Margaret. *Sex and Temperament in Three Primitive Societies.* New York: William Morrow & Co., 1935.

Meissl, Sebastian, Klaus-Dieter Mulley, and Oliver Rathkolb, eds. *Verdrängte Schuld, verfehlte Sühne: Entnazifizierung in Österreich 1945 – 1955.* Wien: Verlag für Geschichte und Politik, 1986.

Menasse, Robert. *Das Land ohne Eigenschaften: Essay zur österreichischen Identität.* Vienna: Sonderzahl, 1992

——. *Selige Zeiten, brüchige Welt.* Frankfurt: Suhrkamp, 1997

——. *Die Vertreibung aus der Hölle.* Frankfurt: Suhrkamp, 2001.

Meyer, Michael, and Michael Brenner, eds. *German-Jewish History in Modern Times.* 4 vols. New York: Columbia University Press, 1996–98.

Mildenberger, Florian. *Die Münchner Schwulenbewegung 1969 bis 1996: Eine Fallstudie über die zweite deutsche Schwulenbewegung.* Bochum: Winkler, 1999.

Mitten, Richard. *The Politics of Antisemitic Prejudice: The Waldheim Phenomenon in Austria.* Boulder, Colo.: Westview Press, 1992.

Moore, Tracy, ed. *Lesbiot: Israeli Lesbians Talk About Sexuality, Feminism, Judaism and Their Lives.* London: Cassell, 1995.

Morris, Rosalind. "Educating Desire: Thailand, Transnationalism and Transgression." *Social Text* 52–53 (1998), pp. 53–79.

Mosse, George. *Toward the Final Solution: A History of European Racism.* Madison: University of Wisconsin Press, 1978.

——. *Nationalism and Sexuality: Middle-Class Morality and Sexual Norms in Modern Europe.* Madison: University of Wisconsin Press, 1985.

——. *The Image of Man: The Creation of Modern Masculinity.* New York: Oxford University Press, 1996.

Müller, Albert and Christian Fleck. "'Unzucht wider der Natur': Gerichtliche Verfolgung der 'Unzucht mit Personen gleichen Geschlechts' in Österreich von den 1930er bis zu den 1950er Jahren." *Österreichische Zeitschrift für Geschichtswissenschaften* 9, no. 3 (1998), pp. 400–22.

Müller, Klaus. *Aber in meinem Herzen sprach eine Stimme so laut: Homosexuelle Autobiographien und medizinische Pathographien im neunzehnten Jahrhundert.* Berlin: Verlag Rosa Winkel, 1991.

Murray, Stephen. *American Gay.* Chicago: University of Chicago Press, 1996.

Myerhoff, Barbara. *Number Our Days.* New York: Simon & Schuster, 1978.

Newton, Esther. *Cherry Grove, Fire Island: Sixty Years in America's First Gay and Lesbian Town.* Boston: Beacon Press, 1993.

Der Novemberpogrom 1938: Die "Reichskristallnacht in Wien — Begleitband zur 116. Sonderausstellung des Historischen Museums der Stadt Wien. Vienna: Eigenverlag der Museen der Stadt Wien, 1988.

Novick, Peter. *The Holocaust in American Life*. Boston: Houghton Mifflin Company, 1999.

Offe, Sabine. "Sites of Remembrance? Jewish Museums in Contemporary Germany." *Jewish Social Studies* 3, no. 2 (1997), pp. 77–89.

Oosterhuis, Harry. *Stepchildren of Nature: Krafft-Ebing, Psychiatry, and the Making of Sexual Identity*. Chicago: University of Chicago Press, 2000.

Pauley, Bruce. "Political Antisemitism in Interwar Vienna." In *Jews, Antisemitism and Culture in Vienna*, edited by Ivar Oxaal, Michael Pollak, and Gerhard Botz. London: Routledge & Kegan Paul, 1987.

——. *From Prejudice to Persecution: A History of Austrian Anti-Semitism*. Chapel Hill: University of North Carolina Press, 1992

Pelinka, Anton. *Austria: Out of the Shadow of the Past*. Boulder, Colo.: Westview, 1998.

Pelinka, Anton, and Erika Weinzierl, eds. *Das große Tabu: Österreichs Umgang mit seiner Vergangenheit*. Vienna: Edition S, 1987.

Pellegrini, Ann. *Performance Anxieties: Staging Psychoanalysis, Staging Race*. New York: Routledge, 1997.

Pinto, Diana. *A New Jewish Identity for Post-1989 Europe*. London: Institute for Jewish Policy Research, 1996.

Pirolt, Karin, Hans-Peter Weingand, and Kurt Zernig. *Was wäre wenn? Eingetragene Partnerschaften von Lesben und Schwulen in Österreich*. Graz: Eigenverlag, 2000.

Plant, Richard. *The Pink Triangle: The Nazi War Against Homosexuals*. New York: Henry Holt Company, 1986.

Poliakof, Leon. *The History of Anti-Semitism*. 4 vols. New York: Vanguard Press, 1965–85.

Prell, Riv-Ellen. *Prayer and Community: The Havurah in American Judaism*. Detroit, Mich.: Wayne State University Press, 1989.

Prieur, Annick. *Mema's House, Mexico City: On Transvestites, Queens, and Machos*. Chicago: University of Chicago Press, 1998.

Pulzer, Peter. *The Rise of Political Anti-Semitism in Germany and Austria*. New York: John Wiley & Sons, 1964.

Purin, Bernhard. *Beschlagnahmt: Die Sammlung des Wiener Jüdischen Museums nach 1938 – Ausstellungskatalog*. Vienna: Jewish Museum, 1995.

Rabinovici, Doron. *Papirnik: Stories*. Frankfurt: Suhrkamp, 1994.

——. "Transparencies and Silhouettes, or, The Visible and the Invisible in Jewish Life." In *Vienna Today: Photographs of Contemporary Jewish Life*.

——. *Suche nach M*. Frankfurt: Suhrkamp, 1997.

——. *Instanzen der Ohnmacht — Wien 1938–1945: Der Weg zum Judenrat*. Frankfurt: Suhrkamp, 2000.

Rabinow, Paul, and William Sullivan, eds. *Interpretive Social Science: A Reader*. Berkeley: University of California Press, 1979.

Rathkolb, Oliver. "NS-Problem und politische Restauration: Vorgeschichte und Etablierung des VdU." In *Verdrängte Schuld, verfehlte Sühne: Entnazifizierung in Österreich 1945 – 1955*, edited by Sebastian Meissl, Klaus-Dieter Mulley, and Rathkolb. Wien: Verlag für Geschichte und Politik, 1986.

Reinprecht, Christoph. *Zurückgekehrt: Identität und Bruch in der Biographie österreichischer Juden.* Vienna: Braumüller, 1992.

Repnik, Ulrike. "Lesben in Bewegungen: Die Lesbenbewegung in Österreich seit den 70er Jahren." In *Der Andere Blick: Lesbischwules Leben in Österreich,* edited by Wolfgang Förster, Tobias Natter, and Ines Rieder. Vienna: Eigenverlag, 2001.

Riedlesperger, Max. *The Lingering Shadow of Nazism: The Austrian Independent Party Movement Since 1945.* New York: Columbia University Press, 1978.

Robertson, Jennifer. *Takarazuka: Sexual Politics and Popular Culture in Modern Japan.* Berkeley: University of California Press, 1998.

Rosa Lila Tip, ed. *Rosa Lila Villa: 10 Jahre Lesben und Schwulenhaus.* Vienna: Eigenverlag, 1992.

Roscoe, Will. *The Zuni Man/Woman.* Albuquerque: University of New Mexico Press, 1991.

———. "How to Become a Berdache: Toward a Unified Analysis of Gender Diversity." In *Third Sex, Third Gender: Beyond Sexual Dimorphism in Culture and History,* edited by Gilbert Herdt. New York: Zone Books, 1993, pp. 329–372.

Rosenkranz, Herbert. *Verfolgung und Selbstbehauptung: Die Juden in Österreich 1938–1945.* Vienna: Herold, 1978.

Rot-Weiss-Rot-Buch – Gerechtigkeit für Österreich: Darstellungen, Dokumente und Nachweise zur Vorgeschichte und Geschichte der Okkupation Österreichs. Vienna: Verlag der Österreichischen Staatsdruckerei, 1946.

Rotenberg, Robert. "May Day Parades in Prague and Vienna: A Comparison of Socialist Ritual." *Anthropological Quarterly* 56, no. 2 (1983), pp. 62–68.

———. *Time and Order in Metropolitan Vienna: A Seizure of Schedules.* Washington, D.C.: Smithsonian Institution Press, 1992.

Rozenblit, Marsha. *The Jews of Vienna 1867–1914: Assimilation and Identity.* Albany: State University of New York Press, 1983.

———. "The Jews of the Dual Monarchy." *Austrian History Yearbook* 1992. Minneapolis: Center for Austrian Studies, University of Minnesota.

———. *Reconstituting a National Identity: The Jews of Habsburg Austria During World War I.* Oxford: Oxford University Press, 2001.

Scharsach, Hans Henning. *Haiders Kampf.* Munich: Heyne, 1992.

———. *Haiders Clan: Wie Gewalt entsteht.* Vienna: Orac, 1995.

———. *Haider: Österreich und die rechte Versuchung.* Reinbeck: Rowohlt, 2000.

Scharsach, Hans Henning, and Kurt Kuch. *Haider: Schatten über Europa.* Cologne: Kiepenheuer & Witsch, 2000.

Schindel, Robert. *Ohneland: Gedichte vom Holz der Paradeiserbäume.* Frankfurt: Suhrkamp, 1986.

———. *Geier sind pünktliche Tiere.* Frankfurt: Suhrkamp, 1987.

———. *Im Herzen der Krätze.* Frankfurt: Suhrkamp, 1988.

———. *Ein Feuerchen im Hintennach.* Frankfurt: Suhrkamp, 1992.

———. *Gebürtig.* Frankfurt: Suhrkamp, 1992.

Scholte, Bob. "Toward a Self-Reflective Anthropology." *Critical Anthropology* 1, no. 1 (fall 1970), pp. 3–33.

———. "Discontents in Anthropology." *Social Research* 38 (1971), pp. 777–807.

———. "Toward a Reflexive and Critical Anthropology." In *Reinventing Anthropology,* edited by Dell Hymes. New York: Pantheon Books, 1972.

Schorske, Carl. *Fin-de-Siècle Vienna: Politics and Culture.* New York: Vintage, 1981.

Seidman, Steven. *Difference Troubles: Queering Social Theory and Sexual Politics.* Cambridge: Cambridge University Press, 1997.

Sered, Susan. *What Makes Women Sick? Maternity, Modesty, and Militarism in Israeli Society.* Hanover, N.H.: Brandeis University Press, 2000.

Shokeid, Moshe. *The Dual Heritage: Immigrants from the Atlas Mountains in an Israeli Village.* Manchester: Manchester University Press, 1971.

———. *A Gay Synagogue in New York.* New York: Columbia University Press, 1995.

Sichrovsky, Peter. *Schuldig geboren: Kinder aus Nazifamilien.* Cologne: Kiepenheuer & Witsch, 1987.

Sorkin, David. *The Transformation of German Jewry, 1780–1840.* Oxford: Oxford University Press, 1987.

Spartacus: International Gay Guide 2000/2001. Berlin: Bruno Gmünder Verlag, 2000.

Spira, Leopold. *Feindbild "Jud": 100 Jahre politischer Antisemitismus in Österreich.* Vienna: Löcker, 1981.

Spiro, Spiro. *Kibbutz: Venture in Utopia.* New York: Schocken Books, 1956.

Steakley, James. "Iconography of a Scandal: Political Cartoons and the Eulenburg Affair in Wilhelmin Germany." In *Hidden from History: Reclaiming the Gay and Lesbian Past,* edited by Martin Duberman, Martha Vicinus, and George Chauncey, pp. 233–263. New York: Meridian, 1990.

Stocking, George. "From Physics to Ethnology." In *Race, Culture, and Evolution: Essays in the History of Anthropology,* pp. 133–60. Chicago: University of Chicago Press, 1968.

Stümke, Hans-Georg. *Homosexuelle in Deutschland: Eine politische Geschichte.* Munich: Beck, 1989.

Sulzenbacher, Hannes. "'Homosexual' men in Vienna, 1938." In *Opposing Fascism: Community, Authority and Resistance in Europe,* edited by Tim Kirk and Anthony McElligot, pp. 150–62. Cambridge: Cambridge University Press, 1999.

———. "Keine Opfer Hitlers: Die Verfolgung von Lesben und Schwulen in der NS-Zeit und ihre Legitimierung in der Zweiten Republik." In *Der Andere Blick: Lesbischwules Leben in Österreich,* edited by Wolfgang Förster, Tobias Natter, and Ines Rieder. Vienna: Eigenverlag, 2001.

———. "Die Diskussion über die Strafrechtsreform 1957." Unpublished manuscript.

Sulzenbacher, Hannes, and Nikolaus Wahl, eds. *Aus dem Leben: Begleitpublikation zur Ausstellung über die nationalsozialistische Verfolgung der Homosexuellen in Wien 1938–1945.* Special issue of *Lambda Nachrichten,* 2001.

Tietze, Hans. *Die Juden Wiens: Geschichte, Wirtschaft, Kultur.* Vienna: Edition Atelier, 1987 [1933].

Tributsch, Gudmund, ed. *Schlagwort Haider: Ein politisches Lexikon seiner Aussprüche von 1986 bis heute.* Vienna: Falter, 1994.

Uhl, Heidemarie. *Zwischen Versöhnung und Verstörung: Eine Kontroverse um Österreichs historische Identität fünfzig Jahre nach dem "Anschluß."* Vienna: Böhlau, 1992.

Utgaard, Peter. "Forgetting the Nazis: Schools, Identity, and the 'Austria-as-Victim' Myth Since 1945." Ph.D. diss., Washington State University, 1997.

Wahl, Nikolaus. "'Dame wünscht Freundin zwecks Kino und Theater': Verfolgung gleichgeschlechtlich liebender Frauen im Wien der Nazizeit." In *Der Andere Blick: Lesbischwules Leben in Österreich,* edited by Wolfgang Förster, Tobias Natter, and Ines Rieder. Vienna: Eigenverlag, 2001.

———. "Forschungsgegenstand Homosexuellenverfolgung — Research Topic: Persecution of Homosexuals." In *Europride Guide,* edited by CSD Wien. Vienna: Eigenverlag, 2001.

Walters, Suzanne Danuta. *All the Rage: The Story of Gay Visibility in America.* Chicago: University of Chicago Press, 2001.

Warner, Michael, ed. *Fear of a Queer Planet: Queer Politics and Social Theory.* Minneapolis: University of Minnesota Press, 1993.

———. *The Trouble with Normal: Sex, Politics, and the Ethics of Queer Life.* New York: Free Press, 1999.

Wasserstein, Bernard. *Vanishing Diaspora: The Jews in Europe Since 1945.* Cambridge: Harvard University Press, 1996.

Webber, Jonathan, ed. *Jewish Identities in the New Europe.* London: Littman Library of Jewish Civilization, 1994.

Weber, Harry. *Vienna Today: Photographs of Contemporary Jewish Life.* Vienna: Böhlau, 1996.

Weeks, Jeffrey. *Homosexual Politics in Britain, from the Nineteenth Century to the Present.* London: Quartet Books, 1979.

Weingrod, Alex. *Israel: Group Relations in a New Society.* London: Pall Mall, 1965.

Weston, Kath. *Families We Choose: Lesbians, Gays, Kinship.* New York: Columbia University Press, 1991.

———. "Lesbian/Gay Studies in the House of Anthropology." *Annual Review of Anthropology* 22 (1993).

Whiteside, Andrew. *The Socialism of Fools: Georg Ritter von Schönerer and Austrian Pan-Germanism.* Berkeley: University of California Press, 1975.

Williams, Walter. *The Spirit and the Flesh: Sexual Diversity in American Indian Culture.* Boston: Beacon Press, 1986.

Wistrich, Robert. *The Jews of Vienna in the Age of Franz Joseph.* Oxford: Oxford University Press, 1990.

———. "The Kreisky Phenomenon: A Reassessment." In *Austrians and Jews in the Twentieth Century,* edited by Robert Wistrich. New York: St. Martin's Press, 1992.

Wodak, Ruth, Peter Novak, Johanna Pelikan, Helmut Gruber, Rudolf de Cillia, and Richard Mitten. *"Wir sind alle unschuldige Täter": Diskurshistorische Studien zum Nachkriegsantisemitismus.* Frankfurt: Suhrkamp, 1990.

Wodak, Ruth, Rudolf de Cillia, Martin Reisigl, Karin Liebhart, Klaus Hofstätter, and Maria Kargl. *Zur diskursiven Konstruktion nationaler Identität.*
Frankfurt: Suhrkamp, 1998.

Wodak, Ruth, and Anton Pelinka, eds. *The Haider Phenomenon in Austria.*
Atlantic Highlands, N.J.: Transaction Publishers, 2002.

Zborowski, Mark, and Elizabeth Herzog. *Life Is with People: The Jewish Little-
Town of Eastern Europe.* New York: International Universities Press, 1952.

Ziegler, Meinrad, and Waltraud Kannonier-Finster. *Österreichisches Gedächtnis:
Über Erinnern und Vergessen der NS-Vergangenheit.* Vienna: Böhlau, 1993.

Zimmermann, Moshe. *Wilhelm Marr, the Patriarch of Antisemitism.* New York:
Oxford University Press, 1986.

Zöchling, Christa. *Haider: Licht und Schatten einer Karriere.* Vienna: Molden,
1999.

Index

Soviet Union, Jewish immigration from, 103–4, 110, 250n57
Sozialpartnerschaft, 3, 90, 225–26n5
spectacular actions, lesbian/gay movement and, 127–28
Spira, Elisabeth, 93–94, 247n10
sports, Jews and, 104–10. *See also* Haboah; Maccabi
Standard, Der, 84, 205
Star of David: antisemitism and, 47, 251n70; Jewish pride and, 1–2, 107, 109, 114, 250n56
Stöcker, Adolf, 43, 232n66
Stonewall Rebellion, 8, 125, 129
Strauss, Johann, 146
Sulzenbacher, Hannes, 145

Tolar, Günter, 211
Torberg, Friedrich, 92
Totalverbot (total ban), 4, 60–61, 64–65, 68–69
Toth, Michael, 136–37
Trotzdem, socialist youth magazine, 93

United Nations Committee for Human Rights, 194
United States: as lesbian/gay model, 120, 122, 124–25, 129, 133, 143, 149, 255n32; as model of ethnic pluralism, 218–19, 223; restitution/compensation pressure by, 262n72

VdU (Union of Independents/Verband der Unabhängigen), 10, 40, 237nn9, 239n43
Verein Christopher Street Day (CSD), 149
Vergangenheitsbewältigung (dealing with the past), 93–94, 191
victim myth, 31–40, 92, 239n35; Austrian Nazism and, 21–23, 31–32, 235nn94,96,98; generational differences regarding, 158–59; "Monument Against War and Fascism" and, 173–75; origins of, 30–32; restitution and, 34–35, 43
Vienna, 182, 189, 236n102, Habsburg Monarchy and, 52–54
Vienna Philharmonic's New Year's Concert, 123, 127, 146
Vienna's Historical Museum, 167
Vranitzky, Franz, 123, 157, 175, 180

Wagner, Richard, 14
Waldheim, Kurt. *See* Waldheim affair
Waldheim affair, 54–56, 159; Jewish public emergence and, 3, 91, 94–96, 97
Wantoch, Erika, 94, 96, 103
Warme Blätter. See Lambda Nachrichten
Weber, Harry, 171–72
Weigel, Hans, 92
Wessely, Paula, 64
Weston, Kath, 8
Whiteread, Rachel, 173, 178, 179
Why Not discotheque, 76
Wiener Antidiskriminierungsstelle (WA), 4, 200–202
Wiener Festwochen, 198
Wiener Zeitung, 167, 205
Wien ist andersrum (Vienna is different) culture festival, 140–41, 257nn67,69,72, 258n79
Wiesenthal, Simon, 40, 177–79
Wochenpresse, 71–72, 82
"Working Group for Cultural Initiatives." *See* Coming Out organization
World Jewish Congress (WJC), 54–55, 242nn79,81

XTRA!, 136–38, 257n61

Zentralbad baths, 75
Zilk, Helmut, 190; Vienna's Jewish Museum, 163–65, 168
Zionism, 50–54, 156
Zwi Perez Chajes School, 102–4, 169, 181, 249nn37,41

Indexer: Greg Jewett
Compositor: BookMatters
Text: 10/13 Galliard
Display: Galliard
Printer and Binder: Edwards Brothers, Inc.